LEADING CHANGE

IN ACADEMIC LIBRARIES

COLLEEN
BOFF AND
CATHERINE
CARDWELL

EDITORS

CONTENTS

Part I. Strategic Planning

Part II. Reorganization

Part III. Culture Change

Part IV. New Roles

Part V. Technological Change

Acknowledgments

Without a doubt, change in academic libraries is difficult. It challenges librarians to rethink missions, visions, organizational structures, operations, and daily tasks. It frequently leads to deep discomfort and anxiety. However, it is what keeps libraries relevant and their work meaningful.

The stories in this book address various types of change in academic libraries from strategic planning and reorganizations to culture change, new roles for libraries, and technological changes. The contributing authors examine their experiences through the lens of Kotter's change model. John P. Kotter originally intended his publication *Leading Change* (1996), which outlined the model, to be a resource for the business community, but its straightforward approach offers a common vocabulary and enough complexity to afford substantive analysis in different environments.

This book would not be possible without the contributing authors' willingness to share stories about their libraries, including the successes and barriers they experienced. We sincerely thank them for their contributions, thoughtfulness, and professionalism. It was a pleasure to work with them.

We also wish to thank Erin Nevius and Judith Lauber, our gracious editors at ACRL, for their expert advice and thoughtful contributions to the project.

The two of us became librarians in the mid-1990s and began working together early in our careers. Along the way, we have experienced significant change, and, though we have taken different professional paths, we remained steady colleagues, eager for new challenges and opportunities. We appreciate the creative, thoughtful, and supportive colleagues and leaders we have known throughout our careers. They have enriched both our professional and personal lives.

Of course, we appreciate our families and their constant support, particularly our partners Bobby and Federico, who have been exceedingly kind, patient, and full of good humor.

This book is intended to provide analysis and guidance for ways forward in academic librarianship, not a criticism of institutions, leaders, or colleagues. We encourage readers to consider the change stories in that spirit and imagine what academic libraries can become.

Colleen Boff
Catherine Cardwell

Introduction

Change in Academic Libraries

Colleen Boff and Catherine Cardwell

Institutions of higher education and academic libraries are no longer the traditional organizations they once were. Instead of being stable, predictable, and generally free from external influences, they are subject to a variety of forces, including shifting and changing populations, technological changes, and public demands for affordability and accountability.

In 2017, Ithaka S+R conducted a survey of 164 senior leaders and experts at colleges and universities, associations, research groups, and philanthropies and published the results in *Higher Ed Insights: Results of the Spring 2017 Survey*. Respondents were generally optimistic about higher education but had immediate concerns about the need to improve degree completion rates, the quality of student learning, and affordability for students. From their perspective, other significant changes in the educational landscape include federal policies affecting affordability, student financial aid, regulation of for-profit institutions, state support for higher education, protection of students at risk, and issues related to diversity, inclusion, and free speech.[1]

In this climate, academic libraries can no longer establish their excellence and ground their missions, visions, and strategic directions using traditional means. Excellence in academic libraries was previously measured first and foremost by size, which required an organizational structure designed to support and manage the collections, not the user experience. Dempsey and Malpas contended that academic libraries are in the process of being shaped by changing approaches to research and learning in the context of their institutions and are shifting to a services-based model to support this transition. Elements of this new model include responsiveness to institutional needs and an emphasis on the user experience, flexibility, and collaborative work. In sum, the service-based model requires engagement. "Libraries are forging a new engagement-based identity which is not anchored in a building or a collection, but rather as a partner in the creative process of learning and research."[2]

In 2018, ACRL identified the top trends in academic libraries that underscore the transition to service-based, engaged academic libraries serving local institutional needs and shaped by external political and economic forces. Academic libraries meet student needs by leading campus textbook affordability and OER initiatives; they meet faculty needs by supporting open access collection development and funding and supporting data management; they meet institutional needs by supporting learning analytics and data collection related to student success. All of these activities come with their own serious concerns that

need specialized attention. Librarians are engaged in ethical issues related to using student data to improve student success, copyright challenges related to the acquisition and use of data sets, and the need to leverage open and licensed content to increase affordability.[3] Set against this backdrop of changing demands, academic library leaders need to create agile, flexible organizations that promote innovation and creativity.[4]

Dempsey and Malpas proposed that "articulating the new story" is essential as libraries transition from collections-based organizations to more flexible service-based institutions and become "partner[s] in the creative process of learning and research."[5] With twenty change stories from a variety of institutions and on a variety of topics, this book responds to their imperative to tell new stories about academic libraries.

A Framework to Analyze Change Stories: Kotter's Eight-Stage Process of Leading Change

This book contains a collection of change stories authored by academic librarians from different types of four-year institutions. Librarians tell the story firsthand of how they managed major change in processes, functions, services, programs, or overall organizations, using Kotter's Eight-Stage Process of Creating Major Change as outlined in his book, *Leading Change*.[6]

Numerous change management models exist,[7] but Kotter's is relatively jargon-free and offers enough complexity to afford substantive analysis of the change process. Credible, research-based studies substantiate it as a highly regarded model. Its eight stages can be grouped into three phases. Note: The terms *model* and *framework* are used interchangeably in the literature for Kotter's process. Readers will find that is the case in this work.

WARM-UP PHASE

1. **Establishing a sense of urgency.** According to Kotter, "establishing a sense of urgency is crucial to gaining needed cooperation."[8] He asserts that in order for change to take root, approximately 20 percent of the organization needs to go above and beyond the call of duty to make change happen[9] but that approximately 75 percent of management needs to grasp this sense of urgency.[10] He also contends that a major reason change fails is due to complacency among the staff. Complacency settles in for a variety of reasons. Chief among them are the following: absence of a major crisis, too many resources, low performance standards, an organizational structure that focuses staff too narrowly, internal measurements that focus on the wrong performance outcomes, "a lack of sufficient performance feedback from external sources," low confrontation culture, denial that there is a problem, and "too much happy talk from senior management."[11]

2. **Creating the guiding coalition.** According to Kotter, teams are important in change leadership, but the members of the team must have the right position titles, expertise, credibility, and combination of leadership and management abilities.[12] He stresses the need to avoid putting staff on the team who have big egos, who will undermine the change process, or who are reluctantly on board.[13] He also stresses the need to build trust among the team members and to establish common goals.[14]

3. **Developing a vision and strategy.** Kotter defines a vision as "a picture of the future with some implicit or explicit commentary on why people should strive to create that future."[15] While he outlines a visioning process, he asserts that the guiding coalition should be responsible for creation of the vision and that the vision should convey "a direction for the future that is desirable, feasible, focused, flexible and is conveyable in five minutes or less."[16]

4. **Communicating the change vision.** When it comes to communicating change, Kotter argues that leaders typically under communicate at a time when staff have the most questions. He suggests that the best strategies for a guiding coalition to follow are to keep the change message simple and easy to recall by employees, repeat it often, and most important, for everyone in the guiding coalition to be on the same page and to send a consistent message.[17]

INTRODUCING NEW PRACTICES PHASE

5. **Empowering broad-based action.** This portion of Kotter's change model is about removing barriers that are preventing employees from engaging with the shared vision of change. These barriers can come in the form of the organizational structures that are in place, not having the appropriate skills in the organization, not having the right systems in place to get the job done, or having ineffective people with positional power.[18] The barriers with employees can be addressed through professional development, reorganization, and active involvement in the change process. He also suggests the importance of addressing issues with managers undercutting the change momentum.[19] Investing in the right tools, especially in libraries, can move change initiatives forward as well.

6. **Generating short-term wins.** In order to hold the attention of employees in the organization, Kotter explains that short-term wins need to be evident within the first six months of the change initiative. Timing matters, and so does the quality of the "win." These accomplishments need to be highly visible to those who work in the organization and should be directly related to the change at hand. These changes don't need to be extensive, but they need to demonstrate forward momentum.[20]

7. **Consolidating gains and producing more change.** At this stage in Kotter's change process, the guiding coalition assesses the smaller wins and increases the momentum of change by identifying larger scale changes that need to be made and by determining who else is needed in the organization to make this happen.[21] Does someone need to be promoted or hired? Kotter underscores the importance of maintaining a sense of urgency for change at this stage and the necessity that project management be emphasized and shared with middle management. Kotter also stresses the importance of examining what he calls "interdependencies."[22] A good example of this in the academic library setting might be a call to question why certain data is being tracked if no one is using it or how a processing workflow could be streamlined.

GROUNDING PHASE

8. **Anchoring new approaches in the culture.** Because Kotter's process follows a particular sequence,[23] he reinforces the importance of this stage coming last.[24] His rationale

is that employees within an organization need to see that the changes are superior to the old ways, but he also explains that it is important to frequently remind employees of these changes and to articulate what these changes are in order to actually change the culture.[25] Not everyone in the organization has a holistic view of the entire organization in the same way that a senior leader does, and employees need to spend some time with the new changes to be convinced of their value. He emphasizes the necessity of making staffing changes when continued, persistent barriers to change negatively influence the transformed culture.

AT A GLANCE

Kotter's Eight-Stage Process of Creating Major Change

Warm-up phase:
- Establishing a sense of urgency
- Creating the guiding coalition
- Developing a vision and strategy
- Communicating the change vision

Introducing new practices phase:
- Empowering broad-based action
- Generating short-term wins
- Consolidating gains and producing even more change

Grounding phase:
- Anchoring new approaches in the culture

Source: John P. Kotter, *Leading Change* (Boston: Harvard Business Review Press, 1996), 21.

Literature Review

Kotter's work on organizational change began with an article published in the *Harvard Business Review* titled "Leading Change: Why Transformation Efforts Fail."[26] It was so well received that he expanded the ideas in his article into his first book, *Leading Change*, published in 1996.[27] He went on to author five more books that delve deeper into the ideas expressed in his first article and book.[28] In 2012, Harvard Business Review Press released a second edition of his first book, with the addition of an updated preface in which Kotter describes the continued relevance and importance of the eight steps for managing and leading organizational change.[29]

Use of Kotter's Framework in Academic Libraries

Kotter's change framework has periodically made an appearance in the library literature over the years, and growing evidence exists to suggest that it is gaining significant traction as a framework that has application within academic libraries. Some have used the framework or an adaptation of the framework as a mechanism to guide change from the outset, while most have used the framework to analyze change after it has taken place. Farkas asserted that "Kotter's model provides a pragmatic paradigm for change" and encouraged further use of the framework in the profession.[30] In a brief newsletter article, Pressley also encouraged librarians to rely on Kotter's framework to propel change in their libraries. She provided two brief examples, one regarding digital scholarship and another regarding emerging scholarly communication practices.[31] In Smith's review of the library literature, he found that Kotter's framework was often used by academic libraries, but he also highlighted Doppelt's less frequently used Wheel of Change model.[32] Novak and Day also found that Kotter's framework seemed popular among academic libraries, as was Bolman and Deal's four frames—structural, human resource, political, and symbolic—to analyze and advance organizational change.[33]

Smith compared different organizational change models, but he did this alongside an examination of various organizational quality frameworks. He drew comparisons between these two sets of frameworks to summarize their commonalities. Smith went into a more in-depth explanation of Kotter's change framework and Doppelt's framework and presented similarities and differences between the two. Chief among them is that the progression of change in Kotter's framework is linear while the progression through Doppelt's framework is not. He also pointed out that both models are intended for use in the establishment of long-term change. To further explain these models in particular, he applied each framework to change at his university across many university functions, including the library.[34]

Novak and Day examined the library literature related to reorganizations and determined that Kotter's framework and Bolman and Deal's reframing model were frequently used by librarians as roadmaps to implement or analyze change. They explained both models in their article and then created their own five-step change model based on overlap between the Kotter and the Bolman and Deal models. They then used the reorganization of their division at their library to explain the nuances of their five-step change model.[35]

DEANS AND DIRECTORS LEADING LIBRARY-WIDE CHANGES

Fox and Keisling described their experience using an adaptation of Kotter's model midstream through a large-scale strategic planning and reorganization change at their library at the University of Louisville. As the newly appointed dean, Fox began by aligning the strategic planning process with the university priorities, gathering some benchmark data from users, and creating a student advisory board. He learned that their spaces and services were outdated, which necessitated a space redesign and a reorganization of staff to provide the appropriate services to users. Fox and Keisling explained how they utilized a modified version of Kotter's framework to overcome barriers and to root change in their organization.[36]

Using Kotter's framework, Horn relayed her change experience as the newly appointed university librarian at Deakin University Library. The sense of urgency for the change in her library came from the campus administration's mandate to align library priorities with the university's priorities and to meet new and more efficient budget targets. These mandates were officially part of the university's operational plan. Because of this, the staff were already feeling a sense of urgency, but Horn made no assumptions and continued to communicate the importance and necessity of this change. She established an executive leadership team and her guiding coalition of middle managers. As a way to build support, she included the team in planning, communicating, and demonstrating accountability. Key outcomes of these change initiatives included structural reorganization and changes to core client services. As a staff, they stopped some activities while initiating others. This approach resulted in eliminating some positions, retooling the skills of staff, and creating new positions. While all aspects of change were not complete at time of publication, they had conducted some assessments to gauge user and staff satisfaction, both of which were positive.[37]

Wheeler and Holmes used Kotter's framework to explain their change initiatives as new directors at two different medical libraries. Though neither stated that she actively used the framework for change initiatives at her library, the framework provided a common language for both directors to describe their collaboration and communication with their staff to establish initiatives, including the creation of an internship curriculum, nontraditional reference services, digital systems, informatics initiatives, and much more.[38]

Sidorko employed Kotter's model to analyze change that had already taken place at the University of Newcastle in Australia. The university's vice-chancellor provided a sense of urgency by asking for an investigation of "better co-ordination in the areas of library, information technology, teaching and learning skills support, educational technology and class room services." These units operated in silos with varying degrees of service quality, which was impeding progress toward the university goal of "expanding choice on what, when, where and how people learned."[39] The guiding coalition included the heads of the three largest units, which were IT, the library, and the Centre for the Advancement of Learning and Teaching. The three directors wrote a report that recommended the development of an "information and educational support unit," the combination of all five units involved in the change process.[40] The director of the IT unit was appointed director of the new division and was tasked with integrating the work of these units while involving the staff to create the shared vision and strategy for change. The director provided open forums, scheduled regular staff meetings, and held workshops that brought staff together in new ways. The first barrier to staff empowerment was getting all the members of the newly formed single unit to work together. The second barrier the director dealt with was redundancy in staffing when the various units merged. Among the short-term wins were library staff getting IT training, the development of a division-wide charter that defined service expectations, and merging library and IT help desks. Failures were prevalent as well and surfaced in the form of change weariness, culture clashes among staff in formerly siloed units, and prevailing cynicism. In spite of continued wins, ultimately the grounding of these changes never came to fruition due to a larger university mandate that shrank staffing levels and dissolved the newly formed unit.[41]

CHANGE RELATED TO A SPECIFIC LIBRARY PROGRAM OR INITIATIVE

Carter and Farkas wrote about Kotter's framework in the context of assessment. Farkas mined the library literature as well as the scholarship published in higher education, organizational behavior, and change leadership to establish ways to create cultures of assessment regardless of positional authority. She described Kotter's framework as a mechanism to outline a strategy to change behaviors toward assessment in libraries.[42] Carter used a case-study approach to describe the change efforts at Auburn University Libraries to incorporate course-integrated information literacy assessment into the library instruction program with seventeen librarians. Though the libraries did not use Kotter's framework as they set out to create a culture of assessment, Carter used the framework to describe their three-year change journey in response to Farkas's challenge to librarians to use this framework more often as a mechanism to describe change in academic libraries. Auburn spent the first year in phase one of Kotter's model. With support from the library administration, the guiding coalition consisted of the library instruction coordinator and three other librarians with varied perspectives and rank on the instruction team. A sense of urgency emerged externally from the library when the university added information literacy as a general education goal. The guiding coalition decided to emphasize with the staff the opportunity for professional development rather than just fulfilling the need to gather data for assessment initiatives. The guiding coalition decided to focus on one learning outcome at a time and to use a combination of authentic assessments and informal classroom assessment techniques popularized by Angelo and Cross. These decisions kept the guiding coalition focused during its small-group planning stage and also served as its vision. Over the course of approximately one year, the guiding coalition developed, tested, and actively used these assessment techniques among the four members before they entered into the two-year implementation phase and started communicating the vision to and preparing resources for the staff in formal meetings and presentations. Participation, at first, was voluntary to give staff the latitude to experiment. Then the guiding coalition required all seventeen reference librarians to try at least two informal assessments from a prepared LibGuide. With positional support from the library administration, the guiding coalition added instruction assessment to the formal evaluation cycle so that individuals could set areas of improvement for the following year. Librarians were then asked to expand assessment efforts the following term to also include two formal assessments. Phase three is still underway, but the librarians at Auburn are now generating their own assessment instruments and actively discussing what they have learned from their assessment efforts, and they know that assessment is there to stay.[43]

In a case study, Hackman described how Kotter's model was actively used and adapted to reorganize the Resource Sharing and Access Services Department at the main library at the University of Maryland. Thirty-two staff members worked together to increase efficiency, staff engagement, and user satisfaction. Instead of beginning with an external or internal sense of urgency, active, direct, and clear communication propelled this change. The primary goal—to more fully integrate staff and services from two other units into the Resource Sharing and Access Services unit—was communicated and included the Information Services department and its Learning Commons department. As a result of this communication, the staff had the opportunity to address multiple issues related to the recent mergers: duplication of effort, competition for resources, overstaffing in some areas, understaffing in other areas, and staff skills mismatched with patron demands. The guiding coalition consisted of department heads and coordinators with supervision responsibilities. This group developed five goals as its vision: the integration of three departments into one, sufficient staffing at two public service desks, elimination of redundancies and improved efficiencies, a better understanding of staffing needs to make the most of staffing resources, and ways to build skills among staff. As part of communicating vision, staff were asked to annotate their job descriptions and to keep detailed logs of their work for a two-week period. Staff were also expected to participate in an interactive retreat with additional activities to elicit staff input. This provided the guiding coalition with the data it needed to generate some short-term wins. These included the development of a new department name and a new organizational chart complete with unit descriptions. Next, staff in each unit were empowered to work in small task forces to develop specific workflows for their areas of responsibility. Department heads updated position descriptions, and the change work was shared and communicated to the wider library audience. Once the changes were rooted in the fully integrated department, efficiencies surfaced, such as improved turnaround times for course reserves and document delivery. Hackman credited the success of this ten-month process to the high levels of trust among staff members but admitted that the latter two stages are still evolving. He pointed out that Kotter's steps are not linear, nor is there much guidance on how to assess the change experience.[44]

A review of the library literature substantiates the use of Kotter's change model within the library setting. An examination of these articles informed the editors and contributed to their approach in shaping this book.

Process for Soliciting, Accepting, Organizing, and Analyzing Change Stories

The editors distributed the Call for Proposals (Appendix A: Call for Proposals) to several email discussion lists, including acrlframe@lists.ala.org, collib-l@lists.ala.org, and ili-l@lists.ala.org. Originally, the focus of the volume was on change stories in four-year institutions in the United States, but it was later expanded to include community colleges as well as institutions in North America.

The response to the call for proposals for this project was overwhelming. The editors received approximately 120 proposals and accepted twenty-three, twice as many as originally planned. They selected chapters based on the quality of the proposal as well as the subject of the change story as a way to balance and shape the collection. The editors asked authors to follow very specific directions for the chapters (Appendix B: Information about the ACRL Monograph Project) to facilitate analysis across chapters. While twenty-three proposals were accepted at the outset, twenty chapters were submitted in the end.

The editors reviewed the first draft of each chapter and, for the second and final submissions, asked the authors questions when more information or clarification was needed. Originally, the chapters were limited to 3,500 words, but in the end, authors indicated that limit was too restricting. The word limit then became 5,000 words. Using the second drafts of the chapters, the editors carefully examined the change stories in each category to identify patterns across each of Kotter's eight stages. The editors used only the information that the authors provided in their chapters for analysis and did not search beyond it for further explanation or clarification. In sum, the editors stress that this volume is not intended to be a critique of the institutions; rather it is intended to use Kotter's model as a tool to help others learn about best practices, common obstacles, and more.

Organization of the Library Change Stories

The chapters fall into one of five broad categories: strategic planning, reorganization, culture change, new roles, and technological change. Contributors come from a variety of public and private higher education institutions of all sizes.

STRATEGIC PLANNING

Academic libraries strive to meet the evolving needs and missions of their home institutions. Strategic planning provides an opportunity to lay the groundwork and set goals to meet those needs. Kevin Messner and Lindsay Miller at Miami University Libraries analyze middle management's role in implementing large-scale, library-wide change after a new strategic plan was complete. At Montana State University, Kris Johnson, Kenning Arlitsch, and David Swedman, along with Martha Kyrillidou, QualityMetrics, LLC, write about their collaborative, holistic approach using the Balanced Scorecard process to plan and map progress. At the University of Tennessee, Knoxville, Michelle Brannen, Regina Mays, and Manda Sexton formed a team charged with formally tracking the libraries' strategic plan and advancing priorities through communication, incentives for participation, and assessment. Diane Klare and Melissa Behney at Wesleyan University recount difficult moments in their libraries' history and the need for program and external reviews to help them envision a new future. Their libraries' efforts created the foundation for a collaborative, bottom-up approach to planning and a renewed confidence in the libraries, particularly from upper administration.

REORGANIZATION

Reorganizations have become common practice as libraries downsize, grow, or change leadership. Miami University Librarian Aaron Shrimplin and brightspot strategy consultants Elliot Felix, Adam Griff, and Emily Kessler explain how a design-thinking strategy helped Miami revise its organizational structure and adopt a "safe-to-try" philosophy rather than one based on perfection. Doug Worsham, Allison Benedetti, Judy Consales, Angela Horne, Nisha Moody, Rikke Ogawa, and Matthew Vest present their team-based, collaborative efforts to centralize the User Engagement division across multiple locations at the UCLA Library. C. Heather Scalf and E. Antoinette Nelson from the University of Texas at Arlington relay their experiences aligning the library with their institution's strategic directions and developing a singular vision for a major library-wide reorganization at a large R1 institution. Julie Garrison and Maira Bundza describe ways the Western Michigan Libraries reorganized a more traditional, collections-based library into one focused on the user experience.

CULTURE CHANGE

Four chapters comprise the culture change section. Renaine Julian, Rachel Besara, and Michael Meth at Florida State University explain their approach to rethinking their unit's daily work in order to increase effort related to engagement with users. Andrew See and Cynthia Childrey at Northern Arizona University present a solution to moving beyond siloed departments by implementing and instituting two cross-departmental user experience groups, one focused on user experience in the physical library and the other on the web experience. Susan Garrison and Jeanette Claire Sewell at Rice University write about creating an intensive homegrown customer service training program after realizing that a more general human resources approach to professional development did not meet their needs. Emma Popowich and Sherri Vokey at the University of Manitoba Canada present their library's approach to creating a model that involved librarians and support staff who needed to revise their work after a major reorganization and budget cuts.

NEW ROLES

Changing the focus from collections to engagement requires new roles for librarians and library staff and provides new opportunities to interact with users. Neal Baker, Kate Leuschke

Blinn, and Bonita Washington-Lacey at Earlham College report on an intensive two-semester information literacy program for first-generation college students. At the University of Florida, Laurie Taylor and Brian W. Keith write about a program designed to make the library a "laboratory," where graduate students in a variety of disciplines have opportunities to explore alternative career paths. Gary W. White and Yelena Luckert write about the transformation of the University of Maryland library liaison program, which now includes a framework outlining new and emerging responsibilities. Carroll Wetzel Wilkinson at West Virginia University Libraries focuses on a collaborative program that promotes success for student veterans.

TECHNOLOGICAL CHANGE

Against this backdrop of change, libraries contend with and benefit from technological transitions. At Stephen F. Austin State University, Jonathan Helmke, R. Philip Reynolds, and Shirley Dickerson recognized that their institutional repository was far too expensive to host approximately thirty documents and that the IR could be far more robust. Their efforts successfully increased the number and type of materials now hosted in their IR, making their investment worthwhile. Jeffrey Graveline and Kara Van Abel discuss a merger of libraries at the University of Alabama at Birmingham, which required the revision of two individual library websites into one unified presence. Jennifer O'Brien Roper and her colleagues Jeremy Bartczak, Jean L. Cooper, Christina Deane, Mike Durbin, Kara McClurken, Elizabeth Wilkinson, and Lauren Work present efforts to improve cross-departmental workflows for digital projects at the University of Virginia Library. Sara Byrd, Richard Stringer-Hye, and Jodie Gambill recount their collaborative efforts to remove barriers and improve communication for all staff at Vanderbilt University Libraries.

Readers will find an analysis written by the editors after each category of change stories, which serves to highlight opportunities, barriers, strategies, common threads, and differences among the stories. For quick access, they will also find in Appendix C: Summary of Resources Used across Change Stories a list of resources the contributing authors used during their change process. Those resources include data sources, readings, frameworks, names of consulting companies, activities, and various tools used.

Conclusion

In sum, authors of these change stories report that change at their institutions was not as linear as the process outlined in the Kotter model. However, the model provided a common framework for the authors to examine change at their own institutions, measuring their successes and areas for improvement, and, in the end, determining whether they were making progress. All of the institutions included in this volume have made some visible progress.

These change stories, taken as a whole, confirm that change is difficult but possible. The authors address some common challenges faced during the process—fear, anxiety, change fatigue, complacency, unexpected changes of leadership, vacancies, and resistance. Many authors found that their perseverance led to a better work-life balance for staff, along with renewed engagement with users, technology, and library staff. Several authors report that their libraries now embrace flexible, nimble, collaborative, and, perhaps most important, safe-to-try and fail philosophies and decision-making processes. This mind-set facilitates the transition from legacy collections-based libraries to forward-looking service-based libraries.

Notes

1. Rayane Alamuddin, Martin Kurzweil, and Daniel Rossman, *Higher Ed Insights: Results of the Spring 2017 Survey* (New York: Ithaka S+R, October 31, 2017), https://doi.org/10.18665/sr.305362.
2. Lorcan Dempsey and Constance Malpas, "Academic Library Futures in a Diversified University System," in *Higher Education in the Era of the Fourth Industrial Revolution*, ed. Nancy W. Gleason (Singapore: Palgrave Macmillan, 2018), 78, https://doi.org/10.1007/978-981-13-0194-0_4.
3. ACRL Research Planning and Review Committee, "2018 Top Trends in Academic Libraries: A Review of the Trends and Issues Affecting Academic Libraries in Higher Education," *College and Research Libraries News* 79, no. 6 (June 2018), 286–300, https://doi.org/10.5860/crln.79.6.286.
4. S. Adams Becker, M. Cummins, A. Davis, A. Freeman, C. Giesinger Hall, V. Ananthanarayanan, K. Langley, and N. Wolfson, *NMC Horizon Report: 2017 Library Edition* (Austin, TX: New Media Consortium, 2017), 6, http://cdn.nmc.org/media/2017-nmc-horizon-report-library-EN.pdf.
5. Dempsey and Malpas, "Academic Library Futures," 78.
6. John P. Kotter, *Leading Change* (Boston: Harvard Business Review Press, 1996).
7. For select examples of additional change models, see Lewin's Change Process of Unfreeze, Change, Refreeze; Doppelt's Wheel of Change; Kanter, Stein and Jick's organizational change model; and Bolman and Deal's Reframing Organizations model.
8. Kotter, *Leading Change*, 1996, 36.
9. Kotter, *Leading Change*, 1996, 35.
10. Kotter, *Leading Change*, 1996, 48.
11. Kotter, *Leading Change*, 1996, 40.
12. Kotter, *Leading Change*, 1996, 57.
13. Kotter, *Leading Change*, 1996, 59.
14. Kotter, *Leading Change*, 1996, 61.
15. Kotter, *Leading Change*, 1996, 68.
16. Kotter, *Leading Change*, 1996, 81.
17. Kotter, *Leading Change*, 1996, 90.
18. Kotter, *Leading Change*, 1996, 115.
19. Kotter, *Leading Change*, 1996, 112.
20. Kotter, *Leading Change*, 1996, 121.
21. Kotter, *Leading Change*, 1996, 143.
22. Kotter, *Leading Change*, 1996, 142
23. Kotter, *Leading Change*, 1996, 23.
24. Kotter, *Leading Change*, 1996, 155.
25. Kotter, *Leading Change*, 1996, 156.
26. John P. Kotter, "Leading Change: Why Transformation Efforts Fail," *Harvard Business Review* 73, no. 2 (March–April 1995): 59–67.
27. Kotter, *Leading Change*, 1996.
28. John P. Kotter, *Accelerate: Building Strategic Agility for a Faster-Moving World* (Boston: Harvard Business Review Press, 2014); John P. Kotter, *John Kotter on What Leaders Really Do* (Boston: Harvard Business Review Press, 1999); John P. Kotter, *Power and Influence: Beyond Formal Authority* (New York: Free Press, 2008); John P. Kotter, *A Sense of Urgency* (Boston: Harvard Business Review Press, 2008); John P. Kotter and Dan S. Cohen, *The Heart of Change* (Boston: Harvard Business Review Press, 2002).
29. John P. Kotter, *Leading Change* (Boston: Harvard Business Review Press, 2012).
30. Meredith Gorran Farkas, "Building and Sustaining a Culture of Assessment: Best Practices for Change Leadership," *Reference Services Review* 41, no. 1 (2013): 14, https://doi.org/10.1108/00907321311300857.
31. Lauren Pressley, "Catalyzing Organizational Change: Strategies and Tools to Implement Your Scholarly Communication Agenda," *College and Research Libraries News* 79, no. 9 (2018): 486–97, https://doi.org/10.5860/crln.79.9.486.
32. Ian Smith, "Organisational Quality and Organisational Change: Interconnecting Paths to Effectiveness," *Library Management* 32, no. 1 (2011): 111–28, https://doi.org/10.1108/01435121111102629.

33. John Novak and Annette Day, "The Libraries They Are A-Changin': How Libraries Reorganize," *College and Undergraduate Libraries* 22, no. 3–4 (2015): 358–73, https://doi.org/10.1080/1069131 6.2015.1067663.
34. Smith, "Organisational Quality."
35. Novak and Day, "The Libraries They Are A-Changin."
36. Robert E. Fox Jr. and Bruce L. Keisling, "Build Your Program by Building Your Team: Inclusively Transforming Services, Staffing and Spaces," *Journal of Library Administration* 56, no. 5 (2016): 526–39, https://doi.org/10.1080/01930826.2015.1105548.
37. Anne Horn, "Strategic Competence: To Soar Above," *Library Management* 29, no. 1/2 (2008): 5–17, https://doi.org/10.1108/01435120810844603.
38. Terrie R. Wheeler and Kristi L. Holmes, "Rapid Transformation of Two Libraries Using Kotter's Eight Steps of Change," *Journal of the Medical Library Association: JMLA* 105, no. 3 (2017): 276–81, https://doi.org/10.5195/jmla.2017.97.
39. Peter Edward Sidorko, "Transforming Library and Higher Education Support Services: Can Change Models Help?" *Library Management* 29, no. 4 (2008): 309, https://doi.org/10.1108/01435120810869093.
40. Sidorko, "Transforming Library and Higher Education Support Services," 310.
41. Sidorko, "Transforming Library and Higher Education Support Services."
42. Farkas, "Building and Sustaining a Culture of Assessment."
43. Toni M. Carter, "Assessment and Change Leadership in an Academic Library Department: A Case Study," *Reference Services Review* 42, no. 1 (2014): 148–64, https://doi.org/10.1108/RSR-05-2013-0028.
44. Timothy A. Hackman, "Leading Change in Action: Reorganizing an Academic Library Department Using Kotter's Eight Stage Change Model," *Library Leadership and Management* 31, no. 2 (2017): 1–27.

Bibliography

ACRL Research Planning and Review Committee. "2018 Top Trends in Academic Libraries: A Review of the Trends and Issues Affecting Academic Libraries in Higher Education." *College and Research Libraries News* 79, no. 6 (June 2018): 286–300. https://doi.org/10.5860/crln.79.6.286.

Adams Becker, S., M. Cummins, A. Davis, A. Freeman, C. Giesinger Hall, V. Ananthanarayanan, K. Langley, and N. Wolfson. *NMC Horizon Report: 2017 Library Edition.* Austin, TX: New Media Consortium. http://cdn.nmc.org/media/2017-nmc-horizon-report-library-EN.pdf.

Alamuddin, Rayane, Martin Kurzweil, and Daniel Rossman. *Higher Ed Insights: Results of the Spring 2017 Survey.* New York: Ithaka S+R, October 31, 2017. https://doi.org/10.18665/sr.305362.

Bolman, Lee G., and Terrence E. Deal. *Reframing Organizations: Artistry, Choice, and Leadership,* 6th ed. San Francisco: Jossey-Bass, 2017.

Carter, Toni M. "Assessment and Change Leadership in an Academic Library Department: A Case Study." *Reference Services Review* 42, no. 1 (2014): 148–64. https://doi.org/10.1108/RSR-05-2013-0028.

Dempsey, Lorcan, and Constance Malpas. "Academic Library Futures in a Diversified University System." In *Higher Education in the Era of the Fourth Industrial Revolution.* Edited by Nancy W. Gleason, 65–89. Singapore: Palgrave Macmillan, 2018. https://doi.org/10.1007/978-981-13-0194-0_4.

Doppelt, Bob. *Leading Change toward Sustainability.* London: Routledge, 2010.

Farkas, Meredith Gorran. "Building and Sustaining a Culture of Assessment: Best Practices for Change Leadership." *Reference Services Review* 41, no. 1 (2013): 13–31. https://doi.org/10.1108/00907321311300857.

Fox, Robert E., Jr., and Bruce L. Keisling. "Build Your Program by Building Your Team: Inclusively Transforming Services, Staffing and Spaces." *Journal of Library Administration* 56, no. 5 (2016): 526–39. https://doi.org/10.1080/01930826.2015.1105548.

Hackman, Timothy A. "Leading Change in Action: Reorganizing an Academic Library Department Using Kotter's Eight Stage Change Model." *Library Leadership and Management* 31, no. 2 (2017): 1–27.

Horn, Anne. "Strategic Competence: To Soar Above." *Library Management* 29, no. 1/2 (2008): 5–17. https://doi.org/10.1108/01435120810844603.

Kanter, Rosabeth Moss, Barry Stein, and Todd Jick. *The Challenge of Organizational Change: How Companies Experience It and Leaders Guide It*. New York: Free Press, 1992.

Kotter, John P. *Accelerate: Building Strategic Agility for a Faster-Moving World*. Boston: Harvard Business Review Press, 2014.

———. *John Kotter on What Leaders Really Do*. Boston: Harvard Business Review Press, 1999.

———. *Leading Change*. Boston: Harvard Business Review Press, 1996.

———. *Leading Change*. Boston: Harvard Business Review Press, 2012.

———. "Leading Change: Why Transformation Efforts Fail." *Harvard Business Review* 73, no. 2 (March–April 1995): 59–67.

———. *Power and Influence: Beyond Formal Authority*. New York: Free Press, 2008.

———. *A Sense of Urgency*. Boston: Harvard Business Review Press, 2008.

Kotter, John P., and Dan S. Cohen. *The Heart of Change*. Boston: Harvard Business Review Press, 2002.

Lewin, Kurt. "Frontiers in Group Dynamics: Concept, Method and Reality in Social Science; Social Equilibria and Social Change." *Human Relations* 1, no. 1 (1947): 5–41.

Novak, John, and Annette Day. "'The Libraries They Are A-Changin': How Libraries Reorganize." *College and Undergraduate Libraries* 22, no. 3–4 (2015): 358–73. https://doi.org/10.1080/10691316.2015.1067663.

Pressley, Lauren. "Catalyzing Organizational Change: Strategies and Tools to Implement Your Scholarly Communication Agenda." *College and Research Libraries News* 79, no. 9 (2018): 486–97. https://doi.org/10.5860/crln.79.9.486.

Sidorko, Peter Edward. "Transforming Library and Higher Education Support Services: Can Change Models Help?" *Library Management* 29, no. 4 (2008): 307–18. https://doi.org/10.1108/01435120810869093.

Smith, Ian. "Organisational Quality and Organisational Change: Interconnecting Paths to Effectiveness." *Library Management* 32, no. 1 (2011): 111–28. https://doi.org/10.1108/01435121111102629.

Wheeler, Terrie R., and Kristi L. Holmes. "Rapid Transformation of Two Libraries Using Kotter's Eight Steps of Change." *Journal of the Medical Library Association: JMLA* 105, no. 3 (2017): 276–81. https://doi.org/10.5195/jmla.2017.97.

PART I
STRATEGIC PLANNING

Chapter 1

After the Consultants Leave

Implementing Significant Library-wide Change

Kevin Messner and Lindsay Miller

Setting the Change Stage

Miami University is a mid-size public research university located in Oxford, Ohio. Miami has a highly residential student body and is known for its commitment to undergraduate education. There are four libraries on the Oxford campus: King Library, the flagship library that houses most humanities and social sciences collections, and three branches—the Business, Engineering, Science and Technology Library; Music Library; and Art and Architecture Library. The system has eighty-two full-time employees.

During the first half of 2017, the libraries conducted a strategic consulting process that considered library-wide service, staff organization, and space renovation. The libraries contracted with Perkins+Will and brightspot strategy to create a framework to define an overall strategic direction for the libraries. This project scope involved the entire system's services and organizational structure, but space recommendations focused on King Library.

The coauthors of this chapter served as members of the three task forces formed as part of the master planning process. In terms of Kotter's model, the libraries leadership team (the dean, associate dean, and two assistant deans) and hired consultants had the bulk of responsibility in the warm-up phase, or Stages 1–4. After the consultants completed their work, a master plan was presented, and in late summer of 2017 the libraries entered the implementation stage, or in the Kotter model, Stages 5–8. This chapter focuses on middle management's role in facilitating, enabling, and sustaining large-scale, library-wide change and on implementation of a broadly crafted organizational plan in the context of a particular department.

I. Warm-up Phase

STAGE 1: ESTABLISHING A SENSE OF URGENCY

Prior to the consultant visits and the reorganization process, there were several recognized concerns within the library organization in need of address. The libraries

leadership team was a party to campus-wide planning discussions and had defined a need for creation of an architectural master plan for the libraries. Staff organization was another recognized priority. Staff turnover had left many unfilled librarian positions and a substantial number of interim, acting, and visiting positions and roles, leading to unclear and unbalanced workloads for many librarians and staff. Another broadly recognized issue was blurred relationships between different units and the existence of organizational silos that impeded collaboration and communication between departments. There was also a heavy reliance on committee structures with unclear reporting lines for management of core library functions such as instruction, collection development, and outreach and event planning.

For librarians with collections, instruction, reference, and liaison responsibilities (the blended librarian model),[1] the realities of a changing environment and evolving professional roles created additional areas for discussion and tension. Active areas of discussion and concern were the ACRL *Framework for Information Literacy*, pressures on library collection budgets, work on a liaison assessment plan, the viability of a desk-based reference service, and our ability to support librarian roles in entrepreneurial service development and delivery. These and other issues were being discussed formally and informally at all levels of the organization. While there was a broad acknowledgement by library administrators of mounting concerns, an inability to expediently reframe positions and responsibilities within the organization was leading to a sense of having fallen behind the curve.

In December 2016, after a selection process, the dean of libraries announced to library staff that contracts were signed with architecture firm Perkins+Will and strategic consultant brightspot strategy to coordinate a comprehensive review of the libraries system. An outside consultant can challenge the status quo and bring a fresh perspective due to not being tied to company culture or tradition. However, external consultants can lack understanding of the culture, history or personnel of the organization.[2] Kotter suggests bringing in outside consultants to help raise the urgency level and to increase buy-in on the need for change.[3] The objective was for the firms to partner with the libraries to develop a master plan to inform decisions about future renovations. The master plan project was intended to be holistic, integrating issues of space, service, and staff to define the future work and overall strategic direction of the libraries.

Though there was some skepticism among staff about the need for and cost of outside consultants and whether they could actually solve the organization's problems, the decision to hire consultants to spearhead the reorganization and master planning process helped to show that the leadership team was ready to make financial and organizational commitments to address systemic issues and move the libraries forward. This helped create a shared sense of urgency for the leadership team and the organization.

STAGE 2: CREATING THE GUIDING COALITION

According to Kotter, an effective guiding coalition must have the right membership, consisting of four key characteristics: position power (enough key managers), expertise (diverse voices), credibility (reputations of members), and proven leadership abilities.[4] The guiding coalition in the Miami Libraries case consisted of Perkins+Will, brightspot, and a Steering Committee. This committee served as the chief deci-sion-making body throughout the process and determined the direction for the team of consultants. The Steering Committee participated in selected staff visioning and organizational strategy workshops. The Dean of Libraries, Associate Dean of Libraries, and the Coordinator of Library Facilities represented the libraries on this team. Other members of the committee were Miami's Facility Planner; Director of Architecture, Planning, and Engineering; Assistant Provost for Budget and Analytics; and Associate Director of Campus Planning. The libraries' Strategic Communications Coordinator served ex officio.

Overall, the Steering Committee was an effective guiding coalition for the first stages of the process. The presence of the dean and associate dean on the committee showed commitment to the project, though it also contributed to an appearance the project was led top down by the dean's leadership team. Kotter warns that without key line manag-ers in the guiding coalition, the guiding team may have difficulty achieving change and overcoming "massive sources of inertia."[5] Kotter also stresses "a guiding coalition made only of managers—even superb managers who are wonderful people—will cause major change efforts to fail."[6] Although additional voices were included in the various task forces discussed in the next section, an additional member or two of the Steering Committee who was not on the libraries' leadership team might have helped contribute to more buy-in among staff.

STAGE 3: DEVELOPING A VISION AND STRATEGY

The vision for change was led by the consultants and Steering Committee. The vision-ing process for the libraries system included a variety of exercises during which the consultant team engaged with Miami University students, faculty, and staff in a variety of teams and settings. The consultants began their project with a site visit, workshops, and meetings in January 2017, beginning a six-month project including subsequent visits and remote work. The consultant team used its visits to gather information, build consensus, and plan and consolidate what it learned into a final document.

Multiple teams with different objectives were formed prior to the first visit. In addi-tion to the Steering Committee, three task forces—Visioning, Service Design, and Orga-nizational Design—comprised of library staff and stakeholders were formed, each with representation from horizontals and verticals across the library system. The consultants also began conducting listening meetings with each library department.

The first task force to meet as part of the change process was the Visioning group, shown in figure 1.1. Comprised of library leadership, including the dean and associate deans, middle managers, and librarians with continuing contracts, the group met with consultants to kick off the information-gathering stage. Participants focused on the desire to work more as a team and to break down barriers that hinder teamwork and accountability. There was also consensus that a high level of service would continue to be a priority.

The Service Design and Organizational Design task forces met in workshops to create the vision for their respective focus areas. The Service Design group compared desirable and undesirable service experiences and developed methods for the libraries

FIGURE 1.1
The Visioning task force meeting

to adopt excellent service qualities. The group developed a service philosophy statement—"We proactively connect our community with the resources and personalized guidance to empower discovery, creation, and success"—and guiding principles—"Welcoming, Understanding, Proactive and Empowering." The Service Design Task Force developed and the Steering Committee prioritized future service concepts. Building on that work, the Organizational Design Task Force created, through an iterative process, four new service categories, shown in figure 1.2.

1. **Create & Innovate:** Services that provide specialized tools and resources aimed at supporting a wide range of user projects and scholarly work.

2. **Advise & Instruct:** Services that connect users to guidance on research, teaching, and learning—whether by appointment or on demand, physically or virtually.

3. **Access & Borrow:** Services that provide short- and long-term access to library materials as well as spaces.

4. **Share & Showcase:** Services that inform the greater community of the work accomplished through the libraries and solicit input on their future.

FIGURE 1.2
New service categories

This led the consultants and Steering Committee to create new departments based on the service categories (see figure 1.3). Other recommendations were to bring together complementary services, improve transactional service delivery, and enhance user and staff spaces with technology. As the departmental structure took shape, one critical conversation in the final organizational design meeting highlighted the fact that the subject liaison librarians considered it important to maintain a mix of research, instruction, collections, and liaison services in their roles.

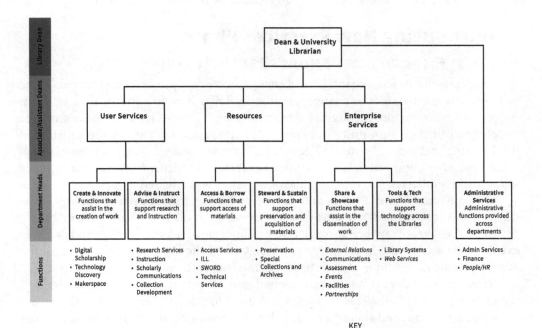

KEY
Items in italics are proposed new functions

FIGURE 1.3
Recommended department structure

A vision for change was articulated in a 260-page document created by Perkins+Will and brightspot. The first section outlined the Facilities Master Plan for a new King Library. The document also included organizational recommendations to dismantle functional committees and group functions in departments, and to integrate branches into the structure by grouping similar branch functions under common departments regardless of location and integrating liaison librarians together. There were also several suggestions to integrate or colocate existing service points.

After the master plan document was finished, the consultants finished their work and the guiding coalition and task forces disbanded. Implementation of the plan was left to library leadership and management.

STAGE 4: COMMUNICATING THE CHANGE VISION

Throughout the entire process of the consultants' visits, transparency was essential. Meeting minutes, consultant slide decks, photographs, supporting documents, and reports were shared with the library community. The Dean of Libraries sent monthly updates between the consultant and task force meetings. Members of each task force shared information with colleagues and direct reports from the workshops, gathering feedback in staff meetings and keeping channels of communication open.

There was a significant period of uncertainty between the final task force meetings and the delivery of recommendations from the consultants. When the final document was finished, it was shared with staff via email and Google Drive. The August all-staff meeting served as the rollout of the change vision by the leadership team.

II. Introducing New Practices Phase
STAGE 5: EMPOWERING BROAD-BASED ACTION

After the consultants left, organizational changes were ready to be implemented. There were quite a few barriers to change, mostly involving how to actually integrate real people and practices into the suggested restructuring. Facilities recommendations were widely seen in the community as being far in the future because of the substantial fund-raising that would be needed. Service and organizational changes were of much more interest to library staff. Uncertainties, rumors, and speculation caused anxiety for many staff members as the new organizational chart was released.

The role of middle managers and supervisors is key in empowering change, especially in this stage. Kotter explains that supervisors can often be what stalls or blocks progress.[7] Conversely, supervisors can also be important drivers of change and can help explain the vision and empower others to act. One of the first priorities was to fill the department head positions in each newly formed department.

After the new departments were named, a draft mission statement was written for each department. The leadership team drafted job descriptions for the six department head positions and submitted those descriptions to Academic Personnel (human resources) for review. The organizational plan and job descriptions underwent review by the Office of Equity and Equal Opportunity (OEEO). Department head positions were filled through a combination of appointment of existing personnel in equally responsible positions and new position searches.

Beyond this and a delineation of which personnel would be placed into which department, relatively little of the operation or structure of each department was detailed in the master plan. While every current member of staff was placed in a department, there were several instances where either the employee or the supervisor thought a staff member had been misplaced in the structure. At the end of June, one of the authors accepted the position of head of the Advise and Instruct department on the condition that there be opportunity to build substructures and additional leadership positions within the department. As the department with primary responsibility for academic outreach, instruction, research services, and collection management, the Advise and Instruct department is home to seventeen full-time-equivalent positions, over half of the system's tenure-track librarian positions, as well as the majority of duties previously managed by library committees.

Weekly department head meetings were established in July, in part to address issues of information siloing. The reorganization expressly hinges on empowered middle managers and open communication between departments, and these meetings have been instrumental in sharing information, making decisions, and clarifying roles and responsibilities. Department head meetings initially included the two assistant deans, officially in the positions of interim department heads while searches were conducted. While intentionally temporary, this arrangement had the benefit of maintaining a regular channel of communication up and down between the leadership team and the departments.

STAGE 6: GENERATING SHORT-TERM WINS

Kotter describes short-term wins as essential to the overall change initiative's success.[8] To encourage change in the department, our change experience had a number of small, highly visible successes that relate back to the goals of the master plan. These wins helped provide evidence that the sacrifices that people were making were paying off. These small successes also served the practical purpose of helping to fine-tune the vision and strategy.

From the authors' perspective, a "push broom" organizational chart with seventeen FTE positions reporting directly to a single department head was an unsustainable prospect, reminiscent of earlier problematic organization in the system. The department heads concurred and advocated for the creation of additional leadership positions within the department, either along the lines of subject areas or along task-oriented lines. Considerations included literature supportive of smaller team sizes[9] and the strong desire of subject specialists to not be split into "instruction" and "collections" positions, while supporting a need for instruction and liaison positions devoted to cross-curricular engagement. A recommendation was approved by the dean for the department head to supervise the approximately twelve subject specialist positions and to develop a position of assistant head with oversight of instruction and outreach functions and supervision of four to five supporting librarians. A national search for Assistant Head of Advise and Instruct was conducted, and an internal hire was made in early 2018. This was a highly visible win that is helping to maintain the momentum for change.

Another significant organizational change was the physical and organizational merger of the King Library reference desk and circulation desk. This initiative had been discussed for years and had been implemented in the branches but was addressed directly as a long-term aim in the master plan. With the departure of the reference desk supervisor, it was decided to revise that position, relocate it within the Access and Borrow (circulation) department, and move forward with combining service points in January 2018. Advise and Instruct librarians remain available on call for research inquiries and as primary respondents to our chat reference service.

In parallel to the broad reorganization, a revisioning of collection development duties within the libraries had been initiated in the fall of 2016. Disruptions in collections budgets had exposed shortcomings in our highly segmented subject fund model, with librarians individually responsible for several impractically small budgets. Concurrent with the broad library reorganization, the collection development committee consolidated funds into four broad-based subject areas, and subject specialist teams share responsibilities. While librarians each maintain liaison roles with distinct academic departments, this model has encouraged a broader view of transdisciplinary collections needs and fostered collaborative decisions. Recently, the teams further consolidated into three subject groups. This successful transition, along with the reorganization of a cross-departmental collection development committee, generated another win for the department. The structure also helps organize the librarians into more ideally sized teams.

STAGE 7: CONSOLIDATING GAINS AND PRODUCING MORE CHANGE

Recruiting, screening, selecting, and onboarding new employees have been a dominant activity in 2017–18, with seventeen hires to date. Significant staff time and energy have been spent on search committee work and, while it was essential to fill new and vacant positions to have a fully staffed library system, it has been difficult to be patient throughout the process. Maintaining momentum when impending change is slow is difficult, but managers can help to handle resistance by continuing to empower their teams and celebrate successes.

Within the Advise and Instruct department, the Learning and Engagement section is taking shape. Led by the assistant head, two Student Success Librarians were hired, one to lead outreach efforts especially for at-risk student populations and another to take on lower-level instruction initiatives such as the Personal Librarian program and first-year-experience and English composition courses. To populate the rest of the team, two librarians with traditional liaison roles transitioned into instructional design positions.

An important part of transitioning existing staff into new roles is taking into account people's strengths and what they are enthusiastic in accomplishing. Involving employees in discussions surrounding organizational change can garner needed feedback and help with buy-in. When possible, the department's practice has been to balance decisions on what the organization needs with existing personnel preferences. Through transparent communication and solicitation of feedback, the department aims to establish trust regarding the new vision and new roles. Multiple searches and alignment of positions have also provided the opportunity to further explain the vision on a more personal level and empower the team with new projects and tasks. Fostering a culture that allows for questions and differing points of view is another way to counter resistance and can lead to increased accountability and engagement.

Strategies employed in this time of change are good practices for leadership in general. Competent employees will become more engaged if they feel valued for the work they are doing. Supervisors, including the authors, began to actively recognize and reward strong performance to motivate employees and increase the likelihood of changes being adopted into the culture. While this hasn't been fully implemented, leaders are asking employees how they'd like to be recognized, acknowledging excellent performance in staff meetings by sharing stories of success, and showing appreciation in one-on-one meetings and via email.

III. Grounding Phase

STAGE 8: ANCHORING NEW APPROACHES IN THE CULTURE

As of this writing the libraries are precisely one year into implementation of the reorganization. Adopting the "anchoring" imagery of Kotter's Stage 8, the department is just arriving into port and dropping anchor after a year of significant change. As has been alluded to, several new hires at the line and management level have been made. The Advise and Instruct department is fully staffed at this time, a benefit for morale that should not be underemphasized. Team training and leadership training plans have been put into place, which hopefully will provide the opportunity for candid conversation among staff and leadership about what is working and what modifications need to be made, in a spirit of continuous improvement.

Analysis and Conclusions

In reflecting back on the change process using Kotter's model, some areas worked well. Consultants provided structure and kept a timeline that avoided losing steam or direction. Communication during the process was effective, and the master plan document was comprehensive and especially useful for facility needs. A multitude of voices was included throughout the process, and the relatively swift pace kept staff from becoming complacent in the earlier stages.

There were points in the process where more support was needed. When forming the guiding coalition, the Steering Committee was heavily weighted with members from Miami's Physical Facilities Department, no doubt to help lead the facilities portion of the project. For balance and another perspective, additional libraries personnel, such as our Organizational Effectiveness Coordinator, could have added a needed voice for the service and staff restructuring portion of the project.

After the consultants left, and the master plan document was completed, the libraries had a well-crafted document but lacked a clear direction in how to implement the change. A strategic plan including assessment metrics, an implementation plan, and the establishment of an implementation committee could have ensured that initiatives were developed and executed to realize the plan's goals. Also, the document was quite long and overwhelming for most of the staff to digest. Kotter describes an effective vision as realistic, focused, flexible, and conveyable in five minutes or less.[10] A one-page summary of the vision to refer to throughout the implementation would have been extremely helpful for both leaders and staff.

When we were communicating the vision and rolling out the master plan, more venues to invite feedback from the community were needed, perhaps in the form of a town hall meeting. Kotter suggests if the community doesn't accept the vision, the next two phases will fail, stating that buy-in occurs only after the community has a chance to "wrestle with it." Kotter goes on to explain that "two-way discussions are an essential method of helping people answer all the questions that occur to them in a transformation event."[11]

Kotter's change model served as a way to reflect back on the change experience, see the process as a whole, and see places where improvements could be made. Some disadvantages of Kotter's model are that it is very top-down and highly dependent on leaders. Employees are expected to follow along, buy in to change, and face removal if they don't toe the line.

The model is also inflexible for situations that use both internal and external change agents or a nonlinear process. The guiding coalition of Stage 2 is assumed to be the same group from start to finish. Additionally, the later steps in the model could be more detailed, particularly in how to create an executable strategy to deliver the vision. Stage 7, Consolidating gains and producing more change, for example, doesn't give much in the way of specific guidance for sustaining change.

In the past year the library system and the Advise and Instruct department have established a baseline and are moving toward securing these changes more firmly in the culture. Next directions will be to reflect on the changes, assess whether the new organization is functioning effectively, and develop metrics and goals to keep the focus on continuous improvement.

Notes

1. Stephen P. Bell and John Shank, "The Blended Librarian: A Blueprint for Redefining the Teaching and Learning Role of Academic Librarians," *College and Research Libraries News* 65, no. 7 (July/August 2004): 374, https://doi.org/10.5860/crln.65.7.7297.
2. Fred Lunenberg, "Managing Change: the Role of the Change Agent," *International Journal of Management, Business and Administration* 13, no. 1 (2010): 1.
3. John P. Kotter, *Leading Change* (Boston: Harvard Business Review Press, 1996), 44.
4. Kotter, *Leading Change*, 57.
5. Kotter, *Leading Change*, 7.
6. Kotter, *Leading Change*, 59.
7. Kotter, *Leading Change*, 112–14.
8. Kotter, *Leading Change*, 121.
9. "Is Your Team Too Big? Too Small? What's the Right Number?" Wharton School of Business, June 14, 2006, http://knowledge.wharton.upenn.edu/article/is-your-team-too-big-too-small-whats-the-right-number-2.
10. Kotter, *Leading Change*, 72.
11. Kotter, *Leading Change*, 99.

Bibliography

Bell, Stephen P., and John Shank. "The Blended Librarian: A Blueprint for Redefining the Teaching and Learning Role of Academic Librarians." *College and Research Libraries News* 65, no. 7 (July/August 2004): 372–75. https://doi.org/10.5860/crln.65.7.7297.

Kotter, John P. *Leading Change*. Boston: Harvard Business Review Press, 1996.

Lunenberg, Fred. "Managing Change: The Role of the Change Agent." *International Journal of Management, Business and Administration* 13, no. 1 (2010): 1–6.

Wharton School of Business. "Is Your Team Too Big? Too Small? What's the Right Number?" June 14, 2006. http://knowledge.wharton.upenn.edu/article/is-your-team-too-big-too-small-whats-the-right-number-2.

Chapter 2

Using the Balanced Scorecard as a Framework for Strategic Planning and Organizational Change

Kris Johnson, Kenning Arlitsch, Martha Kyrillidou, and David Swedman

Setting the Change Stage

Strategic planning processes offer an opportunity to connect foundational practices with a vision for future change. In this chapter, Kotter's eight stages of change are mapped to the Montana State University Library's strategic planning effort (September 2017–February 2018).

Montana State University (MSU) is a land-grant public research university located in Bozeman, Montana. It is listed in the Carnegie Classification as a doctoral-granting university with "Higher Research Activity,"[1] and with a head count of nearly 17,000 students in Fall 2018, it is by far the largest institution of higher education in Montana.[2] The university's annual budget is $201 million, and research and development expenditures exceeded $126 million in 2018.[3] In addition to having its teaching and research missions, MSU is also one of 359 universities in the US awarded Carnegie's community engagement classification.[4]

The MSU Library has one physical location with fifty-five to sixty employees, including approximately eighteen tenure-track faculty and thirty-five classified staff. Led by a consultant who worked with an internal Strategic Planning Group, the library employed

a participatory and community-oriented approach to developing its new strategic plan. The library aligned its planning process with the Balanced Scorecard (BSC) framework, which guided the strategic thinking and formed a foundation for future organizational and individual change.

The BSC is used extensively in business, industry, government, and nonprofit organizations worldwide as a strategic planning and management system. It helps employees align their day-to-day work with a comprehensive strategy, and it helps administrators monitor and measure progress toward implementation of the plan. The BSC outlines objectives and measures that define an organization's success at realizing its envisioned future, and it creates a framework comprising four perspectives: Customer, Internal Processes, Learning & Growth, and Financial. Utilizing the BSC supported a key goal of the MSU Library strategic planning process to include feedback and participation from the whole organization, thus building a strategic plan for which all employees could take ownership while also indicating leadership commitment to a vision.

This chapter will describe the experience of working with the consultant to create a strategic plan utilizing the BSC framework. Throughout the process, individuals from across the library engaged in discussions and stepped into leadership roles beyond the scope of their daily work, which helped the MSU Library create shared buy-in for the new strategic plan. The library is now implementing the plan through the adoption of new processes and procedures shaped by the strategy as well as insights gained from reflecting on Kotter's eight stages of change.

Balanced Scorecard Background and Literature Review

The BSC was introduced as a tool for private business in 1992 by Kaplan and Norton.[5] Initially intended as a performance measurement framework tied to financial success, it later evolved into a full strategic planning and management system, into which an organization outlines how it will achieve success.[6] In 2001 the Association of Research Libraries (ARL) and OCLC brought awareness of the BSC framework to the library community via a three-day workshop.[7] In 2009 ARL launched the Library Scorecard Program as part of an effort to assist ARL member libraries interested in utilizing the BSC for strategic development and inspired by the University of Virginia's (UVA) early adoption in 2001.[8] A 2016 literature review designed to test a series of hypotheses on the main characteristics of the implementation, use, and outcomes of the BSC, by both public and academic libraries worldwide, is recommended.[9] The MSU Library's implementation of the BSC, while not unique in the library profession, was a novel experience for the staff of the library, and the writing of this article was a unique opportunity to reflect on the process in the context of Kotter's eight stages with this chapter.

I. Warm-up Phase

STAGE 1: ESTABLISHING A SENSE OF URGENCY

A variety of environmental and organizational factors contributed to establishing a sense of urgency for the library strategic planning process. In this chapter, internal factors are framed in the context of the MSU Library while external factors are framed within the context of the university and the broader library context within the state of Montana and beyond.

Internal environmental factors included the expiration, in 2016, of the previous strategic plan. An assessment of that plan was completed in 2017, and insights gained from several data collection efforts,[10] helped frame the picture. Other internal factors included an extensive facilities master plan that was completed during the 2015–2016 fiscal year and two highly transformative and all-consuming organizational initiatives: statewide implementation of the Alma library services platform from Ex Libris and digitization of a recently acquired archive.[11] These initiatives led to genuine reflection about the efforts and resources required for future initiatives.

External factors included the conclusion of the seven-year university accreditation process and the imminent launch of a new strategic planning cycle for the university, as well as the early development stages of the statewide academic library consortium, TRAILS, and the continuing success of attracting national funding for library research activities.

The assessment of the 2013–2016 expiring strategic plan was conducted by a group that would later come to be known as Strategic Planning Group 1 (SPG1). The associate dean led the group, which included representation from every library department, and it produced a report highlighting the difficulty of identification and fine-tuning of meaningful, well-aligned measures.

Throughout the process and resulting conversations between SPG1 and the associate dean, much was learned about the value of producing a consistent, coherent, and assessable strategic plan. The dean and associate dean proposed to bring a highly qualified consultant familiar with the BSC, receiving buy-in from the rest of the organization through communications with the library's Executive Team (ET) and the entire library through all-staff meetings.

Through a limited solicitation request for proposals (RFP) process, a consultant was contracted to facilitate the BSC process in September 2017.[12] The consultant received access to various data the library had collected over the recent past, including the assessment report of the previous strategic plan, LibQUAL+ survey data, and the baseline data from ClimateQUAL in 2013. These sources described an organization on a transformative path with capacity constraints, mainly in terms of the staffing. With a creative staff and a strong desire for automation and innovation, the MSU Library was at the crossroads of defining a new path.

Based on advice from the provost, the proposed three-year strategic plan was expanded to a seven-year plan to more closely align with the university's strategic planning and accreditation cycles. Early on, the consultant was introduced to the campus personnel who were responsible for the university strategic planning process and was kept abreast of developments in that area in the interests of aligning the two plans.

In addition, comments solicited during the building master planning process indicated the library was a place that students and faculty value, even while its resources are strained due to increasing enrollment. The need for library space is acute. The realization of the new facilities master plan was envisioned as a long-term process, which also added urgency for a new strategic plan as the funding for such an ambitious project is contingent on successful fund-raising, and the implementation will be staged over a period of years.

Broader strategic conversations were also taking place at the campus level, and it was during the first BSC in-person workshop that the recent results from the accreditation evaluation team from the Northwest Commission on Colleges and Universities were shared. The MSU Library received a commendation (one of only five bestowed upon the university) for its leading role in establishing the statewide academic libraries consortium, TRAILS. The report also identified the need to work on creating more physical spaces that contribute to student success in future years.

Finally, the recent success in securing national grants for library research and digitization were contributing to the sense of urgency for a strategic way of deploying internal resources.

STAGE 2: CREATING THE GUIDING COALITION

The culture of the MSU Library is one in which the staff desire their voice be heard and they frequently advocate for active participation in administrative planning and decision-making processes. Early in the strategic planning process, this "voice" was present in relation to considerations that planning be driven as a democratic, grassroots initiative—that is, from within the organization rather than from the top administrators. As the RFP process unfolded during the summer, the grassroots language was used widely by library administrators as they communicated progress and assured staff that their voices would be heard. However, it became apparent that while the concept of a grassroots initiative was ideal, the reality required an administrative body of some type that could help the consultant understand the library's culture, could facilitate local logistics, and could communicate directly with the staff to counter the concern that the administration was simply going to drive the process from the top. This balancing act is indicative of a constant tension that exists in educational institutions. Administrators are tasked with leading their organizations, but they must find a way to do that in an inclusive and equitable manner respecting diverse voices; otherwise the best strategic plan will fail to gain widespread adoption.

With urgency in mind, the associate dean of the library was tasked with creating a guiding coalition to develop the strategic plan. A second iteration of the Strategic Planning Group, known as SPG2, was tasked to work with the consultant. SPG2 was designed to promote a democratic and empowering dynamic among its members by:
- Including one representative from every department in the library;
- Composing the group of half classified staff and half faculty librarians;
- Giving each representative an equal voice in the process;
- Intentionally excluding the associate dean and dean from the committee (although they took part in the larger process and provided consultation to SPG2 on request)

The consultant rounded out group membership, adding a neutral voice and having the overall responsibility of educating and guiding SPG2 through the BSC process. Following Kotter's Stage 2, this group was intended to guide the organization through the strategic planning process; coordinate the participatory activities associated with this process; and communicate with the organization.

The consultant had a very specific charge, outlined via a formalized contract that detailed expectations for work to be completed, deliverables, and a timeline. The details of this contract were communicated directly between the consultant and the dean of the library, with the overarching goal being to develop a strategic plan and an assessment plan that has measurable objectives using the BSC.

Members of SPG2 knew their work would involve the creation of the next-generation strategic plan, utilizing the Balanced Scorecard approach (BSC), but beyond that, no other roles, responsibilities, or expectations for participation were communicated in advance of the first meeting. A general charge was discussed at the kickoff meeting, but in the spirit of preserving a light administrative touch, SPG2 was left to organize and govern itself.

The process formally kicked off on September 11 with a phone meeting facilitated by the consultant (who was off site) and attended by SPG2 and the associate dean and dean of the library. SPG2 had received an agenda prior to the meeting and came to the meeting looking for further clarification on the process the consultant would be using to guide the organization through its work. It quickly became apparent that roles and responsibilities for all levels of individuals involved in the process, from the consultant through SPG2 and into library administration, needed to be established. It also became clear during this first meeting that the cocreation of a strategic plan in a participatory manner would require a substantial amount of time from SPG2 members during a busy fall semester. Without being tasked or prompted, members of the group identified areas in which they could best contribute to the team, some taking on the role of scheduling, communication, and electronic tool maintenance. Others stepped up to assist with communication, including a spokes-person for the group, sending regular (and specifically formatted) email updates to the library, taking notes and writing the minutes from every meeting, and creating a shared space at the library's intranet to document progress and share content. The group crafted a document called "Roles, Responsibilities, and Expectations" based on their early understanding of the process. This document was presented to and accepted by the administration and the consultant, but it did not specify roles and responsibilities at the individual level for SPG2 members. Thus, members pitched in when they could and helped each other when workloads prevented the fullest participation. Stabilization, common understanding, and agreement were always achieved as the consultant and other members of SPG2 became aware of capacity and compensated as needed. There were moments of creative tension between SPG2 members during the library-wide surveys, while in-person workshops had a more even, collaborative, and convivial tone. This could be due to the primary team (SPG2 and the consultant) absorbing more of the work in order to create the best experience for library personnel. Staff experiences were designed to minimize tension and maximize collaboration and creativity.

By November, when the team began crafting objectives within the formal Balanced Scorecard, it became clear that the absence of the associate dean was a deficit for the group because he had the most internal knowledge of the BSC process. Becoming facile in BSC philosophy, terminology, and processes is a complex process and was difficult to achieve for most members of SPG2, who were simultaneously juggling their other work (no reduction in work assignment was given). Both the dean and the associate dean were asked to participate in the meetings after December as SPG2 and the consultant focused on finalizing the objectives.

Creating the guiding coalition was a critical element of success for MSU; among the lessons learned was the need to allow more time for the guiding coalition to coalesce and come to a clear understanding of the shift from a grassroots approach to a guiding coalition approach. SPG2 had only six weeks and six phone calls with the consultant to do that before the first in-person library-wide BSC workshop in October. A second lesson was the need to allow for a reduction in the normal duties that would permit SPG2 members to focus on the planning task without being distracted by all the pressures of daily work. Creating a guiding coalition of staff members who can communicate, compensate, and support each other was very important for the success of the MSU planning effort.

STAGE 3: DEVELOPING A VISION AND STRATEGY

The process of developing a vision and strategy included frequent communication between the consultant and SPG2, including three site visits aimed at engaging everyone in the library through in-person facilitated sessions, as well as a series of follow-up phone calls aimed at finalizing the strategic objectives, initiatives, and potential metrics.

Mission, Vision, and Values

The MSU Library had well-established mission and vision statements from the 2013 library-wide planning process as well as a statement of values which had been drafted by a past library administration without input from staff. The consultant and SPG2 members reviewed these three statements carefully and agreed that a simple refreshment of these elements would be helpful. However, as the process opened up and feedback was gathered from the whole organization through surveys and discussions of selected readings, it became clear that the staff wanted to spend more time discussing the future of the library with an emphasis on developing a new set of values. The development of values statements took more time and energy than initially anticipated and was brought to closure in December through departmental and all-staff meetings. As a result, the overall strategic plan was completed in March, a month later than originally planned.

An important outcome of the mission and vision statements process was that the entire library staff created its first ever set of values statements, which were designed to align with university values. Despite the additional time this required, one could argue that this process was necessary to help establish a vision to guide our plan; it was a necessary step in creating a solid foundation, regardless of the timeline outlined in the contract. Figure 2.1 lists the 2013–2016 and 2018–2024 mission, vision, and values.

FIGURE 2.1

Mission, vision, and values evolution from 2013–2016 to 2018–2024

2013–2016	2018–2024
The library's mission is to facilitate student and faculty success by providing access to information and knowledge.	We support and advance teaching, learning, and research for Montana State University and the people of Montana by providing access to information and knowledge.

FIGURE 2.1

Mission, vision, and values evolution from 2013–2016 to 2018–2024

2013–2016	2018–2024
We are a progressive research library, integral and committed to student success and the research enterprise of MSU.	We are dynamic, adaptive, and responsive research library. We aspire to build innovative digital and physical spaces where our diverse communities can access and apply information to grow intellectually, build meaningful collaborations, communicate ideas, and envision a better future for Montana and beyond.
Respect Value respect for diversity in all its dimensions. Respect and civility foster collaboration and open communication, which in turn create productive local, regional, and global communities. **Integrity** Value honesty and professionalism in all work. Each individual is personally accountable for his/her work and behavior. **Student Success** Value all students and believe in creating an environment in which they can be successful and reach their full potential. **Excellence** Belief in challenging the MSU community in the pursuit of the highest quality that can be attained.	We are proud to serve the university and the people of Montana, and we strive to do so while embodying the core values of the profession of librarianship (http://www.ala.org/advocacy/intfreedom/corevalues) and MSU (http://www.montana.edu/strategicplan/vision.html). Our values reflect how we carry forward our strategic and operational decisions: we aim to build a more informed, thoughtful, and just world while striving to cultivate an environment that supports the potential for finding joy and meaning in our work. We value: • **Accountability**: We hold ourselves accountable to each other, to the ethics of our profession, and to our statewide supporters. • **Diversity, Equity, and Inclusion:** We seek out diverse perspectives, as they challenge us, help us learn, and broaden our worldview. We work to build spaces and services that are equitable and inclusive to all. We value collegiality and build a culture of care within the Library. • **Empathy:** We promote a culture of empathy and user-centeredness. We invite stakeholders to participate in creating services and resources that are relevant, usable, and desirable. • **Inquiry and Innovation**: We nurture an environment that encourages a collaborative and enthusiastic approach to the pursuit of knowledge. We leverage new technologies and forge cross-disciplinary and cross-cultural collaborations to create new ideas and ways of knowing.

FIGURE 2.1

Mission, vision, and values evolution from 2013–2016 to 2018–2024

2013–2016	2018–2024
	• **Openness and Access**: We believe in openness and equitable access in scholarship and resources. We ensure that information is readily available to our community. People: We respect the humanity, knowledge, and expertise of people in the Library, the university, and the community. • **Teaching and Learning**: We facilitate critical engagement with information and knowledge creation through education and advocacy. • **Transparency and Communication:** We value transparency and clear, open communication in our Library and beyond.

Readings and SOAR Survey

One of the critical organizational readiness exercises implemented early on was an environmental scan in the form of readings and discussions on the future of libraries. SPG2 wanted everyone to prepare to envision the future and encouraged them to read at least two items on the reading list prior to filling out a Strengths, Opportunities, Aspirations, Results (SOAR) survey. SPG2's hope was that these readings would inspire insightful feedback through the survey and future participatory feedback approaches. The articles exposed staff to what is going on outside the MSU environment and highlighted national trends in libraries and higher education useful for the planning process.[13] SPG2 members offered to hold departmental discussions that were scheduled in coordination with the department heads as convenient. These discussions facilitated additional input and catalyzed ideas for the future of the MSU Library.

In-Person Facilitated Workshops

Three three-day site visits by the consultant were spaced across the months of October, November, and December, and each visit included workshops. The rest of the time included meetings with SPG2 and the dean and associate dean. SPG2 developed a method of organizing the days by scheduling two identical half-day workshops so that staff could choose to register for the workshop that best fit into their schedule. SPG2 ensured that each department was represented in order to maximize opportunities for staff conversations across departments. The careful planning of the scheduling allowed for a strategic planning process that was inclusive, participatory, and balanced.

The consultant engaged staff and implemented exercises to gather input for building the MSU Library strategic objectives in all four perspectives: Customer, Internal

Processes, Learning & Growth, and Financial. The result was the development of a change vision in the form of a strategy map described in more detail in the next section.

STAGE 4: COMMUNICATING THE CHANGE VISION

The process of utilizing the BSC approach to create the library's strategic plan represented the process by which the change vision was communicated to the staff and culminated in the final document, also known as the scorecard. Each step in the process, from external readings to in-person workshops, communicated to staff a strategic planning approach that was new and systematic. Each step of the process also built upon the previous, serving to communicate incrementally, through a participatory process, what the BSC was and how it would inform the future of the library. While some in the organization were closer to the process than others (SPG2 for example), everyone in the organization, at varying levels, experienced this changing vision.

Formally, this was communicated strategically and regularly, primarily via email. SPG2 oversaw that process and developed an email template, color-coded, bulleted, and organized for readability. Twenty such emails were sent over a six-month period. Those emails were also archived in a section of the library's intranet devoted to the strategic planning process. Also housed at this site were readings, survey results, workshop agendas, meeting minutes, and more. The strategic planning intranet site served as a location of record for all activities and work products, and it was referred to frequently in the email updates and by SPG2 members when giving updates at departmental meetings. One SPG2 member, a department head, also delivered regular updates at Executive Team meetings to keep that group up-to-date. Culminating updates were also delivered at all-staff meetings and during the in-person discussions of the readings. Through this process, all individuals in the library had multiple opportunities for communication at the individual, departmental, and library level, both in person and electronically.

Two specific steps in the process stand out as having played a significant role in the change vision: (1) creating the Library Values statements and (2) molding the feedback from the in-person workshops into the final set of objectives that comprise the strategy map. Strategy maps help clarify the strategy and the related strategic objectives, whereas scorecards include metrics and targets to measure and manage the performance of the organization against those strategic objectives. As of this writing the MSU Library scorecard is still in development as we have not yet completed a full year of implementation.

As mentioned previously, through participation in the in-person workshops, library staff communicated a desire to spend more time focusing on the creation of the Library Values statements. While this resulted in extending the consultant's work an additional month, SPG2 and administration decided it was important to honor staff's desires in this area. In retrospect, this was an important decision, as it helped staff to more fully participate in shaping the picture of the future library.

More important was the iterative process of finalizing the strategy map. Once the workshops and reading discussions concluded, it was the job of the consultant, a newly formed User Experience and Assessment (UX&A) team (details below under Stage 7), and SPG2 to mold all feedback into something that could become an acceptable strategic plan. This process involved presenting rough drafts of the individual perspectives to various groups (departments, specific stakeholders, administration) through structured meetings, rewriting based on meeting feedback, and communicating the next version of the drafts again, via email and more in-person meetings. The strategy map (figure 2.2) evolved through three drafts, and the organization continued to engage in the process, marking the communication of the change vision as multidirectional and participatory.

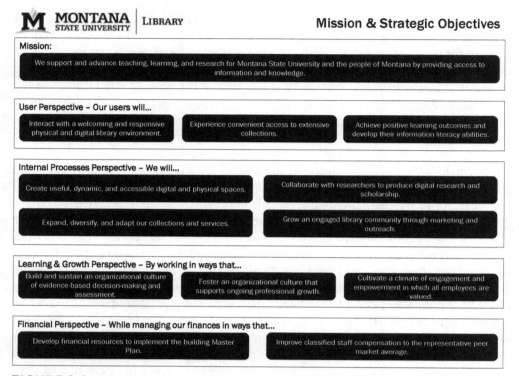

FIGURE 2.2
MSU Library strategy map

Staff feedback regarding our new mission, vision, and strategy has mostly been positive. Staff have publicly remarked that they were greatly appreciative of the participatory nature of the plan's development, and that it possesses "a place for everyone." While there is strong buy-in for the plan at a conceptual level, there is one major concern: How will implementation impact employee workflows, capacity, and expectations?

II. Introducing New Practices Phase

STAGE 5: EMPOWERING BROAD-BASED ACTION

Kotter emphasizes that once the employees accept the change vision, they need to be empowered to act upon it. Within the BSC framework, people in the organization are empowered to act upon the change vision as coordinators of measures or initiatives. These people are responsible for monitoring the performance of a strategic measure or initiative and ensuring that it serves its strategic intent. They are also expected to facilitate strategic collaboration and planning for their assigned measure or initiative by:

- Collaborating across the library and bringing together stakeholder perspectives from different departments;

- Ensuring that there are initiatives that improve the measures [performance indicators] and accomplish the strategic objective;
- Collaborating with the leaders of such initiatives or being a leader for related initiatives; and
- Making recommendations for adjusting the measure, if needed, and proposing new initiatives.

The Strategic Plan Implementation and Assessment Model (figure 2.3) illustrates how coordinators function vis-à-vis other key stakeholders in implementing our change vision.

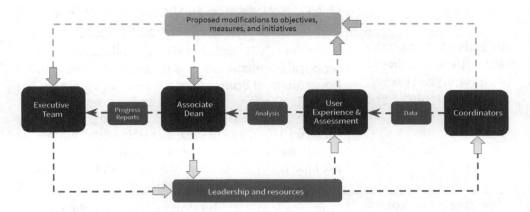

FIGURE 2.3
MSU Library Strategic Plan Implementation and Assessment Model

Over half of the organization's employees have been identified as coordinators. While most of these people have embraced this role, others have expressed trepidation about their capacity to take on these new responsibilities due to the impact it would have on their current work duties. Overall, healthy pondering continues to occur about the staff capacity versus ability to achieve accomplishments. How much and how quickly can staff achieve? How can the library move incrementally in the absence of extra funding? How can the organization gain or maintain momentum despite staff turnover?

STAGE 6: GENERATING SHORT-TERM WINS

Kotter acknowledges that the change process "goes through a series of phases that, in total, usually require a considerable length of time,"[14] but he also stresses the value of short-term wins. Without these wins to recognize and celebrate, an organization risks loss of momentum and declining morale. Kotter further explains that creating short-term wins is an active process that requires deliberate planning and action. The short-term wins described in figure 2.4 were deliberately executed to align with the strategic plan as it developed.

Most of the items described in figure 2.4 are in process, but they all represent significant, and in some cases foundational, milestones toward achieving objectives in the strategic plan. Therefore, they are considered short-term wins that achieve Kotter's aim of creating measurable progress to sustain momentum and staff morale.

FIGURE 2.4

Short-term wins mapped to strategy map objectives

Strategy Map Objective	Short-Term Win
Objective 2.1—Create useful, dynamic, and accessible digital and physical spaces	Created a Digital Accessibility Committee to help ensure that all electronic content managed by the library would comply with accessibility requirements for disabled users. This action aligns with a campus-wide effort after MSU came to agreement with Department of Education's Office of Civil Rights to bring MSU websites and the campus learning management system into accessibility compliance.
Objective 2.2—Collaborate with researchers to produce digital research and scholarship	Submitted CLIR Digitizing Hidden Collections final proposal in collaboration with researchers from the Department of Ecology and the Montana State Library. The six-month proposal process resulted in a $300K award, MSU Library's first funded grant in this category. Hired a CLIR Postdoctoral Fellow in the Digital Humanities. This position will work closely with the Ivan Doig Center, which is managed by the College of Letters and Science.
Objective 2.3—Expand, diversify, and adapt our collections and services	Conversations with the Montana Office of the Commissioner of Higher Education have led to commitment to a statewide OER initiative, in collaboration with TRAILS, Montana's academic library consortium. Several new archival collections have been acquired, and more are on the horizon. The library has dramatically increased the number of interviews in "Angling Oral Histories," a showcase project for MSU's Trout and Salmonid Collection.
Objective 3.1—Build and sustain an organizational culture of evidence-based decision-making and assessment.	Established the UX&A (User Experience and Assessment) program, comprising one full-time librarian faculty member and one classified staff member. UX&A has been charged with coordinating the fulfillment of strategic plan initiatives as well as producing reports that will help communicate progress of the plan.
Objective 3.3—Cultivate a climate of engagement and empowerment in which all employees are valued.	Ran the ClimateQUAL survey in summer 2018 to gather employee input about the organization and their job satisfaction. This survey occurred five years after the initial survey was run to gather baseline data.

FIGURE 2.4
Short-term wins mapped to strategy map objectives

Strategy Map Objective	Short-Term Win
Objective 4.1—Develop financial resources to implement the building Master Plan	Worked with Campus Planning, Design, and Construction to develop a plan that will move part of the general print collection to an external storage facility. An RFI and RFP were issued and a contractor hired, and during late spring and early summer of 2019 the collection was inventoried, a deselection project completed, and a move was underway to relocate a portion of the collection to an off-site annex. This is a crucial initial step of the Master Plan.

STAGE 7: CONSOLIDATING GAINS AND PRODUCING MORE CHANGE

This chapter was originally submitted for publication six months after launching the strategic plan. Since then, personnel in the newly formed UX&A team have assisted the organization in maintaining momentum for the plan. The official mission of UX&A is "to work collaboratively with all library departments to continually measure, assess, and improve users' experiences of library services and instruction, both physical and virtual." UX&A has led the primary efforts to move forward on action items written into the "What's Next" section of the final report for the strategic planning process. The following action items will help the library to consolidate gains and produce more change early in the process:

- Measures Coordinators will work collaboratively with UX&A staff to establish targets in all the measures and monitor trends.
- Initiatives Coordinators will oversee large umbrella initiatives comprised of a series of department-level projects and work across departments as needed to advance initiatives with support from the Executive Team.
- The Executive Team will work with Initiative Coordinators, Measures Coordinators, and UX&A staff to monitor both Strategic Initiatives and Measures—that is, a set of projects that are designed to help the MSU Library to achieve its objectives and targets.
- Initiatives will be defined and prioritized by the Executive Team with input from the Measures and Initiative Coordinators and UX&A staff using project management and prioritization principles as defined in the Project Management and Prioritization Initiative; existing good practices from project management processes currently used in departments will be deployed consistently across departments.
- Measures and Initiatives Coordinators will convene as needed to ensure progress is achieved.
- Review meetings will be held on a semi-annual basis. The review will serve to (1) inform; (2) evaluate the objectives, measures, targets, and initiatives; and (3)

refresh the strategy. Strategy update communication emails may be released in between semi-annual meetings.

- The UX&A program staff will develop a strategic plan dashboard with Tableau visualization software.

III. Grounding Phase

STAGE 8: ANCHORING NEW APPROACHES IN THE CULTURE

The UX&A team has been meeting with measure coordinators to establish detailed processes, refine measures, and define projects to realize targets through the strategic initiatives. There were also discussions during the strategic planning process about changing the departmental annual reports so that they are tied specifically to annual strategic plan progress and clearly showcase how departments contribute to strategy implementation. The role of the library's Executive Team is becoming more critical in the implementation process. The UX&A team works with the organization and the Executive Team, and department heads can make sure the strategy is a living discussion document during departmental meetings. Anchoring this on the leadership of the organization and the leadership seeking to anchor this on the staff is a dialectic and iterative process, ensuring that leadership is listening to staff and staff are listening to leadership in a purposeful and healthy way.

It became clear through the planning process that a systematic project management approach is needed. Certain departments follow more formalized annual planning processes, and SPG2 members were willing to share some of these internal processes that shape departmental cultures. The project management practices that are established in some of the MSU library departments will be a good way to formalize progress for different initiatives and projects across the organization.

Analysis and Conclusion

Creating a seven-year strategic plan in seven months was an ambitious but worthwhile effort, and the objectives articulated in the plan will have long-lasting value for MSU. The objectives are articulated on a one-page strategy map (figure 2.2) that places users at the heart of our desired future.[15] The hope for any strategic plan is that it becomes a living document against which all major initiatives and expenditures of human and financial resources are weighed. The BSC provides a structured framework against which to measure that accounting, and while it is early, we are pleased with the quality of the plan we have produced and the buy-in we have achieved.

Kotter's eight-step change model has helped us reflect on our recent strategic planning process, and in this chapter, we successfully mapped many key aspects of that process to the change model. We have found that the iterative nature of the change model resonates with the iterative and participatory framework of development that we used to generate the strategy map and the BSC at the MSU Library. The authors' desire to capture the change process in this chapter was guided by our reflections, by the contributions of our colleagues to the strategic planning process, and by our commitment to achieve tangible outcomes.

MSU Library has a vision for reporting successes of the strategic plan that will be guided by our shared sense of mission, vision, and values. Through the lens of Kotter's principles for change, we look forward to continuing to foster momentum, morale, and good management and leadership practice.

Notes

1. "About the Carnegie Classification," Carnegie Classification of Institutions of Higher Education homepage, accessed May 9, 2018, http://carnegieclassifications.iu.edu/.
2. Gail Schontzler, "MSU Sets New Enrollment Record—16,902 Students," *Bozeman (MT) Daily Chronicle*, September 24, 2018, https://www.bozemandailychronicle.com/news/montana_state_university/msu-sets-new-enrollment-record-students/article_5c600779-bed9-54ec-bae2-a273f11a2398.html.
3. Gail Schontzler, "MSU Research Spending Totals $126 Million, Second Highest in History," *Bozeman (MT) Daily Chronicle*, September 13, 2018, https://www.bozemandailychronicle.com/news/montana_state_university/msu-research-spending-totals-million-second-highest-in-history/article_47af68f8-f1f7-52e5-afeb-3a718986c0f8.html.
4. "About the Carnegie Classification."
5. Five citations in the bibliography represent the complete series written by Robert S. Kaplan and David P. Norton on the Balanced Scorecard system. Cumulatively, all five present a full philosophy of their approach.
6. Marta de la Mano and Claire Creaser, "The Impact of the Balanced Scorecard in Libraries: From Performance Measurement to Strategic Management," *Journal of Librarianship and Information Science* 48, no. 2 (2016): 191–208. https://doi.org/10.1177/0961000614558078.
7. James Self, "From Values to Metrics: Implementation of the Balanced Scorecard at a University Library," *Performance Measurement and Metrics* 4, no. 2 (2003): 57–63, https://doi.org/10.1108/14678040310486891; Julia C. Blixrud, "Mainstreaming New Measures," *ARL Bimonthly Report*, no. 230/231 (October/December 2003): 1–8.
8. Self, "From Values to Metrics"; James Self, "Metrics and Management: Applying the Results of the Balanced Scorecard," *Performance Measurement and Metrics* 5, no. 3 (2004): 101–5, https://doi.org/10.1108/14678040410570111; Martha Kyrillidou, "The ARL Library Scorecard Pilot: Using the Balanced Scorecard in Research Libraries," *Research Library Issues: A Bimonthly Report from ARL, CNI, and SPARC*, no. 271 (August 2010): 36–40.
9. de la Mano and Creaser, "The Impact of the Balanced Scorecard."
10. ClimateQUAL baseline in 2013 and LibQUAL+ (most recently in 2016) among others.
11. Kenning Arlitsch et al., "Digitizing the Ivan Doig Archive at Montana State University: A Rise to the Challenge Illustrates Creative Tension," *Journal of Library Administration* 57, no. 1 (2017): 99–113, https://doi.org/10.1080/01930826.2016.1251251.
12. The same consultant facilitated a nominal group technique focus group and a series of structured conversations in the library over two days in May 2017. The purpose of this short visit was to assess the MSU Library's organizational culture and attitudes in order to set the stage for the more formal and detailed participatory process in the fall, which would focus on developing a strategy for the future. The structured conversations allowed all staff members to openly discuss with the consultant organizational issues important to them. The consultant then compiled the information into a report that included nine recommendations for ways the library could initiate culture change in areas such as human resource management, project management, and communication. Discussing the current organizational culture was a useful reference point for launching the participatory approach employed during the fall semester.
13. Select examples include: S. Adams Becker et al., *NMC Horizon Report: 2017 Library Edition* (Austin, TX: New Media Consortium, 2017), https://www.nmc.org/publication/nmc-horizon-report-2017-library-edition/; S. Adams Becker et al., *NMC Horizon Report: 2017 Higher Education Edition* (Austin, TX: New Media Consortium, 2017), https://www.nmc.org/publication/nmc-horizon-report-2017-higher-education-edition/; Sue Baughman et al., *Report of the Association of Research Libraries Strategic Thinking and Design Initiative* (Washington, DC:

Association of Research Libraries, August 2014), http://www.arl.org/about/arl-strategic-think-ing-and-design/final-report-of-the-arl-strategic-thinking-a-design-initiative; Brian Mathews, "Cultivating Complexity: How I Stopped Driving the Innovation Train and Started Planting Seeds in the Community Garden," September 2017, VTechWorks, Virginia Tech, https://vtechworks.lib.vt.edu/handle/10919/78886.

14. John P. Kotter, "Leading Change: Why Transformation Efforts Fail," *Harvard Business Review* 73, no. 2 (1995): 59.

15. We created laminated double-sided placemats with the Strategy Map on one side and the Mission, Vision, and Values and the Strategic Initiatives on the other side. These placemats were distributed to all library staff and can also be found in our meeting rooms.

Bibliography

Adams Becker, S., M. Cummins, A. Davis, A. Freeman, C. Giesinger Hall, V. Ananthanarayanan, K. Langley, and N. Wolfson. *NMC Horizon Report: 2017 Library Edition*. Austin, TX: New Media Consortium, 2017. https://www.nmc.org/publication/nmc-horizon-report-2017-library-edition/.

Adams Becker, S., M. Cummins, A. Davis, A. Freeman, C. Hall Giesinger, and V. Ananthanarayanan. *NMC Horizon Report 2017 Higher Education Edition*. Austin, TX: New Media Consortium, 2017. https://www.nmc.org/publication/nmc-horizon-report-2017-higher-education-edition/.

Arlitsch, Kenning, Melanie Hawks, Hannah McKelvey, Michelle Gollehon, and Jan Zauha. "Digitizing the Ivan Doig Archive at Montana State University: A Rise to the Challenge Illustrates Creative Tension." *Journal of Library Administration* 57, no. 1 (2017): 99–113. https://doi.org/10.1080/0193082 6.2016.1251251.

Baughman, Sue, David Consiglio, Lee Anne George, Susan Gibbons, David Gift, Kaylyn Groves, Tom Hickerson, et al. *Report of the Association of Research Libraries Strategic Thinking and Design Initia-tive*. Washington, DC: Association of Research Libraries, August 2014. http://www.arl.org/about/arl-strategic-thinking-and-design/final-report-of-the-arl-strategic-thinking-a-design-initiative.

Blixrud, Julia C. "Mainstreaming New Measures." *ARL: A Bimonthly Report*, no. 230/231 (October/December 2003): 1–8.

Carnegie Classification of Institutions of Higher Education homepage. Accessed May 9, 2018. http://carnegieclassifications.iu.edu/.

de la Mano, Marta, and Claire Creaser. "The Impact of the Balanced Scorecard in Libraries: From Perfor-mance Measurement to Strategic Management." *Journal of Librarianship and Information Science* 48, no 2 (2016): 191–208. https://doi.org/10.1177/0961000614558078.

Kaplan, Robert S., and David P. Norton. *Alignment*. Boston: Harvard Business Review Press, 2006.

———. *The Balanced Scorecard: Translating Strategy into Action*. Boston: Harvard Business Review Press, 1996.

———. *The Execution Premium*. Boston, MA: Harvard Business Press, 2008.

———. *The Strategy-Focused Organization*. Boston: Harvard Business Review Press, 2001.

———. *Strategy Maps*. Boston: Harvard Business Review Press, 2004.

Kotter, John P. "Leading Change: Why Transformation Efforts Fail." *Harvard Business Review* 73, no. 2 (1995): 59–67.

Kyrillidou, Martha. "The ARL Library Scorecard Pilot: Using the Balanced Scorecard in Research Librar-ies." *Research Library Issues: A Bimonthly Report from ARL, CNI, and SPARC*, no. 271 (August 2010): 36–40.

Mathews, Brian. "Cultivating Complexity: How I Stopped Driving the Innovation Train and Started Planting Seeds in the Community Garden." September 2017. VTechWorks, Virginia Tech. https://vtechworks.lib.vt.edu/handle/10919/78886.

Schontzler, Gail. "MSU Research Spending Totals $126 Million, Second Highest in History." *Bozeman (MT) Daily Chronicle*, September 13, 2018. https://www.bozemandailychronicle.com/news/montana_state_university/msu-research-spending-totals-million-second-highest-in-history/article_47af68f8-f1f7-52e5-afeb-3a718986c0f8.html.

———. "MSU Sets New Enrollment Record—16,902 Students." *Bozeman (MT) Daily Chronicle*, September 24, 2018. https://www.bozemandailychronicle.com/news/montana_state_university/msu-sets-new-enrollment-record-students/article_5c600779-bed9-54ec-bae2-a273f11a2398.html.

Self, James. "From Values to Metrics: Implementation of the Balanced Scorecard at a University Library." *Performance Measurement and Metrics* 4, no. 2 (2003): 57–63. https://doi.org/10.1108/14678040310486891.

———. "Metrics and Management: Applying the Results of the Balanced Scorecard." *Performance Measurement and Metrics* 5, no. 3 (2004): 101–5. https://doi.org/10.1108/14678040410570111.

Chapter 3

Staying on Track

Leading Change by Sharing Progress toward Strategic Goals

Michelle Brannen, Regina Mays, and Manda Sexton

Setting the Change Stage

Most academic libraries engage in some type of strategic planning, often primarily or solely because their parent institutions require it. Libraries create plans based on a well-known and well-worn formula—mission, values, vision, goals. The plans satisfy university or college administrators and look good on paper—which in many cases is where they stay. Even the most carefully crafted plans are often forgotten until the next round of strategic planning rolls around. Three to five years, the typical implementation period, is a long time in the life of an academic library. Without some formal system of oversight and follow-up, the chances are low that all individuals throughout a large library will stay focused on an increasingly distant plan.

The University of Tennessee, Knoxville, located in Knoxville, Tennessee, is the flagship campus of the University of Tennessee System. With 22,317 undergraduate students and 6,004 graduate and professional students, the university has an R1 Carnegie Classification. Like many large universities, UT Knoxville requires each of its colleges, including the University Libraries, to create a strategic plan on a regular basis. The University Libraries administer the John C. Hodges Library and two branch libraries, the Webster C. Pendergrass Agriculture and Veterinary Medicine Library and the George F. DeVine Music Library, and have 140 staff in the organization. The Libraries have a history of engaging in strategic planning every three to five years but until recently had not enacted a formal process for monitoring progress toward strategic goals.

In 2016, the Libraries committed to a robust, inclusive, and in-depth planning process that incorporated, as a final step, creation of a group with the formal charge of tracking strategic progress. That group was endowed with the necessary support, resources, and endorsement to achieve the task. This chapter will explore the work of this committee through the structure of Kotter's eight-step process for leading change, first introduced in 1995 in his article "Leading Change: Why Transformation Efforts Fail."[1] This article quickly became one of the most requested articles from the *Harvard Business Review*, and Kotter later expounded upon the model in several published books and articles.

I. Warm-up Phase

STAGE 1: ESTABLISHING A SENSE OF URGENCY

Establishing a sense of urgency about the importance of the Libraries' strategic goals—and therefore the need to carefully monitor progress toward those goals—began with the strategic planning process itself. Library administration formed a small team of six members from across the Libraries to serve as the Strategic Planning Steering Committee. The Steering Committee led a year-long planning process that was more inclusive and comprehensive than any previous planning experience.

The planning process included repeated opportunities for feedback from library staff, partly in response to staff's expressed desire to be more involved in decision-making. Over the course of a year, multiple internal surveys, open meetings, and small focus groups were conducted to garner staff input at every step of the planning process. These were also structured to communicate information to staff. Surveys regularly included explanatory information that respondents needed to comprehend before answering the questions. Meetings and focus groups were similarly structured.

Seeking extensive feedback from stakeholders outside the Libraries underscored the priority the Libraries set on the planning process. The Steering Committee conducted group meetings or individual interviews with key stakeholders including faculty, students, alumni, community members, and university administrators. Individual interviews were scheduled with administrators in every area of the university including the graduate school, research, student life, and so on. It is important that in these interviews, the administrators were not asked anything about the Libraries; rather they were asked what challenges they themselves faced. Their illuminating answers were powerful tools in creating a sense of urgency for setting and reaching strategic goals for the Libraries.

The completed strategic plan (figure 3.1) is organized into five broad strategic areas: Teaching, Learning, and Innovation; Empowering Research; Collaborative Collections; Organizational Excellence; and Sharing Our Story.[2] Within each area is a fairly broad set of goals. The number of goals

Empowering Research

Through investigation and creativity, scholars generate ideas and discoveries that improve our community, our region, and lives around the world. Librarians, as information specialists and stewards of the scholarly record, recognize the power inherent in scholarship and are crucial partners in its creation and dissemination.

2.1 Educate and collaborate with the campus community on emerging forms of scholarly discovery, knowledge management, and research dissemination.

2.1.1 Develop a business and sustainability plan for publishing and preserving born digital scholarship produced or edited by the UTK community.

2.1.2 Highlight campus research that utilizes innovative and open dissemination methods via the Libraries' website and digital displays.

2.1.3 Deploy a team-based approach to liaison service to better support interdisciplinary research teams and programs.

2.1.4 Host the Correspondence of James K. Polk Transcriptions, April 1848-June 1849 in Islandora.

2.1.5 Promote awareness of data-related issues in the Libraries and across campus.

2.1.6 Develop best practices, create documentation, and provide training for liaisons on emerging forms of scholarly discovery, knowledge management, and research dissemination.

FIGURE 3.1

Excerpt from UT Libraries Strategic Plan, 2017–2022

ranges from four to six. Lastly, and crucially, the Libraries' administrative group was responsible for the final piece of the strategic plan: a list of 154 concrete action items to be accomplished over the next three to five years.

Because of this, all the senior leaders in the Libraries shared the sense of urgency that had been fostered among the rest of the staff. Without the support and cooperation of these key players, buy-in from other stakeholders would be unlikely to create change.

STAGE 2: CREATING THE GUIDING COALITION

With library administration serving as a solid foundation for a guiding coalition, the next step was to form a team of individuals who would lead the hands-on work of creating processes for monitoring and reporting progress. In early 2017, the Libraries formed the Strategic Achievement Review (StAR) team. The name was deliberately chosen for its PR-friendly acronym.

The StAR team would be led by the newly minted Coordinator of Strategic Planning and Assessment, formerly assessment librarian. To be a nimble, productive group, the StAR team would include only two other members, one faculty member and one staff member. These members were chosen by the Libraries' faculty and staff advisory councils, respectively. Although it was part of the coordinator's job description to lead this group, the other two members did this as a service to the library, and all three maintained their regular job responsibilities in addition to working on the StAR team. It was important to the success of the group that two of the three members were chosen by other faculty and staff. This egalitarian formation was intended to give the group credibility outside the team and to foster a sense of shared ownership of both the strategic plan itself and of the process of tracking progress.

The last act of the Strategic Planning Steering Committee was to develop a mission and charge for the StAR team that included established goals. While the charge was developed by the Steering Committee, it was given to the team by the dean.

The charge is as follows:

> The mission of the StAR Team is to facilitate keeping the Libraries' strategic goals in the forefront of everyone's minds, by systematically tracking and communicating progress toward strategic goals. The group will accomplish this mission by engaging in the following activities:
>
> - Consult on a regular schedule with Library Administration in order to:
> - Track progress toward strategic goals
> - Communicate progress to the whole organization effectively and regularly
> - Consult with departments and individuals as requested to support the formation and review of goals and action items, and to help identify gaps in progress and/or goals/strategies that are no longer meaningful
> - Collaborate to create and monitor/promote an annual planning calendar

- Maintain the Strategic Plan as a living document and track changes
- Maintain a website for communication about progress toward goals

The team, thus formed and charged, would next turn to developing a vision of the change they were charged to enact and strategies to achieve that change.

STAGE 3: DEVELOPING A VISION AND STRATEGY

Armed with a broad charge and no previous strategy to follow, the StAR team spent the first year exploring ways to make the strategic plan central to the work of individuals and groups—including ways to change it from a high-level guiding document used during annual review and planning periods to a practical, living document that could inform decision-making in everyday work. In order to be sustainable, the process would need to become part of staff workflow. While the team understood that it might require a great amount of work and time on the front end to establish new practices, they also understood that any system that required a large amount of work on a continuing basis—either by themselves or by library staff in general—was unrealistic.

The team's strategy was two-pronged: make the process valuable to individuals by showing them what's in it for them, and make the process as easy and automatic as possible. They looked at ways to "sell" the benefits of reporting progress toward goals, brainstormed tools and processes that could lessen the workload of tracking and reporting, and planned fun and engaging ways to encourage and celebrate success.

The team developed a rough timeline, with the understanding that there would be a lot of trial and error involved. The first year would be devoted to creating a website and developing systems for tracking and reporting progress on a regular basis, including systems for individuals to report progress. In the second year, the team would develop processes for integrating tracking and reporting into the annual planning calendar. In order to maintain the strategic plan as a living document, they would also develop processes for reviewing goals—with the rationale that after a year it would become apparent which goals were no longer relevant or were suffering from stalled progress. The team anticipated that the third year would involve only tweaking, cementing, and continuing successful changes.

The team understood that they would need widespread cooperation, as well as the continued support and approval of library administration. Effective, regular communication would be crucial, and communication would start with communicating the change vision.

STAGE 4: COMMUNICATING THE CHANGE VISION

Since communication is a major part of the change the StAR team sought to create, there is considerable overlap between the steps taken to communicate the change vision and the strategies developed to communicate progress toward goals. The charge to the StAR team included outward promotion of the Libraries' strategic plan. To maintain staff and faculty engagement, StAR consistently communicates with the library as a whole on different actions toward completion.

The hub of StAR's communication strategy is the website the team created. The StAR website publishes an ongoing list of library accomplishments that advance strategic goals. The front page of the site includes a list of the five Areas of Emphasis, their descriptions, and their *medals*. Medals represent the number of reported actions taken toward completion of that Area of Emphasis. Also on the front page are links to the strategic plan with the action items (ten-page document), the StAR Plan, a breakdown of each Area of Emphasis, a link for employees to report their progress, and a Priority Selection Tool (figure 3.2). Visitors to the sub-pages of each Area of Emphasis can expand a pull-down menu to view the action items beneath each goal. Medals are awarded on the StAR website to those who have taken steps toward completing a goal. Action items include a list of the medals with a very brief description of actions taken toward the goal.

Pendergrass Library, 2017-2018's
Personalized List of Action Priorities

Welcome to your personalized plan!
We hope you find this report a useful way to keep track of your contributions to the libraries strategic plan. We have grouped information in a couple of different ways. You are free to use this in any way you wish. If you have feedback, please let us know.

Don't forget to share your story and submit your contributions to the StAR team!
Thanks from the StAR team,
Manda Sexton, Regina Mays, and Michelle Brannen

Dashboard
The dashboard provides you a list of the action priority items you've indicated interest in at a quick glance. Use the numbers to identify items in the Strategic Plan.

Area of Emphasis	Goals	Action Priorities
Teaching, Learning, & Innovation	1.1, 1.2, 1.3, 1.4, 1.5, 1.6	1.1.1, 1.1.2, 1.1.5, 1.1.10 1.2.2, 1.2.4, 1.2.6, 1.2.7 1.3.2, 1.3.5, 1.3.7 1.4.5, 1.4.7 1.5.2, 1.5.6, 1.5.7 1.6.1, 1.6.2, 1.6.3, 1.6.4, 1.6.5

FIGURE 3.2
Report generated for Pendergrass Library using the StAR Priority Selection Tool

Perhaps the most important part of the website is the Tell Us Your Progress Form. The StAR team explored ideas for reporting progress that included gathering feedback in open library meetings and email suggestions from staff, leading to the creation of this form. The form is the easiest way for library staff to alert StAR when progress has been made toward an action item. This form is the first place individuals report accomplishments. One strategy StAR employs to create momentum is to encourage reporting all steps toward fulfillment of a strategic action item.

StAR also encourages staff and supervisors to use the reporting form as a tool to track success library-wide. One practical use StAR suggests is to incorporate the information reported using the Tell Us Your Progress form into annual departmental reports that showcase activities and accomplishments each academic year. A second suggested use has been to utilize the information in individual annual performance evaluations.

The website serves both as a reminder of the shared journey towards the Libraries' goals and as a tangible presence of the StAR team. StAR has been invited to several departments to speak to their involvement with the strategic plan and the process of planning new departmental goals for the coming years. In the near future, StAR hopes to receive training in goal-setting techniques—information they can bring back to library departments. In this way, they can help departments set manageable goals toward strategic priorities and make them easily trackable. These meetings also allow the team to see overlapping departmental goals and connect individuals accordingly.

At least one member of the StAR team serves on Library Council, an advisory body to the Dean of Libraries. StAR has a standing time within the meeting to report on the progress of the team and of the strategic plan as a whole. Feedback from the council helps the team adjust their goals and outreach efforts.

II. Introducing New Practices Phase

STAGE 5: EMPOWERING BROAD-BASED ACTION

The empowerment stage involves removing structural barriers to creating change. In the team's experience, the greatest barrier has been a low level of employee engagement with the new system for tracking progress toward strategic goals. With support from library administration, StAR has been able to explore and experiment with methods for collecting information from individuals and groups, developing tools to make tracking and reporting progress easier, and communicating results back to the organization.

While not every strategy the team explored has been put into use, many have helped generate needed information and have raised awareness of the work of this group within the organization. In addition to the needed input, StAR has taken multiple approaches to communicating progress on goals—including blog posts, email communications, printed documents, presentations, and celebrations. Support from library administration has allowed the StAR team to be creative and to engage with library staff in various ways, generating wins and increasing momentum for the project.

STAGE 6: GENERATING SHORT-TERM WINS

StAR is tasked with recording and celebrating progress made toward the strategic plan, no matter how small the progress may be. Thus, in the medals list, StAR not only acknowledges when an action item has been completed but also lists even small contributions made by individuals or groups, with the thought being that all the small steps are needed to achieve the larger goal. By putting emphasis on these smaller results, the team demonstrates consistent change to skeptics, acknowledges contributions by individuals throughout the organization, and sustains efforts over the long term.

While the tools StAR created have met with positive feedback overall, getting library staff to utilize the tools is another story. The team explored new approaches to obtaining the needed information, such as data mining annual departmental reports. Over time, the team faced the inevitable decrease in employee engagement with the new tracking method. Little to no progress was reported to the group, despite significant, observable progress toward library goals. It became clear that the team needed some different strategies.

Library staff are subject to numerous mandates for reporting and reviews, so it is understandable that individual employees experience reporting fatigue and choose not to interact with the group. As an alternate tactic, StAR decided to take the required annual departmental reports and mine them for progress toward strategic goals. These reports showcase activities and accomplishments made by the department throughout the year and are submitted to Libraries Administration and shared throughout the organization. The team, along with a group of graduate students from the university's School of Information Sciences, spent a day mining departmental reports for progress made toward the action items. Rather than making this an ongoing practice, the intention was to jump-start the ability to show substantial progress and demonstrate to staff the benefits of reporting progress and being acknowledged for their contributions.

STAGE 7: CONSOLIDATING GAINS AND PRODUCING MORE CHANGE

Entering the second year of work with StAR, the team paused to take stock of the work completed and to consider new approaches. Throughout the first year, the team worked very hard to communicate throughout the organization. To keep the strategic plan foremost in the minds of library staff, the team took every opportunity to talk to groups throughout the library. Once per semester, the library holds an all-staff meeting, and the StAR team has made regular presentations at these meetings, offering a helpful in-person reminder for individuals to report their progress and celebrate their

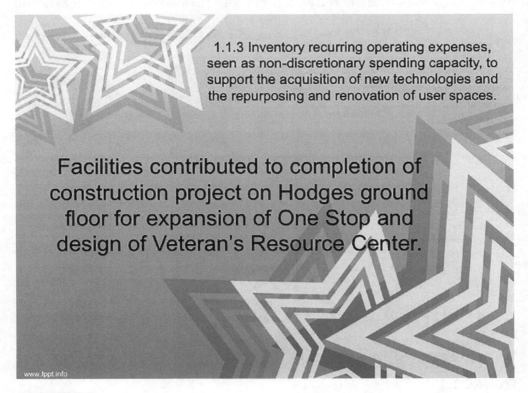

FIGURE 3.3
Slide from StAR celebration documenting progress toward a specific action item

accomplishments. Additionally, team members have attended departmental and working group meetings to discuss goal setting and to tout the benefits of using the StAR reporting features in the planning process. StAR also created a booklet version of the strategic plan, hoping to create a more useful working format for the document.

In January 2018—not quite a year into the process—StAR hosted a party for the entire library to celebrate the accomplishments reported thus far. As staff members socialized, two large screens played a slideshow of accomplishments (figure 3.3). Informal feedback indicated that the slideshow was popular and well-received. It offered positive reinforcement to those who had reported progress and, the team hoped, encouraged more people to report activity to StAR.

Sharing progress through a blog, through email communications, at meetings, and through events such as the party has proved far easier than actually tracking the progress on specific action items and goals. In an effort to consolidate the work achieved thus far, StAR created a spreadsheet of 154 individual action items. StAR worked with administrators to help identify individuals and groups working on each action item. By determining who "owns" an action item, StAR will be able to reach out to the persons responsible for action items where no progress has been reported. This is not an ideal solution to a lack of self-reporting. It represents a tremendous amount of communication work for a team of three. This is a clear sign that StAR needs to concentrate on making self-reporting an expected behavior and a normal part of each individual's work.

StAR also experimented with creating a dashboard to quickly show a snapshot of progress in the five overall strategic areas (figure 3.4). The team used Microsoft Excel and

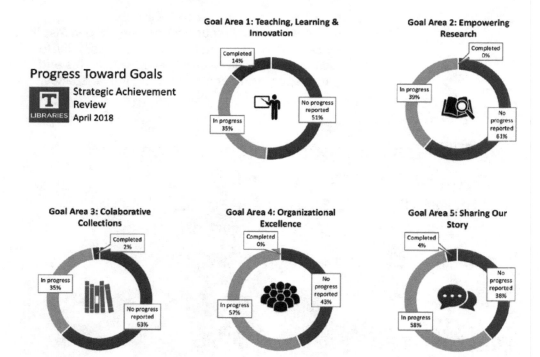

FIGURE 3.4
Dashboard displaying progress reported by April 2018 in each of the five strategic areas

PowerPoint to create the dashboard and shared it initially with Libraries Administration and then with the entire library. Each of the five strategic areas also has a dedicated page on the StAR website, listing all goals and action items. As progress is reported, it is tracked on these pages, providing more frequent updates. Below each action item, a medal icon denotes each reported action, regardless of how large or small. Significant progress or activity is also featured on a blog with links from the action item bullets to the blog entries.

Having the action items owner list also lets StAR explore different ways to view work across the organization. For example, identifying the individuals associated with each action item provides the opportunity to explore tools such as social networking graphs to help provide a clearer picture of how individuals across the organization come together for certain projects.

While the initial dashboard design is not perfect, it is effective in communicating progress and—perhaps more important—the areas where progress has been made but not yet reported. StAR continues to lobby with administrators, department heads, and working groups throughout the library for increased reporting. The team recommends using information reported to StAR to help write annual reports. They hope staff will realize that it need not be extra work: progress reported to StAR now can be used again in official reports later. In order for the Libraries to maintain their momentum on tracking progress, StAR will need to continue to work with people throughout the organization to emphasize the importance of self-reporting.

III. Grounding Phase

STAGE 8: ANCHORING NEW APPROACHES IN THE CULTURE

Creation of the StAR team is a major transformation of the Libraries' strategic planning process. The work of StAR itself is tied directly to the Organizational Excellence area of emphasis in the strategic plan. StAR's mission is two-fold: tracking progress and then communicating that progress. There is starting to be evidence of a shift in the organizational culture: individuals have begun to incorporate the language and structure of the Libraries' strategic plan into their own planning and goal setting. But much work remains to be done to anchor the changes in the culture.

The biggest sign of the need for continuing work in this area is the perpetual struggle to get individuals to adopt self-reporting practices. Mining departmental reports, email communications, and other documentation is not a practical long-term approach. This has served well to seed the progress tracking but is an overwhelming amount of work for a three-person team. Kotter states, "Culture changes only after you have successfully altered people's actions, after the new behavior produces some group benefit for a period of time, and after people see the connection between the new actions and the performance improvement."[3] With this in mind, StAR has enlisted the help of library leaders—administrators, department heads, committee heads—to communicate the importance of reporting progress and the benefit of integrating that information into annual reporting and evaluations.

One way the team is working to anchor the strategic plan and progress reporting in the culture is by developing a template for departmental annual reports. The report template, while providing structure, remains flexible, allowing departments to report on activities important to them, including data in a wide array of formats (text, visualizations, lists, etc.). However, a template will help departments organize their unique information around the areas of emphasis outlined in the strategic plan. As this template is put into practice later this year, StAR plans to work with the individuals tasked with writing annual reports. StAR will demonstrate how the data self-reported by individuals and groups in their area can be repurposed and included in the report. As a result of simplifying the reporting process and organizing all departmental reports in a way that relevance to the strategic plan is clear, the intention is to persuade these individuals of the benefit of self-reporting. They might then become champions who encourage individuals in their departments to report more regularly and to be more active in the StAR process.

The hope is that, by having departmental reports organized around the structure of the strategic plan, individuals across the organization will see how their work directly impacts progress toward overall library goals. This individual connection could go a long way toward encouraging people to keep the strategic plan in the foreground as they work and plan for future work. Thus, the perception of the strategic plan might slowly change from an artifact to be dusted off once a year to a living document that impacts daily work. Overall, progress has been made toward anchoring the strategic plan into the libraries' culture. But there is still work to be done.

Analysis and Conclusions

The Kotter model provides an interesting framework to consider change in academic libraries.[4] For the work of StAR, the Kotter model illuminates the importance of grounding a change in the culture. Reporting progress made by individuals across an organization—even small progress—continues to be a major challenge. Individuals see the reporting process as merely an added step in their very busy workdays. While a challenge, StAR's positive focus on celebrating achievements rather than policing non-reporting, combined with making the reported progress useful for other documents such as departmental annual reports, is slowly gaining proponents among individuals in the organization. For this change to become truly grounded in the culture, StAR will need to expand its base of supporters who believe in self-reporting and adopt it into their everyday workflow. StAR is starting to see evidence that the strategic plan is being utilized more regularly than in previous planning cycles. This is evidenced by interest in the new departmental report template organized around five strategic areas, use of the priority selection tool by committees to focus in on the action items relevant to their group, and by invitations to StAR to work with departments during goal setting and planning. The change to the organizational culture is not complete. But—keeping in mind Kotter's lessons about how changes reverse when not grounded effectively in the culture—the StAR team appears to be on a good trajectory for making the strategic plan a living document relevant to the work of individuals across the organization.

Notes

1. John P. Kotter, "Leading Change: Why Transformation Efforts Fail," *Harvard Business Review* 73, no. 2 (1995): 59–67.
2. "University of Tennessee Libraries Strategic Plan, 2017–2022," University of Tennessee Libraries, August 2016, https://www.lib.utk.edu/about/files/StrategicPlan_Aug2016.pdf.

3. John P. Kotter, *Leading Change* (Boston: Harvard Business Review Press, 2012), 148.
4. Kotter, *Leading Change*.

Bibliography

Kotter, John P. *Leading Change*. Boston: Harvard Business Review Press, 2012.

———. "Leading Change: Why Transformation Efforts Fail." *Harvard Business Review* 73, no. 2 (1995): 59–67.

University of Tennessee Libraries. "University of Tennessee Libraries Strategic Plan, 2017–2022." August 2016. https://www.lib.utk.edu/about/files/StrategicPlan_Aug2016.pdf.

Chapter 4

Building from the Ground UP

Creating a New Vision

Diane Klare and Melissa Behney

Setting the Stage

Wesleyan University, a residential liberal arts institution with a population of approximately 3,100 students, is located in Middletown, Connecticut. In line with its baccalaureate and master's Carnegie classification, the majority of the curriculum is focused on undergraduate education, although there is a small population of graduate students in doctoral programs. There are two libraries on campus, Olin Memorial Library and the smaller Science Library. The library staff consists of sixteen non-tenure-track librarians (including the university librarian) and eighteen support staff. The university librarian in 2014 had been appointed in 2009 upon the retirement of the prior incumbent. Previously, she had been the associate university librarian.

In preparing this chapter, the authors retrospectively utilized John Kotter's eight-stage process of creating change to analyze the impact of events that affected the library's organization. The authors also assessed the actions taken, commencing in fall 2014, by those in library leadership positions to move the library forward. Kotter's model is useful in creating the framework that describes the organizational renewal of the Wesleyan Library.

I. Warm-up Phase

STAGE 1: ESTABLISHING A SENSE OF URGENCY

On August 26, 2014, the provost called an unexpected and urgent meeting of library leaders. They were informed that the university librarian (UL) had been dismissed. The provost asked the assembled group to select someone to communicate the change to library staff. The group selected the head of reference, and the following day, the provost appointed her to serve as interim university librarian (IUL). Despite assurances from the provost that the library had the administration's support, many staff were shocked and did not understand why this leadership change had occurred. Some felt that a diligent defender of library values had been betrayed. Several reacted with anxiety about the

future of the library and their jobs, as well as expressing a deep distrust of the campus administration. Others had been more aware of ongoing issues between the UL and the administration, but had been circumspect in disclosing these perceptions. As staff questioned the provost's true intentions, the newly appointed IUL, facing similar questions, found much work needed to be done to provide reassurance and salvage morale as the new semester began.

In the months leading up to this event, the UL had been put in an increasingly difficult and defensive position as she pushed back against mandated changes to the library. In spite of the UL having just completed a major project initiated by the administration to merge a branch library into Olin Library, campus administrators had lost confidence in the UL. Over time, the library had been marginalized and was operating from a reactionary stance. There was limited delegation to department heads and senior librarians in an effort to insulate them from tense relations with the campus administration. In this environment, the UL's attention was not focused on moving the library forward strategically but rather on trying to maintain the status quo. It had become difficult to explore new avenues that required administrative support, financial or otherwise. After the dismissal, these factors contributed to an urgent need to regroup and find a way forward before staff morale suffered further and the library lost more ground with the administration.

The library faced a leadership crisis compounded by a lack of alignment between library and institutional goals, as the library's annual goals had become insular over time. Earlier in 2014, the provost had mandated a library self-study. The Association for College and Research Libraries' *Standards for Libraries in Higher Education* was used as a framework.[1] A rudimentary self-study plan had been put together by the UL and head of reference, but with few specifics and the looming deadline to close the branch library, little progress had been made. After the leadership transition, the provost outlined a series of questions based on the *Standards* and tasked the IUL to move forward on the self-study. The provost sought answers to eight key areas about the library:

- Educational role
- Discovery of materials
- Collections
- Spaces
- Campus relations
- Collaborations with external institutions or entities
- Library management and administration
- Leadership

The self-study would serve as a precursor to a spring 2015 external review. Hiring a permanent UL was put on hold until after the report by the visiting committee. Ultimately, this resulted in a twenty-two-month period in which the library was in a liminal state and all library staff were dealing with significant ambiguity. If the library were to improve relations with the administration and have a voice in the UL hiring process, the IUL and other library leaders would need to act as a team to articulate the library's contributions and requirements for supporting the academic mission.

STAGE 2: CREATING THE GUIDING COALITION

The IUL chose three additional senior managers from across major areas of the library to assist her with the self-study. The head of cataloging, the director of special collections and archives, and the science librarian had different backgrounds, strengths, experiences, and lengths of service at the institution. Each understood the roots of the crisis and the need to view the library through a critical lens in order to create change. This group had experience working together, respected each other's thinking, and were all deeply committed to serving the best interests of the library. As managers, these individuals could communicate the message that the library was moving in a positive direction and had the provost's support.

The provost's deadline for the first draft was late November, giving the team roughly twelve weeks to gather anonymous qualitative and quantitative input from library staff and other campus constituencies, analyze the results, and formulate a written response to each question. Initial meetings focused on identifying relevant stakeholders and the necessary data to gather. A library staff questionnaire was extant from a previous self-study, and the team modified select questions for currency. Emblematic of their distrust, some staff asked for assurances that responses would be anonymous. Institutional Research assisted by providing existing student survey data and administered a short faculty survey designed by the self-study team. Additional stakeholder surveys were created and two open forums conducted for faculty to share their teaching and research needs. To address library space questions, a campus facilities planner who had previously worked with the library drafted an analysis of library spaces that included deficiencies and recommendations. Finally, benchmark comparison data were gathered from existing external sources.

After reviewing the survey results, the team divided the writing responsibilities, and an initial draft was submitted to the provost on time. But the provost pressed for a more candid and critical assessment, so the team spent the following two weeks addressing the needed changes. Once the revisions were complete, the IUL shared the report with library staff and asked for additional input prior to submitting it to the provost. The final report fully reflected the situation in the library, including the strained relations with the campus administration. As a result, the provost was fully informed of challenges facing the library, including the larger context of academic libraries in higher education.

STAGE 3: DEVELOPING A VISION AND STRATEGY

Concurrent with the self-study preparation, the provost and associate provost invited three senior-level academic library administrators from other institutions to campus in March 2015 to conduct an external review. Based on their findings and using the self-study as background, the reviewers were asked to produce a final report by mid-April that addressed the eight areas of focus.

The external review confirmed many of the issues identified in the self-study. The conclusions were communicated to the library staff, the campus administration, and the library-faculty advisory committee. Among the findings, the review validated the need for a library strategic plan to establish direction and long-term goals and to turn the organization's focus outward.

The IUL led the strategic planning process from September 2015 to April 2016 while the university conducted the search for the next UL. This planning process was important in instilling a sense of momentum. The IUL adapted the steps outlined in John Bryson's *Strategic Planning for Public and Nonprofit Organizations* in order to meet a spring 2016 deadline.[2] Staff were presented with the rationale behind strategic planning, which was to

- Help shape future library directions
- Plan for pending retirements
- Assist the new UL in setting priorities and allocating resources
- Articulate long-term library goals
- Align library goals with institutional ones

The IUL conveyed the inherent fluidity of a strategic plan and emphasized the necessity to adjust it periodically for new conditions. Expecting the strategic planning concept to be met with skepticism by some staff, the IUL designed the process to be bottom-up with widespread staff involvement to gain buy-in and ownership of the final outcomes.

By design, the process spanned several months. Library staff were asked to respond to three questions in distinct phases, and responses were anonymized to encourage honesty and frankness. Although participation was not required, almost 90 percent of staff responded. In phase one, the IUL provided the staff with the university's strategic plan and asked everyone to submit their reflections on the question "How do you, in your job, contribute toward the university's strategic plan?" The library management group, a standing committee whose membership differed from those on the self-study team, organized the responses into overarching categories that naturally mapped to the findings of the self-study and the external review. The resulting themes were discussed and adjustments made to categories based on staff comments at a subsequent meeting.

In the second phase of the plan development, which was built on the foundations of the first, each staff member was asked, "What values are important to our library organization?" This more philosophical question was intended to help articulate the library's ethos and assist the library management group in writing an appropriate mission statement as the last step in building the strategic plan.

As the third question, staff were asked to reflect on the question "What one or two challenges (aka 'strategic issues') are you (individually) or is your department (collectively) facing over the next 3–5 years?" With responses in hand, the library management group described how the library would address and resolve challenges and issues. Building on the thematic points that had emerged from the process, the IUL drafted the document and issued a final request for feedback. The library management group developed a mission statement based on this three-step process. Finally, the plan was discussed with the library-faculty advisory committee and presented to the provost for formal approval. The plan was made publicly available on the library's website.[3]

STAGE 4: COMMUNICATING THE CHANGE VISION

The library's annual retreat in early summer 2015 had already laid the groundwork for strategic planning. This event started the communication process needed to begin reversing the library's reactionary culture, continue to build trust, and inculcate a positive change vision for the library. Soliciting ideas from staff in advance, the IUL and the library management group created goals to help library staff recognize their ability to take on new projects, institute meaningful change, and move the library forward toward long-term objectives while not undercutting the vision of the next UL. Goals that would boost staff morale were given priority and were proposed as pilot projects. Before the retreat, staff selected their preferred projects so planning could begin at the retreat. The retreat would focus on determining action items rather than spending time on goal formation as had been done in the past. The pilot projects were representative of long-deferred aspirations (e.g., full inventory of the library collection) as well as newer priorities (e.g., promoting Wesleyan's unique collections through social media). After initial team-building exercises, the project teams met and designed specific steps, set timelines, and created easily identifiable benchmarks to gauge progress. Each team selected a project leader to report back at staff meetings during the 2015–2016 academic year.

During this same period, the IUL worked with the library management group and the library's collections group on other initiatives to signal a proactive change in direction in providing resources or services. A digital projects librarian, a new position for the library made possible by a retirement, was hired in spring 2015. The IUL worked with the campus administration to identify and reallocate funds within the library budget to outfit a library space with new equipment and furniture to create a digital lab. The library also became a member of the Eastern Academic Scholars Trust and joined HathiTrust to expand physical and digital access to materials.

When the new UL arrived in July 2016, the foundation was in place to continue with the library's change vision, but there were several unaddressed challenges. The strategic plan had been completed, and the new UL had the self-study and external review for reference. One of the new positions validated by the review (the digital projects librarian) had been filled, but the IUL had delayed hiring for positions created by retirements by employing temporary librarians to provide maximum flexibility in future staffing. The logical priority was to identify missing areas of support and define new positions around them. The strategic plan provided a road map toward that priority. In early 2017, the UL began meeting with the library management group to consider alternative organizational models, facilitate internal communication, and create a missing, long-desired senior management level. By late spring 2017, the proposed reorganization, which included two associate university librarians (AULs) to relieve the UL of day-to-day operational tasks, had been approved by the campus administration. In addition, some position descriptions of existing staff changed to reflect the new priorities. The vacancies that remained were reworked and new responsibilities based on the strategic plan were identified so the library could hire appropriately skilled librarians.

During this reorganizational process, the work being done was regularly communicated during staff meetings, and the UL conveyed the progress to the campus administration. Liaison librarians kept their respective faculty departments apprised, in part to reassure them that the library was actively interested in their concerns. By aligning the new organizational structure with the library strategic plan and recommendations of the external review, strong buy-in was achieved inside and outside the library.

II. Introducing New Practices Phase

STAGE 5: EMPOWERING BROAD-BASED ACTION

With library leadership in flux for almost two years, there were practical limitations to initiating specific courses of action. However, the time that elapsed during this interim period resulted in an advantageous opportunity for self-reflection, framed the next steps needed as a result of the review, and allowed time to build a strategic plan that was flexible enough to be adjusted by the new UL. This two-year period, however, precluded lasting and deeper changes that only a permanent UL could make. As it was critical to avoid undermining the agenda of the incoming UL, some legacy issues, such as the ineffective organizational structure, remained in place from August 2014 until the new organization was approved by the campus administration in April 2017. Moreover, the IUL's deliberate decision to fill retirement vacancies with temporary librarians, although a sounder move that allowed a new structure to be created, limited the ability to change responsibilities and focus on new priorities during this intervening time.

Following the UL's arrival, broader changes could not be made or a new structure developed until he had a good understanding of the library's current functions, culture, and critical gaps in skills. Over a period of several months, he met with everyone to assess the situation. Moreover, budget constraints imposed by the campus administration meant that although positions could be re-described and a missing layer of management added, no overall increase to headcount was approved and personnel costs were capped at current levels. The final reorganization resulted in a few areas losing staff while others gained staff. Although the IUL had often apprised the staff that a reorganization would be likely, the resulting changes were not universally well received. In areas where staffing shrank, there were naturally concerns that necessary work might not get done. For the most part, however, these changes were welcome since they signaled progress was being made.

A further challenge to enacting changes more rapidly was the implementation of a new library management system (LMS) during the new UL's first year. Many library staff were deeply involved in this implementation and could not take on any new responsibilities (or easily drop old ones) at the same time. Though the new system would have more robust analytics, streamline workflows, and integrate the wide variety of collections, the implementation process was stressful and highly time-consuming.

By July 2017, the new UL had overseen the planning process to restructure the staff, had appointed the previous IUL as one of the two AULs, and had supported the staff as they worked through the LMS implementation. The library was now prepared to start the next significant step: hiring the second AUL and consolidating functions for acquisitions, cataloging, serials, electronic resources, and systems under that new hire.

STAGE 6: GENERATING SHORT-TERM WINS

Initiating pilot projects during the 2015 retreat generated short-term wins. The pilots allowed library staff to try out initiatives in a low-risk environment and determine the workflow, staff time, and other resources required for full-scale projects. Overcoming hurdles and moving into an action phase gave people a sense of empowerment and achievement.

Because of the LMS implementation during the 2016–2017 academic year, librarians who had not been in leadership roles chaired working groups and served as project managers, sometimes for the first time. The successful implementation and shared sense of accomplishment were a real win. The new system streamlined workflows and also reinvigorated collaborations with consortial partners that resulted in fresh initiatives, such as a shared approval plan. Newly described positions began to be filled according to the approved reorganization plan. The step of hiring the two AULs was the first phase of creating a senior administrative level and realigning library departments to support the long-term vision of the organization, improving communication, and creating more cohesive working groups. It was clear that this was not the same library or staff that it had been before 2015.

After being with the library for only fifteen months, the UL died unexpectedly in September 2017. This was yet another traumatic loss for library staff to absorb at a time when people were beginning to feel a true sense of change and possibility. Shock, disbelief, and anger were common responses as people struggled to find their footing. The AUL for research and access services was again appointed IUL to provide continuity of leadership while people grieved and dealt with another transition and period of uncertainty.

Since preliminary interviews for the AUL for technical and digital services had begun, the hiring process continued after a short delay. Proceeding with this hire signaled that plans for the future were not being tabled, and this somewhat ameliorated uncertainty about changes in the wake of the UL's death. The provost also concurred with the library staff's need for stability and desire to maintain momentum and opened the search for a UL in the fall of 2017. A new UL was named in late spring 2018.

While some of the anticipated promotions and organizational changes were put on hold, those under the purview of the IUL, in her role as AUL for research and access services, moved forward. The library management group prioritized positions from the new organizational chart and developed position descriptions. Both internal promotions and external hires were made and a union staff position reconfigured. Other staffing decisions, such as title changes, promotions, and changing the status of some of the temporary librarians, were put on hold until a new UL was in place.

STAGE 7: CONSOLIDATING GAINS AND PRODUCING MORE CHANGE

From the initial destabilization in August 2014 to the present, the library has advanced to a new place in the view of both its staff and the provost. This was accomplished by these steps: assessment of the state of the library and validation of that assessment by an external review committee, rebuilding of relations with the administration, and development of a strategic plan and model for reorganization. The current provost has determined the library should be the centralized location for a wide range of unique and distinctive collections on campus, and some of these have been moved under the library's oversight. The library is now widely viewed as an organization that can enhance discovery and highlight these collections.

From the beginning of this change, the IUL, UL, and senior library managers communicated to staff the need for and benefits of change. The library management group met regularly to discuss proposed changes. The IUL included all staff in the development of goals and the strategic plan, while reinforcing the message of progress at staff meetings. All library staff members were included and given the opportunity for input when candidates were interviewed. Three of the four original library self-study team members (one having retired) were part of the search committee to select a new UL in 2018.

As with any change process, there were some recalcitrant individuals. As more staff members became directly involved in changes as a result of the reorganization or in roles of project leaders, the hold-outs became a less vocal minority. It remains to be seen how all the staff will respond to the new UL with his own priorities and expectations, but the sense of renewal and momentum has built to a point that everyone recognizes a clear change.

III. Grounding Phase

STAGE 8: ANCHORING NEW APPROACHES IN THE CULTURE

Due to the unusual circumstances of having significant leadership turnover in four years, subsequent adjustments will require a period of evaluation before determining if they are practicable. The new UL will be studying the Wesleyan campus, reaching out to key stakeholders, observing the campus culture and dynamics, and deriving his own conclusions and understanding of the broader opportunities. Conversely, the library staff will need to adapt to the new UL's leadership style and the new structure that includes a senior management level. For everyone involved, the changing leadership has been difficult psychologically, and the heightened workloads due to retirements have compounded the situation.

Anchoring long-term approaches instituted by the new UL will await his assessment of changes already implemented since the self-study, external review, and writing of the strategic plan. Realistically, a review of that plan is advisable since it is already two years old. The efficacy of the new organizational structure has yet to be determined, since a significant portion of position changes occurred under the IUL's second term, and the reorganization has not been fully realized. The new UL will need to evaluate these changes and, with the new management team, decide how to move forward to align with his vision. The UL is keenly interested in developing relationships that will position the library as an integral part of the student and faculty experience and the campus community. Guided by the steps outlined in the strategic plan, this integrative process should spawn new initiatives and fresh approaches.

Analysis and Conclusions

The changes that have taken place in four years at the Wesleyan Library have been significant. Beginning with the initial crisis in 2014, the IUL understood the urgent need to stabilize the library and help the staff regain a sense of trust and safety. When the new UL died after only fifteen months, the continuity of leadership under the previous IUL helped staff grieve and process another sudden loss. The IUL and the library self-study team made good use of improved relations with the campus administration and the provost to address library issues within and outside the library. These issues were acknowledged in the external review. The initial two-year term of the IUL moved the library from a reactionary culture to a more proactive one, improving staff morale significantly. This was done by including staff in the self-study process, implementing several desired pilot projects, and the bottom-up strategic planning process. As a result, the staff had ownership of the library's future.

Unfortunately, the library lacked additional financial support from the campus administration, which would have allowed full implementation of the approved reorganization. Lack of support is also evidenced in areas where the library is still only marginally involved, such as educational policy and changes in use of library buildings and spaces. Both these concerns would be ameliorated if the library were included throughout the decision-making process. The Wesleyan Library plays an active part in educating its students, and it is imperative that the entire campus embrace that role. A deeper understanding of the twenty-first-century academic library is required, as its work goes far beyond outdated perceptions of it being primarily a repository for books and museum collections. While relations with the campus administration are greatly improved, misconceptions still remain and must be addressed to facilitate progress.

In analyzing the change process at Wesleyan, the first three stages of John Kotter's model align well with the work done in addressing the initial crisis, the subsequent library review, and the strategic plan that was developed to provide a future vision. When comparing Kotter's Stages 4 through 6 to the steps subsequently taken at Wesleyan, the elements as prescribed in each of those stages were largely implemented in an iterative rather than linear manner. There were interdependent changes occurring within the library that don't lend themselves to being easily placed into just one of these stages, perhaps because of the reactionary climate under which these changes began. Leadership transitions have inhibited the organization's ability to fully move from the last stage of the Kotter's new practices phase into the grounding phase, but the building blocks are in place for further transformation.

As evidenced in this chapter, library organizations are extremely complex and subject to completely unforeseen forces (e.g., a leader's death). Despite Kotter's framework, bringing about change can be difficult to institute within a precise and logically laid-out model. Humans are complex creatures, and that complexity is evidenced daily as an organization evolves and confronts both planned and unexpected changes. Wesleyan's library provides an example of the intricate issues surrounding substantial changes and adjustments necessitated by abrupt and unexpected events. The deliberative steps required in strategically transforming the library have been time-consuming and are not yet complete, but the outcomes so far indicate the time spent will be well worth the effort.

Notes

1. Association of College and Research Libraries, *Standards for Libraries in Higher Education* (Chicago: Association of College and Research Libraries, 2011).
2. John M. Bryson, *Strategic Planning for Public and Nonprofit Organizations*, 4th ed. (San Francisco: Jossey-Bass, 2011).
3. "Wesleyan University Library Strategic Plan 2016," Wesleyan University, accessed May 16, 2019, http://www.wesleyan.edu/libr/about/2016librarystrategicplan.pdf.

Bibliography

Association of College and Research Libraries. *Standards for Libraries in Higher Education.* Chicago: Association of College and Research Libraries, 2011.

Bryson, John M. *Strategic Planning for Public and Nonprofit Organizations: A Guide to Strengthening and Sustaining Organizational Achievement,* 4th ed. San Francisco: Jossey-Bass, 2011.

Wesleyan University. "Wesleyan University Strategic Plan 2016." Accessed May 16, 2019. http://www.wesleyan.edu/libr/about/2016librarystrategicplan.pdf.

Chapter 5

Analysis
Strategic Planning

Colleen Boff and Catherine Cardwell

Libraries
Miami University (Miami)
Montana State University (MSU)
University of Tennessee, Knoxville (UT, Knoxville)
Wesleyan University (Wesleyan)

Introduction

Each institution's entry point into the strategic planning process is a key component of this analysis. MSU and UT, Knoxville, had guiding documents to work with from the beginning of their change stories. These consisted of expired or already existing strategic plans or data from nationally normed surveys. Miami's story began with a library-wide strategic planning process while the second half focused on middle management's role in implementation after the consultants left. These three institutions, the largest in this category, reported positive relationships with and support from upper university administration on their respective campuses.

The entry point into strategic planning at Wesleyan, a small private institution, was very different from that of the other institutions. It entered into the library strategic planning process having to establish credibility with its campus administration, a step that was not necessary for the other institutions. Consequently, its strategic planning process took much longer, with many stops, starts, and stalls due to its relationship with university administration in addition to extraordinary circumstances.

The scope of strategic planning at each institution varied in this category of change stories. MSU zeroed in on work to develop its strategic plan, while UT, Knoxville, primarily focused on the Strategic Achievement Review (StAR) team's efforts to implement the strategic plan at the institution. The StAR team was responsible for monitoring and reporting progress toward achieving the strategic plan. The change stories at Miami and at Wesleyan spanned the entire process of strategic planning from development to implementation of the strategic plan.

I. Warm-up Phase

STAGE 1: ESTABLISHING A SENSE OF URGENCY

The level of urgency among these strategic planning stories ranged dramatically, from mildly urgent to extremely urgent in the face of crisis. In all of these instances, evidence suggests that strategic planning efforts were moving forward and taking root. Complacency was not a systemic problem in these change stories.

At Miami, campus-wide facilities upgrades sparked change. The dean wanted to create an architectural master plan so that the library could be part of the momentum on campus. The dean also wanted to create a more unified, cohesive library organization. After years of patching holes in its organizational structure, the library needed to redefine reporting lines, remove barriers between departments, and improve collaboration and communication. MSU's reason for change was a strategic plan that had run its course and needed to be updated in addition to the library wanting to participate in change at the university level. MSU chose the Balanced Scorecard Framework to guide its process.

At UT, Knoxville, urgency was self-imposed—it added a specific goal into the strategic plan to create a group to monitor and communicate the progress toward achieving the strategic plan. The library leadership subsequently sent a clear message to the staff by allocating resources, forming the StAR team, and presenting the team with a specific charge.

The urgency for the work at Wesleyan was the most pressing among all of the change stories in this category because the library underwent a comprehensive strategic planning process in response to its leader being dismissed and its college administration questioning the library's credibility. Its administration gave the library a mandate to conduct a self-study and start a strategic planning process. It launched both mandates under extremely tenuous circumstances and with the staff reeling from losing their leader. The sense of urgency was, in fact, unrelenting and continued when the staff at Wesleyan faced another crisis after the unexpected death of their newly hired permanent library director.

STAGE 2: CREATING THE GUIDING COALITION

The guiding coalitions at MSU and Miami included external consultants, with the latter employing consultants from two different firms. Miami's strategic planning steering committee comprised the dean, the associate dean, and two assistant deans of the library but lacked middle management involvement until later on in the implementation process when the task forces were developed. In fact, the initial steering committee had more members external to the library than internal, an unusual approach when compared to the other change stories in this category. Each task force was subsequently provided with a charge shaped by the strategic plan. The guiding coalition at MSU also included a consultant, but the coalition was mindful at the outset of making certain that constituent groups had broad representation. The overall committee was not given a charge, but the consultant was. In a unique approach when compared to the other stories, the guiding coalition worked together to create its own charge.

The guiding coalitions at UT, Knoxville, and Wesleyan were small when compared to the other two institutions. The coalition at UT, Knoxville, consisted of three members who accepted this responsibility in addition to their regular jobs. Unlike any other guiding coalition in this category, they were given a detailed charge by the dean with specific guiding action steps. The guiding coalition at Wesleyan was small but consisted of the interim university librarian and three senior managers who were trusted colleagues of the interim university librarian. This team of four had a history of working together, understood the depths of the crisis at hand, and had a shared interest in moving the organization forward. Instead of a committee charge, this group had the daunting task of conducting a self-study given to them by their provost.

MSU recommended the need for release time for committee members to serve on such committees because of how time-consuming the change process can be. Another constructive piece of advice several of the authors provided was the need to consider who is at the table when it comes to strategic planning committees. The guiding coalition must include people who have the appropriate level of authority, knowledge, and influence.

STAGE 3: DEVELOPING A VISION AND STRATEGY

The visioning process was led by the guiding coalition of consultants and strategic planning committees at Miami and MSU but with a great deal of input from the staff. Through the work of three task forces, Miami was able to develop its service philosophy, guiding principles and new service categories, which ended up serving as its new departmental structure. Its vision and strategy were formed in six months and synthesized into a 260-page master plan to guide the organization through implementation after the consultants left. The consultant experience at MSU differed from Miami's in a few distinct ways. Staff discussed selected readings, filled out surveys, and unexpectedly revised their existing set of value statements, which heavily influenced the outcome of the strategic plan. What started out as a simple refresh of existing vision and mission statements ended in a much more involved exploration as staff examined their values, a step that Kotter warns can be time-consuming and iterative.[1] Another unique aspect of the change story is that MSU completed a Strengths, Opportunities, Aspirations, Results (SOAR) analysis instead of the more common Strengths, Weaknesses, Opportunities, Threats (SWOT) analysis. The visioning process at Wesleyan unfolded very differently from that of Miami and MSU primarily because its situation was so different. After it completed a self-study, its provost mandated that it do an external review. Both processes pointed to the need for a strategic plan, which the interim university librarian developed in seven months. Approximately 90 percent of the staff responded to three specific questions she asked them about their work. From these results, she wrote the strategic plan while the management group crafted the mission statement.

The UT, Knoxville, StAR team had a slightly different challenge from the other institutions because they started with a finished strategic plan and a specific charge. As a consequence, they spent their time strategizing about how to tackle their role of monitoring staff progress toward accomplishing the goals listed in the strategic plan. They approached this monumental task by establishing a timeline spread out over the first two years.

STAGE 4: COMMUNICATING THE CHANGE VISION

Communication typically happens throughout a change story. Therefore, the authors mention communication not only in the Stage 4 section of their chapters, but also refer to communication practices elsewhere in the change stories. The strategic planning change teams frequently sought direct feedback from staff in the form of surveys and during face-to-face meetings with staff.

Miami stressed its commitment to transparency by sharing all documentation related to the change effort with staff. Its dean also sent monthly communications via email. MSU took similar measures by creating an intranet to host all pertinent change documents. It went one step further and branded the emails used for its communications, and it also involved everyone from the library in an iterative process to create many drafts of strategy maps and value statements for a truly participatory experience. Both MSU and UT, Knoxville, had team member representatives who regularly reported their progress to the library administration. In addition to regularly communicating to staff through email and staff meetings, the StAR team at UT, Knoxville, built an interactive, dynamic website for the staff to use. This was the primary way of documenting progress toward achieving the goals of the library's strategic plan. As a result, the team spent a great deal of effort to build in incentives for staff at the library, from the possibility of earning medals to staff being able to extract information from this system to use for other required reporting such as annual reports. Wesleyan took a completely different approach to communicating strategic planning change efforts to its staff. The guiding coalition under the interim university librarian's direction developed project-based goals and worked with the library staff at their annual retreat to develop concrete action steps needed to complete specific projects. This approach was intentionally designed to build teamwork and buy-in among the staff and to begin moving the library forward in visible ways. After they worked together to create their strategic plan, their new university librarian was hired and the work among the leadership team to reorganize the library began.

Readers will find a few words of caution about communicating the vision in these strategic planning stories. The chapter on Miami points out that lag time between staff involvement and the production of a written strategic plan may cause angst among staff. Another issue is that long stretches of time without communication with staff could disrupt buy-in. Actively engaging staff in person via workshops and other face-to-face interactions, such as annual retreats, may foster buy-in more quickly than counting on staff to check in on a website for updates. The latter approach may be easy for staff to ignore if they are busy or if widespread buy-in does not exist. Momentum appears to be compromised when a guiding coalition that involves library administration hands off the implementation of a strategic plan to a team that does not include library administration.

II. Introducing New Practices Phase

STAGE 5: EMPOWERING BROAD-BASED ACTION

Miami's story of strategic planning involved a complete reorganization of its entire structure. After the consultants left, the library faced the daunting task of making this new structure work. The leadership team wrote position descriptions for the heads of the six new departments, some of whom they needed to hire. Each department was asked to create a mission statement to align with the overall vision and to help guide their work. The department chairs started meeting together as a group to avoid recreating silos in their newly formed structure. Middle management at MSU also led the change process at their institution, with more than half of the library staff holding some type of coordinator title. While MSU did not have to contend with a reorganization to the degree that Miami did, MSU still expressed angst at this stage because staff turnover was a barrier to success. Wesleyan recognized that the logical next step in its strategic planning was to reorganize, but it needed to wait until library leadership stabilized and the new leader got his bearings. While the interim university librarian created and hired one new position and filled several others temporarily, it was not feasible for her, as an interim, to address all of the barriers the organization faced.

The change story at UT, Knoxville, provides a stark contrast at this stage when compared to the other institutions. It was up to the small team of three to keep the strategic plan alive among the staff. It is no surprise that employee buy-in was among the primary barriers in this change story, especially since it did not seem as if the middle managers were involved to the degree as were middle managers at Miami or MSU.

The importance of continuous and effective communication at this stage cannot be overstated. In most of these stories, the authors describe how important the role of middle managers was to the change efforts. This usually came in the form of having a seat at the table from time to time with the library management group for regular check-ins about progress toward achieving change efforts. It is also important to note that not all libraries are in the position to hire needed staff, to pay for a consultant, or to purchase new systems. Cash-strapped organizations may not be able to fix some of the barriers but instead must be creative in how they address them.

STAGE 6: GENERATING SHORT-TERM WINS

The teams responsible for strategic plan implementation at Miami had three primary short-term wins. They worked with staff to address burdensome reporting structures in one of their departments by creating a substructure with a new middle management position. They also merged two service points and adjusted the collection development budget and the way staff were organized to approach collection development. These immediate changes demonstrated their desire to adapt to the new structure, to address long-standing problems, to firmly root these changes in the new structure, and to resist the urge to fall into old habits. Library administration support of these changes also signaled commitment to the staff.

MSU experienced six short-term wins that directly aligned with steps taken to achieve its strategic plan. These short-term wins include creating committee structures and finding financial resources to help achieve its building master plan goal. They helped set the stage for anchoring changes in the organization. Wesleyan's use of its annual retreat to focus on projects and action steps toward completing projects helped to unite the staff the most and made them feel a part of moving the organization forward. This was much needed as its momentum as a library was once again disrupted by another tragic event that left it without a leader. While it continued to move forward in the wake of this trauma, short-term wins were episodic and in select areas of the library.

Because staff interest in submitting their short-term wins at UT, Knoxville, had waned, the StAR team devised a strategy to mine the annual departmental reports. This innovative work-around addressed staff complacency but was not sustainable in the long term.

STAGE 7: CONSOLIDATING GAINS AND PRODUCING MORE CHANGE

To strengthen its momentum, MSU created a new user experience and assessment group, the UX&A Team, to ensure that accountability measures for achieving goals in the strategic plan were integrated across all levels of the library. It did not have the opportunity to hire any additional staff for this new work. However, this offered stability and continuity as it implemented its plan. In fact, of the institutions in this category, MSU had the most direct and streamlined timeline for its process. Miami had the opportunity to hire seventeen new staff as a result of staff turnover and unfilled librarian positions. However, hiring, onboarding, and familiarizing new staff with the institution are labor- and time-intensive, and these tasks slow momentum for an organization already in flux. In spite of the significant turnover at Wesleyan at the top ranks, it accumulated large-scale wins, from the completion of a self-study to the creation of a strategic plan. As at Miami, hiring and onboarding caused the change process to be episodic and slower than desired. Spreading these short- and long-term wins out over longer periods of time may also impact staff morale, in both positive and negative ways. The length of time it took to address the organizational structure at Miami frustrated people. However, the length of time that the change process took at Wesleyan worked in its favor. Some staff who had been initially resistant to change began to understand why changes needed to occur, especially once they experienced more support from the university administration and others on campus.

With the strategic planning process complete, the UT, Knoxville, team focused on influencing staff behavior. They encouraged staff to report progress in a couple of strategic ways. First, they intentionally celebrated accomplishments that staff submitted to the StAR team by throwing a party and publicly recognizing accomplishments. Some leadership experts refer to this as "encouraging the heart," a strategy that leaders frequently overlook when immersed in such focused change.[2] Rather than punitive measures, the UT, Knoxville, team used rewards and public appreciation for those who contributed to the system of self-reporting. They also shared an executive summary of the strategic plan in the form of a small booklet and a dashboard that contained five overarching strategic areas distilled from an overwhelming list of 154 action steps. Their strategy to make an administrative document more accessible to everyone was commendable.

III. Grounding Phase

STAGE 8: ANCHORING NEW APPROACHES IN THE CULTURE

With the help of consultants, Miami and MSU moved through the strategic planning process within months. Because Miami also reorganized its entire library and hired so many new people, its next steps to anchor change in its organization were to explore leadership training and to discuss if anything else needed attention in its structure. MSU realized that it needed to agree upon a systematic project management approach in order to make change, so it built its accountability infrastructure through the creation of its User Experience and Assessment (UX&A) team. The chapters on both MSU and UT, Knoxville, mention the importance of building in linkages between the ways staff contribute to strategic plans and to their annual reports. The UT, Knoxville, team even developed an annual report template that mirrored the strategic plan framework to facilitate this process and took the important step of enlisting the library administration's support and willingness to communicate this message. UT, Knoxville, acknowledged a growing need for professional development related to creating measurable goals. Unlike the other institutions in this section, Wesleyan experienced strategic planning born out of reaction to one crisis followed by another. In spite of these circumstances, library leadership worked together to create a secure foundation to position the next leader for success. Wesleyan's story demonstrates that in spite of the unexpected, an organization can be resilient and move along a change process that is just as remarkable as an institution that takes a less pressure-packed approach.

Analysis and Conclusions

The strategic planning process at each of these institutions was holistic and involved the entire organization. However, none of these change stories is complete. Therefore, it is not possible to comment on the final outcome from the strategic planning process at any of these institutions, nor was that the goal. More than one institution reported at the outset failed attempts at strategic planning in the past. These strategic planning efforts are strong and well anchored in their organizations. In order for these efforts to stay strong, it is imperative that the staff understand how library administration will use the results of these efforts in order to continue to buy in to future strategic planning cycles.

Tips for Strategic Planning

- Continuous communication with staff throughout the strategic planning process is important for maintaining the momentum and understanding the reasons for change.
- While the change momentum is swift when consultants are brought in to help with this process, the staff may feel disoriented and uncertain as to how to proceed when consultants leave. A transition plan should be provided by the consultant or crafted by leadership to help with this potential problem.
- Written strategic plans are important and serve a purpose in the strategic planning process. However, it may help library staff to buy in more quickly if large strategic planning documents are distilled to a more digestible format. Large plans in excess of 100 pages or plans that contain more than 100 action steps can overwhelm readers and diminish buy-in.
- Strategic planning often involves multiple committees. It is important to have some overlap of membership from one committee to the next for communication purposes and to make sure that there is adherence to the overall vision.

- It is important to build into the strategic planning process metrics and assessment measures by which everyone will know if the planning process was effective. One way to do this is to use a ready-made framework such as the Balanced Scorecard.

Notes

1. John P. Kotter, *Leading Change* (Boston: Harvard Business Review Press, 1996), 81.
2. James M. Kouzes and Barry Z. Posner, *The Leadership Challenge*, 6th ed. (Hoboken, NJ: Wiley, 2017), 245.

Bibliography

Kotter, John P. *Leading Change*. Boston: Harvard Business Review Press, 1996.

Kouzes, James M., and Barry Z. Posner. *The Leadership Challenge*, 6th ed. Hoboken, NJ: Wiley, 2017.

PART II
REORGANIZATION

Chapter 6

Aligning Services and Staffing

A New Organizational Design for Miami University Libraries

Elliot Felix, Aaron Shrimplin, Emily Kessler, and Adam Griff

Setting the Change Stage

In 2012 upon the departure of its outgoing dean, Miami University Libraries (MUL) took stock of their current situation and recognized an opportunity for change. During her twenty-five-year career, the dean had overseen a network of libraries that had well served this public university and its 19,452 students enrolled on its Oxford campus. Focused on undergraduate research with growing research aims (Carnegie Classification RU/H), the libraries were recognized for their emphasis on customer service, emerging technologies, and partnerships. However, their vision was murky, morale was waning, and legacy services and staffing models were no longer relevant within a rapidly changing environment. In the early days of new leadership, MUL strategy was best described as "emerging." Leveraging a newly created position as coordinator of facilities and space planning, the libraries initially embarked on an updated and revised facilities master plan. However, as the facility planning process unfolded in 2016, it became apparent that Miami University Libraries should consider a plan and vision that incorporated a reimagined service and organizational strategy.

MUL partnered in late 2017 with architecture firm Perkins+Will on the architectural planning, and strategy firm brightspot strategy on the service and organizational strategy to accomplish this fully integrated facilities and organizational master plan. The new integrated master plan would comprehensively transform not only the libraries' facilities consisting of four locations and 192,650 square feet, but the redesign of an organization consisting of seventy-six positions that would ultimately include an additional twenty-six new hires as part of the plan.

In partnership with MUL leadership, brightspot brought its expertise in the changing landscape of academic libraries along with a design thinking methodology to its service strategy and organizational redesign approach. As with other academic libraries, MUL faced an expanded new purpose beyond access of materials to supporting new

experiences and offering new services that enable connecting, creating, and collaborating. This expanded mission, evolved services, and new talent fundamentally challenged the organizational design of MUL. The design thinking methodology that brightspot employed was pivotal in placing users needs as the central focus, then using an iterative process to uncover additional needs through testing and refinement. Indeed, brightspot's approach to organizational design also considered the roles people play, the structure that connects those roles, and the processes used to fulfill the roles—all working together to achieve a purpose and supported by a platform of information, tools, and skills (see figure 6.1). This approach—complemented by close collaboration and a willingness to try new ideas—was critical to MUL's organizational redesign and successful change management process.[1]

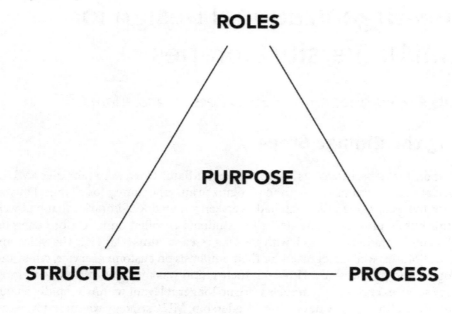

FIGURE 6.1
The approach to organizational design

I. Warm-up Phase

STAGE 1: ESTABLISHING A SENSE OF URGENCY

The new leadership team at MUL recognized an opportunity to re-envision the libraries upon the installation of a new dean, along with the short-term availability of resources. Under the old budget model, MUL was able to carry forward unspent funds. However, a compelling case for using the funds was required in order to receive authorization from the university. Likewise, there was a movement on campus to initiate more strategic planning within departments and divisions as a best practice. A number of divisional deans were engaged in space planning and creating master plans, and the university was coordinating all these efforts and consolidating the plans. MUL leadership recognized the need to be included in larger campus master planning efforts in order to share in any potential funding for capital expenditures.

Internally, the libraries were starting to feel constraints with their existing systems and processes, and staff no longer felt unified around a singular organizational vision. In order to validate assumptions among staff that changes were needed, the libraries looked to data from two important assessment surveys, LibQUAL and ClimateQUAL, administered in 2015 and 2016. The LibQUAL examined the libraries' services by gathering feedback from students and faculty and discovered two significant areas required improvement: web services and library facilities. Data indicated that the libraries were not meeting normally high marks for service quality. Furthermore, the ClimateQUAL survey gathered feedback from MUL staff and faculty, resulting in a 90-plus percent participation rate. Data indicated four key organizational needs: (1) teamwork reframing and refresh; (2) training for supervisors, strategic planning, and vision setting; (3) alignment across departments and their liaison efforts; and (4) professional development opportunities. These findings made the case for organizational change in order to bring about more cohesion within the libraries and deliver the high level of customer service the community was accustomed to receiving.

A robust communications plan explained the unique opportunity to address the issues and set a new vision for the libraries. The communication strategy focused on emphasizing this critical "pivot point" to establish transformational change and create a new vision for a twenty-first-century library. MUL built an extensive set of communications collateral to articulate this new narrative and shared it broadly among all university stakeholders.

STAGE 2: CREATING THE GUIDING COALITION

Broad engagement in both decision-making and content development was required for this large scale of change. brightspot led a participatory and co-creative process with three committees designed to ensure engagement and buy-in across the institution. A steering committee was formed to be inclusive of campus, including the provost and university planning, to ensure support across campus, create ownership of the project, and develop institutional champions. Comprised of MUL and university leadership, this group of eight individuals was responsible for establishing a vision for the project, reflecting on content, and deciding the short- and long-term direction. Having a university perspective on the libraries' greater role on campus helped to establish the context of the libraries as a significant part of the larger ecosystem within an academic institution. Campus-level engagement offered an opportunity for leadership and non-library personnel to learn more about the inner workings of the libraries.

brightspot worked with senior MUL leadership to form two working committees: Service Design Task Force (SDTF) and Organization Design Task Force (ODTF). Committee membership was nearly unique, with some overlap between the two. MUL leadership designed these committees to be inclusive and broad in membership. They included a variety of individuals internal to the libraries with diverse roles, responsibilities, and years of service. Committees were designed to be cross-functional and inclusive of frontline and management staff to build credibility across the organization.

Several students and faculty were invited to participate in order to provide an external stakeholder perspective. These committees were empowered by senior leadership to develop content and make preliminary decisions.

The participatory and co-creative process led by brightspot ensured that MUL leadership and staff would fully own the content they developed and the decisions they made as a group. This methodology builds buy-in and capacity building into the process to establish a higher rate of adoption of the change the organization seeks. In order to better form as teams, brightspot led the committees through a series of activities designed to help promote collaboration. Activities borrowed from improvisational acting classes (such as "Yes, and...") helped set the right tone for working together with minds open to possibilities. Content created in workshops first originated in small-group discussion to create safe zones for the expression of ideas and to better include all voices. After being refined in small groups, concepts were then vetted through large-group discussion to build consensus and understanding.

STAGE 3: DEVELOPING A VISION AND STRATEGY

A project vision can serve multiple purposes in a change management project. First, as a North Star, it can guide decision-making during and after the engagement. It can ensure alignment on the organization's purpose and contribute to higher levels of engagement in and adoption of the change process. A progressive vision can transform an organization as a leader in the field by instigating broader and more creative thinking on impact and implementation.

The vision for this project had three components: (1) a service philosophy, (2) guiding principles to help direct the service strategy, and (3) a vision for the organizational structure, building off of work previously developed by MUL. Clear instructions about when and how to use each were provided to MUL staff. The SDTF and brightspot developed a service philosophy to inform staff of the quality of service interactions and desired future service experience for its patrons. Guiding principles outlined how staff might achieve the aspirational service philosophy. With the ODTF, brightspot constructed a vision to guide the change process and inform the new organizational structure. This vision was adapted from earlier work completed by the libraries and later organized and prioritized by brightspot during workshop sessions.

A component of the project focused on developing new services and service points for a new library facility and reorganizing internally to best support this new direction. A next step was to develop service categories as an attempt to capture the central themes across services offered by the libraries. Working within the framework of the service philosophy and guiding principles, building on organizational strengths, and looking to peer libraries for examples, the SDTF made the strategic decision to create user-centric service categories that were both intuitive and easy to navigate. These categories were designed to facilitate user navigation among services by describing them from the user's point of view rather than the organization's (see figure 6.2).

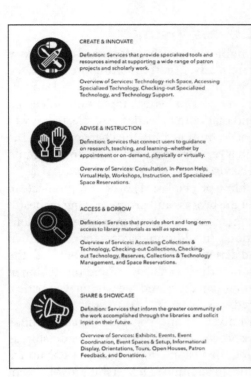

CREATE & INNOVATE

Definition: Services that provide specialized tools and resources aimed at supporting a wide range of patron projects and scholarly work.

Overview of Services: Technology-rich Space, Accessing Specialized Technology, Checking-out Specialized Technology, and Technology Support.

ADVISE & INSTRUCTION

Definition: Services that connect users to guidance on research, teaching, and learning—whether by appointment or on-demand, physically or virtually.

Overview of Services: Consultation, In-Person Help, Virtual Help, Workshops, Instruction, and Specialized Space Reservations.

ACCESS & BORROW

Definition: Services that provide short and long-term access to library materials as well as spaces.

Overview of Services: Accessing Collections & Technology, Checking-out Collections, Checking-out Technology, Reserves, Collections & Technology Management, and Space Reservations.

SHARE & SHOWCASE

Definition: Services that inform the greater community of the work accomplished through the libraries and solicit input on their future.

Overview of Services: Exhibits, Events, Event Coordination, Event Spaces & Setup, Informational Display, Orientations, Tours, Open Houses, Patron Feedback, and Donations.

FIGURE 6.2
MUL service categories

At the time of brightspot's engagement, MUL was seeking to resolve several challenges, namely increasing clarity of roles and responsibilities among MUL staff; providing more consistency in service delivery; and decreasing silos between departments. Hence, aligning front-facing service categories to the internal organizational structure was logical and resolved a number of issues and concerns. The ODTF and brightspot developed a new organizational structure with departments based on the new service categories with clearly defined department heads and simple and straightforward reporting lines. The new structure also anticipated future services to be offered in the new library facility and the corresponding staffing model (see figure 6.3).

MU LIBRARIES ORGANIZATION CHART

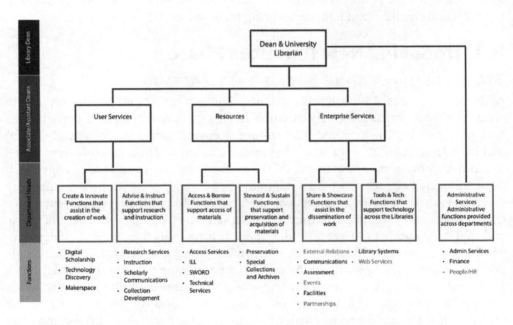

FIGURE 6.3
MUL organizational chart

STAGE 4: COMMUNICATING THE CHANGE VISION

MUL leadership recognized that open communication with staff and effective story-telling were critical to successful change, even in advance of initiating the integrated master plan. Having previously served as mayor in the community, the new dean was a compelling and persuasive communicator. In order to better amplify his voice and that of the libraries, a new communication and marketing position was created. It was a prescient hire considering the importance of communicating the change vision. The new role ensured that MUL communicated in a regular, consistent basis to help build momentum and show evidence of realizing the vision.

The communications strategy had four guiding principles: (1) over-communicate to reinforce the message; (2) be transparent about the process and progress being made; (3) use concrete examples of progress to maintain momentum; and (4) manage expectations about the rate of change to minimize frustrations. In addition to constant communication, multiple channels were used to share and disseminate information about both the process and the vision, such as flash updates, monthly dean's letters, and discussion at biannual meetings. Consistency in both meeting schedules and messaging was critical to ensure that staff were informed and engaged.

Communicating the vision to the wider university and engaging crucial campus stakeholders were crucial to ensuring success. Involving key university leadership as participants in contributing to and developing the vision contributed to their understanding and commitment to the transformation. In addition to leadership's involvement in the master planning process, the dean used his regularly scheduled one-on-one meetings with the provost to keep her well informed. Meeting with and engaging the office of academic personnel in hiring department heads, creating new positions, changing job titles and responsibilities, and serving in an advisory role had also proven invaluable to the success of the master plan. The support of the university as a whole was critical to implementing the vision and empowering broad-based action.

II. Introducing New Practices Phase

STAGE 5: EMPOWERING BROAD-BASED ACTION

With a new vision, the libraries initiated an ambitious hiring and promotion plan to create their new organizational structure. At this time, newly formed departments had yet to develop the processes and culture to ensure successful collaboration, nor had they determined their greatest challenges. Consequently, brightspot introduced the tool of process mapping to the ODTF to uncover and address challenges each department had already or would potentially encounter. During the process mapping exercise, each key step in a process was documented to produce a visual representation of what was occurring over time. For each step, the front of house, back of house, and supporting activities were also identified. This tool was then used to understand and improve work, as well as ensure that work is aligned with organizational goals and objectives. Having outlined the process step-by-step with its related activities, the ODTF was able to begin identifying where processes could be improved given the new departmental structure and revise the process accordingly. By learning this tool, the ODTF could diagnose challenges and solve for barriers on an ongoing basis (figure 6.4).

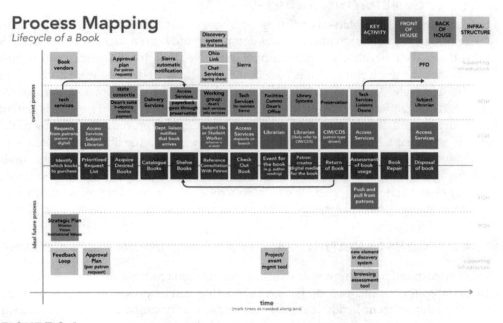

FIGURE 6.4
MUL process map

The integrated master plan also set clear instructions to create new practices and bring greater clarity to each department's role within the organization. These directives required that each department clearly define its purpose by writing a departmental charter; ensure clarity of roles by revising job descriptions; and thoughtfully create new rituals that would foster its new vision for organizational culture. For example, scheduling regular meetings for the six new department heads helped to serve as a model for collaboration and greater transparency.

A significant barrier to action appeared to be an organizational mind-set that sought perfection. There was a widely held belief that any change must be perfectly conceived before acting, as the consequences of getting it wrong were too great. Through participatory engagement and a focus on experimentation, brightspot helped to change the mind-set from "needing to be perfect" to "safe to try." The master plan report aimed to reinforce this shift in culture by emphasizing recommendations as a foundation for further refinement and testing and building in processes for assessment and change at regular intervals during implementation.

Organizations face other hurdles when it comes to a change management process, particularly when its people are hesitant or resistant because they fear loss. It is often easier to add roles or departments than to remove them, which explains many of today's unwieldy organizational charts within academic libraries. The brightspot process provided MUL with the crucial opportunity to consider the libraries holistically and challenge the status quo, as when the pivotal decision was made to reorganize front-of-house services and back-of-house functions from the user perspective. A noteworthy outcome saw branch library functions, previously on their own, absorbed into the larger organizational network, further helping to break down internal silos.

STAGE 6: GENERATING SHORT-TERM WINS

The integrated master plan—consisting of a space plan, vision, and framework to reimagine a next-generation library—was completed and shared in the summer of 2018. At this time, MUL began key organizational initiatives building off service and organizational strategy work completed earlier in the year. Immediate steps were both macro and micro in scale. The libraries transitioned to their new organizational structure (see figure 6.3) and initiated a new hiring plan with priority given to two new department heads, an assistant department head, and three web service librarians. Launching multiple new hires that addressed urgent needs demonstrated that the libraries would move immediately on the report's recommendations. MUL also sought to institute small-scale changes by addressing cultural issues identified in the ClimateQUAL. For example, a new meeting schedule for the libraries was rolled out, providing opportunities to improve collaboration and synergy between the departments.

STAGE 7: CONSOLIDATING GAINS AND PRODUCING MORE CHANGE

The libraries maintained momentum through continuous communication, recognition and championing of early adopters, and supporting and empowering middle management (i.e., department heads) to make decisions. Communications were consistent, frequent, and purposefully repetitive: "We've made lots of progress, we're still on track, and there's a lot more to do." The communications strategy included a "road show" in which the master plan was presented to a variety of university leadership, as well as MUL, student, and alumni groups.

The libraries also recognized and supported the early adopters in an effort to build momentum and counteract complacency among staff. These individuals—many of whom served on the task forces described in Stage 2—were deeply invested in changing the service model and organizational structure and ensuring adoption across the organization. They were recognized by leadership, who found regular and multiple ways to connect with them to maintain their excitement. These interactions consisted of informal meetings or spontaneous conversations. More formal tactics included scheduled one-on-one meetings with the dean or scheduled lunch meetings with senior leadership.

As the hiring plan was implemented, the libraries' deans brought together new department heads as a cohort and actively coached them on leading the change, both by continually communicating the vision and by working to implement it within their departments. It was critical that middle management felt empowered as well as committed to implement the vision. MUL leadership emphasized and foregrounded their work, "sharing the stage with them," to encourage and reward them for taking ownership for implementing the change. All staff meetings would include updates from department heads on their process to date. The dean's monthly update was recently revised to include updates and news from department heads.

III. Grounding Phase

STAGE 8: ANCHORING NEW APPROACHES IN THE CULTURE

Much as expressed in the famous quote often attributed to Peter Drucker "Culture eats strategy for breakfast,"[2] the libraries viewed their culture as an equal force to strategy, interdependent and intimately linked. While the new organizational structure improved the coordinated delivery of services, staff still needed to value and understand how to work together as a team. Although the structure provided clear reporting lines and roles, new department heads required the right leadership skills to effectively manage. Senior leadership recognized that bringing transformational strategy to fruition was dependent on nurturing a new organizational culture with them driving the change and consequently invested significant time, energy, and effort in leadership training. Indeed, the deans were committed to the newly redefined organizational values and purpose and ensured that they were continually discussed in meetings and integrated into practices. Leadership envisioned a new culture that was creative, deeply collaborative, team-oriented, and responsive—one that embraced and learned from risk.

During the master planning process, MUL leadership purposely waited to fill open staff lines and launched the transition plan with a critical mass of openings—nearly 20 percent of the current organization—in order to identify and hire individuals who would best support the new service model and organizational structure. The dean had a strong and trusting relationship with the provost and was able to make a compelling case for moving forward with this strategy. Initially, staff felt overworked while MUL leadership developed a hiring strategy and created roles that aligned with the new organizational structure and emerging service areas. Subsequently, MUL was able to recruit candidates who would thrive and succeed within its culture. New staff joined the team well-informed, able to embrace the vision, and bringing their energy and optimism. During the interviewing process, MUL intentionally communicated this new organizational culture and conveyed that new hires would be responsible for creating it with existing staff. The onboarding process was designed to further reiterate this new culture.

In addition to the implementation of the strategic hiring plan, senior leadership recognized the need for training programs for team members and their managers. Key to the team's success was senior leadership's commitment to finance this training using endowment revenue rather than limited department budgets. Developed between senior leadership and a professional development committee, the training program strove to build relationships across departments; develop skills to be productive; understand and leverage strengths; and understand roles within productive teams. This team member training program began with a full workshop attended by all MUL staff and led by Kristen Hadeed, a "Start with Why" facilitator who helped to build trust among the team and find alignment on organizational purpose.[3]

As of this reporting, the leadership training center program is leveraging the expertise of the university's Farmer School of Business. A series of half-day sessions was recently led by Tom Heuer, a Forsythe Chair in Entrepreneurship and Clinical Faculty and an expert in the Five Practices of Exemplary Leaders Model and its Leadership Practices Inventory.[4] Over the course of several months, senior leadership and department heads will work with Tom Heuer to further develop and refine their leadership skills to facilitate the organizational vision.

Analysis and Conclusions

Success in redesigning their organizational structure was due in large part to MUL leadership and staff engaging in initial analysis, understanding the challenges they faced, adopting a mind-set open to change, and making a public commitment to transform the libraries. With this approach, the libraries were able to successfully align their services with a redesigned organizational structure that put the student experience front and center with departments redefined by function and not geography. Initially overwhelmed by first steps in the process, MUL leadership brought in expertise and support, enabling them to see their challenges more holistically and apply a system-wide lens to the solution. MUL leadership has described brightspot's design thinking methodology as a "game changer," which helped the libraries to shift from a perfectionist mentality to one that encouraged a "safe to try" approach through prototyping and other rapid testing of ideas. Ultimately, the co-created space, service, and organizational plan allowed MUL to move forward with its desired transformation and implement a plan to better serve MU's students and faculty, as well as the libraries' invaluable staff.

Using the Kotter model as a framework to analyze this project, the writers found much alignment with the design thinking methodology employed by brightspot. Indeed, both call on the engagement of stakeholders in the change process to provide insights into the user perspective and to serve as role models who help implement the change (e.g., the guiding coalition). Employing the user perspective can also assist in identifying barriers that might impede change. Kotter's Stage 6: Generating Short-Term Wins speaks directly to design thinking's penchant for prototyping. Both allow for testing of ideas without investing too many resources while building momentum for the change project. Fundamentally, in order for a change project to stick, an organization needs to feel discomfort with the status quo. Otherwise, models and methodologies are useless against a fixed mind-set.

Notes

1. Three principles guided the application of brightspot's approach to organizational design: first align the service offerings and the groups of people offering them; second, think "inside-out" and "outside-in" simultaneously; and third, assume that reorganization is continuous as you try to align all these aspects amid a shifting landscape.

   Principle 1: Align the organization of services to users.
   In the past, defining the library's role, service offerings, and departmental structures could be based on the life cycle of the book: from selection to acquisition, cataloging, shelving, circulating, reshelving, and preserving. With expanded roles in teaching, learning, and research, libraries can no longer be designed exclusively around the life cycle of the book. Many academic libraries' organizational charts are hybrids consisting of roles supporting the book life cycle with new functions such as "digital scholarship" or "emerging technology" added on an ad hoc basis. In order to integrate both traditional and new service areas, libraries should begin with reorganizing their services into categories from the user perspectives, considering user needs, understanding of services, and working processes. As a result, services are intuitive and navigable for users, and the organizational structure becomes simplified.

   Principle 2: Align the staff organization to delivery services.
   By matching service categories to functional departments, an organization may simplify its structure, the way staff communicate, and the way work is accomplished. When staff aren't aligned with the areas in which they are delivering services, they face constraints while creating new structures and processes to communicate and coordinate work across departments. With an organizational design that relates directly to the services and user perspective, staff have a clear purpose, increased incentives related to enhanced impact on users, and better collaboration around both staff and user needs.

Principle 3: Enable organizations to continually evolve.
User needs will continually change, and libraries will need to adapt their organizations in order to respond and best deliver their services. Staff need the right mind-set and skills in order to adapt. Using a design thinking experimental approach, they can build capacity to assess and change their services and create a new mind-set that facilitates organizational change during and after the project.

2. Often attributed to Peter Drucker, researchers have been unable to find any citations correctly identifying Peter Drucker as the author. For an interesting look at the ubiquity of this quote, see Quote Investigator: https://quoteinvestigator.com/2017/05/23/culture-eats/

3. For more information on Kristen Hadeed and the "Start with Why" program, go to "Kristen Hadeed," Start with Why website, accessed May 20, 2019, https://startwithwhy.com/igniter/kristenhadeed/.

4. The Five Practices of Exemplary Leadership™ was developed by Jim Kouzes and Barry Posner. For more information, see http://www.leadershipchallenge.com/About-section-Our-Approach.aspx

Bibliography

Hadeed, Kristen. "Start with Why." Accessed May 20, 2019. https://startwithwhy.com/igniter/kristenhadeed/.

Kouzes, Jim, and Barry Posner. "The Five Practices of Exemplary Leadership™." *The Leadership Challenge.* Accessed July 27, 2019. http://www.leadershipchallenge.com/About-section-Our-Approach.aspx

Chapter 7

User Engagement
A Matrix Reorganization

Doug Worsham, Allison Benedetti, Judy Consales, Angela Horne, Nisha Mody, Rikke Ogawa, and Matthew Vest

Setting the Change Stage

UCLA is a four-year, public R1 research institution with an enrollment of 31,002 undergraduate students, 13,025 graduate students, and 1,401 interns and residents.[1] The UCLA Library employs 524 FTE, including 211 student FTE, and has multiple units and locations throughout campus.[2] The User Engagement division was established during a recent reorganization aimed at bringing together public-facing library services under one associate university librarian (AUL). This affected thirty-five academic and career staff across several libraries, including the Arts Library, Louise M. Darling Biomedical Library, Eugene and Maxine Rosenfeld Management Library, Music Library, Powell Library, Science and Engineering Library, and the Charles E. Young Library Humanities and Social Sciences Division; each of these libraries had differing existing administrative structures and norms. The establishment of User Engagement required those staff to combine and divide units as well as workflow processes in order to successfully integrate and scale public services for patrons. A year later, John Kotter's eight-step model of change provides an excellent framework to analyze the successes and ongoing challenges of the reorganization.

I. Warm-up Phase

STAGE 1: ESTABLISHING A SENSE OF URGENCY

The transformation of academic libraries over the past decade has prompted debate on how to simultaneously maintain relevant service models and develop new approaches. At UCLA this debate has been further complicated by a history of decentralized public services and divergent visions and practices that have negatively impacted user experience and impeded collaboration across units. Frustrated by missed opportunities to connect silos many librarians and staff craved a clear vision, support for collaboration, and empowerment to move forward collectively. Ad hoc and pilot efforts in cross-location collaboration had been occurring for a number of years, though few had the institutional mandate to expand into universal adoption. Many staff recognized the cost of silos in terms of efficiency, user experience, priority setting, and staffing. Previous efforts to standardize had run into challenges in large part due

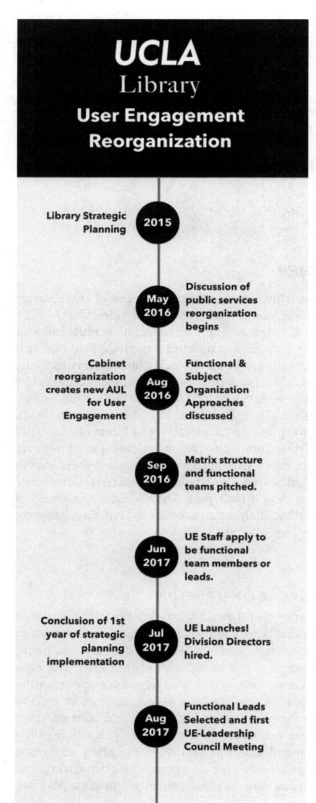

to competing reporting lines, uneven communication, lack of widespread buy-in, and insufficient resources. It was too easy for staff to default to the way they had always worked because each new initiative could be viewed as someone else's project or interest and not their own.

In 2015, revitalization came in the form of a new library-wide strategic plan that emphasized a team-based, collaborative approach to functional areas and called for the elimination of traditional location-based silos common for multi-location library systems.[3] An AUL departure and middle manager attrition had left Cabinet (the library's senior leadership team) stretched thin, impeding efforts to implement larger strategic initiatives. Cabinet recognized multiple urgent needs to reconfigure the portfolios of senior leadership, create a better structure for succession planning, foster new leaders, and enable innovation that would allow the library to grow. To address these issues, they created an improved senior leadership structure and a new portfolio, called User Engagement, that combined most public services under one AUL. At this point, the new AUL for User Engagement (AUL UE) began discussions with stakeholders about a strategy for reorganization (see figure 7.1).

FIGURE 7.1

User engagement reorganization timeline

STAGE 2: CREATING THE GUIDING COALITION

The primary goal in creating the guiding coalition for the reorganization effort was to recruit a diverse group of leaders and stakeholders from within public services, as well as other key partners within the library. In an effort to include wide representation, the AUL UE recruited a group of seventeen librarians and staff to serve as the UE planning working group. Eleven members of this group were internal to UE, and six were from library units reporting to other AULs.

When the working group was formed, the University Librarian articulated a vision of "One Library" across many locations, though the group was initially unsure about how to translate this vision into an organizational chart. The working group also had a set of pre-established objectives that set the boundaries and scope of its efforts. These included the desire to create opportunities for professional growth and leadership; resolution of an unsustainable interim reporting structure; recognition of the connections between UE and the rest of the library; and interest in minimizing the amount of disruption for affected staff.

These parameters still left several areas open to negotiation and allowed the working group to explore a number of possible approaches to creating an organizational chart. The group was also able to develop various approaches for how the reorganization effort could contribute to the "One Library" vision. These included a desire for an improved user experience, more efficient coordination between units, and increased capacity for new services. The development of this shared vision was not always easy or automatic, and it quickly became clear that the group had varying and even contradictory ideas and approaches to effective management, leadership, and teamwork for UE. This diversity of opinions is what the AUL UE had hoped for, in that it reflected the varying backgrounds and experiences of the working group members. The working group found itself struggling to answer a number of challenging organizational questions:

- Should we continue to be organized geographically, by subject, or would a functional approach lead to improved coordination of services?
- How do we divide staffing and designate reporting lines? What impact will this have on staff office locations?
- What degree of hierarchy is needed? Could we use this reorganization as an opportunity to flatten hierarchical structures and foster leadership among all UE staff? Is it possible to lead effectively even if you are not a supervisor?

The constructive tension that resulted from these challenging discussions had costs and benefits. At times it seemed as if factions might be developing within the working group, particularly with respect to geographical versus functional approaches. Some suggestions had personal implications in that areas of authority and responsibility might change as a result of the reorganization. At the same time, the group as a whole had an increasingly shared desire to try something new, and there were signs of progress toward a workable solution. Time for creative thinking in between meetings was essential at this stage. Individual brainstorming, as well as ideas generated through informal conversations after meetings, frequently moved the process forward. In many ways, these ideas, when brought back to the group as a whole, generated the most significant breakthroughs.

STAGE 3: DEVELOPING A VISION AND STRATEGY

Several breakthroughs moved the group towards its ultimate vision for UE. One of these was an exercise to analyze how three proposed organizational structures—subject-based, function-based, and the existing structure—could help UE address a number of known challenges, which included budget allocations, interdisciplinary support, and sustainable services. Each group found pros and cons to its organizational style with no one proposal emerging as the ideal solution. Influenced by other institutions' efforts and the "One Library" vision, group members started working on organizational charts. Using scenarios, the group discussed pros and cons, and over time members coalesced around five primary functional teams and three subject-based divisions. A matrix organizational structure in which staff serve both on a functional team and in a subject-based division became the proposed model for User Engagement (see figure 7.2). Such matrix structures have roots in project management and have been used to leverage project leadership activities while centralizing administrative responsibilities external to the project team.[4] The working group also discussed the potential for the matrix structure to provide opportunities for more staff to develop leadership skills through teamwork and knowledge sharing.

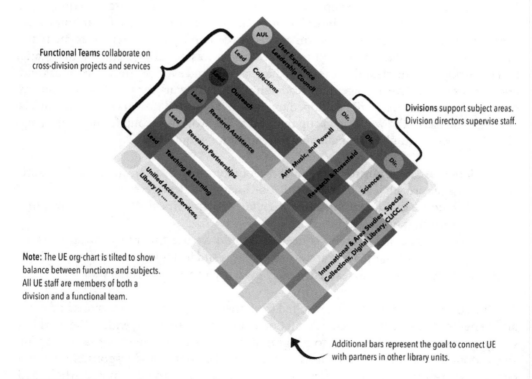

FIGURE 7.2

The User Engagement matrix organizational chart

At this point, the University Librarian attended a working group meeting and gave her input on the proposed matrix model. After receiving positive feedback from the University Librarian, the group shifted focus from idea generation to questions of implementation: Could this work? Would it help create a more formalized coordination of public services across locations? Would it adequately account for discipline-specific needs? Would the divisions have equal staffing? Could we agree on the number and scope of functional teams? Could we agree on priorities? These questions came at a critical time and inspired group members to work together to create the new organization.

STAGE 4: COMMUNICATING THE CHANGE VISION

The working group members varied in the amount and type of information they shared with their peers. Some engaged in active discussions about the pros and cons of possible changes; others simply reported out, occasionally without a great deal of specificity. Staff reactions and engagements were also highly variable. Some staff were skeptical while others were curious and excited about what opportunities a new approach might bring. In addition to face-to-face communication strategies, the group kept all documentation in an open organizational wiki for staff member review. This prompted both planned and spontaneous conversations.

Once the working group had coalesced around the matrix, the proposed structure for the organization was shared with all UE staff. The AUL UE, equipped with the matrix organizational chart and the proposed charges for the functional teams and divisions, embarked on a series of meetings across the library to talk about the vision for her new portfolio. Cabinet endorsed the proposed changes, and the library's Management Council, comprised of the library's middle managers and senior leadership, expressed interest and support and shared their questions about how units outside of UE would interact with and participate in activities and initiatives. In response, the working group added these stakeholder groups to the left and right edges of the organizational chart in order to illustrate UE's goal to connect with partners in other library units. Continuing the communication efforts, the AUL UE went to department meetings for the affected units and spoke at an all-library staff meeting.

The working group members were also part of communicating the vision. The final plan included choices and compromises that meant several staff members would face significant changes in job responsibilities, creating some anxiety. The group tried to be open and provide opportunities for discussion at staff meetings, in individual conversations, and on the organizational wiki, but later feedback indicated that some staff felt this was insufficient. In general, communication was a challenging part of this process. These struggles were indicative of some of the issues that UE sought to address—silos, lack of agreement about priorities, and inadequate leadership.

II. Introducing New Practices Phase

STAGE 5: EMPOWERING BROAD-BASED ACTION

Fostering ongoing opportunities for leadership and staff engagement and empowering broad-based action were important goals of the UE reorganization. The new organizational structure called for eight new leadership positions: three division directors and five functional team leads. These open positions offered staff unprecedented opportunities to consider themselves as potential leaders in a newly integrated organization. In part to facilitate ongoing opportunities for leadership development, the working group decided that functional team leads would rotate every two years, meaning that over time UE staff would have multiple opportunities to take on leadership roles in the organization. While some considered this approach empowering, others asked questions about fairness and equitable access to leadership:

- What if multiple qualified people apply for the same functional lead position? If this happens, are co-leads an option?
- Are leadership positions truly open to all UE staff, or are they open only to librarians? If functional team leads rotate, should division directors rotate as well?
- If some leadership positions rotate and others do not, does this create a power imbalance?

These questions remain relevant as UE works to become an organization in which all members are empowered as team members and leaders.

Each of the functional teams and divisions utilized a set of best practices for team formation developed as part of the library strategic plan. The best practices (see figure 7.3) included five stages, from team definition and formation to decision-making and assessment. Key steps emphasized establishing norms and articulating roles and responsibilities. Though lengthy, this process laid a foundation for a new organizational culture and prepared UE as a whole for team-based collaboration.

Team Formation Best Practices (UCLA Library Strategic Plan, 2015)

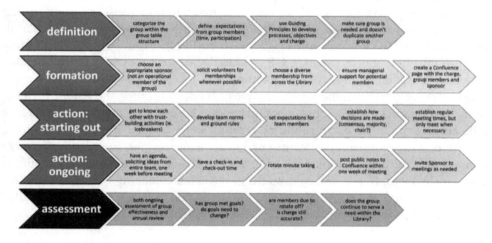

FIGURE 7.3
Team formation best practices

One of these early actions was the establishment of a quarterly all-UE meeting designed to promote active, open, and creative conversations among all staff, including those who were typically less engaged in the past. These meetings are participatory and have helped members identify areas for change and improvement for UE as well as the whole library, including encouraging a risk-taking culture, determining the top priorities for UE's first year, and brainstorming how to create time and energy for new initiatives.

Feedback gathered after the meetings indicates that staff have appreciated the opportunities for connection, the intentionally designed activities, and the ability to provide ideas for improvement:

> Great to hear about what my colleagues are up to and seeing everyone in person.

> Lots of people talking and doing initial self-reflective work with specific current and future actions was practical and hard to do, but sort of essential to a good faith effort to improve the library.

> If the topic is going to be self-reflective, then give continued homework for us to dig a little deeper. This was nice but I'm not sure people got to the point of recognizing individual need to change bad behaviors.

In order to provide multiple ways for staff to address these important topics, divisions and functional teams debrief the meeting to allow for more intimate and specific conversations. Fostering critical organizational conversations multiple times and in multiple venues has been essential to UE's efforts to empower broad-based action.

STAGE 6: GENERATING SHORT-TERM WINS

User Engagement's reorganization has been more than just a restructuring of library units and reporting lines. Throughout the process library staff spoke up about long-standing organizational needs to build community, improve workplace culture, foster constructive collaboration, and build more sustainable service models. Addressing these needs resulted in some short-term wins that built momentum during UE's first year.

Successful community building within UE has involved both large group conversations and opportunities for staff to connect, engage, and collaborate in smaller settings. One early experiment in community building has been Open Mic events, hosted by UE's functional teams. The events are designed to encourage easy and informal idea sharing across the whole library and are different from a traditional brown-bag or staff seminar in that they encourage staff to discuss ideas at any stage of development, without the expectation of preparing slides or formal presentation materials. The format is open, meaning anyone can share an idea related to the theme. For example, staff have shared teaching activities, approaches to reference interviews, new ideas for campus outreach, and collections strategies. At Open Mic events staff have also shared questions and challenges they are facing, which has helped to establish these events as venues for conversation, and even vulnerability. This concept, initially generated by one functional team, gained traction when it was embraced by all of the functional teams. Furthermore, attendees from across the library have provided very positive feedback and encouraged UE to continue offering these community-building events.

Quality communication and opportunities to build emotional intelligence are key success factors in a matrix organization.[5] As a result, divisions and functional teams have been concentrating efforts on building connections between staff inside and outside of UE. The divisions have focused on team building by encouraging "shout-outs" at team meetings, hosting tea time for staff, and giving staff time to share and learn about their colleagues' work. Functional teams have made progress building campus partnerships, improving library-wide workflows, analyzing service structures, and fostering communities of practice. These short-term wins are improving services, building shared understanding, and strengthening community across UE.

STAGE 7: CONSOLIDATING GAINS AND PRODUCING MORE CHANGE

In addition to these achievements, changes in communication practices have been a driver and key component of UE culture, feeding into refreshed views when tackling historic organizational challenges. Throughout the process UE leaders focused on improving transparency through open communication tools, more frequent updates, and increased opportunities for feedback. As with most reorganizations and culture changes, there was complacency and occasionally resistance. Responding thoughtfully to different perspectives and ensuring people felt safe to share opinions honestly was critical to keep momentum moving forward. Further, the increase in open communication, especially in larger meetings, has encouraged colleagues to propose constructive changes to long-held traditions rather than viewing them as impossible to change. In a variety of settings, UE staff have shared their ideas on important areas, including staff review and evaluation, support for leadership development, the review of long-standing services, and new collection development practices, to name a few.

The positive feelings about the promise of the matrixed structure also prompted consideration of the benefits of a more integrated role for scholarly communications (a separate department) in UE initiatives. As a result, about six months into the reorganization, discussions began about folding those librarians into UE. While this integration was ultimately decided against, it is evidence of the influence of the work being done in UE and its potential to foster new approaches to traditional library functions. The collaboration between these groups continues to grow, regardless of the administrative structure, including a cohosted workshop on scholarly communications and the ACRL Framework for Information Literacy for Higher Education.[6]

This year librarians and staff have been increasingly interested in talking about broad issues of librarianship, such as the role of liaisons and how to build collections as a system. Various non-UE units have expressed desire to engage with UE-led initiatives, and library staff members are now better positioned to build on relationships and collaborations with non-library groups across the university. Current initiatives include workshops on advanced research tools and methods, accreditation review, and shared support services for undergraduate research.

Three librarian searches immediately post-reorganization offer further evidence of forward momentum. Previously, searches would have been administratively siloed with a single general invitation to staff outside of that division. This time, the breadth of the new UE structure informed the formation of the search committees as well as interview schedules. Each interview included an all-UE session where candidates met representatives from each functional team and division and were asked prepared questions about how they would contribute to the variety of functions in the UE structure; conversely, finalists received answers to their own questions from a broad swath of UE. Staff members across UE were invited to meetings and meals to demonstrate a unified, multifaceted organization.

Reflecting upon issues of momentum and change, it is worth noting that UE members have varied backgrounds and tenures. Some have been at UCLA for many years and have experienced numerous structural changes. Others have joined the organization within the past few years. It has been valuable to see the process through beginner's eyes, with enthusiasm reinforcing forward momentum. At the same time, those with more tenure provide historical knowledge to inform decision-making and a strong desire to work on long-entrenched challenges. Diversity of experience and viewpoint will be an asset moving forward as UE teams articulate service priorities, develop new initiatives, and improve succession planning.

III. Grounding Phase

STAGE 8: ANCHORING NEW APPROACHES IN THE CULTURE

During the initial year of the new UE structure, much has been accomplished by everyone within UE. The opportunities ahead are wide-ranging and the early lessons substantial. Cultural change takes time and UE leaders are committed to making this new organization as successful as possible. Easily visible ways to anchor this change include bringing transparency to previously obscure processes, while more nuanced methods are discernible in casual conversations between colleagues who might otherwise not have crossed paths.

Leaders at all levels of UE (and outside) are working together to further collaborative, positive successes and move away from the siloed perspectives of the past. Negative conversations that veer toward "We've tried that before and it didn't work" or "Why do I need to do things differently?" are being constructively reframed. Important conversations are more often treated as learning moments for everyone—not just as conversations between managers and staff. Further, UE members continue to improve processes and learn from one another. Hiring is more standardized and candidate interviews involve a broader representation of voices across all sessions. The User Engagement Leadership Council (UELC) developed decision-making criteria that clarify how simple and complex decisions are made and documented. Teams and divisions are taking increasingly coordinated approaches to public services and working together on a wide range of projects and initiatives. In short, although the current UE members can't change the past, all are motivated to help move the organization in successful directions.

As UE members continue to form and improve the organization, some aspects of the change are not yet anchored. It is important that there has been confusion about the role and purpose of the UELC, which brings together the AUL UE along with division directors and functional team leads. Part of the challenge has been that UELC, the five functional teams, and the three divisions all started more-or-less simultaneously, and at a time when staff had services to deliver and active projects to manage. In retrospect, the reorganization would have benefitted from more time during UE's early formation to flesh out core processes and delineate expectations, perhaps with the assistance of a consultant. Instead, UELC's work was sometimes muddled with that of the functional teams and divisions, and it has been unclear whose leadership is primary for some conversations. The need to begin fall quarter services impacted the ability to complete an ideal plan before implementation as UELC members were directly involved in public services roles.

UE's work is further impacted by historical issues that have persisted at UCLA and are still in play, including the lack of shared understanding of liaison roles in the twenty-first-century academic library; differing opinions on levels of emphasis for various user groups such as faculty, professionals, graduate students, and undergraduates; competitiveness between groups seeking financial and staffing support; and challenging interpersonal dynamics.

As the organization moves forward, UELC will need to develop a clear process for leadership cycling. Functional team leads were selected for two-year appointments; this was a deliberate decision to allow for a rotation of new leaders to gain experience, bring new ideas, and address succession planning. Functional team membership was self-selected by library staff with the understanding that the commitment was for a two-year term. This cycling of leadership and membership provides a unique opportunity to bring new perspectives and for staff to explore new professional directions. The ability to honestly reflect upon successes and challenges made during the first cycle will be essential to restarting the cycle of change with the first step, reviewing norms and culture.

Analysis and Conclusions

Although the Kotter framework was not a tool used in this organizational change, revisiting the process through Kotter's linear progression of stages helped the authors reflect on and better understand UE's reorganization. That said, this reorganization effort was more cyclical than linear. At times, it felt as if the UE reorganization was simultaneously in Stage 4, trying to communicate the vision, while also cycling back to the previous three stages because not all stakeholders were in the same place. Stages 1 through 4 of the reorganization planning were conducted mostly among the UE working group, while Stages 5 through 8 involved all of User Engagement and staff in other units of the library. This meant that in order to create meaningful change by bringing all parties into the process, staff had to move through the stages depending on the varying needs of teams, divisions, and individuals. The later stages of the process were cyclical as well. Reflection on Stages 5 through 8 highlights their interdependencies—remove an obstacle, achieve a short-term win, build from there, and then often start again. This is noteworthy because User Engagement cannot succeed by functioning in isolation; as a piece of a larger organization, it is critically dependent on other library units. Finally, revisiting this change through the Kotter framework has highlighted the importance of Stage 8: anchoring cultural change. For UE, cultural change is ongoing as staff come and go and as other parts of the UCLA Library change as well. User Engagement's new approach to its people and their work is about creating an evolving team-based environment that encourages experimentation and allows everyone to lead and develop new skills. In this respect, for UE, Stage 8 is not an anchor. Instead, it is a launchpad for revisiting multiple stages of the organizational change process as UE works toward the goal of creating an innovative and collaborative culture.

Notes

1. "Enrollment," UCLA Academic Planning and Budget, accessed May 25, 2018, https://www.apb. ucla.edu/campus-statistics/enrollment.
2. "Administration and Organization," UCLA Library, accessed October 1, 2018, http://www.library. ucla.edu/about/administration-organization.
3. "Strategic Plan 2016–19," UCLA Library, accessed October 2, 2018, http://www.library.ucla.edu/ about/administration-organization/strategic-plan-2016-19.
4. Mihály Görög and Nigel J. Smith, *Project Management for Managers* (Newton Square, PA: Project Management Institute, 1999).
5. Thomas Sy and Stéphane Côté, "Emotional Intelligence: A Key Ability to Succeed in the Matrix Organization," *Journal of Management Development* 23, no. 5 (2004): 437–55, https://doi. org/10.1108/02621710410537056.
6. "Framework for Information Literacy for Higher Education." Association of College and Research Libraries. Accessed July 27, 2019. http://www.ala.org/acrl/standards/ilframework.

Bibliography

Association of College and Research Libraries. *Framework for Information Literacy for Higher Education.* Accessed July 27, 2019. http://www.ala.org/acrl/standards/ilframework.

Görög, Mihály, and Nigel J. Smith. *Project Management for Managers.* Newton Square, PA: Project Management Institute, 1999.

Sy, Thomas, and Stéphane Côté. "Emotional Intelligence: A Key Ability to Succeed in the Matrix Organization." *Journal of Management Development* 23, no. 5 (2004): 437–55. https://doi. org/10.1108/02621710410537056.

UCLA Academic Planning and Budget. "Enrollment." Accessed May 25, 2018. https://www.apb.ucla.edu/ campus-statistics/enrollment.

UCLA Library. "Administration and Organization." Accessed October 1, 2018. http://www.library.ucla. edu/about/administration-organization.

———. "Strategic Plan 2016–19." Accessed October 2, 2018. http://www.library.ucla.edu/about/ administration-organization/strategic-plan-2016-19.

Chapter 8

Chasing the Hedgehog

An Innovative Process for Reorganization of a University Library

C. Heather Scalf and E. Antoinette Nelson

Setting the Change Stage

The University of Texas Arlington (UTA) is a Carnegie R-1 university located in the heart of the Dallas–Fort Worth (DFW) metroplex. The UTA Libraries serve a current student population of over 54,000, in both on-campus and online degree programs. Prior to 2012, the library was traditional in its structure, having separate public services and technical services staff. Public services included Access Services, Information Services, Information Literacy, and Special Collections departments, as well as branch managers for the two satellite libraries on campus, Science and Engineering and Architecture and Fine Arts. Technical services departments included Metadata Services, Information Resources, and Digital Library Services, with Library Systems and Administration supporting all departments. In 2012, the UTA Libraries hired a new Dean of Libraries. The hiring committee for the new dean actively sought out candidates who were change agents and who expressed a vision of the academic library of the future. The broad perception was that change was necessary in order for the library to increase visibility and remain relevant on campus. The new dean came to the job with a clear mandate to help the library create a more relevant vision that would be more connected to the university's strategic goals. Under the dean's guidance, in 2013 the library's leadership team began a process that used Jim Collins's book *Good to Great* as a framework for setting a new strategic direction and realigning the organization's structure to support this new direction.[1] The entire library staff was invited to change perspective by collectively reading and discussing Jim Collins's book and to join the journey in developing a new vision. This new vision would guide the major reorganization that would take place within the next six months.

I. Warm-up Phase

STAGE 1: ESTABLISHING A SENSE OF URGENCY

The framework provided by Collins' book is based upon disciplined people, disciplined thought, and disciplined action. With new leadership at the library and the university, there was an opportunity for the library to better realign itself for long-term success. In the 2012 Association of College and Research Libraries (ACRL) Research Planning and Review Committee report, ten trends were identified.[2] While all of them struck a chord with the library, the three most immediately relevant were communicating value, prioritizing user behaviors and expectations, and patron-driven acquisition. For example, the need to communicate value to campus partners was very evident because there had been some clear indicators that the library was missing out on critical partnerships across campus. One of these indicators was that, although the library was well respected as a provider of resources and comfortable spaces, no one thought to include the library when planning began for a huge expansion in the online nursing program being offered at the university. Campus leaders making these plans did not think to invite the leadership of the library into the discussions, and thus had no information about the financial and human capital support that the library would provide to the online evidence-based nursing program. This example highlighted the need for the library to be considered an active and strategic partner in the university community. The arrival of a new dean was the beginning of the process that would move the library forward. The dean's participation in the university provost's deans' council was a strong initial step in connecting the library to the work of the campus.

In the first year, the dean created nine task forces, involving over 85 percent of library staff, with charges that were designed to help library staff engage with the idea of a different direction and to ensure that the library had an authentic understanding of the user community. The charges included reviews of best practices in several areas at peer and aspirational institutions and ethnographic observations of facility usage and user activities outside the library related to learning and research. Based on this new information, as well as other data sources from the university and the community, it was clear that the library was not addressing key factors that would increase student success, both academically and professionally. Among the critical needs noted as key to student research and study activity were space and access to power sources, as well as late-night availability of food and coffee.

STAGE 2: CREATING THE GUIDING COALITION

Rather than choosing a small subset of staff or leaders from the library, the dean chose as the guiding coalition for the library's change effort the existing leadership team, comprised of the dean, the associate dean, and the ten department coordinators, as department heads were then called. The departments at the time were Metadata Services, Digital Library Services, Access Services, Information Resources, Information Services, Information Literacy, Library Systems, Library Administration, and two branches—the Science and Engineering Library and the Architecture and Fine Arts Library. Other than the new dean, the leadership team had been working as a group with no changes for more than two years and had established relationships and trust within their departments and the organization. Not unlike the typical academic library, with over one hundred staff in ten departments across five facilities, the library had inevitable silos and areas of opportunity for greater collaboration. Because of the mandate for change that was clearly visible in the dean's hiring process, it was generally expected that there would be some form of reorganization of the library. The involvement of over 85 percent of the staff in the initial task forces greatly contributed to an increased understanding of the need for change, but the unknown final product was also a source of great anxiety for many staff.

STAGE 3: DEVELOPING A VISION AND STRATEGY

The driving goal for the leadership team was the creation of a user-centered organization where innovation was a hallmark. In *Good to Great*, Collins calls this intense focus a "hedgehog." The idea is drawn from Isaiah Berlin's 1953 essay "The Hedgehog and the Fox" and attributed to the Greek poet Archilochus: "The fox knows many things, but the hedgehog knows one big thing."[3] The strength of the hedgehog, as Collins relates, is in its single-minded focus.[4] The leadership team wanted to choose a vision that the library could be passionate about, that the library could be extraordinary at, and that could be sustained. What was the one thing that the library could do better than anyone in the university community?

Using the concept of disciplined thought from *Good to Great*, the leadership team began by confronting the brutal facts. Using a week-long on-site retreat as a catalyst, the leadership team reviewed a variety of data sources to inform the new vision. Beginning with the data that had been acquired from the ethnographic study of the population, the team used a compiled list of things called "What we know and what we think" to guide its understanding of user needs and expectations. Institutional reports such as the National Survey of Student Engagement and the annual Student Experience Survey administered by institutional planning provided a rich local perspective on students' needs and perceptions. The annual survey of the National Association of Colleges and Employers provided clear information about what qualities employers wanted in new employees, which prompted discussions about how the library might engage with student preparation for life after college. Observations of student preferences for space and research support on campus and academic trends at the university and beyond indicated a strong bias toward technology and innovation. Using all of the available data and what it believed that the library could be the best at, the leadership team defined the new vision as CXI—Creation, eXploration and Innovation. The plan was to complete the reorganization and make necessary changes during the summer session so as to have the least impact on users once the new fall semester began. The entire process, from developing the new vision to creating new departments to reflect that vision, took five months from beginning to end. This was the first in a series of changes that would occur regularly over the next five years.

STAGE 4: COMMUNICATING THE CHANGE VISION

While staff broadly understood that change was part of the new dean's direction, many feared what that might look like, and leaders were actively working to bolster confidence and increase communication to support the coming transitions. Coordinators had weekly staff meetings to share all of the available information throughout the first year, and also sent updates via email during the week-long planning process. The dean's weekly "state of the library" email to all staff was designed to keep the communication lines open throughout the library while updating staff on plans and activities and encouraging them to communicate their thoughts and ideas to anyone on the leadership team. As soon as the leadership team decided that CXI was going to be the library's hedgehog moving forward, it began to communicate this information to all staff. At the conclusion of the planning meeting, department coordinators began to meet with their staff and discuss the vision and the process that would help the library to achieve it. The planning process had identified many skills as critical to the achievement of the vision. These skills were then combined into functions, and the functions consolidated into roles. A list of 283 unique skills identified as being those that would move the vision forward was offered to all staff as a self-assessment of knowledge, skills, abilities, and preferences, which we called the KSAP. Additionally, staff were provided a list of roles that would support the new vision from which they could choose (see figures 8.1 and 8.2).

KSAP Skills and Workstyles Preferences Self-Assessment

Workstyles Preferences Self-Assessment

This is a section where you say what your preferences are for a wide variety of situations and aspects of work here in the library. It focuses on what you enjoy rather than what you know.

REMEMBER: there are NO RIGHT OR WRONG ANSWERS. Please be honest! Nobody enjoys everything, and that's ok!

*PR1 Communicating via email
O 1 Dislike   O 2 Enjoy a little   O 3 Enjoy a lot   O 4 Love this!   O 0 Not sure

*PR2 Communicating via IM/text
O 1 Dislike   O 2 Enjoy a little   O 3 Enjoy a lot   O 4 Love this!   O 0 Not sure

*PR3 Communicating by phone
O 1 Dislike   O 2 Enjoy a little   O 3 Enjoy a lot   O 4 Love this!   O 0 Not sure

---

FIGURE 8.1
Work styles preferences example 1

---

*PR107 Analyzing large amounts of data
O 1 Dislike   O 2 Enjoy a little   O 3 Enjoy a lot   O 4 Love this!   O 0 Not sure

*PR108 Teaching information literacy skills
O 1 Dislike   O 2 Enjoy a little   O 3 Enjoy a lot   O 4 Love this!   O 0 Not sure

*PR109 In-depth faculty and PhD student research
O 1 Dislike   O 2 Enjoy a little   O 3 Enjoy a lot   O 4 Love this!   O 0 Not sure

*PR110 Answering statistics, data, or GIS questions
O 1 Dislike   O 2 Enjoy a little   O 3 Enjoy a lot   O 4 Love this!   O 0 Not sure

---

FIGURE 8.2
Work styles preferences example 2

This list included department head roles, but no organizational structure was defined at the time. All library staff were sent two surveys to complete that would inform the dean's decision about their new roles in the library. Along with completing the KSAP, each staff member completed a survey indicating his or her prioritized top seven job preferences and bottom five choices of jobs (figures 8.3 and 8.4), and was asked to select up to four areas of leadership that he or she would like to engage in as part of the new vision. There were sixty-three roles available in support of the vision that encompassed forty-three professional positions and seventy-two classified staff positions. Fifty-three leadership areas were available, and staff also had the opportunity to suggest a new area as part of the process.

RespondentID	First Question: Choose your TOP 7 choices for jobs. These are jobs that you will love doing and that will make you happy. Copy the job position numbers and titles from the list and paste into the textboxes below.						
2654255176	Administrative Assistant	Budget, Accounting Clerk	Human Resources Specialist I	Human Resource Specialist II	Staff Development	Budget Officer	Facilities Assistant
2659549536	Archivist/ Liaison	2. Disciplinary Liaison: Arts & Humanities	3. Book Repair and Conservation Assistant	4. Grant Writer	5. Metadata Specialist	6. Photographic Access Assistant	7. Interdisciplinary Liaison: K-12
2658321305	Archivist/ Liaison	Department Head: Special Collections & Archives	Data Management & Curation	Digital Projects Librarian	Interdisciplinary Liaison: Digital Humanities	Interdisciplinary Liaison: Government Documents	

FIGURE 8.3
Role selection result sample

Second Question: Choose your BOTTOM 5 choices for jobs. These are jobs that you absolutely do NOT want to do and that will make you very unhappy. Copy the job position numbers and titles from the list and paste into the textboxes below. These 5 are in no particular order.				
5 Jobs I Do Not Want				
1. I don't want to do:	2. I don't want to do:	3. I don't want to do:	4. I don't want to do:	5. I don't want to do:
Archivist/Liaison	Liaison	Programmer/Analyst	Serials Acquisitions Assistant	LCD Management
Events Specialist	Communications Assistant	Marketing Coordinator	Exhibits Designer I	Web & Digital Specialist

FIGURE 8.4
Role selection choices sample

All positions were structurally agnostic, as no one except the dean knew the final organizational structure, and every position, except the dean, the associate dean, and a digital research fellow, was on the table. The surveys were sent out in April and were due back in two weeks. After receiving the survey responses, the dean met with all staff members individually to discuss their preferences and role choices so that each staff member would have an opportunity to articulate why he or she selected or did not select a particular role. After these individual meetings were completed, the dean made the decision as to which role each person would fill. Members of library leadership were informed about their new roles on a Friday, and the remainder of the staff were informed the following Monday. The new leadership team created by the reorganization had its first meeting the following week in the form of a two-day leadership development retreat. The overall organizational structure was revealed to the leadership team at the retreat. After clarification and discussion about how the structure would support the achievement of CXI, the structure was released to all staff at the end of that week. After the two-day training, previous department coordinators then met with the staff in their old departments individually to facilitate the transition by explaining roles and answering transition-related questions. One of the key elements that the dean wanted the leadership team to convey to staff was that the change was not an indictment of the past, but a need to focus on the future. The first expression of the new direction was to communicate the library's value to the university community by demonstrating the clear and direct connections that CXI had to the university's strategic priorities. With a new president, the university was embarking on the development of a new strategic plan, and the library's first priority was to align many of its activities with this new plan.

II. Introducing New Practices Phase

STAGE 5: EMPOWERING BROAD-BASED ACTION

The most evident initial barrier to change was the emotional attachment that staff had to doing the jobs that they had been originally hired for and had been doing well for years. New leaders lacked experience in how to manage staff and processes in a time of high transition. Continuing communication about the need for change was required and was delegated down to the department level in most cases. New department heads were challenged to explain to each staff member how his or her past contributions had laid the foundation for the good work required in the future. Additionally, many staff members needed to develop new skills for their new roles and were uncertain as to how they would be evaluated on their performance in those new roles and whether they could even be successful doing the work required. One unforeseen consequence of the reorganization was a shortage of staff to provide research and instructional support. As a temporary measure, the dean asked six librarians who were assigned to non-public services roles and who had indicated that liaison roles were in their bottom five choices of jobs to provide part-time public services support to students and faculty. Although the dean spoke one on one with each of these six librarians, this conflict of expectations impacted their trust in the organization and the leadership moving forward.

A follow-up evaluation of the assignment process showed that 86.5 percent of staff members got a role that was in their top three choices, with 62.8 percent getting their top choice, and no one was permanently assigned to a role that was among their bottom five. One lesson learned after the process was complete was that it was critically important to manage expectations in a time of transition. Some of the organizational challenges inherent in such dramatic change were exacerbated by the perception of some staff that the transition was as simple as stepping from one role into another, without considering the needs of the library's users.

One of the guiding principles for the libraries is "perpetual beta," and the organization itself has continued to change and develop. In some cases, staff chose to change roles or were moved involuntarily to different roles for a better fit, and departments continued to be created, shifted, or realigned to move strategic priorities forward. While every effort was made to honor a staff member's passions in the initial assignments, in some cases the staff member didn't have the necessary skills or abilities, thus requiring additional role changes.

STAGE 6: GENERATING SHORT-TERM WINS

An immediate short-term win was the activity that the new leadership team undertook to begin to develop relationships and trust. An outside consultant came to meet with the team to conduct self-assessments and team-building activities over the following six weeks. Being in an environment where truth telling was encouraged helped leaders to overcome transition difficulties and gain confidence moving forward. Later short-term wins came as a result of the new leadership team's creation of forty-nine initiatives that were divided into three broad categories: Strategic, Operational, and Accountability. These initiatives supported the library's vision and direction of the library leading into the twenty-first-century era of innovation, data, risk taking and the library's overall strategic goals. A very ambitious agenda was set for the first year.

One initial success was in creating an organizational structure that included departments with names and functions that clearly connected to CXI. For example, Information Resources and Metadata Services were merged to become Access and Discovery (A&D). The focus of this new department would be providing access to resources, not ownership. A previously completed analysis of monographic acquisitions for the decade prior had revealed that almost 65 percent of the books that the library had purchased had never been checked out. This analysis was a driving factor in the implementation of a new acquisitions model of patron-driven acquisition (PDA) of resources, instead of the traditional approval plan model based upon what librarians thought the community needed. One result of this change to the acquisition model was the elimination of subject-specific collection development librarians.

Another win for library users was when Access Services became User Engagement Services (UES). With this move was the formation of the Consolidated Service Point (CSP), an initiative that helped combine circulation and reference services into one service point at all library locations. Also included in the CSP was the addition of a help desk in collaboration with the university's Office of Information Technology (OIT). This consolidation was designed to provide users with a single location for technology- or service-related questions and was in response to user comments and feedback during the discovery phase of the reorganization.

An additional significant change was that librarians with reference, information literacy, and collection development responsibilities were joined under one group, Outreach and Scholarship (O&S). The O&S department was broken into three disciplinary areas (Social Sciences, Arts and Humanities, and STEM) with department heads for each area. The task force investigation of the prior year had learned that libraries of a similar size were increasingly adopting a model that combined all three aspects of librarianship and their responsibilities. The library's previous organization had a separate department for each function, which had reinforced silos and encouraged territoriality within the library, rather than promoting a user-centered focus.

During the six months following the reorganization, priority was given to transitioning staff to new roles and in many cases new work spaces, with the continual reinforcement that what was being done was to the benefit of library users. For example, because of the lack of staff in the new UES department, many staff members from the previous Access Services department were asked to fill in at the various service points during the fall semester until new staff could be hired and trained to take over these duties.

Additionally, new departments specifically designed to support the vision were created. In support of the goals of access and discovery, the new Digital Creation department focused on making unique library resources visible, discoverable, and globally accessible. The new Marketing and Communication department was formed to assist in telling the library's stories internally, to the university community, and beyond. A Director of Grants was appointed to increase staff knowledge about grants and to increase grant proposal submissions. With a focus on evidence-based decision-making, three librarians were initially appointed as assessment directors.

Other short-term wins from the first reorganization included the installation of security gates and card swipe access at the entrance of the Central Library; the movement of eighty-three staff to new positions and the related opportunities for them to learn new skills; creation of a graduate student resource delivery service; and the implementation of a graduate student–only study area on the fifth floor.

STAGE 7: CONSOLIDATING GAINS AND PRODUCING MORE CHANGE

The primary strategy used to maintain momentum was one of continual motion. While the previous twelve months had seen major change across the library, a number of areas of strategic focus had not yet been addressed. In order to focus more clearly on creation and experiential learning, the dean and the associate university librarian began planning for a makerspace in the Central Library. This later developed into an MIT-affiliated Fabrication Laboratory, or FabLab. The FabLab's goal was to be a creative applied-learning environment for UTA students and the local community.

Staff from around the organization were hired to develop and then operate the FabLab in its initial iteration.

The liaison model was also reimagined to address experiential teaching and learning rather than traditional information literacy and bibliographic instruction. O&S was dissolved and became two new departments, Experiential Learning and Undergraduate Research (ELUR) and Faculty, Services and Online Engagement (FSOE), designed to focus on services and support for two specific constituent groups on campus.

A sign that an organization is successful is that its staff are highly motivated and positively engaged. The Organizational, Wellness and Development (OWD) program was developed, placing emphasis on creating programs that would increase morale and engagement of library staff.

Change of any kind can be disruptive even to motivated and positive staff. Creating an environment where staff feel valued and are encouraged to grow in their job skills, while cultivating relationships with colleagues and collaborating on projects in support of the library's goals, is key to having engaged staff.

A big step forward in the second year was the hiring of a new administrator, the Associate University Librarian (AUL), who would develop the library's scholarly communications activities. This AUL supervises Special Collections, Digital Creation, and two new groups, Publishing, and Data and Research Services. The Scholarly Communications division expands the resonance of faculty and graduate student scholarship and research by developing, advocating for, and educating about emerging forms of scholarly communication.

III. Grounding Phase

STAGE 8: ANCHORING NEW APPROACHES IN THE CULTURE

In the intervening five years, several steps have been taken to help anchor the changes and propel the library forward. These include the institution of several new staff awards, designed to reward innovation and highlight the values of the organization. Also, the fairly reliable annual merit increase process began to be more clearly connected to the library's values and innovation, as supervisors used a rubric to evaluate an employee's contributions in their recommendations for increases. Additionally, the dean and the assessment director attended many departmental staff meetings to share the "Strategy Tree" (figure 8.5) and discuss how each role and function within the library had an impact on the strategic plan. Weekly meetings of the leadership team continued for the first two years, which increased cohesiveness and understanding about activities across the library.

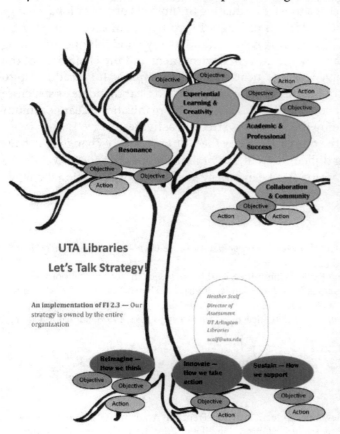

FIGURE 8.5
UTA Libraries Strategy visualization

Analysis and Conclusions

The new organization is dramatically changed from its previous structure and focus. Team compositions changed, leadership changed, and 94 percent of the library staff changed roles. Most staff, including leadership, needed to develop additional skills for their new roles, and this caused a high level of uncertainty during the transition. Several physical spaces were renovated to accommodate newly formed campus partnerships. While there were some short-term wins, the realities of a 24/5 operation combined with resistance to change made momentum slower to achieve. New programs and services have been developed and implemented, and some increase in staff engagement and support is evident. The library continues to tweak its structure to better address its strategic goals. Change has not been without its long-term impact. At the beginning of the reorganization in 2013, 109 staff were employed at the libraries. Eighty-five of those staff members have left over five years, along with an additional thirty-eight who were hired during the intervening time. These departures and the inability to hire new staff to fill gaps has caused a delay in moving the vision forward. As Kotter has reflected, the process of creating and realizing a vision can often take months or even years to complete.[5] Failing to thoroughly complete any one phase will cause subsequent phases to falter as well. While having a perpetual beta perspective is vital for innovation, it can also mean that goals and expectations will rapidly change, causing additional stress.

By using the Kotter model as a tool for evaluating the library's organizational change, we see evidence of the execution of parts of Stages 1 through 6, but success in Stages 7 and 8 is less clearly defined. The guiding coalition did a very good job of confronting the brutal facts and understanding the current environment and the challenges of the future. Initial successes revolved around near-constant communication leading up to and during the initial phases of the change. However, with no clear mandate or structure to continue the hard work of communication after the reorganization, clear communication was quickly subsumed by the ambitious strategic activities.

Using a framework like the one provided by the Kotter model of change may have reduced some of the ensuing difficulties that this organization experienced. While the achievement of the original vision has been largely successful, organizational change is still a work in progress.

Notes

1. James C. Collins, *Good to Great: Why Some Companies Make the Leap—and Others Don't* (New York: Harper Business, 2001).
2. ACRL Research Planning and Review Committee, "2012 Top Trends in Academic Libraries: A Review of the Trends and Issues Affecting Academic Libraries in Higher Education," *College and Research Libraries News* 73, no. 6 (June 2012), 311-20, https://doi.org/10.5860/crln.73.6.8773.
3. Isaiah Berlin, *The Hedgehog and the Fox* (Chicago: Elephant Paperbacks, 1993), quoted in Collins, *Good to Great,* 2001, 90.
4. Collins, *Good to Great,* 2001, 91.
5. John P. Kotter, *Leading Change* (Boston: Harvard Business Review Press, 1996), 23.

Bibliography

ACRL Research Planning and Review Committee. "2012 Top Trends in Academic Libraries: A Review of the Trends and Issues Affecting Academic Libraries in Higher Education." *College and Research Libraries News* 73, no. 6 (June 2012): 311-20. https://doi.org/10.5860/crln.73.6.8773.

Collins, James C. *Good to Great: Why Some Companies Make the Leap—and Others Don't.* New York: Harper Business, 2001.

Kotter, John P. *Leading Change.* Boston: Harvard Business Review Press, 1996.

Chapter 9

Breaking Down Silos through Reorganization

Julie Garrison and Maira Bundza

Setting the Change Stage

Western Michigan University is the fourth largest university in Michigan, located in Kalamazoo. This Doctoral Institution with Higher Research Activity (R2) has over 23,000 students and close to 900 full-time faculty in fifty departments with over 250 undergraduate and graduate programs. University Libraries has a main library (Waldo) and three branches (Maybee Music and Dance Library, Swain Education Library, and the Zhang Legacy Collections Center). In September 2018 there were three administrators, twenty-one librarians, forty-two staff members, three graduate assistants and approximately 100 student employees. Four additional positions were in the hiring stage.

I. Warm-up Phase

Stage 1: Establishing a Sense of Urgency

Library staffing had been in stasis for a long time with recognition that reorganization was needed, as was noted in the 2006 strategic plan. However, a sweep of retirements, including the then dean of the libraries, brought the realization that major changes had to take place.

Fourteen departments operated (see figure 9.1) within the libraries, functioning mostly within their own silos. Staff and faculty made decisions regarding their specific department programs and services, leading to a patchwork of policies and procedures guiding library practices. There was a grassroots way of doing things, with limited mechanisms in place to initiate substantial changes throughout the library. Interdepartmental collaborations worked well, such as the collection development team and local digitization group. In general, there were few organizational strategies or mechanisms in place to reconsider library purpose, work, and processes or nimbly respond to ever-changing academic library needs. For example, despite the transition to acquiring more online and electronic content for our collections, workflows, processes, and staff responsibilities in the library continued to be based heavily upon a print-based model.

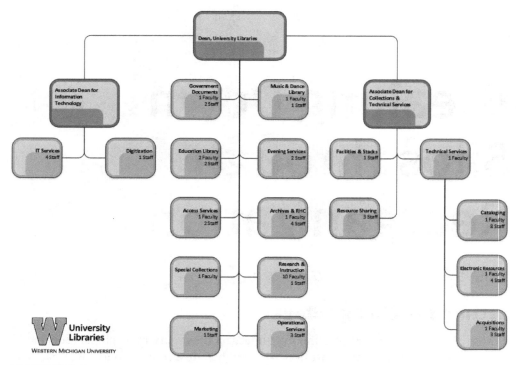

FIGURE 9.1
Western Michigan University Libraries organizational chart, fall 2016

Other factors forced changes upon the libraries. The libraries implemented a new ILS system in 2015, which changed workflows and staff responsibilities in many departments. Work that was once the responsibility of IT professionals was now distributed across a team of individuals with expertise in their functional areas. Other areas of change included a major decrease in physical items coming into the library coupled with weeding projects to make room for more student-centered spaces and a new archives building and storage facility that required major reprocessing work. Statistics showed the decrease in reference transactions, which called for rethinking how to best serve library users. In addition, as part of a university "learner support program review," a thorough analysis of the libraries' information literacy, resource delivery, and research assistance programs had identified opportunities for rethinking aspects of these programs.

Over the past decade, the number of faculty and staff in the libraries had been shrinking. From 2013 to 2016, seven library faculty members retired or left, and only three were hired to replace them. Three additional faculty members announced pending retirements in 2017. Over this same period, two staff positions were eliminated due to budget cuts and several other positions had been left open indefinitely. The new dean started working in March 2016, and all employees in Western's libraries expressed concerns about the eroding workforce and enthusiasm for rebuilding staff and faculty under new leadership.

STAGE 2: CREATING THE GUIDING COALITION

Before the new dean was hired, most departments held conversations about the type of leader they wanted and started discussing their current concerns as well as their visions for the future. When the new dean arrived, she spent the first two months learning about all of the departments' responsibilities and challenges and interviewing every faculty and staff member in the library one-on-one to get to know individuals and learn their perspectives of how the libraries were functioning. The dean sent a list of guiding questions to all staff before the initial meetings:

1. What is your role in the libraries? What does your job entail? Are there ways you would like to see your position evolve? If so, how and why?
2. What do you value about working at WMU libraries? WMU in general?
3. What do you think the libraries are doing well?
4. What are some things you would like to see the libraries do that we are not?
5. What are your expectations of me as the Dean?
6. If the libraries had three new open positions, what would you see as the top priorities for filling these? Why?
7. What does a successful library look like to you? How do you see our libraries fitting your picture of a successful library? Where do you see room to grow?

Questions were adapted from Garrison and Nutefall's 2014 article with advice for new library directors.[1] Some staff prepared written responses and shared these with the dean during the meeting. Other conversations were more free-form, hitting on these topics and a variety of other concerns that were on employees' minds.

A date for an initial library-wide strategic planning retreat with the new dean was set in the summer of 2016, a few months after her arrival. All library employees were encouraged to read ACRL's *New Roles for the Road Ahead* in preparation of the full day conversation about the libraries' future.[2] For the first formal collective conversation, all library employees gathered in June for a full-day conversation. To facilitate the flow of ideas and discussions, the library employees worked in small groups and then reported out on the following questions:

1. In three years, what are the five things you would be sure to do?
2. What are our assets/strengths and what do we need or where does something need to shift?
3. What are your hopes and what needs to stop?
4. What are the environmental factors that affect us, i.e., at WMU and in Michigan, in higher education, in society, in libraries?
5. What should our strategic priorities be for the next three years and our next steps?

Out of all these discussions, five major themes emerged on areas that needed improvement in the next few years—physical space, online presence, the library profile at the university, organizational and communications structures, customer service (or "user experience") culture. One clear message from all staff was that operating in silos prevented us from moving forward and innovating.

Reports of the individual interviews as well as the outcomes from the all-staff retreat were summarized and shared with all staff. The whole team of library staff and faculty understood the need and supported a reorganizational effort to break down silos, identify efficiencies, improve communication, and create a nimbler organizational structure for the libraries' future, ultimately achieving a guiding coalition of the whole.

STAGE 3: DEVELOPING A VISION AND STRATEGY

As a result of the retreat, two task forces were formed: one assigned to create a WMU Libraries strategic plan and another charged with analyzing the current organizational structure. They began their work simultaneously. This paper primarily focuses on the work of the reorganization task force.

The libraries' leadership team set up a large and inclusive reorganization task force that included four administrators (dean, associate deans, and operations manager), seven faculty members, and eleven staff members spanning all units of the library with the exception of Special Collections. At the time, the only employee in the Special Collections department chose to work on the strategic plan rather than the library reorganization. Approximately one-third of all library employees served on the task force, which lent it credibility among the whole staff. Developing a large, inclusive group ensured that all areas had knowledgeable representation and a voice in the process. The charge for the task force was to

> Document all library services and activities currently happening in the University Libraries and examine for continued relevance based upon supporting five identified strategic themes: improve physical spaces, create a more comprehensive and effective, user-friendly online/virtual library experience, enhance Library profile and visibility, redesign organizational communications, operations, structure, and develop a "user experience" culture within the libraries.

The Strategic Planning Task Force eventually translated these major themes into five goal statements, which informed the Reorganization Task Force's final recommendations. These were

1. Make the user experience central to the design and delivery of all services.
2. Develop intentionally designed physical spaces that adapt to users' diverse needs, stimulate collaboration and knowledge creation, and support student success and engagement.
3. Design and implement an intuitive, user-friendly online library experience that promotes discovery and learning.
4. Create innovative library programming responsive to University needs.
5. Reorient the Libraries' organizational structure to better align with our mission and vision, and foster a user experience culture.[3]

The reorganization group strived to bring like functions into closer alignment; streamline workflows; reduce redundancies; eliminate outdated or unnecessary processes, services, and activities; and remove unnecessary layers within the organization.

Dynamics among the members were good, as people were excited about planning a new vision for the library, and only a few seemed reluctant about major changes. The administration had chosen people who had expressed an interest in seeing changes and who would share their thoughts and ideas for how this change could look. Established ground rules for the group included openness to all suggestions, as well as confidentiality within the group. At several steps along the process, there were opportunities for communicating ideas with all library employees and getting their feedback about proposed ideas for structural changes.

The group met every other week from September 2016 to February 2017. The task force attempted various strategies for wading into the conversation and fulfilling its charge. Some conversations and methods proved more fruitful for moving the process forward than others. For instance, brainstorming what a modern library would look like was a good warm-up to get people talking, but did not easily lead to reorganization plans. Often breaking into smaller groups and tackling specific topics helped to facilitate discussions. Methodically, the group used various strategies and addressed these issues:

- Identifying the gaps in the library.
- Visioning what a modern academic library should be.
- Developing a few process maps.[4] While this activity was eye-opening, the group realized that it would take too much time to map everyone's work.
- Creating an inventory of activities and functions and codifying them. This helped identify where efforts were being duplicated.
- Identifying inconsistent policies.
- Exploring main functions: collection management/description, fulfillment, user service/customer support, hiring/training/managing employees, selection, and education/research/technical support/consultation services. This was most revealing when many overlaps were found.
- Creating "ideal" organizational charts and analyzing how they help the libraries achieve the desired vision.[5]
- Reviewing and presenting "What we know" about the different areas, such as branch libraries, back of the house, and so on.

Over the months of conversation, some ideas seemed so logical that they were implemented quickly instead of waiting for the process to be completed. One such example was the closing of a copy center where the libraries offered mediated copying and provided a variety of miscellaneous items, such as stamps, pain relievers, pencils, and so on. The functions of the copy center were no longer central to the mission, and many of the functions had decreased or were eliminated, for example, paying fines.

From all these conversations, the task force developed lists of services and activities and then organized these using sticky notes. Technical services later found an article by Davis that reinforced the group's thinking about grouping particular activities.[6] While there were multiple scenarios that would have worked, the task force settled on one new organizational framework that resulted in restructuring around five main departments. These departments were organized under two associate deans, one focused on education and user services and the other on resource management, IT, and research services. The framework took advantage of the groups that were already informally functioning to move projects and initiatives forward, such as the liaison and digitization groups. Emphasis was placed on putting like functions into the same department, the new User Services and Research Services departments providing the most extreme examples of this because they pulled together the largest number of people from multiple units (see figure 9.2).

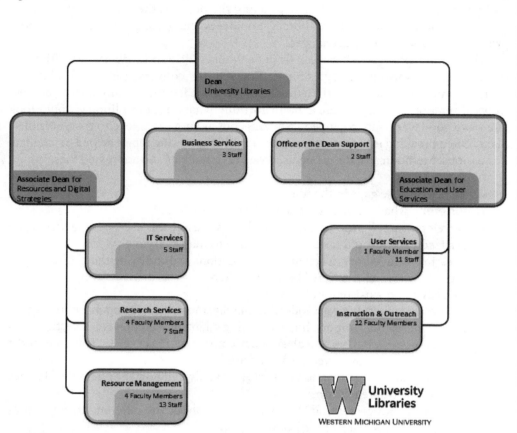

FIGURE 9.2
Western Michigan University Libraries organizational chart, September 2018

STAGE 4: COMMUNICATING THE CHANGE VISION

The task force charge and membership were communicated to all employees at the beginning of the process. The dean included progress reports on the reorganization task force each month and shared general information about activities and topics the group had explored. In February 2017, the full organizational framework, details of the process, decision-making behind the framework, and timeline were shared in writing with all library employees, with the goal of ensuring all employees received the information and explanation at the same time. Everyone was encouraged to consider the proposed changes and ask initial questions based upon the proposed framework with the understanding that a full staff meeting would be devoted to this topic the following month.

While everyone knew that change was coming, for some the changes were larger than for others and produced some anxiety. Based upon the new framework, the administrative team identified where employees would land in a reorganized structure. The dean held individual meetings with those staff and faculty members whose positions would be changing drastically. The dean and others who were part of the task force held conversations with individuals or groups where specific concerns existed. Ultimately, concerns expressed had more to do with unease with the change rather than identifying a fatal flaw with the organizational framework or proposed structure.

An all-staff meeting in March 2017 offered opportunities to review the reasons behind the reorganization and guiding vision used in determining the new framework. While some individuals were skeptical or anxious about the changes, all agreed to move forward with the new organizational structure as presented. The process and timeline were reaffirmed, and in April, initial meetings were set for the new departments.

Each new department was tasked to discuss how they would work together in the new structure. For three departments the changes were less radical—for instance, IT Services remained intact in its current form and Resource Management had already made major changes due to staff losses and the need to evaluate workflows as part of implementing the new ILS system. Their reorganization efforts focused on integrating stacks management into their department and planning for the loss of additional faculty and staff who were anticipating retirements. The Instruction and Outreach team expanded to include liaison librarians in the branch libraries; however, beyond the elimination of the reference desk, the nature of their work changed little. The largest change occurred in the User Services department, where former Access Services, Resource Sharing, Evening Services, and the staff of the education and music branch libraries were tasked to find common ground in serving users. The greatest challenge was consolidating different managerial styles, cultures, training practices, and procedures. A major change also happened with the formation of a new Research Services department, where Archives and Regional History Collections, Special Collections, Government Documents and Maps, Digitization, and ScholarWorks (the institutional repository) were pulled together based upon the focus in curating unique and specialized collections and developing educational programming in support of copyright, open access, digitization, data management, and historical research.

As with all change, concern about the unknown can lead to staff anxiety and worry about how individual work will be impacted and affected. For individuals whose department homes changed completely, there was a sense of loss and some mourning about the structures being dismantled, even when there was enthusiasm for the new structure being proposed. For others, there was some skepticism about how new organizational structures would work or actually improve library operations. From the time the organizational framework was announced through the transitional period, individuals were encouraged to raise questions and offer suggestions to the structure and the process. Libraries administration encouraged departmental teams to communicate openly and share minutes and any other documentation being created library-wide. Individuals were asked to work with the new organizational structure with the promise that there would be opportunities to evaluate the change after one academic year and adjust as necessary. Most of the task force members took an active role in facilitating the conversations in their own departments explaining and promoting the changes during this initial stage.

II. Introducing New Practices Phase

STAGE 5: EMPOWERING BROAD-BASED ACTION

One of the primary reasons for engaging in the reorganizational effort was to break down the structural barriers that hindered communication and effective delivery of services. The resulting consolidated departments collapsed existing structures, which created some initial confusion and presented its own barrier to change. To allow new processes and communication structures to form, the dean defined a four-month transition period for all members of the new departments to come together and define the work of the new unit, identify current strengths and limitations for completing that work, and develop plans for recruiting and developing any needed talent or skills. Departmental groups were pulled together for initial meetings with the dean in April 2017 to kick off this formal transition period. Groups were given some loose parameters and asked to work through the details of organizing as a new department among themselves with the end goal of creating a fully functional, integrated team by the start of the fall semester. During this time, a blend of the old structures stayed in place until new structures for taking their place were determined. Some old structures were completely eliminated as they were identified as no longer necessary.

Going from an organization of fourteen departments down to six left the organization with more department managers or heads than there were formal lead roles to fill. Additionally, to keep from having any particular pre-reorganization culture dominate the way new departments reimagined their work, allowing space for new leadership to emerge in the new structure was critical to the success of the change. To offer each new department space to get to know their new team colleagues, all staff and faculty were asked to work as a community of peers during the transition period. Volunteers scheduled and coordinated meetings and provided a space for open dialogue and decision-making. The goal was to have at least two persons dedicated to coordinating the work of each department. As part of the transition process, there was opportunity for each group to define what they needed in a department leader and make a recommendation for how to fulfill that need. One drawback to this peer-based approach was that individuals tended to tread carefully around topics where there were great differences in opinion. There were also some limits to how far the thinking of the new departments evolved without clear leadership.

While teams worked through transition issues at the department level, simultaneously, the libraries administration developed a job description for department lead responsibilities and began identifying staff positions that needed to be reviewed for potential changes in classification grade and appropriate compensation. Libraries administration crafted guidelines to outline opportunities for faculty to function as term-appointed department leads, ensuring appropriate work-release compensation in exchange for these efforts and compliance with AAUP Agreement parameters. The agreement establishes the chair's responsibility for assigning faculty workload, requiring that this duty remain firmly in the hands of the associate dean/chair positions. Faculty department lead positions were crafted to facilitate department communication and forward momentum while staying clear from any specific faculty disciplinary or workload-related issues. As staff skills, talents, and responsibilities were being outlined for positions, the libraries' administration worked closely to identify areas where responsibilities were out of alignment with job grade and current compensation. These were flagged for review with University Human Resources and upgrades were sought in recognition of impending changes.

STAGE 6: GENERATING SHORT-TERM WINS

The libraries' new organizational framework sought to address critical staff needs, both for shoring up staffing shortages that resulted from trying to cover too many service points with a shrinking number of employees, and for identifying new talent and skills required in new hires to help the libraries achieve strategic initiatives. As part of departmental transition conversations, new positions to fill these talent gaps were identified. Teams fleshed out position descriptions that were then vetted by the libraries' new leadership council for overall merits and to ensure financial resources were available. Once position descriptions were approved, libraries administration quickly began active searches to recruit new talent.

During the 2017/18 fiscal year, the libraries conducted twelve searches, resulting in three faculty and six staff hires. Two faculty searches failed the first time and had to be reposted. One of these failed a second time, leading to a pause to rethink the position before recruiting a third time. In all but two cases, open faculty and staff lines were repurposed or had significantly redefined portfolios to meet the new needs being addressed by the departments.

Reclassification of positions was requested and received in all instances where individuals took on work requiring increased responsibilities or technical expertise. The higher classification for the positions resulted in increases in hourly pay or salaries for twelve individuals.

As new department teams began taking shape, the desire to match workspaces to current needs emerged. Staff consolidating from several dispersed departments wanted to collocate workspace, and current office and work areas were not well suited to accommodate these changes. After evaluating current departmental spaces, plans for renovations were developed and executed to update four staff areas. For User Services this was particularly significant within the main library building where work areas were scattered across several floors and not convenient to the new combined services desk.

STAGE 7: CONSOLIDATING GAINS AND PRODUCING MORE CHANGE

In the course of the first academic year living with the organizational changes in place, there was continual progress in establishing the new structure. New leadership structures were outlined and implemented, from the appointment of the first set of new department leads to the formation of a new decision-making team named Libraries Council. The new Libraries Council is made up of the dean, associate deans, business manager, dean's executive assistant, department leads, marketing specialist, and staff and faculty representatives. Department structures are solidifying, and the work of updating position descriptions and defining the scope of work for the new units is almost complete.

In the fall of 2017, each department was celebrated and recognized with an award for the unique way it was contributing to the success of the new structure and goals of the libraries. All-staff meetings continue to include portions dedicated to focusing on current successes and looking for ways to continually improve. The most recent all-staff retreat covered the topic of quality customer service, recognizing that a vision and shared language around what this means and looks like will be critical to continuing on the libraries' path to build a more user experience–focused organization.

Building capacity for leadership continues. All new department leads were invited to participate in a three-day Library Management Skills Institute. This structured leadership program focused on developing facilitation techniques and management strategies. The new dean encourages more participatory decision-making than was expected or required in the past, and developing trust and comfort with this cultural shift is taking time. At every level of the organization, individuals are learning new ways of contributing to conversations and sharing ideas. Resistance to the new structure is still present, but a growing number of staff and faculty are feeling empowered to push back against those who want to reinforce old behaviors and the status quo.

III. Grounding Phase

STAGE 8: ANCHORING NEW APPROACHES IN THE CULTURE

The change is still in place, and administration has just completed a one-year check-in with all departments. There are areas where individuals are still feeling somewhat unsettled; however, conversations about progress and goals and decisions to anchor the change continue. Positions and work are still evolving as staff continue to live with the new structure for some time and realize some of the original thinking needs to be tweaked. For example, since the Government Documents responsibilities were folded into the job description of the position where there were two failed searches, there was a need to reevaluate the position and where Government Documents best fit into the new structure.

In May 2018 the faculty and staff of the libraries were sent a survey and asked to share the most positive change they think came out of the reorganization, how they have participated, and what other change they might want to see. Almost all employees looked at the survey and even started answering it, and 41 percent completed it.

When asked to share the most positive change achieved by the libraries' reorganization, responses included

- A better interaction among employees, collaboration, synergy.
- The one service desk serves patrons better without making them run around and brought together similar functions.
- Reduced number of departments are more organized.
- Flatter reporting structure providing clear communication and decision-making lines.
- Clear communication, more consistent policies and procedures, budget allocation.
- New trust in the libraries' administration.

When asked how they participated in moving the libraries into the new organizational structure, only a few felt they had not participated. Almost all who responded listed ways in which they have taken an active role to move their new department ahead. A couple had major changes in their job duties, one was just accepting the change and trying to make it work, and one person stated, "It's quite exciting!"

No responses recommended changes to the current structure. However, a few focused on user experience and the need to ensure that the libraries staff are providing the best service to users. One suggested the creation of a user experience team. There was concern expressed that reference questions were not adequately answered, as librarians were not at the front lines anymore. Other individual comments included a need for improving communication between departments, providing more training, and continuing to work on culture changes. One person mentioned a better service desk location. To address these concerns the libraries are working on customer service in the front lines, strengthening the training at the main service desk. An assessment team has been assembled to address user needs. When issues arise, people are brought together from across the libraries, so viewpoints from all departments are considered.

Overall, individuals report that they feel they have stronger relationships and better communication with others from across the organization and that the silos that once existed are no longer barriers. There is awareness of where stronger collaboration and relationships are needed, and staff and faculty are taking ownership of making these connections as the organization moves forward.

The structure has supported forward progress on the libraries' strategic goals. Within User Services, there are great strides in revisiting policies through the lens of the user, resulting in friendly, less restrictive ways of approaching services. The Instruction and Outreach team is spending more time focusing on shared strategies and programming, and Research Services is looking more holistically at digitization and programming than it had when the units were separate.

As a reminder of where the libraries are headed and progress in getting there, regular reviews and discussions around the strategic priorities are taking place within the departments and in libraries leadership council. In some areas, the libraries are making great strides, and in other areas the progress is slower. All department leaders are invested in developing at the department level and considering what success looks like if goals are achieved library-wide.

Analysis and Conclusions

While the libraries did not embark on the reorganization process deliberately using the Kotter change model, many of the commonsense steps the model suggests were intuitively employed. The dean capitalized on the urgency expressed by nearly all staff and faculty to build enthusiasm and excitement for engaging in the change. Throughout the process and even after the change was executed, continual dialogue and reiteration of the reasons behind the change and expected outcomes kept everyone moving forward rather than focusing on past practices. In addition, demonstrating early, positive, visual results from the change have reinforced investment in continuing to make the new structure work.

When the task force first started meeting, the process by which the group was going to move the conversation forward and reach conclusions was somewhat muddied. The group found its own way through the ambiguity and forged a path that worked and achieved an excellent outcome. This was accomplished through trial and error and stumbling upon literature that provided some concrete strategies to employ. The group would have benefited from having an outside expert and consultant facilitate a more structured process for achieving this work. However, as a team, the task force learned through each exercise and built trust in the process by working together closely to find its own way to accomplish the charge.

The Kotter change model provides an excellent reminder about the deliberate and continual effort and diligence required to keep forward momentum when implementing change. Continual communication is important, especially for those who are not as frequently engaged in planning the change. Recognizing milestones and demonstrating the positive outcomes directly related to the change help build enthusiasm and investment moving forward. The Kotter model reminds leaders that change requires continual care and monitoring if it is going to truly anchor itself within the organization.

Notes

1. Scott Garrison and Jennifer Nutefall, "Start by Interviewing Every Librarian and Staff Member: The First Step for the New Director," *College and Research Libraries News* 75, no. 5 (2014): 246–53, https://doi.org/10.5860/crln.75.5.9122.
2. Steven Bell, Lorcan Dempsey, and Barbara Fister, *New Roles for the Road Ahead*, ed. Nancy Allen (Chicago: Association of College and Research Libraries, 2015), http://www.ala.org/acrl/sites/ala.org.acrl/files/content/publications/whitepapers/new_roles_75th.pdf.
3. "Libraries Strategic Plan 2017–2020," Western Michigan University Libraries, accessed May 9, 2019, https://wmich.edu/library/about/strategicplan.
4. Sarah Babrow and Megan Hartline, "Process Mapping as Organizational Assessment in Academic Libraries," *Performance Measurement and Metrics* 16, no. 1 (2015): 34–47, https://doi.org/10.1108/PMM-11-2014-0040.
5. Erin L. Ellis et al., "Positioning Academic Libraries for the Future: A Process and Strategy for Reorganizational Transformation," Proceedings of the IATUL Conferences, 4th plenary session, 2014, paper 13, http://docs.lib.purdue.edu/iatul/2014/plenaries/13.
6. Jeehyun Yun Davis, "Transforming Technical Services: Evolving Functions in Large Research University Libraries," *Library Resources and Technical Services* 60, no. 1 (2016): 52–65, https://doi.org/10.5860/lrts.60n1.52.

Bibliography

Babrow, Sarah, and Megan Hartline. "Process Mapping as Organizational Assessment in Academic Libraries." *Performance Measurement and Metrics* 16, no. 1 (2015): 34–47. https://doi.org/10.1108/PMM-11-2014-0040.

Bell, Steven, Lorcan Dempsey, and Barbara Fister. *New Roles for the Road Ahead: Essays Commissioned for ACRL's 75th Anniversary*. Edited by Nancy Allen. Chicago: Association of College and Research Libraries, 2015. http://www.ala.org/acrl/sites/ala.org.acrl/files/content/publications/whitepapers/new_roles_75th.pdf.

Davis, Jeehyun Yun. "Transforming Technical Services: Evolving Functions in Large Research University Libraries." *Library Resources and Technical Services* 60, no. 1 (2016): 52–65. https://doi.org/10.1177/0961000614558078.

Ellis, Erin L., Brian Rosenblum, John Stratton, and Kathleen Ames-Stratton. "Positioning Academic Libraries for the Future: A Process and Strategy for Reorganizational Transformation." Proceedings of the IATUL Conferences, 4th plenary session, 2014. Paper 13. http://docs.lib.purdue.edu/iatul/2014/plenaries/13.

Garrison, Scott, and Jennifer Nutefall. "Start by Interviewing Every Librarian and Staff Member: The First Step for the New Director." *College and Research Libraries News* 75, no. 5 (2014): 246–53. https://doi.org/10.5860/crln.75.5.9122.

Western Michigan University Libraries. "Libraries Strategic Plan 2017–2020." Accessed May 9, 2019. https://wmich.edu/library/about/strategicplan.

Chapter 10

Analysis
Reorganization

Colleen Boff and Catherine Cardwell

Libraries
Miami University (Miami)
UCLA
University of Texas Arlington (UTA)
Western Michigan University (WMU)

Introduction

The libraries selected for the reorganization section all serve mid-size to large campuses ranging in size of student population from approximately 20,000 to nearly 54,000. Two of the four institutions primarily focus on undergraduate education. The scope of the reorganization efforts at each of these institutions was holistic and spanned several libraries in multi-library systems. UCLA's story was the only one to focus on the reorganization of a particular library function—that of public services. Each change story in this category was written or co-written by the library leader responsible for the change.

I. Warm-up Phase
STAGE 1: ESTABLISHING A SENSE OF URGENCY

Several themes emerged across these change stories that point to the urgent need to reorganize. Chief among the reasons for change was the issue of silos within the library organization due to staff attrition. This was frequently cited as the reason institutions did not feel agile enough to respond to changes in the profession and why some felt that they did not have a seat at the table for important change initiatives or collaborative opportunities taking place on their campuses. There was consistent concern expressed over the pressures to maintain traditional services while having a staff structure agile enough to respond to rapid change in user expectations. This raises the question of how much attrition is too much for an organization to handle before a reorganization is necessary, especially if the intent of the organization is to position itself for continuous change. Keeping the doors open and maintaining business as usual may be more forgiving of a patchwork staff structure, but when it comes to transformational change, our change stories suggest that organizations need to have a clearly defined structure based on current needs, not historical functions.

It is particularly noteworthy that at all of these institutions, there were new hires at the senior level of library leadership. In fact, the hiring committee for the new dean at UTA intentionally sought out a change agent. A strategic plan mandate for reorganization was a driving factor for UCLA and WMU. The need to examine duplicative and inconsistent service models as the result of decentralization was an additional reason for change at UCLA.

Two institutions used specific nationally normed data to help establish their sense of urgency. Miami used data from LibQUAL and ClimateQUAL. UTA conducted ethnographic research to help staff understand user needs. At least two institutions used specific tools in their work with library employees. Miami used a design-thinking approach, while UTA relied on strategies outlined in the monograph *Good to Great* by Jim Collins.

STAGE 2: CREATING THE GUIDING COALITION

Readers will find few similarities across all four change stories in terms of the composition of the guiding coalition. Miami used a consultant who worked with three committees. One was a steering committee that included three top library leaders, with the majority of members external to the library. Their primary purpose was to guide the process and make decisions. Select staff represented the library through service on the other two committees. One committee focused on reorganization, while the other focused on reinventing the service model.

At UCLA, the associate university librarian was a part of the guiding coalition, which included almost half of the staff in the public services group being reorganized along with several representatives from other units. He set a vision for the group and provided objectives to help focus them. Though the new dean at UTA involved nearly 85 percent of the staff in doing their homework to establish the urgency to reorganize, her guiding coalition consisted of the senior library leadership and middle managers. Although the dean was new to this group and to the organization, her team had a history of working together. The dean at WMU was new to her position, but she took a different approach from the others. She met with each staff member individually and held a library-wide retreat so that everyone was involved in the feedback process out of which the need to develop two committees emerged, one to work on a strategic plan and one to reorganize the organization. The composition of the latter committee included the dean and others from the library administrative office as well as faculty and staff who represented all units except the special collections.

STAGE 3: DEVELOPING A VISION AND STRATEGY

At this stage in the change process, the guiding coalitions at Miami, UCLA, and WMU had developed an organizational framework that supported a similar shared vision to improve the user experience, to break down silos among the staff, and to position the library for innovation at their respective institutions. In contrast to the other institutions, the UTA guiding coalition worked only on the establishment of a singularly focused vision to ground the rest of their work. They defined their new vision as CXI—Creation, eXploration and Innovation.

STAGE 4: COMMUNICATING THE CHANGE VISION

Most of these institutions used the typical strategies to communicate change to staff, which included written communications such as newsletter updates, posting materials on an intranet, and emails, as well as face-to-face meetings, either one-on-one with individuals or through presentations at all-staff and departmental meetings. Miami had a unique approach to communicating the change vision because of the timely hiring of a communications and marketing person to help with this step. Most of these institutions leveraged the members of the guiding coalition to help communicate their vision and strategy to the staff. As UCLA points out, this can often present uneven messaging. To remedy this, it created written documents for the guiding coalition to help standardize at least some of the messaging. UTA had only a vision to communicate at this point, but it used this as an opportunity to gather feedback from the staff on what skills, functions, and roles should be present in the new organization. In the end, the dean used this information to construct the new organizational structure that changed the jobs of 94 percent of the staff. This last example was the most widespread, systemic revamping of an organizational structure among the change stories in this category. The dean at UTA, as well as the dean at WMU, was heavily involved with communicating with staff impacted by the reorganization, and to their credit, both took the time to meet individually with staff to ensure alignment between organizational needs and employee interests. It is no surprise that employee anxiety was a prevalent theme among these stories about reorganization. It wasn't so much that the employees disagreed with the new direction for the organization as they were afraid of what it meant for them on a personal level.

II. Introducing New Practices Phase

STAGE 5: EMPOWERING BROAD-BASED ACTION

Miami and UCLA had strategic planning documents that guided staff through this stage and helped them establish rituals and norms in their newly formed units, from writing department charges to establishing new meeting and communication structures. At WMU, each unit was asked to identify training needs to help the staff adjust to the new structure and new roles. WMU mentioned the importance of working with human resources to adjust position descriptions, especially to ensure compliance with union contracts and to make sure employees were fairly compensated for changed job duties. Another noticeable trend at this stage in the change process for reorganizations was the tendency for staff to raise many questions when presented with a new organizational structure. Such was the case at UCLA, particularly in relation to the rotation of leadership opportunities in the new model. UTA was faced with the challenge of resolving the question of how to staff library instruction when not enough people were interested in doing this. UTA underestimated the amount of time and training needed to transition employees into new roles. It, of course, had the added dilemma of how to address the emotional response to such an extreme overhaul of its organizational structure.

STAGE 6: GENERATING SHORT-TERM WINS

Miami was working toward switching to its new structure while developing a hiring plan. WMU was actively hiring twelve new positions as one of its short-term wins while renovating staff spaces to collocate employees in newly formed units. UCLA and UTA were working on team-building exercises among their employees. UTA brought in a consultant specifically to build trust among the new leadership team, while UCLA employees took it upon themselves to develop fun ways to share ideas about ways they could work toward the new vision for the library. With a newly energized leadership team in place at UTA, it generated forty-nine initiatives to support its CXI vision. It set the agenda for the year and provided a framework for the organizational structure. Other short-term wins at UTA included mergers and elimination of functions.

STAGE 7: CONSOLIDATING GAINS AND PRODUCING MORE CHANGE

Miami continued to keep the plan fresh in the minds of the staff by continuing to communicate progress. It rewarded early adopters. WMU mentioned taking the time to celebrate success with staff. The WMU dean put a new leadership council in place and provided leadership development. Change at UCLA began to shift the overall culture as communication between units continued to flourish and break down silos. Forward momentum at UTA came in the form of new initiatives such as the FabLab, an innovative learning space designed to support experiential learning, and a new administrative position in support of the new structure.

III. Grounding Phase

STAGE 8: ANCHORING NEW APPROACHES IN THE CULTURE

Momentum continued at all four institutions that signaled to staff that the reorganization was well rooted and on its way to fruition. Miami launched its hiring plan and began the screening process to fill positions for approximately 20 percent of its organization. It offered professional development to the leadership team. UTA offered staff awards to encourage innovation and adjusted its merit system to better align with its shared vision. UCLA still needs to iron out the rotation of its leadership structure and to define the role of its leadership team in general, but the communication culture was progressing in a positive direction. Perhaps WMU was further along in the reorganization process when compared to the others, but its approach of assessing the change process was unique.

Analysis and Conclusions

Patterns evolved in these change stories that hint at some common trends to consider when embarking upon a reorganization. Interestingly, these themes did not emerge at a predictable and consistent stage in Kotter's change model, which suggests that every change story is unique and nuanced. For example, the stage in the Kotter model at which each institution arrived at a new reorganizational model for their institution differed.

TIPS FOR REORGANIZATION

- Library administration needs to be involved in a library-wide reorganization. Library employees seem to value a leader who has credibility and who can single-handedly or alongside a consultant establish and communicate a clear vision and strategy for the change.
- Middle management is critical in this type of change. They help communicate and spread the shared vision among staff and are essential to setting the strategy and change into motion.
- The use of data and credible information sources with staff is helpful, but staff involvement in the change process is necessary.
- Anxiety and fear among staff may be born out of concern individuals have for themselves. It does not necessarily mean they don't buy into the change vision. Cynicism and complacency may signal that the leadership has more work to do with staff to establish a shared vision. Addressing both of these emotional responses to change takes different approaches and time.
- Two trends may signal the need for a reorganization: changes in library leadership and a disjointed organization structure that has been patched together due to staff turnover and changes in library work.
- An important step in the change process when it comes to reorganizations is to adjust position descriptions and to provide staff training at all levels where needed so that employees are empowered to contribute meaningfully.

PART III
CULTURE CHANGE

Chapter 11

The Evolution of the STEM Libraries at Florida State University

Renaine Julian, Michael Meth, and Rachel Besara

Introduction

This chapter documents the transformation of the STEM Libraries at Florida State University (FSU) Libraries. The authors describe the departmental evolution and its placement in the context of a larger organizational evolutionary process in the Research and Learning Services (RLS) division of the FSU Libraries.

The Florida State University is located in Tallahassee, the capital of Florida. FSU is a Research 1 university according to the Carnegie Classification of Institutions of Higher Education and has approximately 42,000 students and over 1,900 faculty members. FSU's STEM Libraries consist of the Paul A. M. Dirac Science Library as well as the FAMU/FSU College of Engineering Library, which is a joint-use facility between FSU and Florida Agricultural and Mechanical University (FAMU), a historically black college or university. The FSU STEM Libraries also provide library support to various research centers and institutes both on and off campus, including the National High Magnetic Field Laboratory, the Center for Advanced Power Systems, and the Center for Oceanographic and Atmospheric Prediction Studies.

Setting the Change Stage

As is so often the case with organizational change, there is not always a clear date when changes start happening. Organizations are always shifting and changing and responding to their environmental stimuli. This case study begins in the summer of 2014, following a major renovation of the Dirac Science Library and with the appointment of a new director of STEM Libraries. Dirac Science Library was redesigned to better meet the research and learning needs of STEM students and faculty. To support this charge, the

Dean of Libraries asked the new director of STEM Libraries to work on developing a more proactive culture in the STEM Libraries. This charge included an expectation that the director would dedicate time to developing staff skills, recruiting new talent to fill open lines, and empowering the team to increase engagement with STEM scholars.

A new associate dean (AD) for RLS arrived in August 2015. The RLS group includes subject librarians across disciplines and is also responsible for circulation and access services at all library locations. During the first year, the new AD gathered the organization's history and context to understand the current status of the STEM Libraries and to start the development of a vision for the future of RLS. Small changes were made along the way, but by early 2017, a clear picture emerged as to how the division needed to change in order to address inefficiencies, eliminate duplication of services and tasks, and break down silos that had been sources of contention among the various groups in the libraries. A process termed "the evolution of RLS" emerged, which included significant changes in the STEM Libraries.

From the very beginning, the AD regularly met with the director of the STEM Libraries, and a consistent thread in all conversations was a desire to serve FSU's STEM scholars better. The conversations typically centered around themes of how to streamline the operations of the STEM Libraries, find alignment with the services in the central libraries, increase capacity, and address staffing issues. The discussions were shaped by information gathered through a variety of channels such as conversations with library staff, but also through examination of transaction data on instruction, consults, and gate counts. In an effort to build capacity and to shore up the leadership structure of the STEM Libraries, a position for a STEM and Data Librarian was posted in 2016. Not long after being hired, the librarian took on additional responsibilities and was appointed to a newly created position as Associate Director, STEM Libraries. With the increase of capacity at the leadership level, the STEM Libraries' transformation accelerated. However, the leadership faced a new challenge when the Director, STEM Libraries accepted an offer at another institution in 2017. Nonetheless, the team moved forward with formulating a vision, wrote and updated position descriptions, and advertised to fill two vacant librarian positions. Upon the departure of the director, the associate director was promoted to interim director to ensure stability and consistency with the plan that was previously developed. As it turns out, the evolution of the STEM Libraries had to be designed and implemented in a more flexible way in order to accommodate all the changes.

I. Warm-up Phase

STAGE 1: ESTABLISHING A SENSE OF URGENCY

The sense of urgency as defined by Kotter (who looks at organizations through a more competitive lens, i.e. companies operating in a for-profit context have a different sense of urgency than libraries) was not the driving force behind the STEM Libraries' changes. The changes envisioned were a response to the shifting needs of STEM scholars and the changes in personnel in the libraries. The changes coincided with a larger divisional rethink. The RLS organizational structure was developed in prior years by a leadership team no longer in place, and thus the organization was due for a rethink. The departure of key figures in RLS leadership positions created an opportunity to review and update the internal organization. The process that emerged was intentionally titled "the evolution of RLS" to make it clear that this was not a reorganization for the sake of change, but rather a deliberate process to move the organization forward, to create the next model to serve scholars in the best way possible, and to get the library future-ready.

The evolution of the STEM Libraries was included in and aligned with the evolution of RLS. However, one driver of the changes unique to the STEM Libraries was a period of short staffing that needed to be addressed in order to keep the libraries functioning. The short staffing was a result of staff leaving the organization, which presented challenges as well as opportunities. One major challenge was that the entire team, irrespective of title and formal job responsibilities, had to pitch in to run the day-to-day operations of the STEM Libraries. This in turn caused major setbacks in progress toward the goal to increase the scholarly support and engagement with STEM scholars. Thus, STEM Libraries staff were willing and eager to find solutions for their problems in connection with the RLS evolution.

STAGE 2: CREATING THE GUIDING COALITION

The guiding coalition was born out of a shared understanding between the Director, STEM Libraries, the Dean of Libraries, the RLS associate dean, and the RLS leadership team. Discussions over time between the different coalition partners established an understanding of needs, strengths, weaknesses, and opportunities for the STEM Libraries.

In order to develop the vision and plan for the evolution of the RLS and STEM Libraries, the guiding coalition consulted many different stakeholders. However, the majority of the planning and design was in the hands of the RLS leadership team, which included the director and associate director of the STEM Libraries. This leadership group actively engaged among themselves at regular weekly meetings and during special retreats. It is important to note that the changes considered by the STEM Libraries needed to be discussed at the RLS division level since the strategic plan to evolve RLS would produce division-wide decisions and consequences. The key objective for all meetings was to maintain communications and provide ample opportunities for participation and input. In addition to conversations at the RLS leadership level, the RLS associate dean frequently communicated with the dean and peers at the associate dean level. This was done to create opportunities for advice, to inform other stakeholders, and to advocate for the resource needs of RLS. Further, the changes needed in the STEM Libraries were informed by the library's strategic planning process, which was also taking place.

In the STEM Libraries, an important coalition was formed with the hire of the STEM Data and Research Librarian in 2016. The librarian was from a different group in RLS and already had experience with the STEM disciplines. Having worked closely with the Director of STEM Libraries in his previous role in providing data management support, the new STEM Data and Research Librarian was familiar with the values and vision for the STEM Libraries and eager to help achieve the goals. The coalition of the new librarian with the director led to alignment in leadership and opened up capacity for designing and implementing the changes.

Stage 3: Developing a Vision and Strategy

The FSU Libraries' strategic planning process, which started in 2015, identified the STEM Libraries as an area for development. The STEM Libraries were charged with increasing the level of service provided to scholars in STEM disciplines as a priority. In late 2016, a library committee was formed to determine future growth areas for library services and programs for STEM scholars and to advance FSU's leadership in scientific research and education.[1] The group applied the SWOT (strengths, weaknesses, opportunities, and threats) approach to analyze the challenge above. This inquiry identified two weaknesses that were obstacles to increasing the level of support the libraries offer to STEM scholars. One was the relatively small staff of the STEM Libraries, and the other was the fact that the STEM population on campus was relatively unaware of current library services beyond activities in the science library. These two challenges were related to one another. Being charged with operating two library facilities, the team was not adequately staffed, and thus everybody had to pitch in to ensure the library was open and available to patrons. This in turn meant that attention was diverted to administrative tasks, and outreach and user engagement were neglected. As a result, the librarians did not have the capacity to make the campus aware of the resources and programs already available to them, such as research data management and scholarly communication support.

In the summer of 2017, the committee identified six strategies to address the research and learning needs of STEM scholars. Of these six strategies, half were related to outreach and engagement:

1. Raise awareness within FSU community about the library services and programs already available to STEM scholars;
2. Build and strengthen relationships with key stakeholders in FSU community to better serve the research and learning needs of STEM scholars; and
3. Increase levels of outreach and engagement to international students in STEM disciplines.[2]

The committee's final report made two recommendations to aid in achieving the stated goals. The first was related to the focus on cross-functional teams to work toward unique and emerging areas such as research data management and open educational resources. Much of this structure was already in progress at the STEM Libraries, and the committee recommended continuing in that direction. The second recommendation was drafted with the understanding that a larger unit-wide reorganization was forthcoming. In agreement with the future direction of the RLS division, the committee recommended merging the building, circulation, and access management of the Dirac Science Library and the FAMU/FSU College of Engineering Library into the management structure of Strozier Library, which is the main library on campus. This would allow the smaller team of STEM librarians to focus on user engagement and better meeting the needs of STEM scholars.

Stage 4: Communicating the Change Vision

The big test for the vision came in August 2017 when the RLS leadership team organized a special all-staff meeting. At that time, the larger vision for the RLS evolution was communicated for the first time. The approach of having a large all-staff meeting was intentional. Many of the librarians and staff had been aware of upcoming changes, but details were scarce as much of the plan was in development. Some on the team embraced the change, some were ambivalent, and some struggled with the uncertainty. The best way to share the plan and to make sure all heard the complete message at the same time was by calling this all-staff meeting. During the meeting, a slideshow provided clarity on the evolving structure and the changes that were coming. The slideshow was later distributed to make sure all had access to the same source documentation. The presentation was followed by a live Q&A with the RLS leadership team.

The next step was for the STEM director to further explain and share the plan for the evolution with the team and to engage them in conversations so that their hopes and concerns could be heard. The change vision for both RLS and STEM Libraries was communicated through multiple forms of communication to facilitate discussion and gather feedback from everybody. These methods included weekly direct report meeting times which were utilized to communicate strategy and vision and proved useful because individuals were often more comfortable providing feedback in this more intimate setting rather than in a group. The STEM Libraries team also came together weekly and was kept up-to-date during team meetings. During these meetings a team-wide discussion took place to provide opportunities for all to share. By holding weekly meetings, an opportunity was provided for those who wanted to take the time to process the information between meetings to then be able to follow up at the next meeting.

All feedback, even if it challenged the vision, was encouraged and considered. This was largely because the team was empowered to think about the upcoming changes critically and not to keep negative feedback to themselves. Direct report meeting times were used to collect feedback on the plans for change in the STEM Libraries and also to highlight opportunities provided by the RLS changes. This method allowed the achievement of higher levels of credibility and trust between the RLS leadership team and the STEM team. One example where this trust was critical was in the efforts to consolidate the STEM service points into centralized management. As the vision and plan were evolving, many questions remained unanswered and the impact on the STEM Libraries was not quite clear. The STEM Libraries understood that the department heads in RLS were developing a strategy for consolidating library service points. The impact on the STEM Libraries team was not entirely clear, including what types of staffing changes would be necessary for an effective library-wide consolidation. However, due to the level of communication and trust established, concerns were surfaced along the way and considered in the final plan.

II. Introducing New Practices Phase
STAGE 5: EMPOWERING BROAD-BASED ACTION
Empowering broad-based action at the STEM Libraries level required aligning organizational structure with the new vision. The clearest need for organizational realignment was consolidating the library operations and service desks into one unit, which in turn empowered the STEM librarians by freeing them of the responsibility of managing the day-to-day operations of the libraries. With this newly freed-up time, the entire STEM librarians team agreed to a narrowed focus on user engagement and outreach toward

the undergraduate population in STEM disciplines. This was due to an identified lack of undergraduate student engagement and in line with the recommendations that had been made in a previous Libraries strategic planning exercise. In particular, assessment showed that students beyond general studies courses were difficult for the STEM librarians to reach, and thus a deliberate effort was made to approach them.

As the service model was changing and the librarians were focusing on engagement, some challenges occurred. The changes that were happening at the staff level in the organization to consolidate the building and service points management were not moving as quickly as originally anticipated in the STEM libraries. This caused frustration for the library faculty, including the director, because they still had to open and close the building and perform other staff-level jobs while changes in other departments were taking place. However, open lines of communication were set up to explain the delays in achieving the plan. While this did not solve the problems immediately, it did help to alleviate some of these frustrations while the work to implement the changes continued. During this period of change another challenge was that although the vision for change had been explicitly stated, it took some adjustments in expectations to get to implementation. In some cases, the staff were now reporting centrally while still located at the STEM libraries which led to some confusion about the role of the librarians who were previously their managers. This was further compounded with the librarians who were also adjusting to the new model and had to figure out how they were to interact with the circulation desk going forward. There were certainly growing pains, but they were necessary for the evolution of the STEM Libraries as well as the broader RLS division. There were most certainly going to be slips and falls along the way, but empowering the new STEM Libraries team to learn from their mistakes was critical in achieving organizational change.

By spring of 2018, most of the changes to the organizational structure and position descriptions were finalized, which allowed STEM librarians to focus on working toward engaging STEM scholars, since they were now relieved of the responsibility for facilities or circulation services in the Dirac Science Library and Engineering Library. This allowed the director to challenge his team of librarians to spend approximately 25 percent of their time engaging STEM scholars in new ways. Librarians started attending departmental seminars and set up offsite office hours in the College of Engineering as well as in research centers such as the High Field Magnetic Laboratory and the Center for Advanced Power Systems.

STAGE 6: GENERATING SHORT-TERM WINS

One noticeable achievement resulting from the organizational change was the improved work-life balance of the two STEM librarians. Due to not having to worry about opening and closing a building that was open seven days a week reduced the number of hours they were required in the libraries. This sense of relief was an easily identifiable short-term win and energized them to continue toward achieving the strategic objectives of increasing scholarly engagement with the STEM libraries. This change also benefited their work and personal lives, which was also seen as a short-term win. As the team grew and two previously vacant librarian positions were filled in early 2018, the expanded team focused on outreach and engagement. At the time of this writing, the number of research consultations and instruction sessions in STEM disciplines has increased almost four-fold from the previous year. This is a significant win for the team and continues to motivate them to find new ways to engage STEM scholars.

Another short-term win was the service point consolidation. Moving the traditional circulation and access portions of the STEM Libraries' portfolio into a different part of RLS, which was created to focus on these areas, increased the capacity of the STEM librarians to achieve the aforementioned goal of increasing engagement with scholars in STEM disciplines. It also helped the STEM librarians to reach equal status with their colleagues in the social sciences, arts, and humanities (SSAH). The Associate Dean for Research and Learning Services as well as the STEM Libraries director shared areas of success achieved by the SSAH librarians, a team tasked with providing subject librarian and collections support for the SSAH disciplines, which served as motivation to gain departmental buy-in.

While there were plenty of other achievements in the STEM Libraries, we encountered challenges with finding assessments to measure how we did with regards to accomplishing the goals. Broad initiatives such as the strategic plan goal to "engage the STEM scholarly community beyond the walls of the library" are lofty charges, and libraries are not well equipped to assess their success beyond measuring transaction data. Moving forward, the STEM team is developing departmental and individual goals and finding metrics and tools to measure their accomplishments.

STAGE 7: CONSOLIDATING GAINS AND PRODUCING MORE CHANGE

As the RLS—division and the STEM Libraries experience short-term success as a result of significant organizational change, it is important to support these changes so that the STEM Libraries can continue to provide increased levels of engagement with scholars. Establishing measurable goals moving forward is an important part of grounding this change. Additionally, these goals will include challenging the team to aim higher and set loftier expectations for themselves. Challenging the STEM Libraries team to move forward with larger projects and initiatives has largely been met with enthusiasm. For example, in collaboration with other departments in RLS as well as the libraries, a climate science symposium is being planned for the upcoming school year that involves partnerships across campus, including FSU's Office of Faculty Development and Advancement and Office of Sustainability. Moving forward into the next academic year, the STEM team has exciting projects and initiatives planned to better meet and exceed the needs of STEM scholars.

The process of the RLS evolution is ongoing. As a result of the new service model and the changes that have taken place, many job descriptions have been reviewed. The review has often been triggered by one of two main causes. One cause is when positions are vacated. Every position is carefully reviewed before posting in light of the current service model and the new set of expectations. The second is that all staff positions have been systematically reviewed in order to ensure that the job descriptions and classifications are appropriate in the new service model. In most cases this has led to an upgrade in status, responsibilities, and compensation. This is important since the team at all levels is being challenged to contribute and help improve services for our scholars, and the organization has been able to reward and recognize the team for their efforts.

III. Grounding Phase

STAGE 8: ANCHORING NEW APPROACHES IN THE CULTURE

The focus on providing better services to STEM scholars remains, and the STEM team is actively working toward increasing user engagement and reaching out to potential users of the libraries. Forward movement in the evolution of RLS and STEM Libraries has aided the ability of the STEM librarians to spend time meeting scholars in their labs, classrooms, and offices. An important component of leading change moving forward is the anchoring of the new work approaches. Part of anchoring new approaches in the culture of the department and the evolving goals includes intentional partnership building with units, departments, and teams across the libraries so that we, as a library organization, can better meet the research and learning needs of STEM scholars across the entire research life cycle. This partnership building includes partnering with social science and humanities librarians as well as FSU's Office of Digital Research and Scholarship to provide comprehensive and interdisciplinary support in areas such as library instruction, digital pedagogy, and open educational resources.

While many of these approaches are structural, some are more symbolic and are representative of the overall evolution of the unit. For example, at the time of writing, a departmental name change from STEM Libraries to STEM Research and Learning Services is being considered in order to more accurately portray the services and support that the evolved organization provides. Such changes allow the organization to better tell the STEM Libraries' story so that it can further engage with STEM scholars.

Analysis and Conclusions

The FSU STEM Libraries' story is framed in the context of the Kotter model, but it is important to note that the changes discussed in this chapter did not happen in the same sequence as the Kotter model presents them. For example, much of the development of a vision of the STEM Libraries took place during the same time as what was described in the sense of urgency section. Much of this is because the changes envisioned at the RLS level were developed to meet emerging needs rather than responding to a crisis. A further note is to highlight that the chapter was written to capture the different perspectives that informed the design of the evolution. In other words, there was an interplay between the RLS divisional perspective, which highlights some of the bigger picture thinking, and the STEM Libraries perspective, which illuminates the thinking of the leadership of the STEM Libraries at FSU. It is hoped that sharing these two perspectives will give the reader better insights about the decision-making that happened at the respective levels of the organization.

It is too early to close the book on the evolution and provide a complete analysis. As far as evolutions go, this one is ongoing and will continue for a long time. That is the case because the organization has deliberately decided to employ an agile approach in its development.

Here are some of the key takeaways:

1. Communication is key. Finding as many outlets and opportunities as possible to communicate with the various stakeholders was essential in developing buy-in. That being said, communications have to be clearly articulated. Also, it is helpful to be clear whether the communication is merely providing information or is asking for opinions. Furthermore, there are many mediums and formats for communication, and utilizing them effectively is key to reaching different stakeholders.
2. Changes in organizations can be initiated by many factors. In this case, the changing leadership in the STEM Libraries provided the perfect context for the evolution of the team and the service model.
3. Aligning work with personal and professional interests creates higher levels of motivation for participants, making change easier to accomplish.
4. It is important to create an organizational structure and culture that is flexible enough to meet the evolving needs of scholars. It is even more important to express the need for flexibility to employee teams so that the group can achieve a shared vision for organizational change.
5. The work has just started and will be ongoing. As the STEM Libraries enter the grounding phase of organizational change, it is a continuing challenge to stay ahead of the changes and adjust the organization and staffing accordingly. Constant reevaluation and checking in is incumbent on us in order to motivate the entire team.

Notes

1. Rachel Besara et al., "STEM II Balanced Scorecard Initiative: Final Report," September 18, 2017, STEM II BSCI (FSU), Open Science Framework, https://osf.io/5npxh.
2. At the recommendation of the entire STEM Libraries, this focus on user engagement and outreach was shifted toward the undergraduate population in STEM disciplines. Language for these goals has been modified from the original text in the publicly available Open Science Framework project page, https://osf.io/5npxh.

Bibliography

Besara, Rachel, Renaine Julian, Julia Cater, Ginny Fouts, Kelly Grove, Devin Soper, Elizabeth Uchimura, and Trip Wycoff. "STEM II Balanced Scorecard Initiative: Final Report," September 18, 2017. STEM II BSCI (FSU), Open Science Framework. https://osf.io/5npxh.

Chapter 12

Leading Change through User Experience

How End Users Are Changing the Library

Andrew See and Cynthia Childrey

Setting the Change Stage

Cline Library is centrally located on the Northern Arizona University (NAU) campus in Flagstaff, Arizona. The library has a staff of sixty-two, and an additional forty-six student staff. According to the Carnegie Classification of Institutions of Higher Education, NAU is classified as "R2: Doctoral Universities—Higher Research Activity." Founded in 1899 with twenty-three students, NAU is now a public university with over 30,000 under-graduate and graduate students who learn on campus and online, across the state and beyond. NAU has built a reputation for research and scientific discovery, and over 1,000 undergraduates present at the annual Undergraduate Research Symposium. From the beginning, NAU placed students at the center, and students are the driving force behind what Cline Library does.

Through a strategic planning process now underway, users and staff imagine the future for Cline Library as a people-focused experiential learning environment, which is dynamic, is proactive to user needs, and promotes both individual discovery and creative collaboration. The library's newly crafted mission and vision state

MISSION

> We engage our users in the design of discovery, research and learning experiences that advance NAU's mission and strengthen our diverse community. Our expertise, collections, services and spaces elevate learning, scholarship, creativity and innovation in Arizona and beyond.

VISION

> Cline Library is the dynamic center of intellectual inquiry for a highly
> engaged user community that pursues and advances world-class teaching,
> learning and research.

The shift that is placing the user experience at the very center of this collective vision began just three years ago.

To consider the impact of the implementation of Cline Library's user experience program to date, it is instructive to analyze the development of the program and its outcomes utilizing John Kotter's eight-stage process for creating major change.[1] Kotter's model is useful in that it encourages an analysis not only of the impact of the change, but also of the change process itself. The shift in the library's approach to creating and improving its virtual and physical spaces began with the acknowledgement that while the organization was committed to putting users first, there were many individual versions of what was best, and many of those were informed only very indirectly by the end users of the services themselves. In order for a change to take root, it needed to utilize a structured approach that could drive decision-making across departments and engender library-wide engagement. User experience was the approach to test, as it spoke to the library's values and contributed a grassroots voice to service design that cuts through departmental silos.

I. Warm-up Phase

STAGE 1: ESTABLISHING A SENSE OF URGENCY

Several forces contributed to the establishment of a user experience program at Cline Library in late 2015. The library had recently eliminated a layer of its administrative structure, and there were both a need and a desire to transition some programs out of the Office of the Dean, including the library's website. There was also a desire to reduce departmental silos and give rise to decision-making that was more horizontal. Departments, all of which had some responsibility for direct user services, lacked strong pathways to communicate service and system issues to each other. Each department "owned" the services it provided, and feedback across departments was frequently anecdotal. Thus, departmental structures, as well as long-standing policies and processes, served as internally constructed barriers that prevented the library from looking holistically at the end users' experiences and their journeys through our virtual and physical environments.

Departments felt they were acting in the best interest of users, but the library was neither effectively evaluating the data it collected nor collecting the best data for decision-making. Nevertheless, the library was a campus leader in deploying new services and technology-enriched spaces in partnership with student and faculty stakeholders. The physical environment was changing for the better. Assessment of those efforts was spotty, however, and the library staff did not immediately know if they got it right. Meanwhile, NAU was experiencing enrollment growth and responding to a rapidly changing environment. It was time to break down the library's departmental silos and place more responsibility with frontline staff to encourage grassroots assessment and faster, more responsive action based on a deeper understanding of the experiences of all users. The library lacked a structure to improve and enhance its services in alignment with new spaces, and in a way that let user data and voices bring about iterative change in real time. The library had to become more adept at risk taking, moving forward in an uncertain environment.

STAGE 2: CREATING THE GUIDING COALITION

By early 2015, the library began recruiting for a Head of User Services to manage the department previously known as Access Services. By design, his or her responsibilities would extend beyond a single department to provide the leadership necessary to improve and enhance all user experiences. An excerpt from the position posting offers a glimpse of the User Experience (UX) Group, a new initiative empowering users to change the library:

Head, User Services

> Cline Library at Northern Arizona University seeks a forward-thinking, collaborative, and innovative **Head, User Services.** Reporting to the Dean and University Librarian and as a member of the library leadership team, this department head will manage a high-profile customer service program facilitating access to collections, equipment, technology, spaces, and more. With a passion for user engagement and for the exploration and integration of new technologies, s/he will develop and employ an understanding of the library's users through services, spaces, and online environments that promote users' success.

> **The Head, User Services** will work to connect services from across the library into a unified environment that meets or exceeds users' needs and expectations.

> Collaborate with other library units to provide connected, clearly articulated user-centered services. Establish and chair a group with membership from across the library that is focused on providing and enhancing a positive user experience.

By August 2015 there was a new Head of User Services with skill in and a passion for user experience (UX). By September he drafted a charge for the library's first User Experience Group based on conversations with the dean. By November the Library Coordinating Council, the leadership team, approved this new cross-departmental group. Once the charge was approved, a call for membership went out to the library with the intent to select seven to ten members from across departments. With an immediate positive response rate, the inaugural roster was established quickly and constituted representation from nearly all departments. The guiding coalition, led by the Head of User Services, was formed and UX was launched.

FALL 2015 USER EXPERIENCE GROUP

- Head, User Services—Chair
- Library Supervisor, User Services
- Three Teaching, Learning, and Research Services librarians
- Two Content Access and Delivery Services librarians
- Digital Media Technologist from Content Access and Delivery Services
- Head, Library Technology Services
- Archivist from Special Collections and Archives
- Librarian, Coconino Community College

Since the formation of the group in fall 2015, the guiding coalition has evolved organically. During its inaugural year, members learned about user experience approaches by establishing personas and applying newly learned UX processes to its highest priority project, completing an analysis of the library's website. By the end of the year, some members were more intrigued and able to commit time than others, resulting in some attrition by the start of the second year.

After two years, the guiding coalition changed again. Next, two subgroups (UX-Web and UX-Spaces) formed with a total of eleven members. The Head of User Services (who chaired both groups) and the dean agreed on cochairs for each. The UX-Spaces group was tasked by the dean to learn more about how users saw the building in preparation for a possible library master planning process. Membership of the group can rotate on an annual basis to facilitate changes in the focus for UX or when individual workloads and interests fluctuate.

STAGE 3: DEVELOPING A VISION AND STRATEGY

When the UX group was established, staff sentiment was generally apathetic regarding rapid and iterative change and also dubious that such change could be met without considerable institutional barriers. This did not diminish library staff's inherent desire to see positive change. On the contrary, they felt a strong need to make user-centered changes but also felt that they were not empowered to do so. To address this, the group adopted tenets of the design thinking process that Luchs and colleagues defined in their book *Design Thinking: New Product Development Essentials from the PDMA*: to "quickly generate possible solutions, develop simple prototypes, and then iterate on these initial solutions—informed by significant external feedback—toward a final solution."[2] As a result, it was important to clearly define and appoint levels of authority, empowering the group to make change, experiment, and accept failure as a logical step in the design-thinking process, which Mootee noted in his book *Design Thinking for Strategic Innovation: What They Can't Teach You at Business or Design School*: "Design thinking is not an experiment; it empowers and encourages us to experiment."[3]

In creating a vision for the UX group, the Head of User Services and dean worked to establish a charge that included this vision statement:

> The User Experience Working Group will work to ensure that library-wide services are discoverable, accessible, intuitive, automated, and ultimately user-driven.

The focus of the vision was broad enough for the group to move forward with individual initiatives, short-term easy wins that ultimately fed into the larger change initiative. Generating buy-in among committee members was not a challenge, and principles and ground rules were set to establish working parameters and assumptions. To develop strategies, the group approached the work by first understanding these questions:

Who are our users?

Gaining a better understanding of who our users are allows us to better design services that are both useful and accessible to them.

What are user-centered services?

Fundamentally, the answer to this question is that the end-user is at the root of all decisions when it comes to service design. Is the service intuitive to users? Is it useful to them? Are there any barriers to their access to the service?

How do we assess our services?

Data streams come from a wide variety of sources, from our daily interactions with users, to more nuanced usability research. Ultimately, our end-users will answer the question of whether or not our services meet the requirements set forth in the vision; we just needed to communicate with them to find out.

Guiding principles and strategies established, the group reached almost immediate consensus that the library's web presence required the greatest amount of attention. Up to this point, problems with the web environment were tacitly known by UX members. In order to drive change successfully, some significant usability testing and data gathering were needed to collect evidence. Ultimately, the strategy was

- Focus all services through the lens of the end user.
- Conduct testing to see if services are discoverable and intuitively usable by end users.
- Identify pain points.
- Make changes based on findings.
- Retest to ensure changes were successful.

Embracing evidence-based decision-making, the group began a long but successful journey of trust building throughout the library, securing easy wins, and building on those to enact major change in achieving the vision of the group.

STAGE 4: COMMUNICATING THE CHANGE VISION

When the group was created, Cline Library consisted of five departments (User Services; Teaching, Learning and Research Services; Library Technology Services; and Content Access and Delivery Services). Communication about the group was initially disseminated to department heads for feedback and then to the larger library community. The document included a background statement, the charge, reporting structure, membership, scope, and a list of ongoing work. Because the library's web presence is so closely tied to the user journey and is often the sole library experience for distance students, the UX group absorbed the priorities and responsibilities of the library's current web group. As a result, the chair and dean were very intentional in setting the scope of the group:

> **Scope:** Though the group is ultimately responsible for the oversight of the user experience at the Cline Library, it will act collaboratively and proactively with departments on a consultant level. The group will negotiate change with library departments and work to build a library-wide focus on the user experience.

Setting the group's role as that of a consultant and collaborator reduced the chance that cooperation with the UX group would be resisted by staff due to the perception it was somehow hierarchically exceeding departmental autonomy. This in turn broadened departmental engagement. Cross-departmental communication, not surprisingly, had some barriers. The UX group leveraged existing communication channels to reach a broader audience, including

- an open SharePoint site for file storage
- a Microsoft Outlook Listserv
- a ticketing system for staff to use
- regular news items in the monthly newsletter

With established communication pathways in place and a vision firmly established, the UX group set out to begin its work with transparency and a shared understanding.

II. Introducing New Practices Phase

STAGE 5: EMPOWERING BROAD-BASED ACTION

Since the inception of the move to UX, one of its greatest internal wins has been the gradual strengthening of trust both vertically and horizontally within the organization. This development occurred first in approaching the website redesign and in making changes to services offered by the User Services department. User experience work helped to tear down barriers by simply changing the way things were done and the speed with which they could be accomplished. Cross-departmental groups in general, while bringing staff together to complete projects, still had reporting structures that were formal and did not entirely empower the groups to make iterative changes. UX was different in that iterative improvements were the expectation. If changes were not well received by users, the group would know that and immediately make modifications. For example, the website redesign focused on frequent small improvements. There was no waiting, and it was not necessary to compile a list of changes before the enhancements began. The loop of gathering user input during development and then seeking feedback along the way created a continuous process that empowered group members.

It allowed colleagues from across the library to see this approach in action, considering how it might be applied to changes in other programs and services. In the case of disagreement, the user decided, eliminating lengthy discussion over whose version of the user experience was the right one.

STAGE 6: GENERATING SHORT-TERM WINS

The group went about its initial work with a heavy focus on two priorities: establishing personas (figure 12.1) and making changes to the library's website. The creation of user personas, a collaborative effort resulting from a close examination of demographic data about the primary user groups and focus sessions with those groups, served to ground the group's work.

Sophomore, 20 years old, Biology Major

Brianna Carter

About Me
- I grew up in Glendale, AZ and graduated from Glendale High School
- My dad is a Phoenix firefighter and my mom works as a CNA at the hospital
- Neither of my parents went to college. Both my mom and dad took some classes at the community college but never got a degree.
- I am the oldest child. I have a sister and brother in high school. My sister is seeing how I do in college before deciding if she wants to go. My brother wants to be a firefighter like dad.
- I work about 20 hours during the week at Campus Rec and usually a couple shifts on the weekend waitressing at Oreganos.
- I live on-campus in the Suites. They are nice and cheaper than living in a dorm.

In my free time, I:
- Like to go back to the Valley and visit my family and friends from high school whenever I get a chance. Take yoga, use the climbing wall, and lift weights at the gym.
- Camp and hike with my friends.
- Go downtown and listen to music. I can't wait until I turn 21 and can see more shows

Why NAU?
- NAU is affordable, I am a Lumberjack Scholar and that pays my tuition. I still have to pay to live in Flagstaff, and a bunch of fees, but it really helps. My parents can't afford to help out, so I am paying my own way. I also like that I can get to know my teachers and work with them in their labs. I know this experience will help me get a job after graduation. I am hoping to help my little sister pay for college so she won't have to work as much.

FIGURE 12.1
A sample persona

With the website a priority, feedback generated internally from staff and externally from users indicated that there were user interface issues and an overall aesthetic that needed attention. In order to gain greater insight into the problems experienced, usability testing included a significant number of tabling exercises, where users were asked to complete an assortment of tasks compiled from various popular services (e.g., finding peer-reviewed articles, locating books, reserving study rooms, etc.). The group devised scenarios to present to users who were then observed trying to complete the tasks on the website. An example:

Mindset: You are a student in a geology class, and your professor has assigned you to enter and manipulate some data in Microsoft Excel. You don't have a computer, but you've heard that the library has computers students can use.

1. Let's start out with the Cline Library home page. First, just take a look at this page and tell me what you would do to find out about computers to use.
2. Go ahead and use the library website to find a library computer that includes Excel.
3. What are your options? Which computer would you choose? Why?

Data collected through usability testing ultimately played a large role in the group's ability to earn the confidence of administration and staff in general. This shift gave the group more authoritative autonomy to make larger scale changes to the web environment.

As evidenced in figure 12.2, the website as of November 2015 was fairly link-heavy with few pictures. While the site was functional, data collected indicated users desired a more welcoming environment with easier navigation.

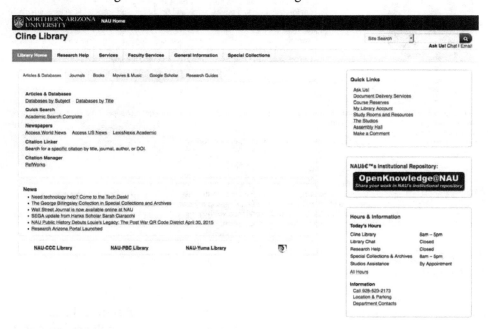

FIGURE 12.2
Cline Library homepage, November 2015

Throughout the FY16 academic year, the UX group conducted usability testing on key services to identify navigational pain points with users. Based on the group's findings, evidenced-based and unambiguous changes were made to the website. Changes included the addition of a new Ask Us! FAQ page, including a portal to the library's popular chat service and other contact information (figure 12.3), and pictures on top-level pages (figure 12.4).

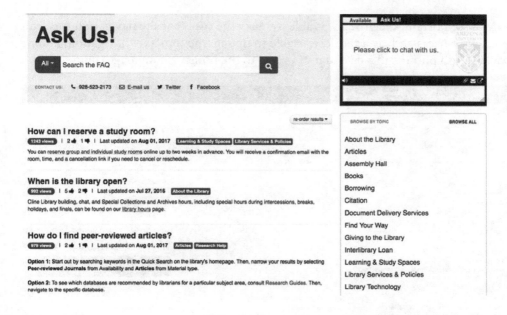

FIGURE 12.3
Cline Library's new Ask Us! FAQ page

FIGURE 12.4
Example of pictures on top-level pages of Cline Library website

Most important, the group was able to make the case that site navigation was troublesome for users and, as a result, was able to update the top-level navigation, adding a background photo and a calendar of events to the library's homepage (figure 12.5).

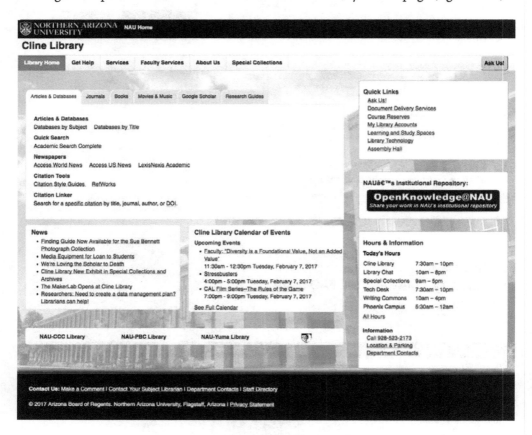

FIGURE 12.5
Cline Library's updated homepage

With a favorable response from users, the UX group gained momentum by rapidly prototyping and deploying changes to the website without bureaucracy acting as a barrier.

STAGE 7: CONSOLIDATING GAINS AND PRODUCING MORE CHANGE

During the summer of 2017, the Head of User Services worked with the dean to divide the UX group into two functioning working groups: UX-Web and UX-Spaces. The heavy focus on web-related UX work was inhibiting the group from spotlighting the user experience in our brick-and-mortar services and spaces. The division of labor allowed the UX-Web group to focus entirely on the redesign of the webpage and simultaneously allowed a new working group to begin an audit of library spaces.

FALL 2017 USER EXPERIENCE GROUPS (UX-WEB AND UX-SPACES)

- Head, User Services & Experience—Chair (UX-Web, UX-Spaces)
- Librarian (Teaching, Learning, & Research)—Co-lead (UX-Web group)
- Librarian (Teaching, Learning, & Research)—member (UX-Web group)
- Library Specialist, Sr. (User Services)—member (UX-Web group)
- Library Supervisor (User Services)—member (UX-Web group)
- Library Specialist, Sr. (Content, Access, and Delivery)—member (UX-Web group)
- Assistant Dean—Co-lead (UX-Spaces group)
- Library Supervisor—member (UX-Spaces group)
- Systems Administrator, Sr. (Library Technology Services)—member (UX-Spaces group)
- Building Coordinator—member (UX-Spaces group)
- Librarian (Teaching, Learning, & Research)—member (UX-Spaces group)

The library began to see substantial progress, assessment, and impacts from the two smaller groups, strengthening the reach of user experience. The UX-Web group also learned that the institution was migrating to the WordPress content management system (CMS). The new marketing template was appealing to the UX-Web group as it boasted a modern look and feel and had a responsive design that worked well across mobile devices. Additionally, the library was migrating onto the new library services platform Alma/Primo through Ex Libris. These factors, coupled with the group's current momentum, were drivers in the decision to become an early campus adopter of WordPress and conduct a full website migration. Working collaboratively with NAU's Information Technology Services (ITS) and leveraging previously collected user data, the group designed and deployed a new homepage featuring the new Primo discovery layer (figure 12.6) in July 2017 with the goal of migrating the back-end content over the FY18 fall academic semester.

FIGURE 12.6

Cline Library's homepage, July 2017

Focus groups were created to guide a data-driven look and feel for the new site, as well as to define its purpose and highlight key services that should be readily available and intuitive to users. Leveraging the success of the group in implementing large-scale change of the web environment through a series of iterative short-term wins, the UX-Web group worked with Information Technology Services (ITS) to rapidly migrate all existing content onto the campus CMS over the winter of 2017–2018. As of this writing, the UX-Web group is conducting an audit of webpages to ensure content is accurate and user-centered. The library's partnership with ITS has grown because of the hard work and dedication of the UX-Web group. As a result of the quality of the library's work, it has been afforded more autonomy in working within the marketing templates, allowing the library to be more iterative in its design and agile in deployment of new website services.

Meanwhile, the UX-Spaces group, in its inaugural year, conducted a myriad of tabling exercises, placed a feedback board (figure 12.7) in various spaces throughout the library, and conducted a library mapping exercise with users. The group found that users were unaware of some key services that could impact their experience in the library. All of these services were prominently marketed on the website, but there was very little marketing of services in the building itself. One example involved a user's reluctance to use an audio/video production studio for a perceived lack of expert help. Help is advertised on the website but not in the physical space. Some users were not aware of the media production studios at all, as they are essentially hidden from sight behind wooden doors. Collaboratively the group designed new signage to fill in these knowledge gaps (see figures 12.8 and 12.9).

FIGURE 12.7
Example of feedback board

FIGURE 12.8
Sign promoting availability of expert help

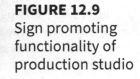

FIGURE 12.9
Sign promoting
functionality of
production studio

III. Grounding Phase

STAGE 8: ANCHORING NEW APPROACHES IN THE CULTURE

Since the formation of the UX group at Cline Library, there has been a paradigm shift in the way staff view change and their ability to become change makers. Using design thinking in strategizing improvements for both the web and the physical building, the UX groups, working alongside departments and stakeholders, have increased the agility of change within the library. Prior to the implementation of UX, change was relatively slow and administered organizationally from the top down or accomplished by project teams charged with major projects but not rapid improvements. By accomplishing several successful initiatives, the UX groups built a layer of trust with staff and administrators that has been crucial to empowering the UX teams to make iterative positive changes to services and interfaces and to rapidly prototype and deploy new services.

Analysis and Conclusions

Although Cline Library's UX program has been wildly successful, the evolution of the UX groups might have been expedited by bringing in a user experience librarian as a consultant to help design the programs and instruct the groups on best practices. However, while this might have brought about more rapid change, it may have slowed the group's ability to learn, grow, and get started. Internally, trust within the group comes down to confidence. Without confidence that the change initiative was based on integrity, data, and a genuine desire for user-centered design, the group would not have had the evidence to change the established paradigm.

Through an open and collaborative communication strategy, the group demonstrated that large-scale change can happen through iterative design, where small failures are OK and no change is seen as a permanent fixture. Using the design-thinking approach, the UX groups empathized with end users by conducting user testing to define problems. The UX groups ideated solutions and either deployed or prototyped solutions for testing and then deployment. This process allowed the UX group to build trust within the library and rapidly make small changes that culminated to large-scale wins. Again, it is not necessarily the win that builds trust, but rather the process itself.

As of the writing of this chapter, the Cline Library User Experience Group consists of two functional working groups: UX-Web, providing oversight for the usability of all aspects of the library's virtual/web environment, and UX-Spaces, currently acting as the research arm for a master plan leading up to a building redesign. Consisting of twelve staff and librarians spanning all departments, the representation is roughly 23 percent of the FTE. What started three years ago as a department called User Services has through effective change management evolved to become the User Services and Experience (USX) department. This is due to UX work and the end-user experience being so closely tied to the core values of the department. USX augments the work of the UX groups by providing student staffing (user experience assistants) to conduct observational data gathering regularly throughout the academic year. It is a partnership that has evolved over the past three years and has some exciting implications for the years to come.

Although the Kotter model was not intentionally used in the construction of the initiative and the development of the process, in retrospect, many of the eight stages outlined in his book were put into practice and, as a result, have successfully changed the paradigm of program and service development for Cline Library. The first phase of the change process benefited from a shared sense of urgency throughout the library and among all levels of library staff. Although the urgency resulted from several reasons, it propelled everyone toward a new approach. Staff working more directly on the front lines with users and those technical staff responsible for the library's systems not only needed better ways to communicate concerns and ideas about the library's website, but also were prepared to take on responsibility and accountability for making changes. The library's leadership had worked with staff to complete a successful major cleanup and overhaul of the website, but it was time to move the overall responsibility for the content of the site out of the Office of the Dean. Furthermore, Kotter's "guiding coalition" was effective and had the support of library leadership. Perhaps most important of all, the guiding coalition had a strong leader with enough knowledge, experience, and confidence to launch UX and get down to work. While the group had a charge that was approved by the library's leadership team and communicated to the staff, the library did not spend an inordinate amount of time discussing the change. The UX group formed and got busy, and it generated immediate products and changes.

The change was also helped by moving responsibility to the right level and to the right staff. As John Kotter plainly observes in his *Harvard Business Review* article "Leading Change: Why Transformation Efforts Fail":

> Because the guiding coalition includes members who are not part of senior management, it tends to operate outside of the normal hierarchy by definition. This can be awkward, but it is clearly necessary. If the existing hierarchy were working well, there would be no need for a major transformation.

Kotter goes on to say:

> A high sense of urgency within the managerial ranks helps enormously in putting a guiding coalition together. But more is usually required. Someone needs to get these people together, help them develop a shared assessment of their company's problems and opportunities, and create a minimum level of trust and communication.[4]

The early wins with the library's website encouraged the formation of a new UX group. Now, one group focuses its efforts on the library's virtual learning environment and a second on its physical learning environment. This is helping to anchor UX further in the library's culture, a step necessary for sustained organizational change.

In closing, having come this far, it seems likely that the library will continue to expand UX into other areas of its programs, circling back through Kotter's model of identifying potential early wins and, if successful, consolidating those to both deepen and broaden the impact of the user in changing the library.

Notes

1. John P. Kotter, *Leading Change* (Boston: Harvard Business Review Press, 1996).
2. Michael G. Luchs, K. Scott Swan, and Abbie Griffin, *Design Thinking* (Hoboken, NJ: Wiley, 2015), xxi–xxi.

3. Idris Mootee, *Design Thinking for Strategic Innovation* (Hoboken, NJ: Wiley, 2013), 32-32.
4. John P. Kotter, "Leading Change: Why Transformation Efforts Fail," *Harvard Business Review* 73, no. 2 (March–April 1995): 62.

Bibliography

Kotter, John P. *Leading Change*. Boston: Harvard Business Review Press, 1996.

———. "Leading Change: Why Transformation Efforts Fail." *Harvard Business Review* 73, no. 2 (March–April 1995): 59–67.

Luchs, Michael G., K. Scott Swan, and Abbie Griffin. *Design Thinking: New Product Development Essentials from the PDMA*. Hoboken, NJ: Wiley, 2015.

Mootee, Idris. *Design Thinking for Strategic Innovation: What They Can't Teach You at Business or Design School*. Hoboken, NJ: Wiley, 2013.

Chapter 13

Strategic Service Excellence

Creating a Holistic Training Program at Fondren Library

Susan Garrison and Jeanette Claire Sewell

Setting the Change Stage

Fondren Library is the main library for Rice University, a comprehensive research institution located on a 295-acre campus in the heart of Houston, Texas. Fondren is the nexus of the campus, and the university's more than 6,700 students affectionately refer to it as "Club Fondy," a place to meet, collaborate, or seek quiet study space to read, write, and reflect. In addition to Fondren, the library system also includes the Gilbert and Ruth Whitaker Business Information Center and the Library Service Center, an off-site, climate-controlled preservation archive used for the storage and retrieval of older library materials. The library staff is composed of 120 individuals, spread across approximately fifteen departments. Staff is somewhat diverse, with a range of ages, years of university service, and ethnicity. Fondren is considered a major research library with more than 2.8 million holdings, but the smaller staff size is unusual compared with many of the library's peer institutions, some of which have 400 or more staff members. Although the library benefits from a small but rich staff culture, agreeing upon a unified communication style, library vision, and approach to service has been an ongoing challenge.

In the summer of 2016, the university vice provost for the library charged a Staff Communications Task Force consisting of nine library staff members to review previous and current modes of communication and propose improvements. As part of that undertaking, the task force surveyed peer institutions to determine how they handled internal communication, what problems they experienced with communication, and what might be some best practices to follow. The task force discussed their findings and then made several recommendations to the library's executive committee. These included incorporating a communication management training component as part of a customer service initiative. At the same time, the vice provost also brought a charge of arranging customer service training for all 120 library staff members. Previous customer service training sessions were not positively received by staff because they did not feel invested in off-the-shelf programs and so were not motivated to attend. Completing

this scenario, the university itself was undergoing a mission, vision, and goals review to chart its next strategic planning course. As part of that initiative, the university embraced updated mission, vision, and goals statements with its Vision for the Second Century, Second Decade (V2C2), stressing the importance of research and service as its key goals for measures of success.[1] The committee experienced a renewed sense of purpose following the announcement of the V2C2, feeling that they were a few steps ahead of the game in anticipating the university's strategic plan. A key question then developed: How could the library be a leader in the area of service and create an initiative that would drive change across the university?

I. Warm-up Phase

STAGE 1: ESTABLISHING A SENSE OF URGENCY

Globally, customer expectations have become increasingly demanding, with many customers turning to social media to voice their compliments or complaints. Customer service in higher education is a complex interaction of developing and consistently showcasing a brand to an ever-changing stream of users while attempting to address all of their unique needs. Libraries have often focused their attention on improving tangibles like creating unique spaces, offering new services such as virtual reality equipment lending, or adding coffee shops. However, as libraries continue to serve populations with diverse needs, providing excellent customer service remains a vital component of organizational structures. Academic libraries can obtain higher service quality satisfaction scores from users if they focus on creating clear policies and strive to provide better, more consistent staff training opportunities.

All of the overlapping initiatives at Rice held a common thread: service. Something bold and innovative would be required to unite library staff. In June 2016, Fondren's Access Services Manager had a spirited conversation with the Senior Organizational and Professional Development Consultant in human resources at Rice, which sparked an idea. Both were new to the university (less than a year at the time), and neither had heard of another department on campus that was using a successful customer service training program. The Senior Organizational and Development Consultant spoke glowingly about having personally completed the Disney Institute training and suggested that there was great potential to create a tailored customer service program that would be meaningful and sustainable for all staff. A homegrown customer service training program would be relatable for staff and could lend itself to becoming a model across the university. As one of the university's key strategic goals was centered on service, it became clear that the library could lead with this initiative.

Additionally, comprehensive new staff orientation for the library did not exist. Although newer staff with less than five years of employment were eager to help the library grow and provide greater service to the community, they also frequently struggled with understanding the underpinnings of the library's organization and culture. Staff who had been with the library for decades were also at times unsure of specific policies, procedures, and documentation. How could staff serve users properly if they themselves were confused about departmental functions? Staff knew that the library had areas of concern to address and that service to users could be improved; however, change would be imperative for improvement to occur.

Early in the process, the Senior Organizational and Development Consultant had conducted a "secret shopper" visit to the library to evaluate the quality and consistency of customer service across several departments. She found that one department provided exceptional customer service, with a staff member exceeding expectations to ensure that her question had been answered and that she was able to find the material she was looking for. In another department, the experience was not quite as expected, and the differences in service were striking. The two managers agreed that the essence of the new program would be one of changing staff behavior to improve customer service both within and outside of the library. Through training and ongoing reinforcement, staff would come to understand that simply knowing their job and their department does not equate to providing a superior customer service experience.

One initial area of concern was that staff members felt isolated and work was siloed. Some staff said that they often did not know what work was performed outside of their department. Customer service was also frequently perceived as relevant only to frontline staff. Literature reviews and web searches conducted by the Access Services Manager and the Database and Metadata Management Coordinator identified very little in terms of successful customer service training programs that did a deep dive into the entire library organization. There was an abundance of niche programs that covered handling exasperated patrons or diplomatically dealing with dysfunctional behavior; however, the Access Services Manager and the Senior Organizational and Development Consultant agreed that a "one and done" approach should not be the goal. Through distinguishing and outlining goals, reviewing department data, and reaching out to peer institutions, among many other tasks, a dedicated force worked diligently to create a customized program that would inform and train staff with the ability to transition knowledge and skills back to the workplace. This training would not simply be about managing the staff-patron interaction. It would be about training staff holistically and providing them with greater knowledge and confidence to provide superior service.

STAGE 2: CREATING THE GUIDING COALITION

According to author John Kotter, it helps to be part of the guiding coalition in order to embody change. A natural fit was to engage members from Fondren Library's Committee for Marketing and Customer Service (C-MACS), an established committee charged with promoting the library and collaborating with other committees to ensure effective and timely communication to library staff and the broader Rice community. Membership of this committee includes two cochairs, one of whom was the Database and Metadata Management Coordinator, another newcomer to the library, and up to eight general members who represent a variety of departments within the library. Several of the members also had served on the Staff Communications Task Force. Members of the current C-MACS team included staff from Reference, Cataloging and Metadata Services, Special Collections, the Digital Media Center, User Experience, and Access Services, among others. A few teams did not have representation, including Acquisitions, Digital Scholarship Services, GIS, Government Documents, and the off-site Library Service Center. In retrospect, it might have been helpful to include a member of the Library Service Center, as its workflow and interaction include users outside of the university, such as area museums and public patron retrieval requests. Additionally, the team also included the Senior Organizational and Development Consultant and the Access Services Manager, who were the drivers for this initiative. The Senior Organizational and Development Consultant's leadership was instrumental in guiding the committee toward creating a customer service program in line with the university's mission, vision, values, and strategic plan, as well as with industry customer service training standards. Although Kotter would argue that change should be led by a "key line manager" rather than someone from HR, it was the combination of the Senior Organizational and Development Consultant's expertise with training and customer service and C-MACS's knowledge of the library and its patrons, policies, and procedures that would eventually help create a training program that was larger than focusing on customer service alone. The Senior Organizational and Development Consultant had originally suggested a small cohort of ten to work on the initiative, recommending that the individuals exemplify recently presented RICE values—R for responsibility, I for integrity, C for community, and E for excellence.

C-MACS meets on a monthly basis, and subgroups were tasked with various deliverables assigned by the Senior Organizational and Development Consultant. She guided C-MACS through various exercises, including exploring existing programs, describing and understanding user personas, reviewing literature regarding customer service in higher education, and reviewing potential customer service videos to be included in training. C-MACS members volunteered for assignments according to their individual skill sets. C-MACS members truly epitomized a "get-to" mind-set, not a "have-to" mind-set.[2] The analogy of a get-to mind-set can be described as an individual choosing to do something in a positive light, rather than feeling coerced or forced. For example, consider the public services staff member who chooses to personalize each and every patron interaction in order to 'get-to' know the community better. Counter this with another staff member who robotically repeats the same greeting to every patron that walks through the library's doors because they 'have-to' converse with them as part of their job. One staff member views their interactions with zeal and sees the benefit, while the other's perspective on the task is endured at best. This mind-set is exactly what C-MACS wanted to convey as the essence of the service excellence program. Staff at all levels should be personifying a "get-to" mind-set in all of their work at the library, regardless of how often they interact with users. This is not to say that all assignments were easy to complete. Gathering information and reporting to the core team was simple. However, determining the actual content, length, and goals for the training program was somewhat more difficult. Concerns arose regarding how all of the compiled content would fit into an actual training program: How would the training be divided and delivered? How many hours or days would the training take? Would participants balk at having to spend a day or more away from their regular duties? Would participants be accepting of training delivered by their peers?

STAGE 3: DEVELOPING A VISION AND STRATEGY

C-MACS, focusing on the customer service excellence program, began meeting formally in December 2016, united behind its purpose. According to Kotter, a vision statement should be something you can explain in five minutes or less and obtain a positive reaction from those you want to adopt the change, or you're setting yourself up for resistance.[3] Many in C-MACS had experienced ineffective customer service training along with little or no orientation to the library. Off-the-shelf programs that had been considered and rejected focused too much on a retail sales perspective, felt too impersonal, or concentrated solely on staff with a public service orientation. The vision that guided C-MACS was one of creating a customer service excellence program with content that would interest all Fondren staff, regardless of longevity or department. The material would be uniquely Fondren, delving into the history of the library, exploring user interactions, determining communication best practices, and understanding the resources that were available to all staff. This approach would place all employees on a level playing field with the same understanding of good customer service.

The Senior Organizational and Development Consultant provided the group with a document titled "Strategy for Service Training Development and Implementation" that borrowed on Seraphim Consulting's "The Road to There" program outlining actions, outcomes, and impacts identified for each actionable item.[4] One example of an action item might be identifying customer personas. The outcome of performing this activity would be to identify customers common to all Fondren staff in order to clarify expectations for these different populations. The impact or result of working through this action item would be improved service to customers focusing on addressing their unique needs in a timely manner. This document was the seed from which all subtasks would germinate and provide the program's structure. Our trainer and participant guides grew from these granular beginnings of understanding our current levels of service to determining what we wanted our outcomes to resemble. C-MACS may not have initially realized that their research and monthly assignments were amounting to anything, yet each time an action item was completed, another iteration of the training document sprang forth. The document swelled from three pages, to eight, to two 30-plus-page guides with additional supporting resources. Working through these action items, C-MACS created Kotter's less-than-five-minute vision statement for the program:

> The administration and staff recognize that excellent service involves all staff, is an ongoing process, and is always enhanced through training and communication. By providing all staff with internally created training, the library seeks to create a unique customer experience that includes positive interactions, and consistent and customized service, so that the needs of all groups served by the staff are met effectively.

The overarching goal was to create a program that would provide current and future staff with a unified approach to customer service excellence. Onboarding for future staff was also identified as a critical need for Fondren. This need helped to ensure that the training included aspects such as a brief history of the library as well as each separate department's responsibilities.

In January 2017, C-MACS members divided into subcommittees to focus on several tasks that would help shape the content and provide next steps for constructing the overall program. The subcommittees began to examine existing service standards and identify examples of excellence within the library. One subcommittee connected with peer institutions to determine what others were doing in this area, and the information that was gathered strengthened C-MACS's conviction that there was no "perfect" training solution. Several meetings focused on creating and understanding user perso-nas (also known as customer profiles), an important step when identifying aspects of the ideal service experience and designing customer service training. The primary purpose, typical needs, common challenges, and unique attributes of each persona were discussed, as well as what would constitute an excellent experience. C-MACS identified four distinct persona groups at Fondren: undergraduates, graduates, faculty, and staff. Identifying and understanding the voice of each of these users as well as their unique library needs helped C-MACS create the program's 4 C approach: providing Courteous, Consistent, Customized, and Collaborative customer service that should be applicable across all departments. This exercise guided C-MACS toward its own set of principles, unique to Fondren Library, which would serve as a road map in designing the training program.

By the end of the spring 2017 semester, C-MACS had spent considerable time developing what service excellence at Fondren should look like. Next came the struggle of how to design the customized training for staff, and the Senior Organizational and Development Consultant guided the group to think in terms of delivering the content in segments. This approach would create a tailored experience, ensuring that all aspects of customer service excellence were included, while also addressing different needs and learning styles of library staff. C-MACS had amassed a considerable amount of content by this time, and it felt like an overwhelming volume of material to deliver. Compiling training documentation took on a life of its own as completed subcommittee work spun itself into several segments, including the benefits of service excellence; department overviews; Fondren's mission, vision, values, and strategic plan; and how the 4 Cs should be demonstrated in the library. The Senior Organizational and Development Consultant then directed the group in creating a participant guide as well as a trainer guide, and sections that C-MACS had diligently researched began to flesh out these documents. C-MACS members also continued to modify the document to offer a more personal touch, with color graphics, diagrams, and cartoons to keep it from becoming too text-heavy (see figure 13.1).

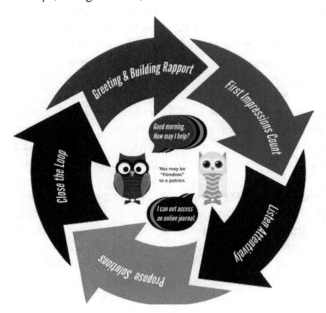

FIGURE 13.1
Graphic example created for Fondren Service Excellence Guide (Courtesy of Jeff Koffler)

With an outline of the training structure in place, team members began the process of evaluating customer service articles, videos, and activities that could be used to round out the training experi-ence. One subgroup focused on reviewing video and webinar offerings, and selected "Dealing with Angry Patrons," offered through OCLC's WebJunction service as a pretrain-ing activity.[5] In discussing what activities would and would not work, the group felt strongly that role-playing exercises should not be included based on previous expe-riences with ineffective training programs. Brief scenario discussion activities were chosen instead, with the intention of creating an opportunity for newer and longtime staff to engage in more effective conversation.

After some delays due to university-wide strategic planning efforts, by October 2017, C-MACS was able to review and revise the training program content multiple times in order to create a trainer guide. Timing and activities were still uncertain, but the majority of the subject matter had been determined. By year end, the group was feeling much more confident about the information that would be delivered; however, the group was uncomfortable with delivering the material themselves. C-MACS team members did not want to appear to be so-called experts or have colleagues who had more years of experience feel patronized. The Senior Organizational and Development Consultant concurred with C-MACS and agreed to act as facilitator for the training. C-MACS team members tackled finishing touches to the program, including finalizing the guides and determining course dates.

STAGE 4: COMMUNICATING THE CHANGE VISION

Fondren holds town hall–style meetings several times a year to share updates with all staff, and details of the training program were discussed multiple times. In addi-tion, the information was shared on Fondren's internal email discussion list. Staff not involved in C-MACS waited in anticipation for a program that had been a long time coming. Some who were frontline staff were eager to learn what would be offered; however, others in departments with less external interaction were indifferent or uninterested. C-MACS knew they would have to work doubly hard to engage those who weren't convinced they needed this training into the fold. Kotter's "bringing the outside in" concept was adopted by building on the momentum that the Senior Organizational and Development Consultant brought as an outsider of the group to keep the project moving along and to gain buy-in.[6] Training had always been an optional activity, but C-MACS did not want their hard work to be delivered to half or less of the staff. According to Gwen Arthur, "To instill credibility and maintain morale, a customer-service program should ideally involve the entire staff and repre-sent a commitment on the part of administrators alike to service."[7] Administration was supportive in their communication to staff regarding the training. All staff were encouraged to attend, and to sweeten the deal, a raffle of a free day off for one lucky attendee was offered to encourage greater participation.

Kotter states that "often the most powerful way to communicate a new direction is through behavior …employees will usually grasp it better than if there had been a hundred stories in the in-house newsletter."[8] C-MACS members knew they would need to epitomize the values of the 4 Cs themselves in order to obtain buy-in from staff. Prior to rolling out the program, C-MACS members were ever-conscious in their daily work to consistently model new behaviors by working hard to be better listeners, going the extra mile for internal and external requests, and reminding themselves to be inclusive.

II. Introducing New Practices Phase

STAGE 5: EMPOWERING BROAD-BASED ACTION

According to Kotter's model, if the process is moving along in a positive manner, C-MACS members would begin to embody a sense of empowerment from their progress. This became evident when the first pilot session of the program was held with the library's executive committee. C-MACS had agreed that the program could not be delivered to the entire staff without executive buy-in. Again, Kotter states that without sufficient buy-in, organizational complacency will creep in, staff won't put faith in the proposed change, and an army of naysayers will crush the dream. By March 2018, C-MACS felt they had sufficiently completed and fine-tuned all of the material and could now present the pilot program. The Senior Organizational and Development Consultant led the session, and C-MACS members observed and took notes. Feedback provided by the executive committee regarding the program content provided incredible support along with a sense of ownership and pride to C-MACS members for their achievement. Although C-MACS members initially had concerns about whether they could create training of such magnitude on their own, the feeling of satisfaction once the program began to take shape was analogous to watching someone work a jigsaw puzzle, as all of the pieces began slipping into their proper spots.

The executive committee via an anonymous survey provided additional feedback at the end of the session. Several tweaks were made to the program in the areas of revising departmental descriptions and decreasing the amount of text presented on some of the PowerPoint slides. The slides were modified to maintain a brief, clean feel to them, absent of distracting PowerPoint animations, to allow the facilitator to better interact with participants. This design allowed the Senior Organizational and Development Consultant the opportunity to intersperse personal examples in the training, which encouraged staff to share their stories, leading to co-teachable moments. Feedback overall was encouraging and positive. A number of activities were enjoyed, including using a set of ExpressPack cards as an icebreaker to talk about what good and bad customer service looked like to participants.[9]

According to Kotter, "Whenever you let up before the job is done, critical momentum can be lost and regression may follow."[10] None of the course modifications were complex, but competing projects, such as overseeing an important staff search, hosting end-of-semester student library activities, and the announcement that Fondren would begin the process of preparing for a library service platform migration, began to draw members away from forging ahead. In addition, scope creep began to sneak into the project. *Scope creep* refers to changes that can occur after a project begins, increasing the scope of the plan, and potentially derailing it from completion. C-MACS was already aware that some staff would be a harder sell on the program. Some teams simply did not see how customer service played a role in their work. As staff remained in positions for greater lengths of time, it became harder to change their fixed mind-sets. These issues were not unique to Fondren. The university as a whole is hierarchical in structure, which often makes change slow to adopt. Time was passing, team members were being stretched, and the venture was losing momentum. Anxious not to have their hard work lost, C-MACS regrouped after the end of the semester and, with an even stronger sense of urgency, determined that training for all staff needed to be completed by summer

2018. C-MACS realized that a longer wait would put the program in jeopardy of never being delivered, as library service platform migration projects would consume most of staff time over the next two years.

C-MACS reconvened in June 2018 to move the program forward. It was determined that four training sessions would be offered. C-MACS spread the sessions over two weeks to provide all staff with attendance options, with sessions scheduled midday, from 10:00 a.m. to 2:00 p.m., including a morning and afternoon break and a thirty-minute working lunch. An initial email was sent to all members of the executive team informing them of the upcoming training. Information about the training was then disseminated in a second email from the library's vice provost. This lent the program credibility and support. Administration also supported the program by offering its largest meeting room for the trainings and by providing all participants with catered lunch. Nearly three quarters of the staff enrolled. Although they did not achieve 100 percent participation, C-MACS conceded that because of summer activities, this initial group would become Fondren's first cohort.

STAGE 6: GENERATING SHORT-TERM WINS

Kotter explains that good short-term wins have at least three components: being visible, unambiguous, and distinctly related to the change transformation.[11] In this project, the program and the supporting documentation were clearly the most physical elements of the short-term win. Even though these pieces were developed nearly a year after the initial meetings, seeing C-MACS's research and small-group tasks culminate in the creation of actual documentation and a viable program was clearly a visible short-term win. Likewise, a second short-term win occurred when the program was delivered to the executive team and received enthusiastically. Finally, a third win was delivering the program to staff, who received the training enthusiastically. Each session included a diverse mix of staff from across the library, which allowed for true transfer of knowledge. Staff who were siloed noted how nice it was to be out of their work area and engaging with others in the library. Staff also commented on the usefulness of the guide and resources, and several stated that they wished they had had these materials when they first started their positions.

C-MACS foresees greater overall customer satisfaction from the delivery and continued support of this program. The committee's plans of following up with super-visors to ensure that all staff receive training, of utilizing the program for onboarding purposes, and of implementing a program to reward those exhibiting desired change behaviors confirm that Fondren is striving for service excellence.

STAGE 7: CONSOLIDATING GAINS AND PRODUCING MORE CHANGE

To ensure that the program would be sustainable and ongoing, C-MACS created post-training activities that were included in follow-up emails to the participants. One activity involved an online scavenger hunt to help staff learn more about services and information offered by the library's various departments, while another activity provided participants the opportunity to explore web services and sites that our customers, use including WorldCat, LibGuides, Rice Digital Scholarship Archive, and the Friends of Fondren membership site. C-MACS did not want participants to feel this would be another over and done training and emphasized that refresher courses would be offered or could be requested by any department. Additionally, C-MACS's intention after the initial training was delivered would be to have all new library employees complete this service excellence training within their first few weeks of employment. This program would stand as part of a new employee orientation to Fondren as well as holding the new staff member accountable to the same service excellence standards as existing staff. It's uncertain in the first round of training whether some staff were reluctant to attend. C-MACS sent follow-up notices to managers informing them which staff members attended and which would need to attend future sessions. This additional effort provided frontline managers with a performance measure to determine whether staff who attended training were demonstrating any of the newly learned behaviors. It also transferred the training stakeholder duty to the participant rather than the manager, as the training clearly identified undesirable behaviors pretraining and desirable behaviors post training.

III. Grounding Phase

STAGE 8: ANCHORING NEW APPROACHES IN THE CULTURE

Kotter states that change becomes part of the culture when behaviors shift to "the way we do things around here."[12] Making change stick requires putting words into action, repeating desired behaviors, and frequently rewarding those who willingly embrace and model the change. However, "Most libraries have not regularly implemented follow-up strategies to support staff's application of new skills on-the-job after their customer-service training programs."[13] In our case, C-MACS created post-training emails that were sent to the staff member's manager as well as the participant. The manager's post training email provided information regarding which staff members had attended training. Managers were asked to encourage staff who did not attend training to schedule a makeup session. Participants' emails thanked them for attending training, thereby recognizing and rewarding them for taking their first step toward change. The email also provided staff with links to a survey to provide feedback, as well as a permalink to the training documentation and post-training activities to reinforce the material delivered in the course. As the saying goes, "Practice makes permanent." Repeat a desired behavior often and well, and it is highly likely the change will stick. C-MACS's intention to continue offering the training on a regular basis, slightly tweaked by participant feedback, is a model that will strengthen the outcome of providing clear, consistent service across all areas of the library. C-MACS's plan to affirm user behavior by recognizing staff embodying the principles taught in the customer service excellence training will encourage cultural change.

Analysis and Conclusions

Kotter states that "change often starts with just two or three people," as was the case for our initiative.[14] Following Kotter's eight-step change model guided the group toward the opportunity of creating a customized customer service program to ensure that cultural change at Fondren Library would become a reality. Our two change agents, despite being extremely enthusiastic, could not have achieved change acceptance without first building a strong corps to shape the vision and create tangible deliverables for the program. Bringing C-MACS into the process bolstered our change agent numbers, afforded additional talents, and created a strong constituency that legitimized the change. While C-MACS experienced periods of negative self-talk, where they doubted their abilities to create a curriculum that could surpass an off-the-shelf program, the group was able to power through these mental barriers by diligently focusing on bite-sized tasks. Piloting the program to senior leadership and receiving accolades and strong support provided C-MACS with short-term wins, as well as sustainability for critical momentum to deliver change to the entire library. Now the hard part begins: instituting and maintaining change. As Kotter says, "Culture changes only after you have successfully altered people's actions, after the new behavior produces some group benefit for a period of time, and after people see the connection between the new actions and the performance improvement."[15] According to Kotter, this can take anywhere from three to ten years. How will we make sure this new service excellence sticks with our staff? We will maintain that eighth stage with frequent reminders, refreshers, and, as Kotter stresses, a lot of talk.

Kotter notes that "organizations everywhere are struggling to keep up with the accelerating pace of change—let alone get ahead of it."[16] Just as C-MACS announced the launch of the service excellence training, Fondren's Strategic Planning Committee announced the start of action planning for the library. Despite the pull of competing interests, C-MACS expedited delivering training, as the entire university was on a trajectory toward change. As Rice University touts itself as having a "world-class infrastructure," C-MACS's work to bring all library staff up to the level of excellence simply furthers that goal.

As the university and the library strive toward the V2C2's mission of contributing "to our world through excellence in education and research," there are many thoughts surrounding how to deliver on these goals.[17] Expanding programs, providing greater outreach, and increasing access, inclusivity, equity, and diversity are just some of the plans. None of these are possible without putting people first. Succeeding with these plans will mean bringing to the table staff who will ultimately be driven to provide the best service possible to our internal and external partners. Creating, delivering, and sustaining a training program for current and future staff to provide the best service possible is a critical step in this plan. Newly trained staff can begin spreading seeds of change throughout the university as they collaborate with other departments, referring back to their tool kit in future interactions. Enduring support and buy-in from the executive team will also help strengthen continued cultural change. Kotter reminds us that "new approaches usually sink into a culture only after it's very clear that they work and are superior to old methods."[18] The library's task now is to implement efforts to make the change become a part of the overall culture by continuing to validate new change practices and re-emphasizing their importance, all while keeping an eye out for our next big opportunity.

Notes

1. "V2C2: Vision for the Second Century, Second Decade: Rice University's Strategic Plan," Rice University, accessed May 10, 2019, https://v2c2.rice.edu/sites/g/files/bxs956/f/V2C2-Supporting-Document.pdf.

2. John P. Kotter, *Accelerate* (Boston: Harvard Business Review Press, 2014), 23.

3. John P. Kotter, "Leading Change: Why Transformation Efforts Fail," *Harvard Business Review* 73, no. 2 (March–April 1995): 63.

4. "The Road to "THERE"" Seraphim Consulting and Training Solutions website, Products page, accessed July 2, 2019,
   http://www.seraphimconsulting.net/id70.html.

5. "Updated Course: Dealing with Angry Patrons," WebJunction, May 18, 2016, https://www.webjunction.org/news/webjunction/updated-course-dealing-with-angry-patrons.html.

6. Kotter, *Accelerate*, 118.

7. Gwen Arthur, "Customer-Service Training in Academic Libraries," *Journal of Academic Librarianship* 20, no. 4 (1994): 220,
   https://doi.org/10.1016/0099-1333(94)90102-3.

8. John P. Kotter, *Leading Change* (Boston: Harvard Business Review Press, 1996), 95.

9. "ExpressPack," Trainers Warehouse, accessed May 10, 2019, http://www.trainerswarehouse.com/expresspack.html.

10. Kotter, *Leading Change*, 133.

11. Kotter, *Leading Change*, 126.

12. Kotter, "Leading Change: Why Transformation Efforts Fail," 7.

13. Arthur, "Customer-Service Training," 221.

14. Kotter, *Leading Change*, 59.

15. Kotter, *Leading Change*, 156.

16. Kotter, *Accelerate*, 1.

17. "V2C2: Vision for the Second Century, Second Decade: Rice University's Strategic Plan," Rice University, accessed July 2, 2019, https://v2c2.rice.edu/.

18. Kotter, *Leading Change*, 157.

Bibliography

Arthur, Gwen. "Customer-Service Training in Academic Libraries." *Journal of Academic Librarianship* 20, no. 4 (1994): 219–22. https://doi.org/10.1016/0099-1333(94)90102-3.

Kotter, John P. *Accelerate: Building Strategic Agility for a Faster-Moving World*. Boston: Harvard Business Review Press, 2014.

Kotter, John P. *Leading Change*. Boston: Harvard Business Review Press, 1996.

Kotter, John P. "Leading Change: Why Transformation Efforts Fail," *Harvard Business Review* 73, no. 2 (March–April 1995): 59–67.

Rice University. "V2C2: Vision for the Second Century, Second Decade: Rice University's Strategic Plan." Accessed May 10, 2019. https://v2c2.rice.edu/sites/g/files/bxs956/f/V2C2-Supporting-Document.pdf.

Seraphim Consulting and Training Solutions. "The Road to "THERE"." Products page. Accessed July 2, 2019. http://www.seraphimconsulting.net/id70.html.

Trainers Warehouse. "ExpressPack." Accessed May 10, 2019. http://www.trainerswarehouse.com/expresspack.html.

WebJunction. "Updated Course: Dealing with Angry Patrons." May 18, 2016. https://www.webjunction.org/news/webjunction/updated-course-dealing-with-angry-patrons.html.

Chapter 14

Moving from In Person to Online

Effects on Staffing in a Large Academic Library System

Emma Popowich and Sherri Vokey

Setting the Change Stage

The University of Manitoba (U of M) is a research-intensive medical and doctoral-level university and a member of the U15 Group of Canadian Research Universities, which includes fifteen of Canada's top research universities. In support of the U of M's strategic priorities, distributed campuses, and over 100 programs, the University of Manitoba Libraries (UML) comprises eleven libraries that are distributed over two campuses within the city of Winnipeg. While most of the libraries' general operations, physical collections, and staff are located at the Fort Garry campus, the Health Sciences Library is housed at the downtown medical campus.

In 2015–2016, the UML reported a staffing complement of 180 librarians and support staff.[1] Organizational changes were instituted in June 2016 that affected many areas within the libraries, and they were felt acutely in public services where support staff positions were reduced. Traffic, circulation, and reference trends at the UML closely mirrored those reported widely within academic libraries: services and resources are increasingly moving toward online environments, and after several years of consistent decreases in face-to-face informational and circulation transactions, frontline service staff in academic libraries are being reduced and redeployed.[2]

A sweeping reorganization of the UML's public services staffing model was instituted in an effort to be responsive to these trends. In addition to the layoff of support staff across multiple units that left managers struggling at times to keep libraries adequately staffed and open, remaining service desk staff were expected to refocus their priorities. Support staff, who for so long were evaluated on and lauded for their commitment to public service suddenly felt devalued and questioned their future in academic libraries. At the same time, librarians who were endeavoring to support new faculty services and library-based initiatives were left clamoring for support from library assistants who were now in short supply.

I. Warm-up Phase

STAGE 1: ESTABLISHING A SENSE OF URGENCY

The discontinuance of library support staff positions in public services and subsequent reorganization of roles presented a number of challenges for library unit heads. The impact of the staffing reduction on the institution remains contentious. Several sources reported that close to forty support staff positions were lost due to restructuring,[3] though the university librarian stated that "30 low-level, part-time positions" were lost, the equivalent of "about nine full-time slots."[4] Unions representing both support staff and librarians decried the negative impact that the restructuring had on morale, workload, and services provided in support of research, teaching, and learning at the university.[5]

Any restructuring initiative, especially one involving the loss of colleagues, will have deep ramifications for individuals directly impacted by layoff and for those who remain. A report published by the Conference Board of Canada used the phrase "survivor syndrome," defined as "a marked decrease in motivation, engagement, and productivity of employees that remain at the company as a result of downsizing and workforce reductions."[6] After layoffs were finalized and restructuring complete, many UML support staff reported mourning the loss of their colleagues and feeling stressed by the impact on their unit and individual workload. Moreover, many reported feeling that the security of their employment was in jeopardy because the layoffs made them feel expendable, especially when the libraries seemed to be moving increasingly in the direction of self-service options, such as self-checkout kiosks, reserve and holds lockers placed outside of library spaces, online room booking software, and self-guided video tutorials intended to reduce the number of face-to-face lab and classroom contact hours between students and library staff.[7]

While they were working to reorganize workload and responsibilities, it became apparent to library unit heads that many staff were feeling decreased satisfaction in their work life and ambivalence toward their employer. Unit staffing levels had been reduced to a bare minimum required to cover hours of opening, and while daytime staff struggled to attend to needs at service points and attend to off-desk duties, evening staff were underutilized. Librarians found their support staff colleagues were now largely unavailable to them, due either to misaligned hours of work or to increased time spent covering tasks previously completed by discontinued staff.

Unit heads began to meet regularly with librarians and support staff to identify the roadblocks to achieving strategic goals and priorities. Librarians were clear in their need for assistance from support staff in areas such as chat reference, instructional support, collections management, and website maintenance. Support staff were frustrated at their inability to assist due to hours spent staffing evening and weekend hours with little to no patron interaction.

After gathering similar feedback from units across the system, the head of the Elizabeth Dafoe Library and the head of the NJM Health Sciences Library advocated for a modified schedule of staffed and unstaffed hours. Further, they requested a greater degree of communication from administration about strategic directions in the area of self-service technologies and the future of user services at the UML in order to allay concerns about job security and value within the organization. Modest improvements have been made in efforts to communicate change and library priorities to faculty librarians via council meetings, but little change has been felt in practices around communication with all staff system-wide. This is compounded by the fact that the library system remains without a strategic document to guide such discussion.

STAGE 2: CREATING THE GUIDING COALITION

The head of the Elizabeth Dafoe Library and the head of the NJM Health Sciences Library initiated a project with the goal of advocating to administration for changes that would improve service and morale. The team was motivated by resolve and desperation to improve a chaotic and burdensome staffing arrangement that was bringing undue hardship upon support staff, librarians, and managers. Libraries Administration gave consent for the two heads to move their agenda forward, but it was not interested in delving into the details of these changes. So long as there were no associated costs or negative consequences, the process could move forward without supervision from the administrative team. These two heads represented two of the three largest library units, and together represent the two main U of M campuses. The head of the third largest unit was invited to join the team, but declined. While having the "big three" units represented would have been ideal for pulling together a strong and robust guiding team, it did not detract from the achievement of the team's objectives. Staff were very familiar with the heads who were involved and were keen to see some response to their concerns. In this sense, support staff and librarians saw the changes led by the two heads as representing their interests.

The team established four priorities: (1) reduce staffed hours to allow for an increase in staffing during peak and in-demand service hours; (2) increase support to librarians from support staff; (3) increase the amount of fulfilling, high-level work for support staff; and (4) improve morale and work satisfaction.

STAGE 3: DEVELOPING A VISION AND STRATEGY

The heads created a vision that anchored proposed changes in the creation of cohesiveness between support staff and librarians. The vision involved creating a sustainable support staff service model that allowed this group to fulfill dual roles: to contribute to student success through reference work, and to support librarian activities by working collaboratively with their librarian colleagues. The upshot of greater collaboration would be an improvement in overall job satisfaction in the newly restructured environment, while remaining committed to the evolving strategic priorities of the UML. The core tenet of this vision and plan centered around a significant reduction in staffed hours at service desks.

The development of the vision and strategy needed to reflect the needs of the UML system as a whole, the university librarian's priorities, and the university's strategic plan. In order to move forward, the team needed to demonstrate how proposed staffing changes would provide additional support to significant UML priorities such as research support and instructional services. Financial accountability was also key, as a reduction in costs and in library closures due to staffing shortages was fundamental in securing the university librarian's support. Furthermore, the head of the Elizabeth Dafoe Library and the head of the NJM Health Sciences Library needed to convey to library administration that by accepting the proposed changes, the UML would be in lockstep with staffing strategies found across comparable Canadian university libraries.

The two heads wrote a staffing proposal for the university librarian in April 2017 that reviewed Canadian U15 library staffing and service models. They discovered that across Canada, U15 libraries were overwhelmingly moving to a tiered service level model with staffed information desks closing earlier in the evening while the library building remains accessible late into the evening or "after-hours" without library staff.[8] The premise of a tiered model involves staffing information service points strategically and during times of peak demand, primarily during the day and early evening.

The two heads argued that by using a tiered service model, the UML could reduce staffing costs, such as overtime, while providing longer hours of opening, access to space, and self-serve options. This involved limited staffed library hours with unstaffed, after-hours access made available in conjunction with security services. Further, they argued that a tiered model would help staff see the adoption of self-service options not as a threat, but as a net advantage to their work lives. Through the adoption of the heads' proposal, support staff would be freed from staffing service points during non-peak times and instead would be working at hours that correspond with those that are most impactful for students. The tiered service model also allowed support staff to see themselves as supporting librarians in more challenging roles instead of staffing study halls or empty buildings. An increase in the concentration of staff during core daytime hours translated into greater support for higher-level work and the development of new initiatives. Fortunately, both administration and library staff understood and accepted this strategy.

Stakeholders from outside the libraries, primarily deans and department heads, were also consulted during this process. The proposed changes were explained with a view to highlighting the overall increase in their library's hours rather than the reduction in staffed hours. Affected deans were supportive of the proposed changes and in fact stated a preference for increased support staff and librarian assistance for research and teaching over longer staffed hours.

With major stakeholder support secured, the head of the Elizabeth Dafoe Library and the head of the NJM Health Sciences Library embarked on a three-phase approach to implementing our proposed changes. The reduction in staffed hours was planned within a multiphase, multiyear time frame. Each phase required that specific strategies and steps be followed in order to successfully see us through to the following phase.

Phase 1

In September 2017, the three largest libraries (Sciences and Technology, Health Sciences, and Humanities and Social Sciences) reduced their staffed hours while extending overall hours of access to library space. This was accomplished by supplementing staffed hours with unstaffed hours with the assistance of private security. In the new model, large libraries would be staffed from 8:00 a.m. to 8:00 p.m., and remain open and unstaffed until 1:00 a.m., or for twenty-four hours during exam periods. This meant that staff who had previously worked until closing at 11:00 p.m. in the larger units would have their shifts moved into the busier part of the day. Smaller units would see staff moved up even earlier, with staffed hours running from 8:30 a.m. until 6:00 p.m. and unstaffed hours extended to 10:00 p.m.

While an overall increase in hours of access to the large unit libraries was well received by stakeholders, it did present immediate implications for some library services. For example, the UML's chat reference service, which had traditionally been monitored by support staff while they worked at the service desk, was now without staffing in the later evening hours. With service desk staff ending their workdays earlier, chat reference hours would also need to be reduced. The head of the Elizabeth Dafoe Library and the head of the NJM Health Sciences Library investigated new ways of providing chat service, and although allowances were made for reduced chat reference hours for an interim period (2017–2018), there are plans to assign a dedicated chat reference staff member from September 2018 forward.

A reconsideration of safety and security in this new context also became an important component of the staffing plan. As managers, the two heads were concerned about staff finding themselves in situations where they were working alone. Through consultation with library support staff, support staff supervisors, and heads, the team concluded that staff working in large, multilevel units could not be permitted to close libraries alone. They liaised with the university's Environmental Health and Safety Office in drafting a "Working Alone Statement (Policy)" for all public service staff.[9] The policy was approved by the libraries' management committee and now works to ensure that staff are protected from risk while working alone.[10]

Phase 2

The second phase began in April 2017 and entailed a change in the type of work assigned to support staff. No further changes to the hours were made, but rather a reduction of time spent on desk with an increase in non-desk duties was instituted. This included assigning higher-level work to support staff in line with their areas of interest and skill level.

With an increase in the number of self-service options being rolled out across library units, support staff were vocal about wanting new and challenging work. At the same time, newly articulated organizational priorities centering on research support and learning and instructional support services were overloading librarian workloads. The head of the Elizabeth Dafoe Library and the head of the NJM Health Sciences Library began to look at ways to shift to support staff some traditional liaison work that included but was not limited to collections management assistance, LibGuide (website) maintenance, events promotion and communication, and social media. The key to the success of this phase was in assigning work mindfully and in consultation with the support staff involved. Staff were consulted by unit heads and supervisors about their willingness to take on new work and their preferences and comfort levels. This step allowed staff to view the experience as a positive, self-directed change.

Phase 3

In the third phase, beginning in September 2018, the team reduced the staffed hours and increased overall opening hours in the remaining eight unit libraries in the UML system that were not initially impacted in phase 1. In this stage, allowances were made for these smaller unit libraries to be open and unstaffed all day on weekends and during non-peak times, which is a first in the UML system. This involved relying on security services to open these libraries and secure the space with no library staff on site. This model is tethered to self-service options such as self-checkout and also to a centralized online chat reference service that can be accessed by students should they require assistance. We chose to use this unstaffed model to make units that previously had no opening hours during weekends to now be open and available, while at the same time reducing staffed hours in other units as a way to mitigate a negative perception of a reduction in staffed service. Student response to the change was positive and the overall increase in opening hours was seen as a direct response to student need by university administration. By the time of the final phase, support staff and librarians also understood the benefits of the transformation at hand.

STAGE 4: COMMUNICATING THE CHANGE VISION

It was understood that the key to support of the vision would rest on effective communication, especially with frontline support staff and librarians. Staff commented repeatedly that one of the largest sources of discontent surrounding the 2016 reorganization was the lack of communication from library administration. The head of the Elizabeth Dafoe Library and the head of the NJM Health Sciences Library developed a communication plan for informing key stakeholder groups. Support staff would be informed as early as practicable and at regular intervals as progress was made through the stages. This group of frontline staff would receive the most in-person communication and the most thorough explanation of how the changes related to the evolution of libraries in keeping with UML strategic directions. Librarians would receive an overview of the change and how it would positively impact their work, but would be kept informed only at important and necessary junctures. Libraries Administration would be kept informed through our monthly management committee meetings and via email, but have preferred to be contacted only as needed during this process. Deans and department heads would require a more in-depth and in-person explanation of changes, primarily at the beginning stages of change implementation, but would not be inundated with detailed updates.

The head of the Elizabeth Dafoe Library and the head of the NJM Health Sciences Library developed consistent messaging for staff that was used at meetings and in discussions and directives by either of the two unit heads. They referred consistently to the future direction of academic libraries in general and to a commitment to moving the University of Manitoba's priorities forward when discussing the plan with staff. In other words, changes weren't being proposed or implemented without context, evidence, and thoughtful decision-making. Support staff received the highest amount of messaging, and individual unit staff and larger groups of support staff were met with regularly to discuss changes. Library supervisors were empowered to communicate the vision and to not be afraid of speaking out of turn about high-level priorities, which they tended to be excluded from. Librarians were also kept abreast of changes in meetings, but librarians have more daily communication with heads, and many of these discussions happened organically in conjunction with conversations about project deadlines and requests for support. Communication to Libraries Administration was more formal and often via email to make staffing requests such as alterations to job descriptions and reclassifications. Finally, communication with deans and department heads was done via an initial first meeting to present the groundwork for upcoming changes and then through email to update and ensure continued support.

Whenever discussing an issue, solution, or outcome with staff, the head of the Elizabeth Dafoe Library and the head of the NJM Health Sciences Library made sure to reference it in the context of our priorities and goals as a system. Through these conversations, they came to learn that many support staff were not aware of the University of Manitoba's strategic plan or how it informed decisions at the library unit level. Initially, it may have appeared excessive, but consistent and contextualized messaging meant that support staff and librarians were never taken by surprise by any of the steps that were taken. Whether goals are defined internally within the libraries or externally within the university's articulated priorities, it is essential that staff be aware of these goals as an anchor to and reason for decision-making at the unit level.

II. Introducing New Practices Phase

STAGE 5: EMPOWERING BROAD-BASED ACTION

Perhaps one of the most challenging aspects of bringing the proposed changes to fruition involved empowering all of the affected staff to act in the interest of change. While a critical step in the change management process, it is one that was found to be largely out of the team's reach. Several barriers to organizational change were present and centered around hierarchical decision-making, organizational culture, vacancy management and succession planning, and fear of obsolescence.

Though the head of the Elizabeth Dafoe Library and the head of the NJM Health Sciences Library were responsible for articulating the proposed change, they often did not have the authority to make it a reality. Implementation of the plan was often subject to stops and starts while decisions and directives rested with library administration. A lack of nimble decision-making during crucial junctures presented challenges to sustaining momentum and confidence. At times the team took silences to be equal to assent, and by working as advisors to library administration, we were sometimes able to advocate for courses of action that would mitigate some organizational barriers.

The team often sensed that we were colliding with some staunchly held beliefs from UML staff and librarians around change: namely that the initial restructuring wasn't required and that the only solution was to revert to traditional models. Bringing people to accept that change is a necessary part of remaining relevant within the profession and continued growth was no small feat. Changing an organization's culture is challenging to say the least, and there were people who remained skeptical and unsupportive throughout, but they were not a majority. Being prepared with a solid communication plan and evidence to back up the proposed vision served to mitigate or quiet most of the opposition.

Throughout the project, the head of the Elizabeth Dafoe Library and the head of the NJM Health Sciences Library faced major obstacles around vacancy management at all levels in the organization, and discussions around succession planning were notably absent. This led to an inability to adequately involve supervisors and managers in the change management plan, as many of those positions either sat vacant or were being temporarily staffed by people who might not be there for a substantial period of time.

After enduring unexpected layoffs, support staff were fearful of further job losses and had endured a period of rapid change in a relatively short amount of time. The head of the Elizabeth Dafoe Library and the head of the NJM Health Sciences Library strongly encouraged library administrators to post permanent library assistant positions within the first few months of our project to allow for greater staffing stability.

Additionally, some librarians were resistant to delegating tasks to library support staff for fear of becoming obsolete in *their* positions. The UML was initiating conversations around the dissolution of the traditional liaison model in favor of functional roles and responsibilities, and librarians were learning that they would soon divide their time between traditional liaison work and an additional functional role in areas like open journal software, data management, accessibility services, and so forth. This created some uncertainty for librarians and skepticism of the team's project. However, further clarification from administration regarding librarian priorities and strategic directions compelled librarians to become more involved in new tasks around research and instructional support. As they become more involved in these new ventures, they were less insecure about losing other tasks to support staff.

STAGE 6: GENERATING SHORT-TERM WINS

Barriers will always be present and introduce unwanted complexity to any change initiative. The head of the Elizabeth Dafoe Library and the head of the NJM Health Sciences Library were aware of the need to create visible successes as soon as possible post-implementation in order to sustain and continue to build momentum with key stakeholders. To that end, they were able to generate four short-term wins.

Approved Reclassifications

Support staff who moved into new and more demanding roles were rewarded with reclassification, often to the highest level (4) when in new positions providing reference services, providing support to librarians, performing supervisory duties, and so forth. This helped to bolster the support for the change that the team was leading.

Assignment of Dedicated Chat Reference Staff

The head of the Elizabeth Dafoe Library and the head of the NJM Health Sciences Library advocated forcefully for a dedicated staff member to assume responsibility for oversight of a nascent chat reference service, especially in the context of a reduction in staffed evening hours. Assigning someone to this role has helped solidify the idea that chat reference was a priority for the system. It further demonstrated that the voices of frontline librarians and support staff have been heard, as they had been very vocal about this need for a few years.

Student Satisfaction

The greatest fear for all participating in the change was the potential for disservice to students, who might have less in-person access to assistance. Increased opening hours were key to obtaining support of students, who saw the increased access to group study rooms, printing services, and collections as a fair trade-off for a model with reduced staffed hours.

Improved Work-Life Balance for Support Staff

With support staff no longer working past 8:00 p.m. on any night of the week, there has been a marked decrease in the perceived inequity of shift distribution. This is perhaps the single most positive and impactful outcome that has led to vastly improved morale and job satisfaction among support staff. It has resulted in increasing overlap of staff during daytime hours and has meant that staff may now attend professional development events, collaborate with librarians and other support staff, and so forth.

STAGE 7: CONSOLIDATING GAINS AND PRODUCING MORE CHANGE

The achievement of short-term gains was viewed as a big win by the team, though they recognized that in order to sustain forward movement and not risk falling into complacency, they needed to push for further organizational change. Much of the proposed plan focused on support staff and hinged on increasing their support and, by doing so, creating more challenging and rewarding work for them.

The head of the Elizabeth Dafoe Library and the head of the NJM Health Sciences Library have more recently refocused on the librarian model. Most librarians are tied to a traditional liaison model that organizes their work and priorities in a very specific way. This particular orientation to professional duties does not always prioritize the kind of innovative and synergistic team-based approach to work among support staff and librarians that the team was hoping for. In November 2017, health sciences support staff and librarians took part in an immersive two-day retreat and focused on how they could achieve greater collaboration. After much discussion and debate, the group came to consensus on the issue of librarian roles and advocated for a realignment of librarian duties around core strategic priorities. Each team will have at least one support staff member on board, and this is currently in the process of being deployed. Other units within the UML are looking to follow this approach and transition to a functional librarian model.

III. Grounding Phase

STAGE 8: ANCHORING NEW APPROACHES IN THE CULTURE

Throughout the three-year process of implementing a new staffing model, the head of the Elizabeth Dafoe Library and the head of the NJM Health Sciences Library modeled consistent communication and consultative, collegial decision-making. Librarians and support staff have come to expect effective and timely communication around changes and have begun to initiate conversations around change management themselves. In addition to increased communication, silos between librarians and support staff have been eroding, with teams forming organically within units in order to tackle new initiatives.

The upskilling and reassignment of support staff to other off-desk duties remains a work in progress as new services are developed and rolled out to faculty and students. As the UML continues to evolve, greater opportunities for participation in higher-level work for support staff are presenting themselves. A number of librarians have transitioned into new roles as coordinators of identified priority areas such as Research Services.[11] With the development of these new roles comes a host of new challenges and issues in which support staff must become skilled and conversant. In the case of Research Services, upskilling for support staff is taking place around bibliometrics, persistent identifiers, and repository deposits, to name just a few. Though by nature the coordinator positions are cross-functional and system-wide in their scope, those occupying the new roles have taken steps to adopt the transparent and timely "culture of communication" that the head of the Elizabeth Dafoe Library and the head of the NJM Health Sciences Library have been keen to model throughout their change process. This has involved the use of blogs,[12] consultations with heads, and direct messages to all staff via email as appropriate.

Analysis and Conclusions

A number of key issues arose throughout this process that have been reframed as crucial aspects to successful change. It cannot be overstated how critical consistent and transparent communication is to the change process. Kotter and Rathgeber illustrate this point expertly in their book *Our Iceberg Is Melting*, in which the role of thinking and feeling is pivotal to effectively bringing people on board and sharing in the vision.[13] *Thinking* differently can help change behavior and eliminate resistance. However, people need to be provided with adequate and logical communication in order to get there. In this case, the head of the Elizabeth Dafoe Library and the head of the NJM Health Sciences Library presented support staff and librarians with a rationale, vision, and strategy at the outset in order to create understanding among those affected by the change. Getting people to *feel* differently can lead to even more impressive returns. Again, in order to help people feel positively about change and even champion the plan as presented, it is essential for leadership to create a compelling picture of the future and everyone's role on that journey.

The head of the Elizabeth Dafoe Library and the head of the NJM Health Sciences Library encountered several instances where staff were unaware that the university had strategic priorities that served as a link to what was being proposed under the new service model. The two heads have endeavored to instill a new culture of change in which people are informed, engage with work collaboratively, and are unafraid to face change. This culture can take root only in a context where a vision of the library in the future is communicated as something for all staff to work toward.

Kotter's eight-stage process for leading change served as a valuable tool in the analysis of the changes that the head of the Elizabeth Dafoe Library and the head of the NJM Health Sciences Library instituted at the UML. Specifically, it reinforced how essential the first two steps, creating a sense of urgency and creating a guiding coalition, were to the successful progression through the later stages. Without a knowledgeable and motivated team who were positioned and ready with a well-researched call to action, there very likely would not have been any movement beyond the warm-up phase.

While the analysis of the case proceeds very linearly from step to step, in reality, there were many bumps and setbacks that found the team either waiting or circling back to previous steps or phases. Implied in the Kotter framework is the notion that successful change comes from following each of these steps, in order. The head of the Elizabeth Dafoe Library and the head of the NJM Health Sciences Library felt at times that there was some necessary fluidity in their process that is not a hallmark of Kotter's industry-focused approach. While Kotter's work may be less aligned with the comparatively flatter organizational cultures than are found in higher education, any library embarking on a process of organizational change would be well-served by following the steps laid out in this process.

Notes

1. Canadian Association of Research Libraries, *CARL Statistics | Statistiques de l'ABRC 2015–2016, Salaries | Salaires 2016–2017* (Ottawa, ON: Canadian Association of Research Libraries, September 2017, rev. October 24, 2017), http://www.carl-abrc.ca/wp-content/uploads/2017/10/CARL-ABRC_Stats_Pub_2015-16-v2.pdf.
2. "Graph 1: Service Trends in ARL Libraries, 1991–2015," from *ARL Statistics 2014–15* (Washington, DC: Association of Research Libraries, 2015), http://www.arl.org/storage/documents/service-trends.pdf.
3. Nick Martin, "U of M, Union Disagree Strongly on Library Staff Cuts," *Winnipeg (MB) Free Press*, June 10, 2016, http://www.winnipegfreepress.com/local/u-of-m-union-disagree-strongly-on-library-staff-cuts-382525141.html; Laurie Morris, "AESES Position Discontinuances at the University of Manitoba," email, June 10, 2016, http://aeses.ca/um-libraries-correspondence/#aesesjune10.
4. Mary-Jo Romaniuk, quoted in Garett Williams, "The U of M Library Jobs Cut in Staff Restructuring," *Manitoban*, University of Manitoba, August 15, 2016, http://www.themanitoban.com/2016/08/u-of-m-library-jobs-cut-in-staff-restructuring/28779/.
5. Mark Hudson, "UMFA's Open Letter to All AESES Members," email, June 9, 2016, http://aeses.ca/um-libraries-correspondence/#umfajune9; Morris, "AESES Position Discontinuances."
6. Stephanie J. Creary and Lara Rosner, "Mission Accomplished? What Every Leader Should Know about Survivor Syndrome," Conference Board of Canada, executive action report, June 11, 2009, 2, http://www.conferenceboard.ca/e-library/abstract.aspx?did=3084.
7. Laurie Morris, "AESES' Response Letter to President Barnard," letter, July 7, 2016, http://aeses.ca/um-libraries-correspondence/#aesesjuly7.
8. This model is currently employed by eleven of the U15 libraries in Canada. All libraries included in the analysis employed security services during the hours when information desks were not staffed by library assistants. Others also included some of the following: closed or limited stack access, swipe card access, and student patrols.
9. "Working Alone Statement (Policy)," University of Manitoba Libraries, February 17, 2017, accessed on the University of Manitoba Libraries staff intranet, http://staff.lib.umanitoba.ca/index.php?q=workingalone.
10. The UML's "Working Alone Statement (Policy)" is hosted on a staff-only intranet. Contact the authors for access.
11. "Library Support for Researchers," University of Manitoba Libraries LibGuide, last updated May 2, 2019, http://libguides.lib.umanitoba.ca/researchservices.
12. *RSDS Blog*, University of Manitoba Libraries, accessed May 10, 2019, http://libguides.lib.umanitoba.ca/researchservices/rsdsblog.
13. John P. Kotter and Holger Rathgeber, *Our Iceberg Is Melting* (New York: St. Martin's Press, 2006).

Bibliography

Association of Research Libraries. "Graph 1: Service Trends in ARL Libraries, 1991–2015." From *ARL Statistics 2014–15*. Washington, DC: Association of Research Libraries, 2015. http://www.arl.org/storage/documents/service-trends.pdf.

Canadian Association of Research Libraries. *CARL Statistics | Statistiques de l'ABRC: 2015–2016, Salaries | Salaires 2016–2017*. Ottawa, ON: Canadian Association of Research Libraries, September 2017, rev. October 24, 2017. http://www.carl-abrc.ca/wp-content/uploads/2017/10/CARL-ABRC_Stats_Pub_2015-16-v2.pdf.

Creary, Stephanie J., and Lara Rosner. "Mission Accomplished? What Every Leader Should Know about Survivor Syndrome." Conference Board of Canada, executive action report. June 11, 2009. http://www.conferenceboard.ca/e-library/abstract.aspx?did=3084.

Hudson, Mark. "UMFA's Open Letter to All AESES Members." Email, June 9, 2016. http://aeses.ca/um-libraries-correspondence/#umfajune9.

Kotter, John P., and Holger Rathgeber. *Our Iceberg Is Melting: Changing and Succeeding under Any Conditions*. New York: St. Martin's Press, 2006.

Martin, Nick. "U of M, Union Disagree Strongly on Library Staff Cuts." *Winnipeg (MB) Free Press*, June 10, 2016. http://www.winnipegfreepress.com/local/u-of-m-union-disagree-strongly-on-library-staff-cuts-382525141.html.

Morris, Laurie. "AESES' Response Letter to President Barnard." Letter, July 7, 2016. http://aeses.ca/um-libraries-correspondence/#aesesjuly7.

———. "AESES Position Discontinuances at the University of Manitoba." Email, June 10, 2016. http://aeses.ca/um-libraries-correspondence/#aesesjune10.

University of Manitoba Libraries. "Library Support for Researchers." LibGuide, last updated May 2, 2019. http://libguides.lib.umanitoba.ca/researchservices.

———. *RSDS Blog*. Accessed May 10, 2019. http://libguides.lib.umanitoba.ca/researchservices/rsdsblog.

———. "Working Alone Statement (Policy)." February 17, 2017. Accessed on the University of Manitoba Libraries staff intranet. http://staff.lib.umanitoba.ca/index.php?q=workingalone.

Williams, Garett. "The U of M Library Jobs Cut in Staff Restructuring." *Manitoban*, University of Manitoba, August 15, 2016. http://www.themanitoban.com/2016/08/u-of-m-library-jobs-cut-in-staff-restructuring/28779/.

Chapter 15

Analysis
Culture Change

Colleen Boff and Catherine Cardwell

Libraries
Florida State University (FSU)
Northern Arizona University (NAU)
Rice University
University of Manitoba (U of M)

Introduction

Each of these stories takes place at a large, public R1 or R2 university, one of which is in Canada. It comes as no surprise that culture change related to library employees is at the heart of these stories since people are central to a culture in an organization. Some aspect of public service unites these examples, from an emphasis on library users at Rice University and NAU to repurposing the work of employees at the other two institutions. The common thread among these stories is how to serve stakeholders or users better while breaking down silos among employees and library departments. What differs from institution to institution is the degree to which employees embraced these changes. Culture changes at FSU and U of M took place across multiple libraries, whereas the changes in culture at NAU and Rice primarily took place in a single library.

I. Warm-up Phase
STAGE 1: ESTABLISHING A SENSE OF URGENCY

The catalyst for change at three of the four institutions in this category was intentional and part of a broader planning process. Strategic planning was a driving force for culture change at NAU, where newly crafted mission and vision statements clearly put engagement with users at the forefront of library operations. Strategic changes to the wider Research and Learning Services (RLS) division were driving change at the STEM libraries at FSU. However, the library administration specifically called for a task force to examine modes of communication in the library at Rice in response to strategic planning at the university level. Although culture changes at these three institutions stemmed from hunches that they could do better for their users, the changes at U of M were in response to a much more urgent and dire situation. Services to patrons were in jeopardy due to unexpected staff layoffs. Library employees at this last institution were

169

dealing with low morale, fear, and anxiety to a much greater degree than employees at the other institutions where entry into culture change was much more gradual.

STAGE 2: CREATING THE GUIDING COALITION

Except for U of M, new leadership was at the helm of these change stories. The guiding coalition at FSU was a collaboration between a new associate dean of the library-wide RLS division and the STEM library director. Together, they crafted a much-needed position for a STEM data and research librarian, who was hired from within and quickly became an integral part of the guiding coalition. Together, this team of three led the change until the STEM library director took a position elsewhere and the STEM data and research librarian became the director. Library administration at NAU hired in the talent they were seeking to support their change. They selected a head of user services, who had oversight for the new User Experience (UX) Group with library-wide representation. Though the guiding coalition at Rice consisted of members of the existing marketing and customer service committee with fairly broad library representation, the drivers behind the customer service program that this group worked on were the new access services manager and the organizational and development manager, another recent hire who worked in human resources. The guiding coalition at U of M consisted of two head librarians from the three largest libraries in its library system. Trusted to do so, they stepped up to lead others through the chaos. Their library administration approved their plan to find ways to reduce hours the library was staffed, increase staff during peak hours, increase support to librarians, provide more fulfilling work for support staff, and improve morale and work satisfaction.

STAGE 3: DEVELOPING A VISION AND STRATEGY

As the result of a larger library-wide FSU strategic planning process, the STEM libraries were charged with increasing the level of service provided to scholars as a major opportunity and as their top priority. A STEM library committee was formed to work on this, and through the Balanced Scorecard process, they decided to raise awareness of library services and programs to their community, build relationships with stakeholders, and increase outreach to international students at the undergraduate level. They also wanted to continue the momentum with a few emerging initiatives. To do this, they needed to centralize some of the day-to-day access functions of building operations with the main library as part of an RLS-wide reorganization. In a similar vein, the team at U of M was trying to get a handle on staffing issues related to day-to-day operations and in support of user needs. Their vision was to create a sustainable support staff model—one built on collaboration and designed to support student success and the librarians. The guiding coalition wrote a staffing proposal that called for a tiered model where staff would be moved to peak hours during the day. During less busy times, private security guards would provide oversight of the library. They sought and got approval from deans and department heads within the library and external to the library as well. Phase 1 of their plan called for a pilot in one of the libraries to expand the hours but reduce the staffed hours. Phase 2 called for giving support staff fewer desk hours and more meaningful work to offset librarian loads. In phase 3, they replicated what they had tried in the pilot with the rest of the libraries. The vision at both of these institutions was to change the roles and responsibilities of individual employees in order to create a culture where employees felt that they were moving forward with new initiatives and going beyond the routine operations of keeping the doors open.

At NAU and Rice, the vision and strategy were centered around the creation of a new assessment approach at the former institution and a new customer training program at the latter. Employees were skeptical of efforts to shift the culture because of earlier attempts or ingrained habits that suggested significant barriers. The dean and new head of user services at NAU created the vision, which also served as the charge for the guiding coalition. The group worked together to explore the design-thinking process, learn more about their users, and establish some guiding principles specifically around making their website more accessible. The working group at Rice had a similar trajectory in that they set about their work through the development of personas for each of their customer stakeholders. After they created a vision statement, they divided into smaller groups and started to build content that eventually served as a custom-built, institution-specific training manual.

Stage 4: Communicating the Change Vision

Readers will find typical communication strategies in these change stories, such as presentations at staff meetings, department visits, email communications, intranet posts, and newsletter updates. A few unique approaches are important to highlight. In their charge, the leadership at NAU specifically referred to the UX group as consultants. This careful wording was intentional and signaled to staff that members of the UX group were partners and collaborators rather than decision-makers. At Rice, the planning team communicated customer service exemplars by actively modeling them in their daily interactions with others. Finally, at U of M, the two heads created a communication plan, which was especially important given that infrequent communication in the past contributed to the morale problems the team was trying to remedy. This team also stressed the importance of contextualizing communications by reminding employees of how changes are related to appropriate library and university planning documents.

II. Introducing New Practices Phase

Stage 5: Empowering Broad-Based Action

FSU and U of M experienced similar barriers when making changes to staff responsibilities. The employees at U of M seemed to have higher levels of anxiety due to recent and unexpected layoffs. From a leadership perspective, the two head librarians expressed frustration with delays because they lacked the authority to make decisions autonomously. Other frustrations included staff wanting to revert to old ways of doing their jobs and having to contend with vacancies. Some librarians at U of M were reluctant to delegate some of their responsibilities for fear of becoming obsolete and losing their jobs too, while librarians at FSU were uncertain of what to do with the time they gained from not having to do the daily operations. At FSU, the librarians are now expected to engage with department faculty for 25 percent of their job responsibilities, yet these engagements were not well defined.

The UX group at NAU began to change the decision-making culture at their library by conducting usability testing with users to make small changes to their website. The user became the decision-maker for changes rather than the staff, who were used to following a more hierarchical decision-making process. After a few successes, they began to gain confidence in this approach to website changes. At Rice, the customer service team gained confidence by piloting their training with the leadership team, who responded positively to the experience with a few minor suggestions for improvement.

STAGE 6: GENERATING SHORT-TERM WINS

In spite of the turmoil taking place behind the scenes at U of M, the student response to increased access to the libraries was positive. The head librarians leading the culture change at U of M were able to get some of the support staff position descriptions reclassified, which resulted in equal or higher compensation. Perceived inequities among employee groups were diminishing, and job satisfaction and morale were increasing. At FSU, work-life balance for the STEM librarians was better now that they did not have the burden of keeping the facility open with too few librarians. Their individual appointments and instruction increased, and they were able to hire two new STEM librarians to further their mission to engage more meaningfully with department faculty.

The UX team at NAU created personas of their various users to ensure they understood their users. They also solicited feedback from staff and users about their suggestions for changes to the website. This information was used to design the usability studies. Most of the changes they made to the website were small and aesthetic, but all changes were informed directly by users. Rice's short-term wins included a successful pilot of the training session with library administration and a high participation rate for the training session they conducted with staff. In spite of failed attempts in the past to conduct customer training, the reaction to their custom training materials was positive.

STAGE 7: CONSOLIDATING GAINS AND PRODUCING MORE CHANGE

After many short-term wins that amounted to improved service and employee satisfaction, the head librarians at U of M have begun working with employees to move away from traditional tasks and toward new initiatives. STEM librarians at FSU embraced a spirit of continual evolution, a change in their culture, as they are finding concrete ways to collaborate with others on campus. They have reviewed more positions and have a commitment to rework vacated positions in support of the new service model and culture.

With a few successes under their belt, the UX group at NAU split into two subgroups: UX-Web and UX-Spaces. The former group agreed to collaborate with campus ITS to be early adopters of their new CMS while also migrating to a new discovery layer, ultimately resulting in a complete overhaul of the library homepage. They continued their work with the user at the center of decision-making. Through focus groups, they defined key services that should be readily available on the newly designed website. The UX space group gathered input about the physical library from users by placing whiteboards throughout the library and asking for comments. They also conducted a library mapping exercise with users. They learned that they needed to improve signage at the point of service within the building rather than solely relying on students to go to a website for details. Just as UX was becoming the cultural norm to facilitate change at NAU, the culture was changing at Rice too. All new library staff at Rice are expected to take the customer service training within three weeks of starting.

III. Grounding Phase

STAGE 8: ANCHORING NEW APPROACHES IN THE CULTURE

The culture at FSU continues to evolve as the STEM librarians discover new ways to serve the faculty and students. They are even beginning to collaborate with librarians in other disciplines. Silos are eroding at U of M, and teams are beginning to form organically and tackle new initiatives. A culture of distrust and uncertainty has been replaced by one where employees feel that they meaningfully contribute and that they are safe to offer new ideas. Though upskilling and reassignments are still in progress, consistent and contextualized communication has begun to change the culture at U of M.

The customer training program at Rice was successfully implemented and delivered with the expectation that newcomers will engage with the materials. The team has plans to offer refreshers, too. Orchestrating change through the lens of the user has altered the culture at NAU, from one where decisions were made through a traditional hierarchical structure to one where decisions are made faster, with user input, and without fear of reprimand for failure. NAU's UX team thought they would have benefited from hiring a consultant to help them with UX methodology, but one could argue that a team of people learning through short-term wins and small failures was beneficial and helped them build community. They also anchored this new approach by hiring and training student employees to serve as user experience assistants to help them gather data.

It is also worth noting that department name changes—to User Services and Experiences Department at NAU and to STEM Research and Learning Services at FSU—signaled that these new approaches were becoming rooted in their culture.

Analysis and Conclusions

A common complaint among contributing authors about the use of Kotter's model is that libraries are not typically competitive entities like businesses, nor does change happen in a linear fashion as he describes in his model. The authors of the change stories in this category referenced these same criticisms. FSU pointed out that their change is still underway. It is safe to say that this is likely the case for the other institutions as well. U of M emphasized the importance of Stages 1 and 2, as does Kotter. Their mantra of consistent and contextualized communication served them well as they emerged with a much stronger culture. NAU gives credit for their success to their exploration of UX, their creation of a new organizational structure to support it, and trusted employees who were able to run with their new responsibilities and deliver results.

TIPS FOR CULTURE CHANGE

It comes as no surprise that the tips in this section focus on people and their interactions internally with the library and externally with users.

- The librarians at Rice stress the importance of modeling the type of behavior they wanted to see from library staff. They sent thank-you notes to participants, sent follow-up emails to those who participated in their customer service training, and continued to reinforce the material offered in their training. Library staff at FSU and U of M exhibited fear and anxiety throughout the change process as they transitioned away from historical organizational structures and processes, even though those structures and processes were unsustainable. Both institutions report that their staff members experience better work-life balance and a better work environment now that they have implemented new approaches to meet the needs of a service-based library. It may be helpful if change leaders help people understand how change can improve their experiences in and out of work when they let go of historical approaches.
- Barriers exist between departments in a library as well as between a library and its external users. When breaking down departmental silos, change leaders should also consider ways to break down silos between libraries and their users. NAU accomplished this with its UX groups examining its website and physical library and allowing more nimble decision-making based on user needs.
- A theme throughout all of the change stories is a move toward collaborative, consultative decision-making and away from top-down decision-making. While it may require more communication and time, it helps people get on board and contribute to the change process. NAU went so far as to describe its UX groups as consultants who worked broadly across departments, not as decision-makers. Librarians at U of M also modeled the kind of consultative decision-making needed to implement the changes they desired.

PART IV
NEW ROLES

Chapter 16

Mission Renewal

Information Literacy as a Campus Diversity and Inclusion Program

Neal Baker, Kate Leuschke Blinn, and Bonita Washington-Lacey

Setting the Change Stage

Looking to demonstrate library ROI and value to the campus mission? Seeking to tie your library to student success? Dreaming of partnerships with other units? Earlham College in Richmond, Indiana, reframed part of its information literacy outreach as a diversity and inclusion strategy for first-generation students—the Library Immersion Fellows Teams (LIFT) Program.[1] This reframing strategy benefits the college, the library, and underrepresented first-generation students. The strategy is political, calculated to impress administrative stakeholders and donors by showing how the library can impact the retention rate for an "at-risk" student demographic. As such, it tries to actualize the logic of Megan Oakleaf's influential 2010 publication, *The Value of Academic Libraries: A Comprehensive Research Review and Report*.[2] At the same time, the LIFT Program is sincerely practical with an eye to social justice. Librarians lead a coordinated effort that now spans the offices of the Academic Dean, the registrar, the Writing Center, the Center for Career and Community Engagement, and the Center for Global Education.

The LIFT Program's emphasis on first-generation students is in alignment with the Earlham College ethos. A private, residential national liberal arts school with an enrollment of approximately 1,100 undergraduates, Earlham has the Carnegie Classification "Baccalaureate Colleges; Arts & Science Focus." An Earlham education is shaped by the perspectives of the Religious Society of Friends (Quakers). Core principles and practices include respect for persons, peace and justice, and community. Even so, foundational tenets can be problematic as acknowledged by the campus "Diversity Aspiration Vision Statement":

> Earlham College exists within a history of systemic cultural and economic oppression that has denied certain groups equal access to education and power. To help redress such injustice and to make our college community more representative of our society and world, we seek to promote the presence and voice of groups that have been historically oppressed because of such factors as race, ethnicity, sex, gender, sexual orientation, socioeconomic class, and physical ability.[3]

In this view, the LIFT Program is a resource commitment to help retain a higher percentage of underrepresented first-generation students from the United States.

I. Warm-up Phase

STAGE 1: ESTABLISHING A SENSE OF URGENCY

The LIFT Program arose out of a January 2013 faculty retreat. A plenary presentation convened by the Senior Associate Vice President for Academic Affairs (SAVPAA)/Registrar shared a longitudinal analysis of student retention data, including that of various compositional groups (e.g., international students, student athletes). The data suggested that certain groups were less likely to persist with their Earlham education, based on retention rates keyed to milestones such as the start of third and fifth semesters. Among other findings, there was a persistence gap involving first-generation students that reflected national trends. One way to summarize the Earlham version of the persistence gap between first-generation and continuing generation students is via comparative retention averages over a seven-year period:

- Average Entering Class Cohort Persistence, Returning to 3rd Semester, 2006–2012
  - O Continuing Generation Students   84.7%
  - O First-Generation Students   79.0%
  - O Difference between Two Groups   5.7%
- Averaging Entering Class Cohort Persistence, Returning to 8th Semester, 2006–2012
  - O Continuing Generation Students   73.0%
  - O First-Generation Students   65.7%
  - O Difference between Two Groups   7.3%

The SAVPAA/Registrar's presentation of the data ended with a call for assistance on retention efforts. Although the call for assistance was pitched to the entire Earlham faculty, only the library responded. The Library Director went to the SAVPAA/Registrar and offered to prioritize librarian outreach to first-generation students if suitable arrangements could be found. The offer was situated within a campus tradition of library instruction, pioneered by head librarian Evan Ira Farber between 1962 and 1994—"his profession's most articulate spokesman for college librarianship and bibliographic instruction."[4] The campus tradition continued with head librarian Thomas G. Kirk between 1994 and 2009, recognized by ACRL as 2004 Academic/Research Librarian of the Year.[5] Led by Kirk, Earlham received the 2001 Excellence in Academic Libraries college category award for "almost 40 years of excellence in contributions to student learning; in partnering with faculty; and in the transformation of the educational program of Earlham College."[6]

STAGE 2: CREATING THE GUIDING COALITION

The SAVPAA/Registrar was enthusiastic about librarian contributions to student learning and partnering with faculty. Earlham librarians are regularly assigned first-year advisees and serve in key campus governance roles such as chairing major committees and presiding as the chair of the faculty senate equivalent. Similarly, Earlham librarians are entrusted to routinely teach first-year seminars and often teach upper-level courses based on their educational backgrounds (e.g., GIS courses; courses in art, religion, and media studies). Moreover, Earlham librarians frequently lead credit-bearing, off-campus programs for entire semesters or during August and May.

The SAVPAA/Registrar and the Library Director assembled a teaching team that started with the library liaisons. The team was accustomed to providing library instruction and teaching in the curriculum and over time grew to include the Writing Center Director and the director of the federally funded McNair Program for underrepresented students seeking graduate school matriculation. This same group served as a decision-making team that functioned via consultation and consensus, in keeping with Earlham governance. The SAVPAA/Registrar and the Library Director co-led the team, soliciting their combined campus trust network that included senior leadership, faculty, and alumni. In so doing, they received initial funding approval from the Academic Dean and the president.

Team dynamics have always been congenial, factoring in disparate tolerances for consensus decision-making processes in the first place. Not everyone shares the same expectation about the merits of often lengthy conversational decisions. Mutual admiration always wins out, happily, and no single person or office could make LIFT happen alone. The teaching/leadership team now coordinates with other campus units as the program seeks to build additional partnerships that will be discussed below. In so doing, LIFT will probably draw in colleagues from Student Life that are usually associated with first-generation student success initiatives, yet were absent at the outset due to the relative strengths of the library and other student priorities for personnel involved with, for example, residential and multicultural affairs.

STAGE 3: DEVELOPING A VISION AND STRATEGY

The vision was originally established by the SAVPAA/Registrar and Library Director. In a March 2013 memo to the Academic Dean, they requested authorization to help the overall admissions yield and retention rate by inviting fifteen to thirty admitted first-generation students to participate in the LIFT initiative. As a targeted strategy, the LIFT initiative matched four small groups of first-generation students with a personal research librarian during the first eight weeks of fall semester. Every LIFT student was awarded an iPad Mini to use for their four years at Earlham and beyond. Meeting for ninety minutes one night per week with their librarian, LIFT students took a one-credit tutorial in information literacy learning outcomes—"the ability to know when there is a need for information, to be able to identify, locate, evaluate, and effectively and responsibly use and share that information for the problem at hand."[7] The tutorial occurred within the context of assigned weekly readings, research, and discussion based on current events, using media like the *New York Times*, the *Economist*, *Scientific American*, the *Earlham Word*, and TED Talks. To gain more perspectives on current events, students utilized a tool kit of library search engines including LexisNexis Academic, JSTOR, the *Earlham Word* student newspaper archive, and subject-specific databases (e.g., PsycINFO) and encyclopedias. The result was such that students engaged with trending issues while acquiring research competencies, library experience, and personal connections with an Earlham administrative faculty member and a few of their classmates in a small-group setting.

The strategy was built out by the teaching team. They developed specific assignments and met a few times during the first semester to calibrate their teaching efforts. As the semester progressed, and during debriefings afterward that incorporated student feedback, the strategy started to shift to emphasize the power of the peer cohort arrangement. In other words, the librarians quickly realized that the affective impact of bringing together a small group of first-generation students with an Earlham employee was arguably more valuable than information literacy outcomes per se. The simple act of meeting weekly as a peer learning community seemed to be as important as any of the weekly content. While the phrase "structuring tension" might be a bit overstated, the interplay between connecting first-generation students with one another and with library content became a productive dynamic undergirding the LIFT Program from the first 2013 classes onward. On any given week, students engaged with an information literacy topic and with each other. Getting to know about aspects of the library and about research contexts also involved getting to know fellow first-generation classmates and a librarian. So in a given LIFT session, the students would spend part of the time building relationships (e.g., weekly sharing about challenges faced; structured discussions about family, ethnicity, and other identity categories) and part of the time building information literacy competencies (e.g., how to search a database, how to use Zotero).

STAGE 4: COMMUNICATING THE CHANGE VISION

Internal communication to campus colleagues began at the fall 2013 faculty retreat, where faculty were asked to reach out to incoming first-generation students and refer them to the LIFT team. Over the next years and continuing up to now, the annual faculty retreat became a venue to summarize LIFT developments. Meanwhile, every summer the team works with admissions to identify admitted first-generation students and send a letter to their families and invite them to join LIFT. While senior administrators within the Academic Affairs division are aware of LIFT, the details escape most faculty members. Beginning in 2015, the team approached the campus Marketing and Communications department to publish information about LIFT in the alumni magazine, and in 2016, the Library Director was approached by a Senior Gift Officer in Institutional Advancement to meet with a prospective donor. A trip to meet the donor in New Orleans led to a $120,000 initial gift that would fund three consecutive years of all-expenses-paid off-campus May Terms for LIFT students, many of whom have never or rarely had the opportunity to travel away from home or campus. Each May Term is co-led by a librarian/faculty pair.

Building on the momentum of the $120,000 gift, the team began to ramp up external communication in 2017. LIFT was featured as a chapter in ACRL's *The First-Year Experience Cookbook*[8] and the first LIFT presentations were delivered during the next several months at numerous conferences.[9] To support these efforts, and to supplement internal communication at the same time, Earlham Marketing and Communications created a LIFT website in 2018. The website includes an application form, an overview of the program, and student testimonials. It will be updated as LIFT and its students develop and figures into a hybrid sort of internal/external communication as the team reports on developments to members of the Earlham Alumni Council and board of trustees.

II. Introducing New Practices Phase

STAGE 5: EMPOWERING BROAD-BASED ACTION

The introduction of the off-campus May Term for students in 2017 changed the context for the first-semester seminar. LIFT instructors continued to teach the same content, balancing Earlham-specific transitions and resources with applied information literacy. While the potential of a travel opportunity was a good draw for students to join LIFT, that future focus added to the challenge for instructors trying to help students focus on the present and engage with the LIFT curriculum.

Another challenge was the limited opportunity itself. Based on funding, not all students who completed the fall semester could be invited to travel for the May off-campus program. An application process, including preliminary questions and in-person interviews, was created. This served as a skill-building and practicing opportunity for the students, highlighted the magnitude of the opportunity, and allowed the program leaders to choose among the applicants. The first program was in Montreal in 2017; based on the available budget, all fourteen students who applied were invited. For the Hawaii program in 2018, a higher cost-per-student meant that ten out of fourteen applicants were invited.

Determining the criteria for participation was a challenge. Program leaders consulted extensively with other LIFT instructors and team members about the discernment process. In order to be as inclusive as possible, the original budget for eight students was adjusted to allow ten students to travel. The leaders invited students for whom they felt that the program would be most impactful, which meant in some cases favoring those who had not already had experiences traveling or living away from home.

Both the Montreal and Hawaii programs were successes in terms of creating opportunities for transformative change in students' lives. Student reflections on their learning as it happened in a particular place far from home and campus bear out the uniqueness of the experience and their appreciation for the change itself. For example, during our orientation to the 2018 Hawaii program, we invited a Hawaiian Earlham student to be our teaching assistant, and she taught the students a chant in Hawaiian. The chant (E Ho Mai) is meant to be used to ask for permission to enter and to learn from the place you are entering. When the students were practicing at Earlham, they were awkward and giggling singing in front of each other. But when we stood at the foot of the stairs in front of Iolani Palace and chanted E Ho Mai, and then an older, very experienced docent sang a reply chant welcoming us in, the students were proud and sincere. We also heard young men at the Polynesian Cultural Center, in the Hawaiian section, chanting the same thing, and the students reflected on that as part of our discussion of tourism, education, and authentic engagement with the place. With reference to the 2017 Montreal program, one LIFT participant reports that she is now certain that she wishes to attend graduate school at McGill University based on her time in the Québécois metropolis.

STAGE 6: GENERATING SHORT-TERM WINS

Some LIFT instructors introduced the creation of a digital story into their first-semester course assignments. These were open-ended prompts, usually on the positive and constructive theme of telling a story about some moment when the student "was first" or when they did something for the first time. The stories they created were often about being a first-generation student or their first days at Earlham.

While teaching and learning the digital storytelling software could have taken up several class sessions, instructors focused on the content of the stories instead of the technical details and required students to learn the software independently.

When the donor came to Earlham's campus for the closing LIFT dinner, late in the fall semester of 2017–18, one instructor shared several of the digital stories that students had made. They were personal stories, endearing in their imperfections and remarkable for the stories of growth and reflection they shared. The donor also met with the students who had traveled to Montreal. These in-person and digital interactions led the donor to extend her support for an additional two years of funding.

Also in 2017, collaboration with the Alumni Council created a short-term win, the opportunity for LIFT students to work with alumni mentors. These interactions connected students with Earlham alumni without specific goals beyond the connection itself and the sharing of academic and career advice. Earlham alumni were excited about the opportunity to "give back" to the college of their time and insight, especially as part of the program for students who might not have many adults in their lives who had completed college.

STAGE 7: CONSOLIDATING GAINS AND PRODUCING MORE CHANGE

The team of LIFT instructors and supporters faced several challenges to implementing a program that continued to change each year: communicating across departments and units of the college, understanding the short- and long-term needs and concerns specific to first-generation first-year students, and offering an engaging curriculum that met the needs of those students.

Communication across units of the college, including Academic Affairs, admissions, the registrar's office, athletics, teaching faculty, Alumni Development, and Marketing and Communications, is essential to the cultivation of the LIFT cohort, the support of individual students, and the growth of the program. Individuals from these units, which have separate reporting lines and structures, must share a common understanding of the program and be able to accurately communicate it to potential students, their parents, and other constituencies.

While the program was created for first-generation students, different instructors used different tactics to engage with students about that aspect of LIFT. For some it was a mere mention in the first meeting session, acknowledging that the students had only one characteristic in common (their first-generation status) and that they had many individual characteristics and histories that they also brought to bear. For other instructors, engaging with the idea of first-generation student status meant asking the students to read an academic article about the characteristics of first-generation students. Discussing the article allowed students to talk about how their own individual experiences matched or differed from the generalizations described in the article as well as to engage with the idea of stereotypes, misunderstandings, and labels as they operate within the academic world of student support.

The teaching team met each August before the fall semester and began to plan for the fall semester. These meetings were moments of strategic reflection on the outcomes of the prior year and the changes that had taken place since then on campus. The SAVPAA/Registrar generally attended these meetings, building in communication about the vision of the program as well as specifics about the incoming group of students.

The instructors also met for strategic reflection and sharing in the middle of the fall. This second meeting also included some attention devoted to planning the important closing dinner and reflection that marks the end of the LIFT fall program. The students have been meeting in their small groups for several weeks, and the dinner reunites them with the other sections of LIFT students, instructors, and the SAVPAA/Registrar. The structured sit-down meal provides an opportunity for LIFT students to reflect on and share about their experience and their perception of the value of the program (students also complete standard course evaluations). Students often describe their growth and changes they've felt over a few short weeks as they transition into college. They describe specific successes that they attribute to LIFT, such as feeling more comfortable accessing or understanding academic papers for course assignments or speaking up in their class discussions. And they describe ongoing challenges, such as learning to find their place in the campus community and the ways that the interactions in their small LIFT cohorts helped them grow in confidence. Their reflections are always remarkably sincere, emotional, and positive.

A final meeting after the fall semester course ended provided instructors the opportunity to debrief and share their own joys and concerns. Sharing ideas for specific activities and readings at the second and third meetings was an important strategy for overcoming frustration, aligning priorities, and maintaining momentum.

III. Grounding Phase

STAGE 8: ANCHORING NEW APPROACHES IN THE CULTURE

The LIFT Program continues to thrive and to change. Each year, LIFT instructors invite students from previous cohorts to visit class to talk about their experiences openly with the first-year students, proving that coming back as a sophomore or junior is possible and that other students around them are also first-generation students. As the first cohort of LIFT students graduated in 2017, the first-year students going to Montreal the next day served as graduation ushers. Watching those students successfully complete their college years at Earlham and walk across the stage to receive diplomas was another moment of meaningful motivation for those students who had completed their first year and continued to face their own challenges. Seeing the graduating seniors, connecting with upperclassmen, hearing the reflections from the cohort of students as they complete the fall semester course—all these moments helped create a change in the culture of first-generation students in the Earlham community.

Analysis and Conclusions

The strategies employed by the teaching team and the other members of college departments that support LIFT and LIFT students continue to be successful—using both collaborative brainstorming and decision-making and allowing individuals (e.g., the

SAVPAA/Registrar or Library Director) to take advantage of opportunities as they arise, just as they did when the program was originally created. Currently, the LIFT leadership team is considering how to respond to support and interest from the college's board of trustees, which requested a presentation of LIFT and offered financial resources going forward. As of August 2018, a LIFT data point to leverage with an eye to future consolidation involves the May off-campus programs. Cohort retention for 2017 Montreal participants was 93 percent (13 out of 14, with one student not returning due to dire family circumstances unrelated to Earlham), and 2018 Hawaii retention appears to be on track to match or exceed that level. In May 2019, LIFT students will travel to Italy with a librarian and a biology professor. Meanwhile, we're in discussion with Earlham's Center for Career and Community Engagement about ways to create a semester of vocational exploration for LIFT participants that builds on information literacy competencies.

Using the Kotter framework to reframe Earlham's LIFT Program was informative. In particular, we came to realize the importance of the warm-up phase. The hard work needed to convey urgency, assemble a coalition, articulate a vision and viable strategy, and then communicate it to other stakeholders are all determinative stages. Each stage comes with political and operational complexities that often mean negotiating multiple stakeholder agendas, and the affective angles can be vast and deep. The LIFT Program vision was (and is) atypical for just about any academic library as it is hands-on "student success" initiative territory often associated with residential life units or diversity and inclusion offices, and not librarians. The affective angles—primordial feelings that arise from notions of ownership, turf, threat, and the perception of being left out of the loop, and so on—can in fact have results that resonate for years in all sorts of unexpected ways. While the LIFT implementation happily managed to avoid affective disasters, as we look to grow the program in tandem with new unit partners, we will be extremely mindful of what is essentially a second, all-important warm-up phase.

Notes

1. "LIFT: Library Immersion Fellows Teams," Earlham College, accessed May 24, 2019, http://www.earlham.edu/lift.
2. Association of College and Research Libraries, *The Value of Academic Libraries*, researched by Megan Oakleaf (Chicago: American Library Association, 2010).
3. "Diversity Aspiration Vision Statement," Earlham College, accessed July 28, 2018, http://www.earlham.edu/policies-and-handbooks/general/diversity-aspiration-vision-statement/.
4. Richard Hume Werking, "The Library as an Instrument of Education: Appreciating Evan Farber," in *College Libraries and the Teaching/Learning Process: Selections from the Writings of Evan Ira Farber*, ed. David Gansz (Richmond, IN: Earlham College Press, 2007), v.
5. American Library Association, "Tom Kirk's Acceptance Speech," July 7, 2006, accessed August 3, 2019, http://www.ala.org/acrl/awards/achievementawards/librarianoftheyear/kirkspeech.
6. "ACRL Selects 'Excellence in Academic Libraries' Winners," news release, American Library Association, February 2001, accessed August 3, 2019, http://www.ala.org/Template.cfm?Section=archive&template=/contentmanagement/contentdisplay.cfm&ContentID=9374.
7. "Information Literacy VALUE Rubric," Association of American Colleges and Universities, accessed July 28, 2018, https://www.aacu.org/value/rubrics/information-literacy.
8. Neal Baker and Jane Pinzino, "A Reserved Table for First-Generation Students," in *The First-Year Experience Cookbook* ed. Raymond Pun and Meggan Houlihan (Chicago: Association of College and Research Libraries, 2017), 59-60.
9. "First-Generation, Continuing Generation…. All Generations: Improving Support for Endurance and Success," HEDS Annual Conference, Cincinnati, OH, June 2017; "Earlham College LIFT

Program," Global Liberal Arts Alliance: Border Studies in the Liberal Arts Workshop, Franklin University, Switzerland, July 2017; "Mission Critical: Information Literacy Reframed as a University Equality and Diversity Initiative," LILAC 2018, University of Liverpool, UK, April 2018; "Building Competencies, Connections, and Persistence with First-Generation Students," WILU 2018, University of Ottawa, June 2018; "LIFT: A Library-Instructional Technology Program for First-Generation Students," EDUCAUSE Annual Conference 2018, Denver, CO, November 2018.

Bibliography

American Library Association. "ACRL Selects 'Excellence in Academic Libraries' Winners." News release, February 2001. Accessed August 3, 2019. http://www.ala.org/Template.cfm?Section=archive&template=/contentmanagement/contentdisplay.cfm&ContentID=9374.

———. "Tom Kirk's Acceptance Speech." July 7, 2006. Accessed August 3, 2019. http://www.ala.org/acrl/awards/achievementawards/librarianoftheyear/kirkspeech.

Association of American Colleges and Universities. "Information Literacy VALUE Rubric." Accessed July 28, 2018. https://www.aacu.org/value/rubrics/information-literacy.

———. *The Value of Academic Libraries: A Comprehensive Research Review and Report.* Researched by Megan Oakleaf. Chicago: Association of College and Research Libraries, 2010.

Baker, Neal and Jane Pinzino. "A Reserved Table for First-Generation Students." In *The First-Year Experience Cookbook*, ed. Raymond Pun and Meggan Houlihan, 59-60. Chicago: Association of College and Research Libraries, 2017.

Earlham College. "Diversity Aspiration Vision Statement." Accessed July 28, 2018. http://www.earlham.edu/policies-and-handbooks/general/diversity-aspiration-vision-statement/.

———. "LIFT: Library Immersion Fellows Teams." Accessed May 24, 2019. http://www.earlham.edu/lift.

Werking, Richard Hume. "The Library as an Instrument of Education: Appreciating Evan Farber." In *College Libraries and the Teaching/Learning Process: Selections from the Writings of Evan Ira Farber*, edited by David Gansz, v–xiv. Richmond, IN: Earlham College Press, 2007.

Chapter 17

Creative Collaborations for Change

A New Take on an Old Idea Produces Unique Transformative Library Internships for Grad Students

Brian W. Keith and Laurie N. Taylor

Setting the Change Stage

Libraries are adjusting to evolving academic and research environments. This requires new technologies and services and the inclusion of professional expertise and abilities from multiple disciplines. Concurrently, the declining market for tenure-track academic positions and increasing competition for other professional positions are challenging both to graduate students, seeking career opportunities aligned with their long and costly educational experience, and to graduate programs, seeking to place their graduates in positions utilizing their hard-earned skills, knowledge, and abilities. In this environment, students need exposure to alternative careers to expand their professional horizons and their opportunities to gain marketable work experience.

The coauthors, from the University of Florida (UF), recognized this nexus. UF is a major comprehensive, public land-grant institution, with an R1 Carnegie Classification ("Doctoral Universities—Highest Research Activity"). The 2016–17 total twelve-month enrollment at UF was 58,993 students, with 21,142 graduate students. In the 2016–17 academic year, UF awarded 4,101 master's and 2,008 doctoral degrees.[1] The George A. Smathers Libraries at UF form the largest information network in the state of Florida, which is the third most populous state in the United States. The libraries have traditionally supported individual unpaid and paid internships related to specific projects. Faculty and staff at the department level generally administered these internships. The pay, if any, and the assigned duties and learning outcomes varied considerably from one

internship to the next. It is likely some internships were not aligned specifically with career-advancing, professional-level, experiential learning outcomes in mind.

The coauthors identified an opportunity and envisioned an opportunity to enact change to improve internships for all stakeholders and served as the catalyst for a cross-departmental team to radically remake the graduate internships conceptually and programmatically into a formal, organized program within the libraries. Through collaboration with teaching department faculty and faculty across the libraries, the leaders developed a design for the new graduate internship program, where unique, purposeful internships are proposed and led through collaboration between librarians and academic faculty. Awards are made via a supportive but competitive process, and the outcome for the students must include "CV-worthy" accomplishments oriented to their learning and professional prospects.

The coauthors recruited collaborators, communicated through established channels and informal settings to gain input, refined the program concept, and developed advocates and champions to implement the vision. The result was the UF Smathers Graduate Student Internship Program, launched in 2015–2016, with the first awards announced in spring 2016. The program began with the creation of supportive infrastructure and policies and an Internship Program Committee to implement, steward, and improve the program.

I. Warm-up Phase

STAGE 1: ESTABLISHING A SENSE OF URGENCY

Both coauthors had previous experience in leading transformative change, including integrating UF's Health Science Center Libraries into the University Libraries, and with programs for the digital humanities and digital scholarship.[2] The coauthors had frequently collaborated on projects and programs related to changing needs and structures for academic and research libraries. They had also collaborated on opportunities to align with greater university needs, including on the Digital Humanities Working Group and Digital Humanities Graduate Certificate.[3]

The specific catalyst for the new internship program came together from several concurrent events within the libraries, including

- the Smathers Libraries' strategic planning process and the resulting release of the 2014–2017 *Strategic Directions*, which emphasized "transformative collaboration"[4]
- participants in internships recognizing that internships within the libraries were inconsistent experiences and lacked optimal support, with each intern director creating training, providing onboarding, and securing funding
- major changes to the workforce in the libraries with the highly successful placement of several new hires possessing advanced degrees in their subject areas or from other technical fields, and not library or information science degrees

Simultaneous to these library developments, the Great Recession from 2007 to 2009 and dramatic declines in academic institution hiring for faculty across the US fostered important campus-wide discussions on the need for additional career-training opportunities and especially for internship programs for humanities graduate students.

Within their numerous campus collaborations, the coauthors worked closely with teaching faculty in the arts and humanities. Those collaborations included the Digital Scholarship Librarian serving on the Arts and Humanities Graduate Coordinators group, which discussed the critical need for graduate student internships in its August 2015 meeting. Participants discussed the need for graduate student internships in the context of problems and opportunities facing humanities graduate education and academia more broadly. The discussion included the shared desire to foster a more positive and productive environment for better engendering collaboration for mutual aid and benefit while graduate students are undertaking their studies and for improved employment outcomes. The Digital Scholarship Librarian shared the notes from the meeting with the Associate Dean in the libraries; he recognized the potential opportunity for the Smathers Libraries in the form of more structured internships. Their subsequent conversations led to the generation of a programmatic concept and to the Digital Scholarship Librarian and the Associate Dean becoming the core of the guiding coalition for realizing this concept.

STAGE 2: CREATING THE GUIDING COALITION

Within the libraries, the core team for developing the Smathers Graduate Student Internship Program was initially comprised of the two coauthors of this chapter: Brian W. Keith, Associate Dean for Administrative Services and Faculty Affairs, and Dr. Laurie Taylor, Digital Scholarship Librarian. They frequently collaborate for change initiatives. These include initiatives to foster transformative partnerships and coalitions for changes. This work to foster partnerships is in recognition that partnerships and coalitions are essential for libraries to support communities of practice, including developing new technologies as embedded with the sociotechnical community needs, and research and resource development to support the changing workforce within academic and research libraries, as with the ARL Position Description Bank.[5]

Acting on their vision for an internship program, the Associate Dean and Digital Scholarship Librarian met with Dr. Elizabeth Dale, a professor in the UF Department of History and Fredric G. Levin College of Law and at that time the Graduate Coordinator for History. Dale was at the forefront of efforts at UF to address the need for improved professional opportunities for UF graduate students. The purpose of the meeting was to solicit Dale's input in order to develop the program idea and establish a model for best supporting graduate internships in the libraries. Beyond achieving this goal, the meeting with Dale resulted in an enthusiastic endorsement for the proposed program from a senior faculty member in the largest college at UF. Building upon this, in August 2015, following consultation with various collaborators within the libraries and in teaching departments, the Associate Dean and Digital Scholarship Librarian drafted a proposal for the internship program.

STAGE 3: DEVELOPING A VISION AND STRATEGY

At this point, the coauthors had arrived at a clear vision for an internship program, which would benefit the libraries, students, and teaching departments. The program vision recognized the voids in libraries for expertise and in graduate education for paid professional internships. The vision for the internship program was to transform the library into a career laboratory and professional learning space and to maximize benefits for graduate students, libraries, and teaching department collaborators. To implement this program, the Associate Dean identified a strategy of first gaining the support at various administrative levels in the libraries and then seeking funding from the dean of the libraries. This proposal was reviewed with the libraries' associate deans in order to solicit input that might improve it and to gauge interest and generate support for the idea of a new program of this kind. Following success at this stage, the Joint Chairs Committee vetted the proposed program through a discussion at their meeting, a recurring meeting of library unit-level administrators, in September 2015. Based on a positive reception at these levels, the leaders formally presented the program to and gained approval by the Dean of University Libraries, along with the formation of a new Internship Program Committee charged with implementing and supporting the program.[6]

The libraries established the committee with six members, including the Associate Dean and Digital Scholarship Librarian. The other members were associate chairs from the Special and Area Studies Collections, Humanities and Social Sciences, Science, and Health Sciences libraries. Each was a trusted, respected, and credible colleague supportive of graduate education, internships, and library goals, including fostering transformative collaborations. It was important that these new coalition members, when combined with the Associate Dean and Digital Scholarship Librarian, represented the diverse areas within the libraries.[7] The initial committee goal was to promote the program within the libraries and ensure ongoing feedback for improvement as the program developed, with a secondary purpose of ensuring library and academic unit stakeholders understood and embraced the vision.

STAGE 4: COMMUNICATING THE CHANGE VISION

Within the libraries in fall 2015 and spring 2016, representatives of the Internship Program Committee presented on the program and continued discussions to share and refine the programmatic design. The committee met regularly to create the website, and refine program materials.[8] They paid special attention to conveying the key outcomes for the program and individual internship experiences:

- complementing the graduate student's academic career and provide for their professional development
- creating benefit for the libraries
- fostering transformative collaborations across campus
- providing a supportive environment for librarians wishing to gain experience conceptualizing, writing, and administering internship projects

The key "wins" for each stakeholder were central to all communications, including presentations. To promote the program, the committee chair presented to the Library Faculty Assembly (the faculty governance body) and at other meetings. Additionally, the committee sent numerous announcements and reminders for the program to all library faculty and professional staff. These activities occurred while the group was preparing for the review cycle for the first round of proposals, starting in spring 2016.

II. Introducing New Practices Phase

Stage 5: Empowering Broad-Based Action

The committee members engaged the campus community informally and formally throughout the rapid development process. Additionally, the leaders collected information on prior one-off internships within the libraries. They documented the benefits and need within the libraries for a fully formed program to best capitalize on the opportunities from working with students for mutual aid and shared benefits and to reducing impacts incurred from individually run internships, which lacked the same community of support. With the strong foundation and momentum made possible from data and engagement, a great deal of work was required to establish and promote the new internship program, but there were not significant barriers to its implementation. On the contrary, the Smathers Libraries had historically encouraged librarian engagement with academic units. Whether modeled as liaisons or subject specialists, or a combination of these concepts, the librarians' established relationships with academic faculty would support the broad-based recognition of the opportunities afforded by the collaboratively developed internships.

Stage 6: Generating Short-Term Wins

The first round of proposals for the new internship program was due in spring 2016 for internships starting in summer or fall. The Internship Program Committee promoted the program, and members contacted various individuals based on projects and known needs and expertise. Members also met with individuals to support internship development to ensure that potential internship directors developed and submitted proposals, as the members had identified the inaugural awards as critical in building program momentum. As a result of these efforts, in the first award round of the internship program, five internships were awarded serving a total of six students across eleven semesters. This exceeded expectations, and these early wins cemented the concept of the new program as not only viable but also as a key support for achieving the important outcomes described above. Specifically, for the first eligible semester, summer 2016, the program funded two pilot internships. These first internships focused on the Digital Library of the Caribbean and Library Publishing. The Digital Scholarship Librarian served as the internship director for both, with the collaborating academic faculty member for the Digital Library of the Caribbean internship from the department of English and the collaborator for the Library Publishing internship from the department of history. The program awarded these initial internships to graduate students in the English and religion departments. The initial success of these internships served as opportunities to refine and expand the program.

The committee remained engaged during the internships, hosting an orientation event and tracking student outcomes. For the orientation event, the committee invited interns, internship directors (librarians), faculty collaborating partners, and key library personnel to orient the community to the program, the libraries, and the larger goals for transformative collaboration, workforce capacity building, and community cultural change. The orientations served to connect members from the full library and UF community and celebrate the new internships. As the program has grown over time, the orientations are also times to celebrate outcomes from past internships.

STAGE 7: CONSOLIDATING GAINS AND PRODUCING MORE CHANGE

The committee established a regular calendar for the internship program moving forward, including regular announcements and reminders for proposal development and submission, as well as for the orientations and for acknowledging awarded internships. The stewardship role of the committee included ongoing refinement to both improve processes and expand the impact for stakeholders and sustainability of the new program. A key development for the internship program was the introduction of a requirement for interns to deliver presentations on their internships with a focus on results and outcomes for the libraries and for themselves. These intern-led presentations or talks are widely advertised and have ensured ongoing promotion and outreach, as well as supporting the interns in their professional development as they learn to better articulate their accomplishments. Subsequently, the program expanded the internship work activities to include an interview with the libraries' Public Information Officer so that these exciting library-student engagements could be captured and shared with external stakeholders, including current and potential library donors. The committee has supported numerous additional changes since the conception of the program. The libraries' Human Resources Office conducts a curriculum vitae/résumé workshop for the interns each semester. Additionally, coauthor Keith and a representative from the UF Career Resource Center offer a presentation on job searching and interviewing, and job opportunities in academic and research libraries. The librarian internship directors attend a required workshop on mentoring and supervising, including evaluating job performance and feedback. To continue driving the program forward, new supports evolved over time, including a template for proposals to ease proposal development, and a standardized report to ensure communication on the program.[9] These ongoing changes aggregated into a more effective program aligned with stakeholder needs and oriented toward greater opportunities to advance the programmatic objectives.

III. Grounding Phase

STAGE 8: ANCHORING NEW APPROACHES IN THE CULTURE

Running in parallel to the internship program and leveraging these experiences, Keith and Taylor continued discussions on internships with faculty in teaching departments to develop the program and to foster transformative collaboration. In October 2015, the National Endowment for the Humanities announced the new Next Generation Humanities PhD Grant Program.[10] This grant program focused on changing graduate programs in the humanities, requesting innovative and collaborative approaches, but not specifically including internships. UF's ongoing discussions on internships positioned the campus community for collaboration to submit a grant proposal for this new program.[11] The proposal detailed the problems facing humanities graduate education, and academia more broadly, in terms of needing to foster a more positive and productive environment for better engendering collaboration for mutual aid and benefit while graduate students are undertaking their studies and for improved job placement outcomes. Professor of history and law Elizabeth Dale led development of the proposal in strong collaboration with the libraries. The grant development process included meetings across multiple colleges and departments and with outside constituents for broad and deep support. The proposal featured the Smathers Graduate Student Internship Program as an asset and method for making needed changes for next-generation humanities PhD programs. For the final proposal, the UF president committed to a more than 200 percent match of internal funds. The wealth of data included in the proposal detailed urgent and important problems, and the opportunities for improvement through graduate internships. While ultimately, NEH did not fund the proposal, the work for the proposal development and the new internship program changed conversations within the libraries and across campus.

Analysis and Conclusions

To date there have been twenty-nine awarded internships with forty-four semesters of appointments, totaling over $100,000 in funding, with foci such as public relations, preservation, 3-D printing, data management, archives and Wikipedia, collaborative grant seeking, assessment, digital humanities, digital pedagogy, digital scholarship, instructional design, and exhibits.[12] Over the past two years, these internships resulted in cultural change within the libraries and dozens of transformative partnerships between librarians and colleagues in academic units. In addition, multiple former graduate student interns have accepted faculty or other professional positions in libraries and academic institutions.

The team did exceptionally well in this change process because of the long-term history of trust, collaboration, generosity, mutual aid, and understanding of shared goals for the institution, academic and research libraries, academia, and the public good. Because the guiding coalition collectively possessed multiple decades of academic experience at the same institution, they were able to navigate smoothly with different communities and constituencies to share information, ensure productive engagement, keep open communication, and foster broad and deep support for the new program. In addition to the strength of the coalition, the design of the internship program was well suited for the objectives and the mutually positive outcomes for the stakeholders. The program also furthered an existing culture of librarian and academic faculty engagement, aligned with an articulated strategic direction of the libraries: transformative collaboration. All of these factors greatly enhanced the likelihood of success.

Another key factor in the success of the introduction and continuation of this program has been the support of library administration. The libraries launched the new program with a vague and modest expectation of the number of internships that would be proposed and ultimately awarded. The actual numbers have greatly exceeded those expectations. The committee vets proposals, and the library deans make the ultimate award funding decisions. Despite the internships exceeding the expected funding requirements, the deans have been extremely supportive of the awarding of internships and allocated additional funds, based on the well-communicated positive outcomes identified in the proposals. Additionally, each semester the deans have lunch with the current intern cohort and are engaged in their orientation. The deliberate and mindful cultivation of this leadership support by the guiding coalition has enhanced the scale of success for the Graduate Student Internship Program.

Kotter's Eight-Stage Change Model for Leading Change provides a highly effective model for considering the case of the Smathers Graduate Student Internship Program's implementation and stewardship.[13] All of the major phases are represented in the coauthors' experiences: creating a climate for change, engaging and enabling the organization, and implementing and sustaining the change. In this case study, it is important to note that the phases and the underlying steps significantly overlapped and some of the guiding coalition's efforts exist in multiple steps. For example, the vision (or at least its articulation) was still being refined while the coauthors were seeking buy-in. The overlap between these steps might be less the case for a change initiative that could be launched based on a leader's authority as opposed to the internship program, which by its nature would require broad, voluntary participation in order to succeed. Further, as discussed above, this programmatic change was stimulated by and occurred in a climate in which the coauthors were active, but it was not a change environment that they created themselves. One can assume many change initiatives would develop similarly. Despite these departures from its tidy step structure, the Model for Leading Change is a very serviceable basis for considering the change management efforts and activities of those engaged in the successful change represented by the Smathers Graduate Student Internship Program. The resounding success of the change fostered by the Graduate Student Internship Program has led to a new opportunity. For example, the library administration has charged the committee to serve as the guiding coalition to create a new paid undergraduate fellowship program to expose students from underrepresented groups to the career opportunities in academic and research libraries—with the goal of contributing to the diversity of the field.

Notes

1. IPEDS, Integrated Postsecondary Education Data System, "University of Florida," National Center for Education Statistics, US Department of Education, accessed October 1, 2018, https://nces.ed.gov/ipeds/.
2. Brian W. Keith, Cecilia Botero, and Michele Tennant, "Mergers and Acquisitions: A Roadmap for Effective Organizational Change" (presentation, ALA Annual Conference, Chicago, IL, June 27–July 2, 2013), http://ufdc.ufl.edu/AA00016004/00001; Laurie N. Taylor and Blake Landor, "Intertwingularity with Digital Humanities at the University of Florida," *dh+lib*, July 23, 2014, https://acrl.ala.org/dh/2014/07/23/intertwingularity-digital-humanities-university-florida/.
3. Laurie N. Taylor et al., "Digital Humanities as Public Humanities: Transformative Collaboration in Graduate Education," in *Digital Humanities, Libraries and Partnerships: A Critical Examination of Labor, Networks, and Community,* ed. Robin Kear and Kate Joranson (Cambridge, MA: Chandos, 2018), 31–44, preprint: http://ufdc.ufl.edu/AA00048267/00001.
4. George A. Smathers Libraries, *Strategic Directions* (Gainesville: University of Florida, October 2014), http://ufdc.ufl.edu/IR00004144/00004.
5. Brain W. Keith, Laurie N. Taylor, and Lourdes Santamaria-Wheeler, "Broadening Impact for Library Exhibitions and Speakers," *Journal of Library Administration* 57, no. 4 (2017): 389–405. https://doi.org/10.1080/01930826.2017.1288977; Brian W. Keith, Bonnie J. Smith, and Laurie N. Taylor, "Building a Collaborative Digital Archive and a Community of Practice," *portal: Libraries and the Academy* 17, no. 2 (April 2017): 419–34, https://muse.jhu.edu/article/653214.
6. George A. Smathers Libraries, "Smathers Graduate Student Internship Program: Committee," University of Florida, accessed May 9, 2019, http://cms.uflib.ufl.edu/interns/committee.
7. George A. Smathers Libraries, "Smathers Graduate Student Internship Program: Committee."

8. George A. Smathers Libraries, "Internship Program Resources," Smathers Graduate Student Internship Program: University of Florida. Accessed Oct. 1, 2018, https://cms.uflib.ufl.edu/interns/application

9. George A. Smathers Libraries, "Smathers Graduate Student Internship Program: Committee."

10. "NEH Announces New Next Generation Humanities PhD Grant Program," news release, National Endowment for the Humanities, October 21, 2015, https://www.neh.gov/news/press-release/2015-10-21.

11. Elizabeth Dale et al., *Publicly Engaging and Employing Scholars in the Humanities* (Gainesville: University of Florida, 2016), http://ufdc.ufl.edu/AA00038894/00001.

12. Smathers Graduate Internship Program Committee, "Internships Awarded in April 2018, Fifth Award Cycle," Smathers Libraries Graduate Student Internship Program, University of Florida, accessed May 9, 2019, http://ufdc.ufl.edu/AA00037247/00021.

13. John P. Kotter, *Leading Change* (Boston: Harvard Business Review Press, 1996).

Bibliography

Dale, Elizabeth, Sophia K. Acord, Leah R. Rosenberg, Laurie N. Taylor, Jordana Cox, and de Farber, Bess. *Publicly Engaging and Employing Scholars in the Humanities.* Gainesville: University of Florida, 2016. http://ufdc.ufl.edu/AA00038894/00001.

George A. Smathers Libraries. "Internship Program Resources." Smathers Graduate Student Internship Program: University of Florida. Accessed Oct. 1, 2018. https://cms.uflib.ufl.edu/interns/application

———. "Smathers Graduate Student Internship Program: Committee." University of Florida. Accessed May 9, 2019. http://cms.uflib.ufl.edu/interns/committee.

———. *Strategic Directions.* Gainesville: University of Florida, October 2014. http://ufdc.ufl.edu/IR00004144/00004.

IPEDS, Integrated Postsecondary Education Data System. "University of Florida." National Center for Education Statistics, US Department of Education. Accessed Oct. 1, 2018. https://nces.ed.gov/ipeds/.

Keith, Brian W., Cecilia Botero, and Michele Tennant. "Mergers and Acquisitions: A Roadmap for Effective Organizational Change." Presentation, ALA Annual Conference, Chicago, IL, June 27–July 2, 2013. http://ufdc.ufl.edu/AA00016004/00001.

Keith, Brian W., Bonnie J. Smith, and Laurie N. Taylor. "Building a Collaborative Digital Archive and a Community of Practice." *portal: Libraries and the Academy* 17, no. 2 (April 2017): 419–34. https://muse.jhu.edu/article/653214.

Keith, Brian W., Laurie N. Taylor, and Lourdes Santamaria-Wheeler. "Broadening Impact for Library Exhibitions and Speakers." *Journal of Library Administration* 57, no. 4 (2017): 389–405. https://doi.org/10.1080/01930826.2017.1288977.

Kotter, John P. *Leading Change.* Boston: Harvard Business Review Press, 1996.

National Endowment for the Humanities. "NEH Announces New Next Generation Humanities PhD Grant Program." News release, October 21, 2015. https://www.neh.gov/news/press-release/2015-10-21.

Persaud, and Leah R. Rosenberg. "Digital Humanities as Public Humanities: Transformative Collaboration in Graduate Education." In *Digital Humanities, Libraries and Partnerships: A Critical Examination of Labor, Networks, and Community.* Edited by Robin Kear and Kate Joranson, 31–44. Cambridge, MA: Chandos, 2018: 31-44. Preprint: http://ufdc.ufl.edu/AA00048267/00001.

Smathers Graduate Internship Program Committee. "Internships Awarded in April 2018, Fifth Award Cycle." Smathers Libraries Graduate Student Internship Program. University of Florida. Accessed May 9, 2019. http://ufdc.ufl.edu/AA00037247/00021.

Taylor, Laurie N., Poushali Bhadury, Elizabeth Dale, Randi Gill-Sadler, Brian W. Keith, Prea

Taylor, Laurie N., and Blake Landor. "Intertwingularity with Digital Humanities at the University of Florida." *dh+lib,* July 23, 2014. https://acrl.ala.org/dh/2014/07/23/intertwingularity-digital-humanities-university-florida/.

Chapter 18

Developing a New Model and Organizational Framework for Liaison Librarians

Yelena Luckert and Gary W. White

Setting the Change Stage

In 2013, the University of Maryland Libraries undertook a major revisioning of its liaison program as a result of two converging task forces. As with many other academic libraries, the University of Maryland Libraries realized that rapid changes in higher education necessitated a reconceptualization of the existing liaison program in order to address emerging needs and to develop core competencies and methods of assessment to evaluate librarians' work. The results of both of these task forces have converged into a new model of liaison librarianship that is integrated into the new Research Commons (RC) organizational unit. This chapter will discuss the planning and implementation of these task force recommendations and how these reports led to a broader vision for the University Libraries.

The University of Maryland (UMD) is a large public research university located in College Park, Maryland, just a few miles outside of Washington, DC. The university is the flagship campus of the University System of Maryland and has a total enrollment of over 26,000 undergraduates and 10,000 graduate students and close to 100 undergraduate majors and over 200 graduate programs. It is a Carnegie Research 1 University with over 1,500 tenured or tenure-track faculty and over 4,400 total faculty members. The University Libraries at UMD consists of eight libraries, including McKeldin Library, the main library on campus. The libraries broadly support the research and teaching mission of the university and are ranked at 42 on the Association of Research Libraries' 2015–2016 ranking of research libraries by expenditures with a budget of nearly $29 million.[1]

I. Warm-up Phase

STAGE 1: ESTABLISHING A SENSE OF URGENCY

In recent times, much has been written about the roles of liaison librarians. In 2009 the Association of Research Libraries (ARL) published a special report on liaison librarian roles, which addressed the emerging roles for liaison librarians and how institutions started to develop strategies to support such programs.[2] Four years later, in 2013, a new ARL report by Janice Jaguszewski and Karen Williams, *New Roles for New Times: Transforming Liaison Roles in Research Libraries,* noted further changes in the library environment, including shifts in student learning, technology, and scholarly engagement, which contributed to further transformation in the roles of liaison librarians. The focus has shifted from what librarians do to what users do.[3]

At the same time, measuring impact and accountability have become second nature to higher education across all areas. It also has become increasingly important for libraries to assess all operations and services, including liaison work. *Assessing Liaison Librarians: Documenting Impact for Positive Change* by Daniel C. Mack and Gary W. White examined how academic libraries evaluate their liaison activities and offered recommendations on how to document impact.[4] In 2015, Columbia University, Cornell University, and the University of Toronto partnered with ARL on a first-of-its-kind library liaison institute where subject librarians of these institutions discussed future models for structuring liaison work in their workplaces.[5] *Evolution of Library Liaisons* by Rebecca Miller and Lauren Pressley offered case studies of liaison programs from about seventy ARL member libraries.[6] "Transforming a Library: Strategies for Implementing a Liaison Program" by Yelena Luckert provided practical solutions for the change.[7]

There has also been a great deal of literature on how librarians can effectively support various components of the research life cycle, with a smaller number of pieces focusing specifically on the development of RCs or related concepts such as scholars' commons or digital scholarship centers. The Coalition for Networked Information presented on this concept at its 2016 membership meeting, outlining the work at Ohio State University.[8] There are several case studies, including those at Duke University, UNC Chapel Hill, and Florida State University.[9]

With a knowledge of national trends in liaison librarianship, the library administration sought to investigate the current roles and activities of our liaison librarians and to conduct a study to examine how librarians could best support researchers in an environment with rapidly changing technologies, pedagogies, and publishing models. As part of this study, the libraries were interested in exploring how to best support desired new liaison responsibilities as well as developing an assessment program to evaluate liaison activities. At the same time, the libraries were aware that campus resources to support research were widely dispersed without an overarching framework. This resulted in researchers having to navigate a complex ecosystem in order to identify and find support for the various aspects of the research life cycle.

STAGE 2: CREATING THE GUIDING COALITION

The administration of the Public Services Division charged two task forces with an overarching goal of providing outstanding support for research on campus. The two task forces were created simultaneously in 2012 to make recommendations for reengineering our liaison program and to explore the development of the RC. The scope of these studies varied. The work of the liaison task force was largely internal, led by liaison librarians in the Research and Learning Department. The RC task force, while consisting of members of the libraries from several different units, also recognized the need to coordinate with other major units on campus, including the Office of Research, the Division of Information Technology, and the Graduate School.

The liaison task force was charged with examining how our liaison program could be revised to address contemporary needs in supporting faculty and student research and teaching and to develop a model of assessment that could be used to improve our liaison activities. As part of their work, the members of the task force examined national trends, emerging literature, and models in place at peer institutions in addition to internal documents and data related to liaison activities. The RC task force used a similar approach and also conducted interviews with stakeholders and other institutions as well as administered an internal survey to UMD faculty and students. As part of the overall planning, these projects were reviewed and approved by the library administration and were shared in the planning and execution stages with the entire library staff.

The liaison task force was comprised of four library faculty, including the Associate Dean for Collections Strategies and Services, the Head of the Research and Learning Department, and two subject specialists. The RC task force consisted of five subject librarians, the head of our Teaching Department and one graduate assistant. While a variety of others from various departments and units were consulted by both of these groups, in hindsight having a member of the Information Technology Department on the RC task force would have been useful. Both groups were formally charged by the Associate Dean for Public Services and given a written charge, which included stated goals and a timeline. Both task forces were led by strong leaders in the libraries who were recognized by others in the organization as credible and knowledgeable librarians, and thus their recommendations were readily accepted by the administration and the vast majority of librarians and staff. Both teams operated very efficiently and worked very well together, a dynamic that we believe was the result of having given the task force members clear guidelines and responsibilities.

STAGE 3: DEVELOPING A VISION AND STRATEGY

For both of these groups, there was a very broad but not overly defined vision. The first, for the liaison group, was to develop a robust liaison program that encompassed the variety of work that our liaisons do and to develop a framework of core competencies, methods of assessment, and a training program and other professional development tools to assist our liaisons in meeting some of the new challenges of their roles. The vision for the RC was similar in that it was broad. The RC task force was asked to create a suite of services and spaces in conjunction with other campus partners that would support researchers at all stages of the research process. We referred to this as a vision for a "one-stop shop," where researchers could find support for any aspect of the research life cycle in one location, rather than the very dispersed and confusing array of services in multiple locations across campus.

It was during the initial phases of both groups that the leaders of the task forces and library administrators discussed how these two initiatives were merging into a more unified vision than previously expected. The work of the liaison task force revealed that many facets of liaison librarianship were directly related to the research life cycle and the desire to offer more effective, streamlined services. The concept of the RC and its implementation were likewise very dependent on the work of our liaison librarians as well as their support. At this juncture, Public Services administration decided to begin communications with librarians around the work of both task forces, with a recognition that the outcomes of the two task forces would be separate but with a great deal of interconnectivity.

STAGE 4: COMMUNICATING THE CHANGE VISION

The two task forces completed their work in 2013, the liaison task force in May and the RC task force in July. The liaison task force presented a framework of core competencies in five broad areas: collections content and access; reference and research consulting and mentoring; teaching, learning, and literacies; outreach and engagement; and scholarly communications and research data services. For each of these five areas, the task force presented an overview of the work, a list of concrete expectations, behavioral guidelines, and methods and resources for assessment and evaluation. The task force also included sample liaison job descriptions and sample liaison best practices.[10] The RC task force's report provided a service model including staffing and a gradual implementation plan. It also included a space plan addressing design aspects and staffing. The report included a detailed three-phase implementation plan to take place over several years as well as a marketing plan that could be used to communicate the vision to both internal and external audiences.[11]

During the late summer, we held several forums for each group to present and discuss their findings and recommendations. Both groups also presented their work to the library's administrative team, getting approval to proceed with the implementation of recommendations. Communicating and garnering support for the work of the liaison task force from among liaison librarians was the most challenging aspect, detailed in Stage 5. In fall 2013, the library administration discussed both plans with both the provost and the Senate Library Committee. During this time, the library administration also initiated and conducted meetings with the leadership teams of the other colleges on campus. All of these discussions served to gain approval and to also communicate the vision for these changes to campus constituents. At the same time, they were a reminder to campus leaders of how much the library can support research activity on campus.

II. Introducing New Practices Phase

STAGE 5: EMPOWERING BROAD-BASED ACTION

In the process of implementing the liaison and the RC models, we have encountered a number of obstacles, some more significant than others, but typical to other organizations. We understood early on that in order to find solutions that will work for the UMD Libraries, we would need to tackle these challenges one at a time. We set up building consensus and support for each step in the process. At the same time, we took careful steps to avoid anxieties and burn out, which often lead to resentment of change on the part of the staff.

Some of these obstacles were purely organizational in nature and required single-handed administrative solutions, such as the restructuring within Public Services. Each one of the libraries located directly on the College Park campus, including the main one, is defined by its concentration of subjects and houses subject librarians serving students and faculty in those disciplines. Before the reorganization, each of these locations had varied expectations of its librarians, which contributed to staff concerns about equity. As the first order of business, all subject librarians were administratively combined into a single department, Research and Learning (R&L). Although branches still remain units within R&L managed by their unit heads, administrative unification of everyone into one department under single leadership enabled standardized expectations and deliverables for all subject librarians. Being in one department promoted and increased cooperation and coordination across locations and purposes, allowed for more system-atic annual review and assessment processes and moved the liaison implementation forward. The department also went through unifying exercises to define the mission, vision, and goals, as well as strategic priorities.

Other barriers were rooted in human nature. Among these were the usual overall reluctance to change; concerns about redefining of duties, spaces, practices, expectations, and professional identity; stress over changes in work environment; and difficulties in understanding new concepts, for example, "What is the Research Commons?" We used multifaceted approaches to deal with these issues. Most gratifying is our success in creat-ing a transparent, consensus-building decision-making process that involves everyone in R&L. With a large and dispersed organization such as ours, it is not an easy task. We use standing committees with membership by representation, task forces, public forums, email lists, one-on-one conversations, visits to units, open-door policies, and other methods available to us. New initiatives are presented at R&L heads meetings, a group that consists of all managers in R&L. From there they are vetted by all units within R&L, then at the R&L forums, and finally by the administration. Our monthly R&L forums discuss issues that affect the day-to-day work of R&L librarians and encourage a free exchange of ideas. We provide a great deal of other internal and external training, which helps staff overcome barriers. Our annual review and assessment process for liaison librarians is perhaps one of the most effective ways by which we can help empower our staff to move forward by identifying concrete individual needs and specific ways they can achieve organizational goals.

STAGE 6: GENERATING SHORT-TERM WINS

Transitioning to a new liaison system and RC model is a process. As such, it has to be evolving and flexible, with an implication that deliverables happen gradually and with purpose. We are already in our fifth year of reorganization, and during this time we have seen a fair number of small and large victories.

In establishing the new liaison system, we started by developing the framework for annual reports, including guidelines and forms, which were based entirely on the liaison task force's final report.[12] The format followed the report, but in the first year (2014), we asked liaisons to demonstrate accomplishments in three out of five categories of liaison activities identified by the report. We decided to use this approach in order to ease staff into the process. In the next annual cycle (2015), we changed that to full compliance as we moved further in the implementation stages. Moreover, we layered the process for liaison assessment on the already existing cycle of annual merit review of the libraries with which people were very familiar. From the start, we wanted our assessment to be meaningful, manageable, and sustainable. It aimed to be broadly discussed with and approved by supervisors and connected to the libraries' and university's strategic goals, as well as to the libraries' policies and procedures for faculty promotion and tenure review. Thus these assessments were designed to be actionable, to let us know what impact individuals are having in their specific areas, to point to the areas of needed improvement and how to get there, and to highlight individual achievements. And at the same time, these annual assessments were to be flexible; responsive to changes in our environment, strategic priorities, and growth; in all to be a reflection of the individual and the organization. With broad support from our librarians, we have achieved what we aimed for, a functional annual assessment system that is helping us move forward. It is important to mention here that the newest librarians on our staff were the first and most vocal supporters of this system.

The development of the RC was slow until we identified a dynamic and proactive individual to lead the charge in 2014. She took upon herself to really understand the environment on campus outside the libraries. In the libraries, we often do not perceive the differences in which various campus communities and populations think of even most common concepts. For example, it was a real surprise to us to realize the meaning of "research" for different stakeholders. By learning and understanding the vocabulary and the true nature of needs of different units and staff on campus, she was able to establish a number of significant campus partnerships that provided the libraries with high-level campus visibility to a degree we had not experienced before. Integrated Research Resources on Campus, or IRRoC, is one of the earliest and most significant examples of what the RC can do for the University.[13] A result of the partnership between the UMD's Division of Research, Division of Information Technology, and University Libraries, it provides a unified, central access point to connect the UMD research community with resources and services across campus. It was a huge win for the Libraries, both internally and externally, with strong praise from the campus administration.

One of the most difficult issues we faced is how subject librarians, who administratively do not directly report to RC, will fit into the overall concept and services of RC. To address this issue, we had conversations and training opportunities at the R&L forums, but we also have taken some proactive solutions in establishing the norms. A "Meet Your Subject Specialist" webpage, complete with the Google Scholar Profile for UMD librarians and Subject Specialist Directory, is administered by the RC, providing a sense of belonging to all subject librarians.[14] Some of the well-regarded event series established before the RC by small groups of librarians, such as Speaking of Books… Conversations with Campus Authors, have been moved under the umbrella of the RC.[15] Now they provide greater access and opportunities to all librarians to host faculty from their departments across the board. Finally, we had some wins in redefining the day to day work functions of librarians, including removing librarians from service desks; introducing student-centric learning, blended and flipped classroom teaching; and modernizing teaching spaces.

STAGE 7. CONSOLIDATING GAINS AND PRODUCING MORE CHANGE

The development of the framework for liaison librarians complete with functional annual assessments, changes in work responsibilities and expectations, and development of the RC have cumulatively added up to a major change in attitudes and perceptions. Today our RC is no longer just a concept and a virtual space. It occupies much improved space on the fourth floor of the main library, complete with a beautiful new formal reading room; large, flexible event/study space; a silent room; a reference alcove; GIS/GeoSpatial Lab and offices; areas for statistical consultations; a series of workshops for graduate students; and offices for our subject librarians and the Teaching and Learning unit. These spaces and services are in constant use and demand. Under the umbrella of the RC, we are in the process of developing themed "commons" based on the focus of a particular location, with Research Commons@McKeldin, our main library, as headquarters. We have already established the science-focused commons on the STEM side of campus, Research Commons@STEM, and are currently in the process of implementing the performing arts commons at our performing arts library, Research Commons@MSPAL. All the heads of our commons, including the learning commons, which is administratively outside of R&L, meet regularly to coordinate and develop new services and ideas. The overarching activities, like building partnerships with campus communities at large, are under the headquarters, but then each one of these locations offers specialized services. For example, Research Commons@STEM offers 3-D printing and skeleton models desired by the STEM students, and Research Commons@MSPAL provides a sewing machine and has experimented with space for interactive performances in the stacks.

Similar transformations have been happening to the liaison model as well. While previously only a few of our subject librarians could be considered embedded in their departments, now this is across the board. Besides our traditional duties, librarians are often providing nontraditional support, such as help with copyright issues and data research, and are full participants in the initiatives of their departments, organizing conferences and mounting exhibits and library-centered events in support and coordination with their faculty. Besides Speaking of Books, which is the only campus forum for faculty to present their latest works, the librarians through RC run a very successful and well-attended series, Interdisciplinary Dialogues, which brings the campus community together to discuss pressing issues in academia, including such topics as big data, immigration, and sex on campus.[16] In effect, the UMD Libraries are becoming a recognized intellectual hub on campus.

We have done this by using the transparent decision-making model. We work on these initiatives step by step, listening to those directly involved, constantly improving and adjusting as we move forward, and that in turn keeps the momentum going. We empower librarians to be independent professionals, but we also nurture a highly collaborative learning environment. We celebrate successes by communicating them to the entire department, the libraries, and even to patrons. For example, our "Meet Your Subject Specialist" page boasts a Google Scholar profile for UMD Libraries and a Kudos section where we post individual praises received from students and faculty, although stripped of identifying information. The liaison annual assessment process offers an important opportunity to celebrate individual progress, but also to handle complacency and other performance issues. We find that providing honest, specific, and direct feedback in combination with ways of improvement enables people to work through difficulties and reach positive outcomes.

III. Grounding Phase

STAGE 8: ANCHORING NEW APPROACHES IN THE CULTURE

The work that we have done thus far gives us great confidence that the changes we implemented have taken root. The key factors here are that we have applied the changes incrementally, building on already existing good practices and professionalism of our staff, soliciting a lot of feedback throughout the process, adjusting things as we progress, creating a cooperative work atmosphere and learning organization, and successfully communicating change and doing things in direct response to the needs of our campus community. We have created an environment flexible and nimble enough to adjust to new demands as they come. This has become our new normal in doing work.

Creating a new assessment program was not an easy undertaking. Communicating this process as incremental and developmental, rather than punitive, was key. The rollout of this program was constantly situated within the context of providing better services and with the notion that everyone has both areas of expertise and areas needing additional development. By actively addressing concerns and fears and by offering substantial professional development opportunities, the libraries have shown that we can go in new strategic directions in a positive manner and with less resistance. By going through this major organizational change, our librarians and staff have experienced how organizational learning occurs, and we have since seen numerous examples of how this has changed people's willingness to accept and even embrace change.

Analysis and Conclusions

We now are a different organization from the one of five years ago. Now the libraries are fully aware of how much we are intertwined with the constantly changing external environment and our need to adapt as changes occur. We are in a much stronger position to react and even affect some of these changes. As we first embarked on this mission, we were not initially considering Kotter's framework as our steps for the process of change. However, looking back at our journey, we realized how closely we have been following this framework in our daily work and progress. We conquered one step at a time, ensuring success and long-lasting change. We are building on the foundation we have already established, moving forward toward our goals of creating excellent services and an educational support system for our students and faculty, of which liaison services and Research Commons are an integral part.

Notes

1. Shaneka Morris and Gary Roebuck, *ARL Statistics 2015–2016* (Washington, DC: Association of Research Libraries, 2018).
2. Karla Hahn, ed., *Research Library Issues: A Bimonthly Report from ARL, CNI, and SPARC*, no. 265 (August 2009), special issue on liaison librarian roles, http://publications.arl.org/rli265/.

3. Janice M. Jaguszewski and Karen Williams, *New Roles for New Times* (Washington, DC: Association of Research Libraries, 2013).

4. Daniel C. Mack and Gary W. White, *Assessing Liaison Librarians,* ACRL Publications in Librarianship, no. 67 (Chicago: Association of College and Research Libraries, 2014).

5. Barbara Rockenbach et al., *Association of Research Libraries/Columbia University/Cornell University/University of Toronto Pilot Library Liaison Institute: Final Report* (Washington, DC: Association of Research Libraries, November 2015), http://www.arl.org/storage/documents/publications/library-liaison-institute-final-report-dec2015.pdf.

6. Rebecca K. Miller and Lauren Pressley, *Evolution of Library Liaisons*: *SPEC Kit 349* (Washington, DC: Association of Research Libraries, November 2015), http://publications.arl.org/Evolution-Library-Liaisons-SPEC-Kit-349/.

7. Yelena Luckert, "Transforming a Library: Strategies for Implementing a Liaison Program," *International Information and Library Review,* 48, no. 4 (2016): 294–300.

8. Alison Armstrong, Meris Mandernach, and Joshua W. Sadvari, "Connect. Collaborate. Contribute: A Model for Designing and Building a Research Commons," PowerPoint slides (presentation, Coalition for Networked Information Spring 2016 Membership Meeting, San Antonio, TX, April 4–5, 2016), https://osf.io/ky2mt/download.

9. Travis L. Jones, "Giving 21st Century Researchers a Place in the Library: A Study of the Research Commons Planning Process at Duke University and the University of North Carolina at Chapel Hill" (master's thesis, University of North Carolina at Chapel Hill, 2016), https://cdr.lib.unc.edu/record/uuid:3603617a-da73-40f6-a712-d23f53363104; Gloria P. Colvin, "The Scholars Commons: Spaces and Services for Faculty and Graduate Students," *Florida Libraries*, 53, no. 1 (2010): 6–8.

10. Yelena Luckert et al., *Liaison Librarian Task Force 2012–2013, The University of Maryland Libraries, Final Report* (College Park: University of Maryland Libraries, May 31, 2013), http://drum.lib.umd.edu/handle/1903/17456.

11. Kelsey Corlett-Rivera et al, *Final Report, Task Force on McKeldin Library Research Commons* (College Park: University of Maryland Libraries, July 2013), Retrieved from https://drum.lib.umd.edu/handle/1903/20733.

12. Luckert et al., *Liaison Librarian Task Force.*

13. Integrated Research Resources on Campus homepage, University of Maryland, accessed May 28, 2019, https://irroc.umd.edu/.

14. "Meet Your Subject Specialist," University of Maryland, University Libraries, accessed May 28, 2019, https://www.lib.umd.edu/rc/meet-your-librarian.

15. "Speaking of Books… Conversations with Campus Authors," University of Maryland, University Libraries, accessed May 28, 2019, https://www.lib.umd.edu/rc/speaking-of-books.

16. "Interdisciplinary Dialogue Series," University of Maryland, University Libraries, accessed May 28, 2019, https://www.lib.umd.edu/rc/interdisciplinary-dialogue.

Bibliography

Armstrong, Alison, Meris Mandernach, and Joshua W. Sadvari. "Connect. Collaborate. Contribute: A Model for Designing and Building a Research Commons." PowerPoint slides. Presentation, Coalition for Networked Information Spring 2016 Membership Meeting, San Antonio, TX, April 4–5, 2016. https://osf.io/ky2mt/download.

Colvin, Gloria P. "The Scholars Commons: Spaces and Services for Faculty and Graduate Students." *Florida Libraries* 53, no. 1 (2010): 6–8.

Corlett-Rivera, Kelsey, Barbara Dickey Davis, Zaida Diaz, Cynthia Ippoliti, Lara Otis, Karen Patterson, and Nedelina Tchangalova. *Final Report, Task Force on McKeldin Library Research Commons.* College Park: University of Maryland Libraries, July 2013. https://drum.lib.umd.edu/handle/1903/20733.

Hahn, Karla, editor. *Research Library Issues: A Bimonthly Report from ARL, CNI, and SPARC*, no. 265 (August 2009). Special issue on liaison librarian roles. http://publications.arl.org/rli265/.

Jaguszewski, Janice M., and Karen Williams. *New Roles for New Times: Transforming Liaison Roles in Research Libraries.* Washington, DC: Association of Research Libraries, 2013.

Jones, Travis L. "Giving 21st Century Researchers a Place in the Library: A Study of the Research Commons Planning Process at Duke University and the University of North Carolina at Chapel Hill."

Master's thesis, University of North Carolina at Chapel Hill, 2016. https://cdr.lib.unc.edu/record/uuid:3603617a-da73-40f6-a712-d23f53363104.

Luckert, Yelena. "Transforming a Library: Strategies for Implementing a Liaison Program." *International Information and Library Review* 48, no. 4 (2016): 294–300.

Luckert, Yelena, Daniel C. Mack, Svetla Baykoucheva, and Patricia C. Cossard. *Liaison Librarian Task Force 2012–2013, The University of Maryland Libraries, Final Report.* College Park: University of Maryland Libraries, May 31, 2013. http://drum.lib.umd.edu/handle/1903/17456.

Mack, Daniel C., and Gary W. White. *Assessing Liaison Librarians: Documenting Impact For Positive Change.* ACRL Publications in Librarianship, no. 67. Chicago: Association of College and Research Libraries, 2014.

Miller, Rebecca K., and Lauren Pressley. *Evolution of Library Liaisons: SPEC Kit 349.* Washington, DC: Association of Research Libraries, November 2015. http://publications.arl.org/Evolution-Library-Liaisons-SPEC-Kit-349/.

Morris, Shaneka, and Gary Roebuck. *ARL Statistics 2015–2016.* Washington, DC: Association of Research Libraries, 2018.

Rockenbach, Barbara, Judy Ruttenberg, Kornelia Tancheva, and Rita Vine. *Association of Research Libraries/Columbia University/Cornell University/University of Toronto Pilot Library Liaison Institute: Final Report.* Washington, DC: Association of Research Libraries, 2015. http://www.arl.org/storage/documents/publications/library-liaison-institute-final-report-dec2015.pdf.

University of Maryland. Integrated Research Resources on Campus homepage. Accessed May 28, 2019. https://irroc.umd.edu/.

University of Maryland, University Libraries. "Interdisciplinary Dialogue Series." Accessed May 28, 2019. https://www.lib.umd.edu/rc/interdisciplinary-dialogue.

———. "Meet Your Subject Specialist." Accessed May 28, 2019. https://www.lib.umd.edu/rc/meet-your-librarian.

———. "Speaking of Books… Conversations with Campus Authors." Accessed May 28, 2019. https://www.lib.umd.edu/rc/speaking-of-books.

Chapter 19

New Outreach and New Roles

Veteran Students and Change in an Academic Library

Carroll Wetzel Wilkinson

Setting the Stage

West Virginia University is a public land-grant institution in Morgantown, West Virginia. Founded in 1867, it has a current enrollment of 31,442. It is ranked as a Research University (Highest Research Activity)—R1—in the 2015 Carnegie Classification of Institutions of Higher Education. Students at the Morgantown campus come from 108 nations, all 50 US states (plus D.C.), and all 55 West Virginia counties; 13,986 are West Virginia residents.

The WVU Libraries (WVUL) encompasses seven libraries statewide. Facilities in Morgantown include the Downtown Campus Library, Evansdale Library, Health Sciences Library, Law Library, and the West Virginia and Regional History Center. Onsite collections include more than 2.4 million books, over 600,000 e-books, and 117,000 e-journals. The library faculty includes forty librarians.

In fall of 2018, the student veteran enrollment of WVU students attending school with support from the Post 9-11 GI Bill was 861.

I. Warm-up Phase

STAGE 1: ESTABLISHING A SENSE OF URGENCY

At WVUL there were two parts to establishing a sense of urgency about veterans. First, in the fall of 2014, the newly appointed Dean of Libraries noted that the libraries intentionally served student groups, including international and at-risk students, as well as students in the two required English classes. But no outreach to student veterans had ever existed, and he wanted that to change as quickly as possible. He challenged me, in my role as Director of Strategic Library Initiatives, to act on this project. In partnership with the WVU Office of Veterans Affairs, we immediately opened a tutoring room at the Downtown Campus Library, initially a dedicated space for tutors and student veterans studying the STEM disciplines. Funding for tutors was provided by AT&T Corporation.

Because this initiative lacked implementation funds, I sought outside funding to support the creation of a program for veteran students beyond the tutoring room. First, I collaborated with the campus Director of Veteran Affairs and the grant writer for Student Affairs in identifying the Institute for Museum and Library Services' (IMLS) SPARKS! Grant program, intended to "encourage libraries and archives to prototype and evaluate specific innovations in the ways they operate and the services they provide resulting in new tools, products, services, or organizational practices."[1] Each grant provides $25,000 for one year to give incentive for relevant program development.

In our application to IMLS, I proposed a multipart outreach program to enhance the academic success of veteran students. Our application was successful. The funding period began October 1, 2015. Work began immediately to implement the outreach program described in the application.

The second part of the sense of urgency came when, as principal investigator of this federally supported grant, I began working to accomplish its goals. I was not only leading an effort to make change for the WVU Libraries, but I was also responsible to an agency of the federal government. Now there was not only the dean's mandate but also the stated outcomes of the federal funding to achieve.

STAGE 2: CREATING THE GUIDING COALITION

Kotter's "guiding coalition" was not something I conceived of initially. Instead I was simply thinking of those on campuses and within the libraries with whom I would either continue to work or initiate contact. Good working relationships are key to success, and I wanted to build new ones and sustain ones I already had. My initial network included the WVU Director of Veterans Affairs, the grant writer for Student Affairs, the members of the established network of campus advocates for student veterans in the student counseling center and in the academic advising center, as well as library staff who handle student hiring and management of grant funding, among others.

Identifying students to work with me on the grant was an important early step in developing the second guiding coalition. Luckily, a graduate student in the English department's PhD program was a captain in the Army and a veteran of two tours in Afghanistan. Having received a fellowship that required forty volunteer service hours each semester, he agreed to work with me to establish a veterans' outreach program. Together, we developed a job description for a part-time student coordinator of social media.

We selected six finalists for interviews whose résumés matched our needs. From that group we selected one undergraduate student, a business and finance major and an Army veteran, who established and maintained our Facebook page, Twitter feed, and a working relationship with the campus WVU Vets club. Both student veterans provided credibility for the developing program, and their perspectives were invaluable as we proceeded to design a survey of student veterans' needs and interests in using the libraries' facilities, services, collections, and expertise.

A third hire, a National Guard veteran and student in the master's program in the English department, analyzed our early survey results, which revealed that over 60 percent of respondents (97 student veterans) wished to see a research buddy program established. Together we attempted to develop such a program.

Others in this second guiding mini-coalition included one resident librarian who had selected the dean's office and specifically my program of strategic initiatives as the focus of her work during her second year with WVUL. The wife of the Dean of Libraries, a US Army Desert Storm veteran and an employee of the local office of the Red Cross, joined as well. Finally, the libraries' Head of Web and Digital Services worked with me and the resident librarian to create a dedicated webpage for student veteran services with links to generic library services as well as new ones such a LibGuide called "Resource Guide for Student Veterans."[2]

Near the end of what turned into a two-year period granted by IMLS to finish accomplishing our goals, I established a third coalition, a working group exclusively of librarians who are to this day an essential part of the final guiding coalition. One is a US Air Force veteran; one has worked with the student veteran community at Potomac State College, a divisional campus of WVU; one is the wife of a veteran; and another is a widow of a veteran. They work with me to establish a sustained program of outreach to student veterans completely integrated into the permanent organizational structure of WVUL.

In summary there were three mini-coalitions developed during the two years of the grant at different times as a need came up. Each offered guidance and a sense of direction, thus developing a collective sense of ownership of the program.

STAGE 3: DEVELOPING A VISION AND STRATEGY

My vision of the organizational context was best expressed in the aspiration statement of the IMLS grant proposal: my vision of an outreach program for veteran students that had never existed at WVUL before. It was also a vision of change within our library system's organization. The accompanying goals and objectives constituted a strategy for establishing the first few years of a new library program.

Here is part of the vision statement I originally wrote for this project:

Veterans who return home to begin college have lives that are starkly different than most students.[3] "The constituency of veteran students includes women as well as men, students who have served one or more tours of duty, many have dependents including spouses, partners, and children, and many have service related disabilities requiring institutional accommodations. Many have been out of school for a while, are 'academically rusty,' and most are seasoned individuals with an eye on returning to the US workforce after completing college."[4]

Until 2014, student veterans as a user group were underserved by WVU Libraries. First year students, international students, first generation students, students at risk, and students with disabilities are examples of groups that have received special programming, focused instruction, and targeted orientations by librarians. Veterans may have been in some of those groups, but our instruction and other programming did not address them directly. The academic success of all students is our mission and our instruction, facilities, resources, and expertise all contribute meaningfully toward that goal. The development of critical thinking about information sources is one proficiency that benefits all students as they engage with their academic programs. Broadly defined, information literacy, which is fundamentally what the Libraries teach, is a set of abilities that allow a person to recognize when information is needed and to effectively and efficiently act on that need.[5] We want the veteran students to receive the benefit of this type of instruction as well as the revitalized instruction possible through the use of the *Framework for Information Literacy in Higher Education, 2016.*[6]

Accomplishing the IMLS grant's goals and establishing a permanent program within the existing organizational structure of the WVU Libraries is something else altogether. The working group mentioned in Stage 2 is trying to do the following:

- Establish an engaged librarian in the developing network of Engaged Librarians within the WVUL system whose job calls for maintaining all forms of outreach to student veterans.
- Maintain a network of relevant contacts with campus veteran advocates for student referrals as needed throughout the library system and on campus.
- Establish a program fund on which the designated engaged librarian could draw for outreach efforts, collection development, and educational programs as needed.
- Work with the Director of Library Development to recruit donors for a Veterans Program fund at WVUL and write a position description for a Veterans' Services Librarian to submit to the Dean of Libraries for consideration.
- Recommend a representative and permanent structure in our library system that unifies efforts on behalf of veteran students that eventually reports to the Associate Dean of Libraries.

STAGE 4: COMMUNICATING THE CHANGE VISION

Sharing information from library leaders regarding decisions and challenges in the organization is one type of communication. Another is transmitting news of all kinds as broadly as possible. I did not share the contents of the grant application with everyone in the library system, only the fact that I had applied. Administrators who supported my application knew what was going on. None of us extracted what I would call the "change vision" and shared it broadly. However here is what the introduction to the grant application said: "West Virginia University Libraries are proposing a pilot project that will address challenges faced by the student veteran community through campus partnerships, expanded services and the development of processes and resources tailored to these students."[7]

Upon the grant application's acceptance, a press release went out in early September 2015 to everyone in the university community saying that IMLS had awarded WVUL $25,000 for this initiative. None of the details of the project's application were shared broadly. Perhaps that was a mistake. At the time it did not seem practical, nor did it seem that there would be interest enough yet to make that sort of effort. The press release was the beginning of broad communication, though admittedly, a press release is not thoroughly read by everyone. Deeper needs for organizational communication lay ahead.

I began sharing an action plan for WVUL through both the Veteran Advocate network coordinated by the WVU Director of Veterans Affairs and the libraries' leadership team led by the Interim Dean of Libraries. Each had monthly meetings, so I prepared and delivered periodic progress reports as we accomplished early goals.

Here are the goals stated in the grant proposal for action:

- With assistance from the Office of the Registrar, assess the enrolled veterans and dependents to determine perceptions of their needs regarding library use, research effectiveness, and overall awareness of current services at the campus libraries of West Virginia University.
- Increase understanding of the library staff about the characteristics of the community of student veterans and their special needs.
- Increase understanding of faculty members who teach veteran students about campus services available to students for mental and physical health, tutoring, financial aid, research support, and other sources of support on campus and promote referrals to these services where needed.
- Install additional equipment in the Veterans Tutoring Room and distribute useful information for student veterans that relates to academic success and library use.
- In collaboration with the University Relations, have the Television Department create a recruitment video that will encourage student veterans to become active users of the facilities, resources, services, and expertise of the University Libraries while also becoming savvy users of information.[8]
- Increase student veteran library use through the video, a website, and program planning and evaluation documents.[9]
- Share results with other academic libraries for use as a model for their own outreach productions and programming.
- Adopt the following definition for student veterans throughout the work of the WVUL campus program development: "A student veteran is any student who is a current or former member of the active duty military, the National Guard, or Reserves regardless of deployment status, combat experience, legal veteran status, or GI Bill use."[10]

Another goal that we established, once funding was in hand, was to articulate the WVUL's aim of increasing the academic success of student veterans. We intended to do this by improving direct services to that community and developing a program that could serve as a model for other academic libraries interested in student veteran outreach.

In the early months, it was necessary to focus on organizing a support staff. Steps included the following:

1. Identifying a graduate student veteran with a fellowship that required forty hours each semester of volunteer work who agreed to work with the outreach implementation.
2. Identifying a second graduate student veteran who agreed to accept paid part-time employment with our outreach program.
3. Creating a job description for an undergraduate coordinator of social media who could set up a Facebook page and a Twitter account for the WVU Libraries' Veterans' Outreach Program (WVUL_VOP) and post regular program announcements.

4. Establishing a formal acronym/Wordmark to identify and brand the new program. It became WVUL_VOP.

The three student veterans in the new positions helped shape communication on campus and directly with the student veterans themselves. They also provided credibility to the program as their rapport with other student veterans increased the effectiveness of the communication process overall.

We were now able to post announcements to the Facebook page of the WVU Vets Club. With help from the WVU Director of Veterans Affairs and later direct support from the University Registrar, we gained access to a more comprehensive list of names and email addresses of registered students who self-report their status as veterans.

As time went on, communication to the campus and libraries included invitations to an open house, announcements of a survey of veteran awareness of library services and desires for new services, and messages about upcoming programs on, for example, mindfulness, conversations with women veterans, and the Research Buddy program. The first open house in February 2016 welcomed approximately twenty student veterans and twenty campus advocates for veterans. The advocates communicated the services they offered, met each other, and talked with a small number of student veterans who elected to come.

Regular attendance by the Director of Library Strategic Initiatives at the monthly meetings of the campus Veterans Advocate group allowed time for progress reports and statistics on library services usage and enabled colleagues to view the newly developed LibGuide "Resource Guide for Veteran Students" and webpages for student veterans.[11] Overall, these meetings provided a forum for the libraries to remind others regularly of our commitment to student veterans and share the actions we were taking on their behalf. We had an opportunity in these meetings to communicate the basic message of dedication to the interests of the veteran students and our determination to break through any misguided perceptions that this was not the territory for libraries.

Taking a long view, the early months of the IMLS grant at WVUL focused more communication outward to the relevant officials and advocates on campus and the student veterans themselves. Internal communication to the library staff and faculty to build internal buy-in and commitment to the student veteran constituency was not as strong. For example, a new library newsletter, *Off the Shelf*, began publication during this time. It included short articles to keep library and staff informed about the ongoing successes and challenges of the grant. Yet the pressures of external projects and goals did not allow time for needed internal communication.

II. Introducing New Practices Phase

STAGE 5: EMPOWERING BROAD-BASED ACTION

The IMLS grant goals were not achieved fully in one year due to circumstances beyond our control involving one of our campus partners: University Relations. Perhaps the most ambitious goal of the grant (the video recording) was not achieved during year one. However, we were able to hire an outside firm to do some library service orientation videos, including interviews with student veterans0.[12] These were completed during the summer of 2016.

That goal was collaboration with the University Relations Television Department to create a recruitment video that will encourage student veterans to become active users of the facilities, resources, services, and expertise of the University Libraries while also becoming savvy users of information.

The stark reality of UR's inability to record on schedule necessitated an application for a one-year, no-cost extension of the IMLS grant, which was extended to September 30, 2017.[13] So eventually we were able to complete the video recording with UR's help.

Another goal developed during the second year of WVUL_VOP: to create a plan for a permanent program of outreach to the veteran students of WVU from the WVUL as part of our Engaged Librarian program. Developing such a plan required outreach to an internal team of librarians linked by their interest and experience in and with military service. This group (mentioned earlier in the Guiding Coalition section of this chapter) is working on a recommendation to the Dean of Libraries for such a permanent program. Funds from IMLS allowed us to create an excellent learning experience and foundation of outreach to student veterans. Now in 2017–18, it became time to integrate what we learned and make it permanent and sustainable through WVUL-supported funds and human resources.

This team of librarians is identifying the internal obstacles that need to be removed before we can achieve total success. We are going to recommend a structure that facilitates action and success, and we are encouraging innovative approaches to build buy-in throughout the culture of WVUL.

STAGE 6: GENERATING SHORT-TERM WINS

Receipt of the IMLS grant in 2015 was the first short-term win in this process of change. The activities of the grant provided more short-term wins including the following:

- Funds to support program development
- Funds to support part-time employment for two WVU student veterans: one undergraduate and one graduate student
- Funds to support several video productions
- Funds to support book and video collection development to address veteran interests
- Funds to support hardware purchase for the door to the Veteran Study Room to convert to swipe card access for veteran students only

Internal library funds supported other short-term wins. They included the following:

- Remodeling and furnishing the tutoring and study room for veteran students.
- Staff time and expertise to create an early survey of veterans' overall knowledge of libraries and interests in new services, resulting in a relevant LibGuide and a webpage providing relevant information about library use for veteran students.
- Staff time of the libraries' Development Director to obtain university funds to support a campus visit by a scholar/librarian from Texas A and M University who had recently co-written a book on library services to student veterans.[14] She presented two programs: one for the Campus Veterans Advocates group and the other for the Library Leadership Team. Both promoted the improvement of services offered to student veterans.

- The libraries' Development Director also found university funds to support remodeling and furnishing a second study room for campus veterans at the Evansdale Library.
- Staff time and expertise of the Director of Strategic Library Initiatives to organize public outreach programs such as "Mindfulness 101: Student Veterans and Mindfulness"; a three-month series of conversations between female staff and faculty veterans with women student veterans; one open house in the libraries and a collaboration on a second more comprehensive event at the WVU Alumni Center.
- Staff time and expertise of the Interim Director of Strategy and Planning (a new appointment title for me as of July 1, 2017) to join other campus service representatives in best practices training programs for academic advisors serving student veterans campus-wide.[15]

There are other examples of short-term wins that have not yet received the recognition they deserve. For example, the members of the early mini–guiding coalitions have not been publicly recognized for their important contributions. This suggests that the Working Group of librarians, mentioned in the sections of this chapter on Stages 2 and 5, needs to advocate for such visible recognition by the Dean of Libraries. All those (including the members of the Working Group) deserve acknowledgment for stepping up to support and sustain this important initiative as part of the organizational change underway.

STAGE 7: CONSOLIDATING GAINS AND PRODUCING MORE CHANGE

Once the recommendations of the Working Group of librarians (the third guiding coalition) are implemented, more changes will happen. These involve the following:

- Promoting buy-in for support by library staff of the student veteran community, its aspirations and needs, and explaining the reasons for continued outreach to this special population.
- Building a Confluence page (content collaboration software that changes how modern teams work) on the libraries' intranet site explaining background rationale for library services to veteran students and sharing relevant documents such as the original grant application, the grant's final report and appendices, and other information of importance to transparency about the creation and implementation of the outreach program in the first place.
- Identifying a librarian who can serve as coordinator of the continuing program of outreach to student veterans.
- Establishing goals for the program of future veteran student outreach and defining a strategy for accomplishing these goals.
- Working to offer instruction to interested veteran students reflecting the ideas and challenges of the *Framework for Information Literacy for Higher Education*.[16]
- Establishing a permanent group of library staff and faculty to advise the veteran student outreach librarian coordinator, including representatives of the Tech/ Beckley and Potomac State campuses.

- Offering two or three programs per year on relevant subjects for student veterans, university colleagues, library staff, or the public as recommended by the Advisory Committee.

III. Grounding Phase

STAGE 8: ANCHORING NEW APPROACHES IN THE CULTURE

The Working Group is recommending that the Associate Dean of Libraries (once hired) become the administrative official overseeing this initiative. The Working Group will morph into a representative Advisory Committee (one member being the engaged librarian coordinator of student veteran library outreach) to report to the Associate Dean. Together they will assess service usage and changes; review user statistics, especially of the study rooms; update the LibGuide and webpage as needed; design, deliver, and assess the effectiveness of programs; and revise any service delivery.

Annual productivity reports of those involved will include references to services to veteran students as evidence of librarians' involvement in addressing university strategic initiatives. Should the coordinator of the veteran outreach program leave WVUL, a replacement will be appointed in a timely manner to continue seamless services to the student veterans in the WVU community.

Analysis and Conclusions

Parts of the story of the creation of the WVUL_VOP did not fit neatly into the Kotter eight-stage model. The Kotter analysis did raise critical areas of focus that were inadvertently left out of the original project implementation. They included, for example, the importance of extensive external *and* internal communication of the change vision and recognition of the mini–guiding coalitions. But some factors were omitted.

What were these factors?

First, the results of the analysis highlighted obstacles and challenges we could not have anticipated. Reporting them in the context of this chapter cannot fully follow the objective conventions of scholarship because of their personal nature. To share these considerations, I have written instead a narrative here of lived experience of one kind of change in an academic library system over more than three years. This project has helped me become realistic about what is possible as I have worked to create change for WVUL. Other factors we could not have known in advance include the unique difficulties of the financial aid process for student veterans; the negative attitudes of student veterans about each military branch they did *not* serve in; and each individual student's goals and aspirations.

Second, getting a grasp on the full complexity of the student veteran community has not been easy because as a pacifist librarian, I was not familiar with military life. It has been a valuable experience to get to know the students while developing new library services. Knowing them has deepened my perception of the value of real engagement with a previously underserved group of students and has demonstrated that an outsider *can* make a significant and empathetic contribution to change.

There is a distinct military culture, and to communicate effectively with its members, an appreciative and respectful approach is essential. Higher education has a culture too, and the transition from military culture to an academic life is daunting for many veteran students. I also learned that the student veterans often have attitudes about other students that they call "the traditionals" (by which they mean the students ages eighteen to twenty-two who view university life as part educational and part social at best, and who are perceived as naïve about the real world). This knowledge helped me to understand why services such as dedicated physical space are meaningful in establishing good working relationships with veteran students.

An academic librarian who is also a veteran has written the best introduction to what makes student veterans tick. In a paper for the ACRL 2015 conference, Sarah LeMire lists five characteristics that distinguish veteran students from other nontraditional students.[17] Veterans share a sense of camaraderie, are accustomed to contributing, are busy people, often have unique needs, and *do not* want to be seen as needier than other students. I consult Lemire's insights often.

Third, and perhaps the most complex factor, is the challenge of military and higher education cultures colliding in the student veterans' experience. The two hierarchies are vastly different as military authorities give orders and expect dedication to the team. Higher education professors expect individual accomplishment and self-direction.

As a person without military experience, I saw cultural dissonance between the faculty and student veterans manifested in student fears of faculty politics. Some students sensed possible faculty suspicions about the reasons for their class absences even though the absences were because of active duty calls. Also, the students sensed that faculty's perceived liberal political leanings meant antimilitary sentiment. As the opportunity has presented itself, I have raised these concerns in discussion groups with other campus veteran advocates. Together we are searching for solutions to these unfortunate realities.

A fourth discovery that did not come out in the Kotter analysis was that our university is not as far along in developing cohesive support of student veterans as I had expected. This became clear upon discovering that comprehensive enrollment data for both undergraduate and graduate student veterans was incomplete. The lack of a centralized campus center was also a real problem for the students. As of 2018 one is at last under development. There is also a President's Action Group for Veterans at work since November 2017 assessing services for veteran students. Many WVU veteran advocates are hopeful this will produce meaningful results and more academic success for student veterans.

Academic libraries are still in the early stages of addressing the development of services for student veterans in the United States. Sarah LeMire goes so far as to say that "academic libraries have been slow to develop efforts to engage this special population."[18] Perhaps this analysis of leading change will advance the progress.

The importance of consistency of practice demonstrating commitment over time to the student veterans was not a goal we identified at the beginning of this change. Neither was it a stated goal to network with campus advocates for veterans in departments and co-curricular offices across the university. But both results were critical to building belief in and the authority of the libraries' role in addressing student veteran needs. The time it takes to address these kinds of changes effectively is significant, and benefits may be observed only after several years of focus and determination.

Some in academic libraries may assume that singling out a group of students for special services is wrong because it plays favorites. This underlying assumption surfaces especially when dedication of physical space is involved. Yet librarians recognize special needs in other subgroups of students, for example, international students, students at risk or with disabilities, and commuter students, to name a few. Engagement implies outreach to all and an expanded definition of diversity and inclusion.

The diversity among veterans and the special characteristics they manifest, including their nontraditional ages and the extraordinary nature of their experience before college, must be understood to provide relevant services and create transformative change in organizational culture on their behalf. University libraries can give better service as they demonstrate concern for the uniqueness of *each* group of students they serve, including student veterans.

Transformative change has been referred to as second-order change because it (1) alters the culture of the institution by changing select underlying assumptions and institutional behaviors, processes, and products; (2) is deep and pervasive; (3) is intentional; and (4) occurs over time.[19] WVUL is aiming for second-order change as we continue to develop effective and permanent outreach to the student veterans of West Virginia University.

In his final chapter, Kotter shares his positive view of organizations that focus on future growth rather than clinging to past successes.[20] He discusses leadership focus on the future and building capacity in the people who work in organizations. He suggests that these actions engender the ability to embrace change. These essential components encourage successful organizational outcomes.

At WVUL our elements of change (though not precisely in the order Kotter recommends) were

- the Dean's sense of urgency
- the original grant proposal
- the funding
- the steps of grant implementation
- the work of both the early guiding coalitions and the later guiding coalition
- the programs we offered to student veterans
- creation and then expansion of the veteran study room followed by plans for a second such room at the Evansdale Library
- the campus networking
- the trust building with student veterans
- the programmatic efforts made over two years
- the program attendance
- the final grant report
- the development of the Working Group's recommendation to the Dean of Libraries for a permanent WVUL_VOP

These function as evidence of the process of real change for student veterans at WVUL and organizational outcomes within WVUL.

Using Kotter's eight stages of leading change as an analytical tool has made it possible to see that the change initiative at WVUL to create a sustainable and permanent WVUL_VOP is on its way toward real success. Though more remains to be done, outreach to a deserving group of students who never received focused library attention in the past is happening now. We are demonstrating that our library culture has expanded its definition of inclusion through mindful attention to veteran students. We hope other academic libraries will integrate this relatively new outreach role into their organizational structures in the years ahead.

Notes

1. "Grant, Notice of Funding Opportunity," SPARKS! Institute for Museum and Library Services, October 2014, accessed 10/13/2014, http: www.Grants.gov
2. This chapter refers to student veterans' webpages, which are located under "Services for Student Veterans" within the WVU Libraries' pages at https://lib.wvu.edu/services/veterans; the chapter also refers to a LibGuide accessible through the WVU Libraries' webpages: "Resource Guide for Student Veterans," West Virginia University Libraries, last updated March 21, 2019, http://libguides.wvu.edu/studentvet.
3. Rae Helton, "Diversity Dispatch: Libraries—An Important Campus Partner for Student Veterans," *Kentucky Libraries* 74, no. 3 (August 1, 2010): 14
4. Wilkinson. IMLS SPARKS! Grant Application, 2015. (Submitted through Grants.gov 2/2/15).
5. Ilene F. Rockman, *Integrating Academic Library Information Literacy into the Higher Education Curriculum* (San Francisco: Jossey-Bass, 2004), 1.
6. Wilkinson, IMLS SPARKS! Grant Application, 2015. (Submitted through Grants.gov 2/2/15).
7. Ibid.
8. West Virginia University, University Relations Department, "Student Veterans Speak Up about the Libraries' Impact," recruitment video for WVU Libraries, 3:11, uploaded to YouTube February 21, 2017, https://lib.wvu.edu/services/veterans.
9. Library service orientation videos are found within the student veterans' site (see note 2).
10. David T. Vacchi, "Considering Veterans on the Twenty-First Century Campus," *About Campus* 17, no. 2 (May–June 2012): 15-21
11. See note 2.
12. See Evansdale Library and Downtown Campus Library Tours, found within the student veterans' site (see note 2).
13. Carroll Wetzel Wilkinson submitted an Institute for Museum and Library Services application for a no-cost grant extension August 2016. The extension was granted.
14. Sara LeMire and Kristen T. Mulvihill, *Serving Those Who Served* (Santa Barbara, CA: Libraries Unlimited, 2017).
15. As part of a Diversity for Equity Grant, this two-part series in February and March 2018 served as a training opportunity for faculty and staff advisors for veteran students. Topics addressed how to better serve WVU's student veteran population by academic advising through best practices collaborations with departments across campus including the libraries, Student Health and Wellness, and Mental Health Resources, among others.
16. The Working Group of Librarians mentioned in this chapter is recommending eventual relevant course-based information literacy instruction in collaboration with interested faculty based on the *Framework for Information Literacy in Higher Education* (Association of College and Research Libraries, *Framework for Information Literacy for Higher Education* [Chicago: Association of College and Research Libraries, 2016].
17. Sara LeMire, "Beyond Service: New Outreach Strategies to Reach Student Veterans," in *Creating Sustainable Community: ACRL 2015, March 25–28, 2015, Portland, Oregon: Conference Proceedings*, ed. by Dawn M. Mueller (Chicago: Association of College and Research Libraries, 2015), 68–70.
18. LeMire, "Beyond Service," 67.
19. Susan R. Komives, Wendy Wagner, and Associates, *Leadership for a Better World* (San Francisco: Jossey-Bass, 2009), 103.
20. John P. Kotter, *Leading Change* (Boston: Harvard Business Review Press, 2012), 194.

Bibliography

Association of College and Research Libraries. *Framework for Information Literacy for Higher Education.* Chicago: Association of College and Research Libraries, 2016.

Association of College and Research Libraries. "Member of the Week: Sarah LeMire." *ACRL Insider,* May 4, 2015. https://www.acrl.ala.org/acrlinsider/archives/10212.

Atwood, Thomas, Michael Farmer, Krista McDonald, Brianne Miller, Eileen Theodore-Shusta, and Elizabeth J. Wood. "On the Front Lines: Serving Ohio's Best." *Journal of Academic Librarianship* 42, no. 2 (March 2016): 172–80.

Helton, Rae. "Diversity Dispatch: Libraries—An Important Campus Partner for Veterans. *Kentucky Libraries* 74, no. 3 (August 1, 2010): 14-15.

Komives, Susan R., Wendy Wagner, and Associates. *Leadership for a Better World: Understanding the Social Change Model of Leadership Development.* San Francisco: Jossey-Bass, 2009.

Kotter, John P. *Leading Change.* Boston: Harvard Business Review Press, 2012.

LeMire, Sarah. "Beyond Service: New Outreach Strategies to Reach Student Veterans." In *Creating Sustainable Community: ACRL 2015, March 25–28, 2015, Portland, Oregon: Conference Proceedings.* Edited by Dawn M. Mueller, 66–71. Chicago: Association of College and Research Libraries, 2015.

LeMire, Sarah, and Kristen T. Mulvihill. *Serving Those Who Served: Librarians' Guide to Working with Veteran and Military Communities.* Santa Barbara, CA: Libraries Unlimited, 2017.

Library Journal. "Veteran Librarian." *Library Journal,* March 17, 2017, 39.

Mills, Chloe Persian, Emily Bounds Paladino, and Jacqueline Courtney Klentzin. "Student Veterans and the Academic Library." *Reference Services Review* 43, no 2 (2015): 262–79.

Ohio State University Libraries. *A Framework for the Engaged Librarian: Building on Our Strengths.* Columbus: Ohio State University Libraries, 2016.

Phelps, Sue F. "The Veteran Student Experience and the Academic Librarian." *Journal of Academic Librarianship* 41, no. 3 (May 2015): 236–40.

Rockman, Ilene F. *Integrating Academic Library Information Literacy into the Higher Education Curriculum.* San Francisco: Jossey-Bass, 2004.

SPARKS! "Grant, Notice of Funding Opportunity." Institute for Museum and Library Services. October 2014. Accessed 10/13/2014, www.grants.gov

Vacchi, David T. "Considering Veterans on the Twenty-First Century Campus." *About Campus* 17, no. 2 (May–June 2012): 15–21.

West Virginia University, University Relations Department. "Student Veterans Speak Up about the Libraries' Impact." Recruitment video for WVU Libraries, 3:11. Uploaded to YouTube February 21, 2017. https://lib.wvu.edu/services/veterans.

Wilkinson, Carroll Wetzel. "Community Salute: Creating a Culture of Community, Discovery, and Learning for Student Veterans at West Virginia University Libraries. "*Up Next Blog,* Institute of Museum and Library Services, November 10, 2016. https://www.imls.gov/blog/2016/11/community-salute-creating-culture-community-discovery-and-learning-student-veterans.

Chapter 20

Analysis
New Roles for Libraries

Colleen Boff and Catherine Cardwell

Libraries
Earlham College
University of Florida (UF)
University of Maryland (UMD)
West Virginia University (WVU)

Introduction

The institutions in this category include Earlham, a small private liberal arts college located in the Midwest, and three large, research-intensive public universities located in Florida, Maryland, and West Virginia. Some aspect of library instruction is common among these stories, yet the intended audiences for these new initiatives differ considerably. Earlham's Library Immersion Fellows Team (LIFT) is designed specifically for first-generation, first-year students. Veterans are at the forefront of the new program at WVU, while graduate students are the focus at UF. Liaison librarians are the primary audience for the change at UMD with a re-visioning of the liaison librarian program. The initiatives at Earlham, UF, and UMD rely heavily upon partnerships with offices, units, or departments outside of the libraries. Regardless of institutional size at Earlham, UF, and WVU, the programs implemented at these institutions involve a segment of the overall student population.

I. Warm-up Phase
STAGE 1: ESTABLISHING A SENSE OF URGENCY

Librarians at Earlham and at WVU started their new programs after top leadership issued a challenge to create new initiatives for underserved populations. The act of presenting a program idea as a possible solution to an administrator's challenge creates its own sense of urgency. The impetus to develop the LIFT program at Earlham came in response to a senior administrator's campus-wide challenge for assistance with solving the retention problem they had with first-generation students at Earlham, a problem shared by many institutions nationwide. In addition to being the only one to respond to this challenge, the library instruction program at Earlham had a long and rich history of innovation thanks to highly effective instruction program leadership. Both of these

factors fueled the urgency with which it approached the implementation of this new program.

Similarly, the pressure to respond to a challenge from the new library dean along with the pressure that comes with being a principal investigator on a federal grant, as was the case at WVU, is ample cause for motivation to succeed. The director of strategy and planning at WVU started this new initiative by partnering with the office of veterans affairs to dedicate a space in the library for veterans to study and seek tutoring. Recognizing the need for more, she subsequently applied for and received an IMLS grant to expand this program.

The programs initiated at UF and UMD evolved from looking inward at library practices. Primed by a goal to create transformative collaborations identified through their strategic planning process, the librarians at UF wanted to address library staff concerns about the administration of graduate internships in the library. They recognized that the timing was right to act on this goal with newly hired talent in place at the library and conversations among the arts and humanities faculty about the need to create internships for their students in order to provide career exploration and CV-worthy experience. The librarians at UMD were similarly engaged with a conversation taking place in the professional literature about the changing landscape of librarian liaison programs. They saw the need to reinvent their liaison program to respond to the changing needs of scholars on their campus. In both instances, these new initiatives were the result of librarians taking a step back from the day-to-day tasks of running libraries to respond to the conversations taking place around them.

STAGE 2: CREATING A GUIDING COALITION

The guiding coalitions at UF and WVU include a few people from the library who championed the initiative and formed partnerships outside of the library to bring the initiatives to fruition. The director of strategy and planning was initially the only person from the library involved with the implementation of the veterans program at WVU. She collaborated extensively with a wide range of staff outside the library, however. An associate dean and the digital scholarship librarian within the library at UF partnered to work on the creation of an internship program proposal, but they also sought external partners when they solicited input from a faculty member who served as the graduate coordinator for the history department.

With more involvement among library employees, the library dean and the senior administrator who made the initial call for help cochaired and identified the team at Earlham. They selected liaison librarians as members because of their long-standing tradition of involvement with campus governance, advising, and teaching semester-long courses. The involvement of two senior-level administrators on this team meant that the team had a wider reach on campus and that it was better situated to spread the word about the program, to raise financial support, and to reach alumni. The guiding coalition at UMD was more complex and consisted of two task forces formed by the associate dean of public services. The liaison task force had four members and was charged with making recommendations for how to improve services to faculty and students. The research commons task force actively sought feedback from stakeholders through interviews and surveys to determine needs.

STAGE 3: DEVELOPING A VISION AND STRATEGY

One or two librarians initiated and articulated the vision for each of these new initiatives, but their strategy evolved to include others. The cochairs' vision for their project at Earlham was to divide the initial cohort of fifteen to thirty students into four small groups with a staff member assigned to each group. The teaching team worked on a shared curriculum where students came together for a ninety-minute meeting each week to discuss readings, to build information literacy competencies, but most importantly, to build relationships with each other. The leading partners at UF presented their internship plan to the library management and leadership stakeholders to get buy-in, which resulted in the formation of the internship program committee that ultimately included some of the key library stakeholders. The goals of the committee were to promote and explain the program to others. The vision for the two task forces at UMD was broad and interconnected. The liaison group was charged with the development of a framework for the liaison program that included core competencies for liaison librarians, methods to assess those competencies, and the professional development needed to be successful in their new roles. The research commons task force was charged with the design of a one-stop shop for researchers to access all services related to the research process. At WVU, the director of strategy and planning lobbied, as part of her vision, for dedicated library funds and a dedicated library staff position to work with the veteran population.

STAGE 4: COMMUNICATING THE CHANGE VISION

Communication efforts at Earlham and WVU were outwardly focused with the intention of reaching the audiences for whom their programs were intended. The teaching team at Earlham used a wide range of outlets to recruit interest in the LIFT program. They started with an annual presentation at a faculty retreat, promotion of their program through the admissions office, and a promotional piece in their alumni magazine. The latter blossomed into a significant donation that enabled them to expand the program offerings with funds to support an off-campus learning experience for LIFT students. Likewise, the director of strategy and planning at WVU spent her time putting the structures in place to recruit veterans to library services and offerings. She did this by recruiting and hiring veterans to help her get the word out through social media and other outlets.

Communication at UF and UMD started among library employees. The committee members at UF spent an academic year developing a website, creating program materials, and working with library staff to promote the benefits of their internship program for graduate students. The two task forces at UMD completed their charges and shared their written reports with library administration and with library staff through open forums. Their library administration, in turn, shared the written reports with campus administrators and with leadership teams in other colleges on their campus as a way to seek feedback. It was a means to remind their campus colleagues of how the library supports research activity on campus.

II. Introducing New Practices Phase

STAGE 5: EMPOWERING BROAD-BASED ACTION

The chapter authors describe barriers they faced in refining the programs at Earlham and WVU. The teaching team at Earlham had the difficult task of developing selection criteria and methods for the travel opportunity due to limited funds. The teaching team also had to contend with keeping students grounded in the curriculum with the distractions created by the travel opportunity. The director of strategic planning at WVU had the frustration of requesting an extension for a grant deliverable when an office she relied upon to produce a promotional video delayed progress. She also had to figure out how to sustain outreach efforts initially afforded by a seed grant. She did so by working with a team of librarians from their embedded librarian program.

The barriers associated with undertaking a new librarian liaison model at UMD were more complicated than the barriers encountered at Earlham or WVU because the change initiative involved many more library staff and the change was personal. In order to move forward with the project and with internal communication efforts, the UMD libraries began with a reorganization to put all subject librarians in one department. In addition to fostering regular communication among middle management, the libraries held monthly forums where all subject librarians could exchange ideas. Most importantly, the libraries provided professional development training and incorporated into their annual review process assessment measures and goal setting for liaison librarians. Unlike the other institutions in this category, the internship program committee at UF felt that they had few barriers to contend with thanks to the many existing relationships the library had with academic departments. While they still had a great deal of work to do to create an actual program, they had a solid foundation on which to build.

STAGE 6: GENERATING SHORT-TERM WINS

Short-term wins at Earlham, UF, and WVU demonstrated continued growth with their projects intended for their respective populations. The teaching team at Earlham integrated a digital storytelling project into their shared curriculum, which led to more funding when one of the librarian instructors showed her students' videos at an alumni event. They worked with the alumni office to set up a mentor program between alumni and LIFT students. The veterans' project at WVU received additional funds from the library administration to build upon the work completed as a result of securing an IMLS grant. Combined, these funds enabled the director of strategy and planning to continue shaping programming, collections, and services for veterans. Short-term wins at UF came with the launch of two internships in the summer of 2016. This enabled the internship program committee to operationalize their planning with their first orientation event. Short-term wins were realized at UMD over a longer period of time because the UMD libraries were changing existing behaviors rather than starting a new program. The liaison framework was phased in over two years and was done through the creation of an annual assessment system. The liaison librarians were expected to demonstrate accomplishments in five categories of liaison activities. Credit for gains in the research commons side of the change initiative was attributed to a dynamic individual who stepped up to lead. Under this umbrella, a one-stop shop website was created along with online librarian profiles. Adjustments were also made to librarians' day-to-day work expectations to make room for the new services offered under the RC, and library spaces were modernized to reflect new active learning teaching methods.

STAGE 7: CONSOLIDATING GAINS AND PRODUCING MORE CHANGE

Regular planning meetings among the teaching team at Earlham before the term, in the middle of the term, and after the term kept the LIFT curriculum grounded and moving forward. Momentum continued at WVU with the help of the engagement librarians, who conceived of continued outreach and programming solutions for veterans now that they had dedicated spaces for this population in their library system. In addition to an orientation experience, the internship program committee at UF launched even more experiences for their interns, such as a required end-of-experience presentation and a résumé-building workshop. The committee streamlined the proposal submission process, posted a calendar of deadlines for applicants, and offered training for librarian internship directors.

Finally, the small seeds of change to the librarian liaison model and research commons at UMD blossomed into a complete culture change. Most of the librarian liaisons became embedded in their departments, while specialized RCs emerged in various libraries around campus. The synergy of these two efforts has aligned to the degree that faculty and students now look to the libraries as a place for all aspects of research assistance.

III. Grounding Phase

STAGE 8: ANCHORING NEW APPROACHES IN THE CULTURE

Each of these programs has been underway for a few years now. Earlham has only grown stronger through the creation of intentional intersections between upper-class students and first-semester students affiliated with the program. The upper-class students serve as role models to first-year students while students across cohorts come together to celebrate those who graduate. UF's internship program committee applied for an NEH grant to strengthen collaborations as a means to improve job placement for graduate students. Though they were not recipients of the award, the work that the librarians put into writing the grant proposal raised the visibility of their work with the president, who provided funding for them to address some changes needed for graduate students enrolled in humanities PhD programs. At WVU, structural changes have been suggested to anchor the work with veterans into the libraries' organization, including a reporting line to the library administrative office and the creation of an advisory board. The changes at UMD, which included the shift to a new librarian liaison framework and a research commons, are well anchored and now a part of the culture. The authors attribute this shift to a gradual implementation process and the creation of a learning culture among library employees.

Analysis and Conclusions

Momentum continued at Earlham, where the libraries have been awarded more funding from the board of trustees to continue increasing the retention rate for first-generation students. Reflecting on the use of the Kotter framework as an analytical tool, the authors at Earlham found value in taking particular care at the warm-up phase, especially when working on a project that is not the exclusive domain of the library. They stress the importance of the warm-up phase, which helped them take stock of the political dynamics on their campus when stepping up to take on a new and unusual role. The library at WVU entered new territory as well with taking the lead on campus to provide services to veterans, an idea met with some skepticism. UF attributed its record of awarding twenty-nine internships over forty-four semesters and taking the lead to transform graduate education to the existing relationships the librarians had with faculty from the outset. These relationships were invaluable throughout the program development as it gained credibility. Though there was a degree of cultural change within the library in each of these stories, the cultural change was most widespread with the transformation of the librarian liaison program at UMD because of the number of librarians it impacted.

TIPS FOR NEW ROLES FOR LIBRARIES

- New projects require seed money, but actively seeking long-term financial sustainability during the change process is also important. The work at Earlham and WVU shows that this can be done by showcasing small wins to the right stakeholders at the right time.
- In most of these new initiatives, the guiding coalition used early successes to fuel program growth incrementally. Typically, the new initiatives started out small with only a partially formed vision, but through an iterative cycle of evaluation and assessment, the initiatives were scaffolded into a more robust program.
- A prevalent theme throughout the stories in this category is the importance of the guiding coalition remaining agile, responsive, and flexible throughout the change process. Having a rigid strategy in place may result in missed opportunities to collaborate with new campus partners.
- Libraries have opportunities to step in and solve campus problems even when the problem does not fall within the traditional scope of the library. Librarians at Earlham solved the retention problem with first-generation students. Librarians at UF changed the educational experience of graduate students through their internship program. The library at UMD is now the go-to place for all aspects of research through its research commons. WVU is setting an example in the field for how the library can serve veterans. Libraries need to take care when they embark on solving these larger campus problems. Not only do they need to gain trust and credibility among their campus counterparts, but they also need to make sure they consider the political ramifications of boundaries and territories. They can address this issue by building the right relationships.
- At least with the stories in this category, a few leaders who will be continuous champions of the vision can best nurture new roles for libraries. Communicating the vision and mission within the library may be of less importance than identifying key library stakeholders and keeping them informed along the way. Critical to all of these stories was connecting with stakeholders outside of the library and building relationships. Keeping library administration involved helped with financial sustainability in addition to furthering the reach of the program initiatives in administrative venues outside the library.

PART V
TECHNOLOGICAL CHANGE

Chapter 21

Repository Reboot

Jonathan Helmke, R. Philip Reynolds, and Shirley Dickerson

Setting the Change Stage

Stephen F. Austin State University (SFA) is located on a beautiful campus in the heart of east Texas in historic Nacogdoches. Nacogdoches, population of almost 40,000, is known as the "oldest town in Texas" and thrives as a college town that also appeals to retirees. SFA has a Carnegie Classification of Basic with a fall enrollment of 13,000 students. The university offers over 120 areas of undergraduate study, as well as over forty masters' programs and three doctoral degrees. In addition to programs at the main campus, select programs are offered at offsite area institutions of higher education (i.e., Houston Community College System, Lone Star College System, Panola College, and LeTourneau University).

The Ralph W. Steen Library building, erected in 1973, is named for Dr. Ralph W. Steen, the university's third president. It supports academic programs and research initiatives by providing an array of informational, educational, and research support services. The library is widely supported by the university administration, faculty, and students; therefore, library faculty acquire a collection that supports the teaching, research, and creative mission of the university. Additionally, the library serves as a community resource, providing access to historical and genealogical collections as well as being a repository for Texas and federal government documents.

The library developed a reputation in the community as an early adopter of technology. Steen Library established the first open computer labs on campus. The first web development office for the university was created and managed by the library. An award-winning peer-tutoring center, at no cost to students, was created to offer supplemental and one-on-one instruction.

In the early 2000s, digitization that supported institutional repositories (IRs) was being implemented at colleges and universities around the country. The first attempt to create a digitization or digital service was supported by a 2003 grant from the Institute of Library and Museums Services (IMLS). In 2006, the incoming library director created a digital projects department, reassigning four librarians from the reference department and archives and special collections. Due in part to the lack of a shared mission and vision, the digital projects department did not gain wide appeal and support from many academic units and was dissolved.

In 2013, the Center for Digital Scholarship (CDS) was created with the following department mission statement:

> To support the scholarly activities and intellectual output of the SFA community, CDS provides support regarding scholarly communications issues, (i.e., open access, copyright and authors' publishing rights), media migration, and increases visibility of SFA's scholarly research in the institutional repository.[1]

One of the services provided is ScholarWorks, the IR maintained by CDS. This department has one full-time scholarly communication librarian and a half-time staff member who helps with various projects in ScholarWorks in addition to her duties in supervising various digitization projects.

This chapter focuses on several aspects of change that impacted the library and the entire campus. These changes include

- initial development of the IR to meet the demand of providing access to faculty and student scholarship,
- what changes were made to the program to address issues and problems after the first implementation, and
- continued development of the program to meet the current and future demands.

I. Warm-up Phase

STAGE 1: ESTABLISHING A SENSE OF URGENCY

The most common mistake in creating change is not spending enough time on building a sense of urgency among enough people before moving on to the other steps.[2] One of the major challenges in building the IR was in developing a strong sense of urgency for the project beyond the walls of the library. While it had been discussed for some time, interest in the project was still limited to a small group in the library. Once the decision to create the IR occurred, the project still lacked the key element of urgency for creating change. A lack of urgency resulted in the IR being assigned as an additional duty for the librarian already responsible for the university archives and records management.

One motivator for the development of the IR was the fear of being left behind by other institutions of higher education that were developing repositories of their own. Steen Library had an established reputation to uphold as a regional and even national leader in integrating progressive, cutting-edge service and technology. The professional literature, as well as library professionals, presented the development of this new service designed to capture and showcase the research of faculty at their respective institutions. Library administrators and professionals recognized the value of the IR to showcase and make accessible faculty research. A leadership change in the organization influenced our experience at Steen Library. Initially, a novice science librarian approached the outgoing library director about creating an IR. The outgoing director had led the organization through the implementation of the online catalog in the late 1980s and the installation of a 150-seat computer lab in the 1990s before these services were mainstays of libraries. The outgoing director knew the great amount of time and energy needed to build a coalition to support these efforts. Subsequently, the incoming library director focused the library's resources, human and fiscal, on the development of a new website. By chance, the East Texas Research Center (ETRC), which serves as the archival department within the library, identified a hosted solution for an IR, and the new director agreed to a subscription to begin the initiative. However, the urgency to develop an IR was over-shadowed by competing needs within the organization; therefore, there was a lack of importance attached to the development of the IR. The library's existing organizational structure did not support the creation of an IR.

In the fall of 2013, the Associate Director for Information Services submitted a proposal to the library director for the creation of a separate department that focused on digital initiatives. The library at the time provided support for digital services in the ETRC as part of its digital imaging of archival resources. In order to meet the needs of the entire university and support new digital initiatives, the director proposed a reorganization of our internal digital experts to create the Center for Digital Scholarship. This involved pulling librarians and staff from the ETRC and the Research and Instructional Services (RIS) department. With these resources, the center could play a vital role in responding to shifting scholarship needs among academic stakeholders.

In the beginning, the lack of a clear and compelling vision communicated frequently inside and outside of the library meant that few knew about the IR and those that knew saw no particular benefit in participating. The barrier of asking faculty to self-submit content to the IR left many asking themselves what was the point of doing all that extra work. This put the onus on the university faculty, who had no sense of urgency or clear and motivating vision as to why, to populate the IR themselves. Some workshops were given about open access (OA) and how to submit papers, but OA was a poorly understood concept outside of the library and, therefore, a poor motivator of faculty to contribute to ScholarWorks. Likewise, there was complacency among the librarians regarding the success or failure of the IR. Other work was more urgent, and accountability for other work was reinforced by annual evaluations. Few if any of the new tasks and responsibilities relating to an IR were included in annual evaluations. It became clear that something had to change to move ScholarWorks forward.

Despite these shortcomings, the librarian responsible for the IR implemented the instance of the Digital Commons platform for the university's IR and made valiant efforts putting into place many features of the service. Inevitably, though, complacency overshadowed the launch and roll-out of ScholarWorks.

A sense of urgency began to emerge again when one of the librarians realized that the library was paying $30,000 a year to house 300 documents in the IR—a cost of $100 per document. At the time this was not written down for fear of who might see it, but clearly, it was unsustainable. A major change needed to occur. A repository reboot was needed.

Library administration needed to bring down the cost per document quickly, ensuring sustainability. The library also had a reputation as a regional leader in many ways and needed to show success and competence in following through with this new investment. Additionally, the library needed to show campus administration that the IR was a success.

Because of the library's several constituencies, a sense of urgency needed tailoring to different stakeholders' interests simultaneously. Since each of these groups in many respects has different interests, different methodologies were required to create the needed sense of urgency. Within the library, there was a need to show significant progress in order to gain the support of other librarians, especially those whose departments had lost personnel in creating the CDS. Library administration also needed to see sufficient progress to justify the cost of the IR and the decision to move these particular staff members. Outside of the library, the university administration needed a different approach. Administrators needed to see how the IR could raise the profile of the university so that they would support the efforts of the CDS with the faculty. Faculty needed to know that the IR was going to benefit them and their work. The focus with them was on the worldwide reach of the IR and the usage statistics of items in the IR. They also needed to see how the IR could be more than just a bibliography of articles. Image galleries, the journal-hosting functionalities, video, and 3-D images were all part of the presentations. This often sparked ideas with the faculty about ways they could use the IR for their projects and generated interest in working with the CDS on a wide range of projects.

STAGE 2: CREATING A GUIDING COALITION

In November 2014, the library administration escalated the level of urgency for the IR through a reorganization led by the Associate Director for Information Services. The associate director identified and reassigned librarians in the Research and Instructional Services (RIS) department and the East Texas Research Center and moved them to create the Center for Digital Scholarship (CDS). This shift moved the lead responsibility of the IR from a part-time effort of a single librarian to that of a department consisting of three librarians (department head, scholarly communication librarian, metadata librarian) and a paraprofessional, which signaled the elevation and urgency of an impactful, campus-wide digital presence as a goal.

The CDS coalition needed a strong sense of urgency to create the new department and solidify the newly reassigned positions with a thriving effort. The team also needed to know that they were seeing substantial progress and receiving recognition for frequent short-term wins. Additionally, they needed to establish their credibility within and outside of the library. This was done through continual presentations to departments and in one-on-one interactions in which CDS made several very public promises to provide services. These included efficiently ingesting articles from faculty CVs into the IR, building an online presence for research centers on campus to display their work, providing a home for digital humanities projects, providing a platform for the publishing and management of peer-reviewed journals created by faculty, and many other faculty-driven projects ranging from the sciences to the fine arts. In the presentations, these possibilities were shared with faculty all across campus. Within a year, these potentialities were realities and solidified the CDS's ability and credibility in the following year's presentations. The public nature of these widely communicated services and mission was a strong motivator for the department to succeed. If this service failed to live up to these promises, the team's and the individual librarians' credibility in and out of the library would be in jeopardy.

STAGE 3: DEVELOPING A VISION AND STRATEGY

The first order of business was to articulate the department's mission. An early version of the department's mission tended to focus efforts on textual content, failing to exploit the full functionality available on the Digital Commons platform. A revision of the vision was changed to read with intentionality and clarity: "ScholarWorks will archive and showcase the intellectual and creative output of the university."

This vision was much more flexible and inclusive than the old one and opened the IR for the integration of content not normally found in IRs. The emphasis went from how we can get more articles into ScholarWorks to how can we "archive and showcase the intellectual and creative output of the university." While this supported numerous agendas, including the university's mission along with many other desired outcomes, it all boiled down to getting more content into the IR.

STAGE 4: COMMUNICATING THE CHANGE VISION

The newly formed CDS department bonded behind a shared urgency to establish its credibility within and outside of the library, which resulted in the development of a unifying tactic that would characterize all communications beyond the walls of the library about the change vision. Through continual department-customized presentations and one-on-one interactions with faculty and university administrators, the collective efforts of the department remained on perfecting the message about the department's vision.

Faculty meetings and new faculty orientation were obvious venues for reaching large groups to share information about ScholarWorks and to invite participation. There was success with the early adopters largely because recruitment focused on relationship building with faculty who were also prolific writers. Significant early adopters of the IR were from the College of Fine Arts, College of Forestry and Agriculture, and the College of Liberal and Applied Arts, which demonstrates the multidisciplinary aspects of ScholarWorks and more than doubled the content in ScholarWorks within a year (see figure 21.1).

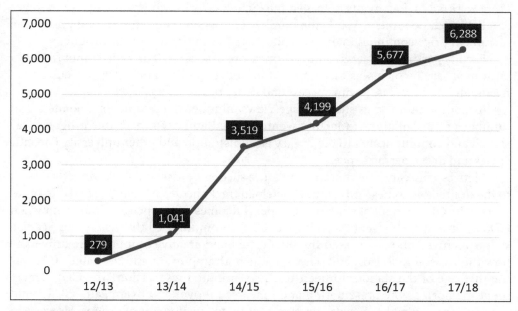

FIGURE 21.1
Number of documents in the institutional repository by academic year (September through May)

II. Introducing New Practices Phase

STAGE 5: EMPOWERING BROAD-BASED ACTION

The newly formed CDS department revisited the vision statement, the collection scope, the faculty engagement opportunities, and the self-submission process of the previous attempt to establish an IR. The removal of these self-imposed obstacles, along with the assignment of primary and common responsibilities within the department, greatly increased faculty participation. The message about the newly named ScholarWorks espoused its value as a repository of multidisciplinary scholarly research outputs of the university's faculty, staff, and students.

The repository reboot overcame the limitations mentioned above primarily in two ways. First, the CDS staff decided to elicit ideas from faculty regarding the IR's collection scope. This was a fundamental paradigm shift from libraries excluding faculty input about their needs in an IR to eagerly inviting faculty discussion with librarians concerning their needs and vision for "their" IR. At the start of the reboot, the nature of faculty meetings went from librarians simply soliciting articles for deposit to librarians engaging in conversations with faculty to explore future possibilities to shape a broader vision of ScholarWorks.

STAGE 6: GENERATING SHORT-TERM WINS

The most tangible evidence of immediate wins was seen in the growing number of documents added to ScholarWorks and the number of downloads from the IR. Prior to the relaunch, ScholarWorks had a total of 300 documents, which averaged about $100 a document based on the annual platform costs. As of this writing of this chapter, there were 6,890 documents uploaded into ScholarWorks, whose annual cost averages less than $5 a document. While the number of documents continues to increase, the document price continues to drop despite increases in the cost of the product.

Faculty participation was an outside measure of success. It provided input from our "customer base," which was instrumental in understanding and acting on customers' needs, and that increased with success and drove productivity.

As additional metrics such as page views, number of documents uploaded, and number of presentations to faculty were gathered and examined, this progress was shared and communicated to the library administration and other university constituencies and drove performance.

Metrics were carefully chosen to measure success by assessing tasks directly related to the desired outcomes. This approach helped track the department's actual outcomes and not just the amount of work being done. Outcomes were especially important when CDS evaluated the presentations it gave. CDS communicated the vision that Scholar-Works archived and showcased the intellectual and creative output of the university, how the IR would do this, and why this was both important and desirable. This was the message of the standard fifteen-to-thirty-minute presentation. The CDS department memorized the presentation and rehearsed it over and over again. CDS could easily go out and make an excellent presentation to any number of groups. However, a well-delivered presentation was not considered a success. A well-delivered message was just the baseline of what was expected. For the presentation to be considered a success, faculty hearing the presentation would need to send their CVs, request the creation of a new journal, or take advantage of one of the other IR services with a new project or content. In this way, CDS measured the true goal, not how well CDS could memorize the presentation, but how many commitments and how much follow-through in actions from the target audience occurred. One of the relatively less impressive performances of the presentation actually resulted in the entire academic department submitting their CVs. This was therefore considered a huge success. By measuring the response of faculty to the presentations instead of just counting the number of presentations given, CDS was able to keep complacency about the presentation at bay and ratchet up the urgency through meaningful goals while simultaneously realizing there were always more faculty to persuade.

These presentations led to many short-term successes that were clear and meaningful. While the number of presentations was counted, it was the number of items added to the IR, the percentage of faculty participation (see figure 21.2), and the number of journals published that became the measures of short-term success.

Academic Year	12/13	13/14	14/15	15/16	16/17	17/18
Growth of IR	279	1,041	3,519	4,199	5,677	6,288
Percentage of Faculty Participation	2%	8.2%	20.8%	24.5%	24.5%	25%
New Journals Published	0	0	2	6	0	0

FIGURE 21.2
Faculty participation rate by academic year (September through May)

STAGE 7: CONSOLIDATING GAINS AND PRODUCING MORE CHANGE

One of the most effective tactics the team used to build momentum was to demonstrate new and successful projects during the presentations. Initially, CDS would talk about the capabilities of the Digital Commons platform but could show only the few citations that were in the repository and showcase projects at other universities. As mentioned earlier, it was decided to remove the roadblock of limiting content placed in the IR by allowing faculty to tell the CDS staff what they wanted to put in the IR. To encourage this, CDS showed successful projects from SFA that were more than just bibliographies of articles. Faculty had all seen bibliographies and databases before, and it was felt they would not respond to just looking at them in our presentation of ScholarWorks. This would also limit their view of what could be done with the IR. As CDS successfully implemented new items, including student capstone projects, new journals, photography projects, academic centers, retiring faculty research, and video from events, faculty became excited and creative in ways the CDS would have never thought of.[3] Demonstrations of ScholarWorks not only encouraged faculty to submit their CVs but also spawned new ideas on how the IR could be used. Some of these ideas included student films, grant-funded faculty projects, inclusion of campus research centers, and 3-D models of Caddo pottery.[4] Each of these in turn were added to the presentations that maintained faculty interest and spawned new ideas and new success to build on.

Those outside of the CDS and outside of the library could see these outputs. This resulted in the university provost praising the IR and the library at the annual faculty meeting one year. The success of CDS and ScholarWorks was widely accepted.

III. Grounding Phase

STAGE 8: ANCHORING NEW APPROACHES IN THE CULTURE

After experiencing several years of accelerated success in growing the IR, the library organization was forced to compete even more aggressively for dwindling funds alongside other university departments. The early successes in achieving name recognition for ScholarWorks, however, did not translate into campus-wide buy-in, with one major exception: electronic theses and dissertations (ETDs). Each year, new incoming faculty, in particular, questioned why ETDs had not been implemented at SFA. Institutions of similar size in the state had established ETD programs. It was a recurring topic at professional library conferences; yet the culture at SFA at the time was entrenched in tradition that impeded a profitable uninterrupted campus conversation about the value of an ETD program to students as well as the potential value to the research community. Once ScholarWorks was implemented and faculty could actually use the platform, it was easier to demonstrate to faculty and students the various advantages of putting ETDs into ScholarWorks. The move from paper to electronic theses and dissertations represented a major change experience in microcosm. Many across the library and across campus were eager to see this change implemented. A coalition of departments, including CDS, the acquisitions department, library administration, the College of Deans, the Graduate Office, and the provost, all wanted to see this happen. The stakes were very high to gain the trust of the university administration, faculty, and students. Therefore, nothing was spared to ensure a smooth rollout of the migration of theses and dissertations to a digital environment. Early on, the CDS department realized that each success fueled the engine that helped to build toward future successes. The success of the ETD program was predicated on forming meaningful alliances with college administrators and faculty as well as the School of Graduate Studies. The ETD success helped to anchor ScholarWorks into the campus culture in all graduate programs.

Analysis and Conclusions

The CDS department's team effort was critical to sustain the sense of urgency that propelled them toward their shared vision. However, internal departmental urgency alone was not enough to anchor interest and support in the campus culture.

Untimely exits of four of the five CDS personnel through retirement and resignations caused the level of productivity to plummet. The successes achieved with ScholarWorks ultimately fell victim to decisions of the incoming university administration to not allow those positions to be filled. Reasons given were related to shrinking university resources and the need to direct resources to support strategic priorities. Despite the crippling upset to the CDS department, the Scholarly Communications Librarian and the paraprofessional looked for opportunities to engage with the university's initiative to promote undergraduate research. ScholarWorks was an established platform to host graduate and undergraduate research, including journals. The library will collaborate with the various academic departments and the Office of Research and Graduate Studies to support this program.

With limited staff resources, it is challenging to continue on the trajectory that the CDS coalition had experienced. The library administration continues to advocate to university administration to support further development of the platform as well as ongoing engagement with the academic community. In this current environment, the work continues and the vision is clear. There is a growing backlog of research waiting to be loaded in the CDS and ScholarWorks. One of these steps is realizing that a lot of hard work, even very good work, can lead to complacency among staff and administration. Without a sense or voice of urgency, other voices for other projects, other changes, or even the status quo will drown out the need for fully supporting another repository reboot.

The needed urgency can be achieved if the department and specifically the IR are aligned more closely to broader university goals. These include recruitment and retention of students and of quality faculty. By adopting changes that demonstrate a less tenuous connection between the work of CDS and the major change efforts of the university, the library can tap into the existing sense of urgency of these other change efforts on campus. The library needs to bombard the university with examples of the rewards of capitalizing on opportunities offered by supporting change in the CDS and the IR and how these changes are in line with broader changes being attempted across the university.[5] These could include student engagement and transformation through the publication of undergraduate research journals, as well as the inclusion of student capstone projects and honors theses in the IR along with other notable undergraduate work unique to the institution and its programs. By showing an ability to contribute positively to change efforts on campus, CDS should receive administrative support by owning its part in the university's change efforts.

Notes

1. Stephen F. Austin State University, *General Bulletin for 2015-16* (Nacogdoches, TX), 20, http://www.sfasu.edu/documents/general-bulletin-2015-2016.pdf.

2. John P. Kotter, "Leading Change in Higher Education," online video, 57:40, hosted by David E. Goldberg, June 28, 2018, https://www.voiceamerica.com/episode/86150/john-kotter-leading-change-in-higher-education.

3. Olivia Bufalini, "Senior Interior Design Exhibit 2018," Interior Design Senior Projects, 37, ScholarWorks, Stephen F. Austin State University, accessed July 10, 2018, https://scholarworks.sfasu.edu/interior_design_projects/37; James I. Perkins College of Education, Department of Human Services, Stephen F. Austin State University, *Journal of Human Services: Training, Research, and Practice*, accessed July 10, 2018, https://scholarworks.sfasu.edu/jhstrp/; Christopher Talbot, "The El Camino Real de los Tejas National Historic Trail Photograph Gallery," ScholarWorks, Stephen F. Austin State University, accessed July 10, 2018, https://scholarworks.sfasu.edu/talbotcaminoreal; National Center for Pharmaceutical Crops,"Arthur Temple College of Forestry and Agriculture, ScholarWorks, Stephen F. Austin State University, accessed July 10, 2018, https://scholarworks.sfasu.edu/ncpc/; Elizabeth Rhodes, "Project Folklórico: Dance in Panama and Bolivia," ScholarWorks, Stephen F. Austin State University, accessed July 10, 2018, https:/scholarworks.sfasu.edu/folklorico/; Center for Digital Scholarship, Ralph W. Steen Library, Stephen F. Austin State University, "Authors and Publishing Issues Forum," Authors and Publishing Issues, ScholarWorks,

Stephen F. Austin State University, accessed July 10, 2018, https://scholarworks.sfasu.edu/authors_publishing_issues/.

4. Robert Z. Selden Jr, "3D Scan Data for Caddo Ceramic Vessels from the George C. Davis Site (41CE19)," ScholarWorks, Stephen F. Austin State University, accessed July 10, 2018, https://scholarworks.sfasu.edu/crhr/237/.

5. John P. Kotter, *Leading Change* (Boston: Harvard Business Review Press, 2012), 44.

Bibliography

Bufalini, Olivia. "Senior Interior Design Exhibit 2018." Interior Design Senior Projects, 37. ScholarWorks, Stephen F. Austin State University. Accessed July 10, 2018. https://scholarworks.sfasu.edu/interior_design_projects/37.

Center for Digital Scholarship. Ralph W. Steen Library. "Authors and Publishing Issues Forum." Authors and Publishing Issues. ScholarWorks, Stephen F. Austin State University. Accessed July 10, 2018. https://scholarworks.sfasu.edu/authors_publishing_issues/.

James I. Perkins College of Education. Department of Human Services. *Journal of Human Services: Training, Research, and Practice*. ScholarWorks, Stephen F. Austin State University. Accessed July 10, 2018. https://scholarworks.sfasu.edu/jhstrp/.

Kotter, John P. *Leading Change*. Boston: Harvard Business School Press, 2012.

———. "Leading Change in Higher Education." Hosted by David E. Goldberg. Online video, 57:40. June 28, 2015. https://www.voiceamerica.com/episode/86150/john-kotter-leading-change-in-higher-education.

National Center for Pharmaceutical Crops. Arthur Temple College of Forestry and Agriculture. ScholarWorks, Stephen F. Austin State University. Accessed July 10, 2018. https://scholarworks.sfasu.edu/ncpc/.

Rhodes, Elizabeth. "Project Folklórico: Dance in Panama and Bolivia." ScholarWorks, Stephen F. Austin State University. Accessed July 10, 2018. https:/scholarworks.sfasu.edu/folklorico/.

Selden, Robert Z., Jr. "3D Scan Data for Caddo Ceramic Vessels from the George C. Davis Site (41CE19)." ScholarWorks, Stephen F. Austin State University. Accessed July 10, 2018. https://scholarworks.sfasu.edu/crhr/237/.

Stephen F. Austin State University. *General Bulletin for 2015-16*. Nacogdoches, TX. http://www.sfasu.edu/documents/general-bulletin-2015-2016.pdf.

Talbot, Christopher. "The El Camino Real de los Tejas National Historic Trail Photograph Gallery." ScholarWorks, Stephen F. Austin State University. Accessed July 10, 2018. https://scholarworks.sfasu.edu/talbotcaminoreal.

Chapter 22

University of Alabama at Birmingham Libraries' Website Design and Launch

Jeffrey Graveline and Kara Van Abel

Setting the Change Stage

The University of Alabama at Birmingham (UAB) is an urban research university located in downtown Birmingham, Alabama and is classified as an "R1: Doctoral Universities—Highest Research Activity" institution in the Carnegie Classification of Institutions of Higher Education. UAB is home to numerous nationally ranked professional programs in the UAB Schools of Medicine, Dentistry, and Business as well as a world-renowned medical center and teaching hospital. The UAB Libraries support a student body of nearly 20,000 undergraduate, graduate, and professional students and the teaching, research, and patient care needs of more than 2,600 full- and part-time faculty and clinicians. The UAB Libraries consist of the Mervyn H. Sterne Library, the university's main academic library, and the Lister Hill Library of the Health Sciences, and employ seventy-one full-time employees. Also falling within the UAB Libraries organization are the Lister Hill Library at University Hospital, the Alabama Museum of the Health Sciences, the Reynolds-Finley Historical Collection, and the University Archives.

In 2014, a new Dean of Libraries was hired and given a mandate to merge the libraries into one cohesive unit to be known as the UAB Libraries. Until then, the Mervyn H. Sterne Library and the Lister Hill Library of the Health Sciences operated as independent academic units, completely siloed from one another. Over the next several years, most pieces of the libraries were merged, both functionally and administratively. With the merger nearly complete, the time was right to launch a single website under the UAB Libraries banner. Until this time, each of the individual entities within the library organization had its own website. This resulted in a fragmented user experience, confusion over information about the libraries and their collections, and redundant website maintenance costs. It was against this backdrop of change and consolidation that

planning began for the new UAB Libraries website in late 2016. The resulting website, launched during the fall 2017 academic term, marked the final step in consolidating UAB Libraries into a single, unified entity.[1]

A library's website plays a critical role in that library's success. It is the online public face of the library, serving as a gateway to the library and its resources. Because it was such a crucial resource, we viewed the website merger as an opportunity for UAB Libraries to streamline our services and policies, improve usability, and update our digital presence.

Librarians are often inclined to provide more and more information for our users, causing what has been called infoglut or information overload.[2] This tendency toward information overload can often be seen in library websites, and our old sites were no exception. A poorly designed website is problematic for a myriad of reasons. A cluttered or overcrowded website makes it difficult for users to locate the information they need. Hidden or buried resources may get little or no use because they are not readily discoverable. These design problems can result in discouraged or frustrated users who forego the library's website entirely and simply look elsewhere for what they need. Knowing this, the UAB Libraries were committed to making sure their new website offered improved functionality. The design and launch proved to be large undertakings, but the resulting website served all of the library's users and met their information needs. Usability testing performed after the launch found that users felt the one-stop website for the UAB Libraries was an improvement and made it easier to locate the information they needed.

I. Warm-up Phase

STAGE 1: ESTABLISHING A SENSE OF URGENCY

As the three-year mark on the libraries' merger neared, there were still some staff who resisted this change. This gave the project an extra sense of urgency. It was critical to create a single, unified website for the UAB Libraries. Creating a unified website would further anchor the libraries' merger and make it more difficult to undo in the future. It would also signify an important milestone in the merger process.

Both of the libraries' existing websites were old, dated, and in need of complete redesign (figures 22.1 and 22.2). For the most part they contained only information about that particular library and did not include anything about the broader UAB Libraries. Because the websites were siloed, there was no single place library patrons could find information about the entire UAB Libraries organization or search across all of the UAB Libraries' content. At the beginning of the project both libraries were also running standalone catalogs, meaning patrons had to search two places to determine if a resource was owned by the libraries. As part of the merger, the libraries acquired a single Alma/Primo discovery system that was being implemented at the same time the new website was being developed. The new website would not only centralize information about UAB Libraries but would also include the Primo discovery tool, which would allow users to discover all of the libraries' content using one search box.

STAGE 2: CREATING THE GUIDING COALITION

Initial discussions between the Dean of Libraries and the Associate Dean for Research about developing the new website began in late 2016, and UAB Digital Media was

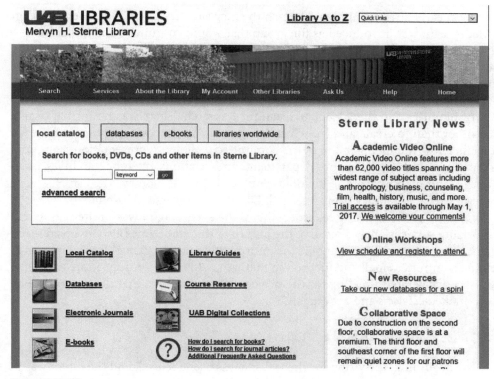

FIGURE 22.1
The Mervyn H. Sterne Library website before the merger and redesign.

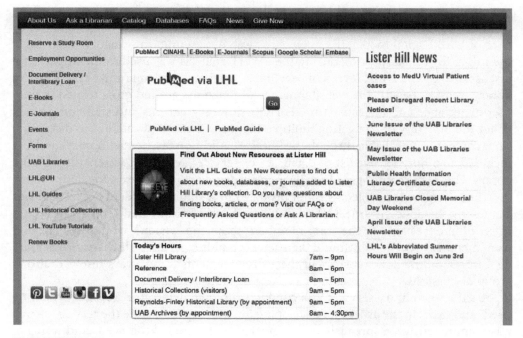

FIGURE 22.2
The Lister Hill Library website before the merger and redesign.

retained in early 2017 to build and launch the new site. In March 2017, the UAB Digital Media team was introduced as the group that would coordinate and build the new website at a town hall–style meeting that included all library faculty and staff. A SWOT analysis of UAB Libraries was conducted at this time to solicit feedback from everyone about needs for the new website.

The following week, the official website committee was selected and formed by the Dean of Libraries and the Associate Dean for Research. There was no formal charge given other than to create and launch an integrated and functional library website for UAB Libraries. The membership of the committee included representation from both library faculty and staff in various departments and locations: reference, archives, circulation, IT, and members of the Reynolds-Finley Historical Library, Mervyn H. Sterne Library, Lister Hill Library, and Lister Hill Library at University Hospital.

The focus of the committee, especially in the early stages, was on itemizing and categorizing services offered by all of the libraries. This sometimes also involved reaching out to non–committee members for information and assistance. The intent was to keep the committee small and focused so that we could tackle projects more efficiently. Given the accelerated timeline for the project, it was essential that the committee be able to make decisions and act quickly.

STAGE 3: DEVELOPING A VISION AND STRATEGY

From the beginning, the vision for the website was user-focused, and the intent was to create a more functional website that would make accessing content from the libraries simpler and more straightforward. The committee extensively discussed what the best design would be for the website. Information from a variety of sources was used to guide the direction of the project. This included reviewing the UAB Libraries' Strategic Plan and past website usability studies and relying on the extensive knowledge and experience of UAB Digital Media, the university's web design unit. Information gathered at the initial town hall meeting during the SWOT analysis was used as the impetus for discussions, and informal review of peer and aspirational academic and health sciences library websites began. The website merger was planned around goals related to both user experience and infrastructure. For years, library patrons and staff complained about the difficulty of navigating multiple library websites and catalogs to determine what content was available through the libraries. Additionally, neither library's website included a comprehensive list of databases or services available to users through the library. These shortcomings led to low perceived and actual user experiences.

The vision for the project was not provided by a single individual but instead was shaped by the collective ideas of UAB Libraries' faculty and staff. There were sometimes differences among the team members about the "vision" for the website, and team members occasionally found themselves at odds regarding which services should be featured on the new website, but these disagreements were always resolved during group discussions.

A survey of library services was conducted to help determine website formatting needs and to begin the process of developing the site map. To ensure the services survey was comprehensive, a spreadsheet was created that included the needs and wants of each library department and unit. Input was solicited from each of these departments and units and was used to create the master library services spreadsheet from which the site map was created. We found there was significant overlap of services among the main libraries, as well as some diverging policies. Taking these things into consideration when planning the new site map, a simplified menu of services was created and new policies were drafted to bring the libraries into better alignment. A rough timeline was developed at this time, and the original launch date of August 25 was set to coincide with the beginning of the fall 2017 semester. The timeline and launch date would be altered many times as the project progressed (figure 22.3).

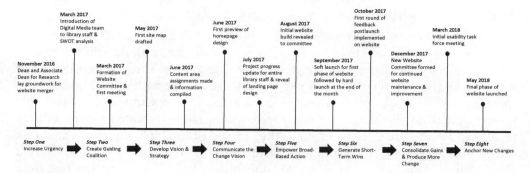

FIGURE 22.3

UAB Libraries abbreviated timeline for website merger implementation

STAGE 4: COMMUNICATING THE CHANGE VISION

Communication regarding the development and progress of the website was limited and, in retrospect, inadequate. At the time, the committee members were caught up in decision-making and information gathering. Despite a few sincere efforts from the committee and Digital Media to provide updates on the project, there wasn't a great deal of emphasis placed on informing library faculty and staff about the progress.

The landing pages for the individual libraries were shared with all library faculty and staff for the first time at the libraries' annual retreat in July 2017. At this time, Digital Media was invited to give a presentation on the project that was intended to lend more transparency to the process. This attempt at transparency, though well received by most of the staff, was not continued. Additional attempts at communication via email were also sporadic and were only occasionally sent to library faculty and staff throughout the build and launch of the website.

Post-launch there was a more focused effort on communication as feedback for improving user access and functionality was sought from the staff. This process included creating a submission form for reporting comments and problems. The form received a lot of use and proved invaluable in discovering and resolving issues with the new website.

Communication to the larger institution about the changes to the library websites was also lacking. There were efforts to have the UAB Libraries' Public Relations and Marketing Committee get the word out, but instructions to this group were unclear. In the end, a series of flyers and posters were distributed within the libraries and to the wider campus promoting the new website. A news item was also added to the libraries' existing websites that a newly redesigned website should be expected and was "coming soon." It was difficult to communicate the changes without knowing exactly when the new website would launch or what it would look like, and there were valid concerns about generating a lot of questions that most library faculty and staff could not answer about the project. In retrospect, communication was an area of the project that was not handled well. For future projects, improved communications both within the library and across campus will be a priority.

II. Introducing New Practices Phase

STAGE 5: EMPOWERING BROAD-BASED ACTION

The launch of the new library website was arguably one of the largest changes to come out of the merger and affected all areas of the library (figure 22.4). As with any change, there were many barriers to overcome, both small and large. The new website launch came at the end of a several-year period of intense change within the libraries, and there was a sense of change fatigue among many faculty and staff members. Not only were people tiring of change, but many were feeling overcommitted as well. Library faculty and staff were stretched thin as they served on multiple merger-related task forces, working groups, and committees. Getting buy-in from an already overtaxed staff was a challenge but was certainly not the only hurdle faced. Other barriers that were encountered can be divided into three broad categories: personnel, technical, and timing.

Barriers posed by library personnel were the most pervasive and difficult to overcome. A significant minority of faculty and staff were opposed to the library merger from the beginning, a number of whom pushed back on nearly every change regardless of how large or small. The new website simply represented another change to oppose. Despite best efforts, very little could be done to get these individuals on board, so the committee was left to work around them. Others who had been involved in the design and maintenance of the original websites sensed a loss of power and opposed the new site because they felt their responsibilities were being diminished. The ongoing development and maintenance of the new site were being outsourced to Digital Media, so these individuals would have little involvement in the day-to-day control of the new site. Still others felt their voices and opinions were not being heard by the website committee. And finally, not everyone liked the design of the new site. While they were not necessarily opposed to it, these individuals may not have shown as much enthusiasm for the new site as would have been liked and did not champion the changes.

Another significant area in which barriers were faced was technology. Specifically, the libraries lacked the technical expertise and IT staffing within the organization to develop the kind of website that was envisioned. Plans were also underway to simultaneously launch a new discovery system and a new suite of Springshare products for both libraries, which added additional layers of complexity to the project. These technology changes, along with others outside the scope of this chapter, led many to feel a technology change overload. To pass this barrier and to address this feeling of overload, it was ultimately decided to outsource all website design, development, and maintenance to another unit on campus.

The final area in which barriers were encountered was with the timing of the project. Both the new website and the new discovery system were to be launched at the same time, prior to the beginning of the new academic year. Because website development did not begin until early spring and classes were scheduled to begin in the late summer, work proceeded on a highly abbreviated timetable. Not only did a complex website need to be developed, but much of the content that was to be used on the new site needed significant revision or needed to be created from scratch. This proved to be a significant hurdle and resulted in a delayed launch of the site. In hindsight, it is clear that not enough time was allocated to adequately complete the work.

While none of these barriers alone were insurmountable, together they created a sense of stress for many on the web committee. Certain steps could have been taken early on to avoid some of these barriers. For instance, better communication to library staff before and during the process could potentially have alleviated some of the opposition that was encountered. And while additional people were added to the team as the project progressed, more people could have been involved to ease some of the burden on team members and speed up content revision and creation. Finally, the committee could have insisted on a more concrete deliverables schedule from Digital Media so they were not left scrambling at the end of the project, which led to an ultimate delay of the launch.

One of the lessons learned during this process was that too few broad-based actions were employed to encourage buy-in of the project. Early on, the committee tried to encourage input from a variety of library staff, but this did not continue as work on the website intensified throughout the summer and into the fall. There was too little communication with library staff and library users, and there were insufficient opportunities for staff involvement and review throughout the entire process. This was clearly one of the project's shortcomings and is a definite area for improvement on future projects.

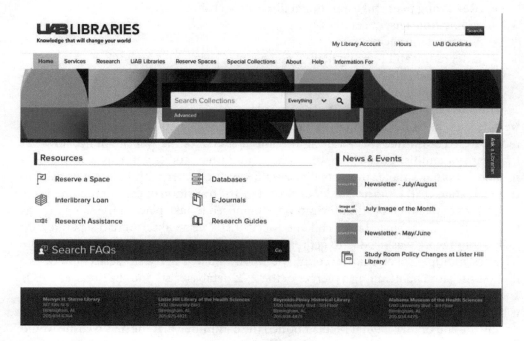

FIGURE 22. 4
The new UAB Libraries website presents users with a unified and streamlined interface.

STAGE 6: GENERATING SHORT-TERM WINS

Short-term wins are defined by Kotter as being visible, unambiguous, and clearly related to the change effort.[3] While the project started with several clear short-term wins, other short-term wins throughout the project were few and far between. In fact, it often felt that setbacks outnumbered wins. The first significant short-term win came when the library administration agreed not only to create a single website for the UAB Libraries but also to outsource the development and maintenance of the new site to Digital Media.

A second significant short-term win came not long after that when approval was secured from the university to create a new third-level domain name for the website at library.uab.edu. This win was particularly significant for several reasons. First, this new URL put the UAB Libraries more in line with other research libraries around the country that use a similar naming structure. It was also significant because the libraries had recently merged all of their Springshare products and planned to use this new domain name for them as well in the form of askus.library.uab.edu and guides.library.uab.edu. After the website was launched, positive feedback was received from users, which could also be considered a short-term win.

STAGE 7: CONSOLIDATING GAINS AND PRODUCING MORE CHANGE

Most of the committee's work on the project was completed early in the process between March and June:

- Assessing UAB Libraries' and users' needs
- Reviewing peer and aspirational libraries' websites
- Compiling a list of services
- Creating the site map
- Integrating and revising library policies
- Compiling from inventory
- Assigning content areas

Toward the end of the summer, the library had made significant progress toward the website launch. By July, most of what was requested by Digital Media had been submitted and the committee was awaiting the initial results of the website build; however, that was not an idle time. There were other committees and task forces working on a number of other smaller projects that would work together with the new website to truly integrate UAB Libraries under one banner. The transition of the libraries' multiple collections and launch of Alma/Primo were supposed to take place at the same time as the website launch. Since Lister Hill and Mervyn H. Sterne libraries had separate catalogs, a lot of work was needed to get ready for the new catalog and discovery tool. The libraries' multiple Springshare accounts were consolidated into a single account before the website launch, including a merger of the A–Z database lists and the libraries' FAQs. The libraries also adopted Springshare's LibChat, which was intended to go live along with the new website.

By the end of July, Digital Media notified the committee that the new website would be launched in phases due to the different needs of the various libraries and the scope of the project. Phase one would include the launch of the main website and landing pages for Mervyn H. Sterne, Lister Hill, and Lister Hill at University Hospital libraries. The old pages for Archives and Special Collections would also be linked on the new website until new pages for these units were complete. Later phases of the project included the launch of new pages for both Archives and Special Collections as well as a new page for the Alabama Museum of the Health Sciences. Phasing the website launch made the project more manageable for the Digital Media team. The time between the "soft launch" and the actual launch of the website was another window with increased activity by the committee. It conducted a thorough review of the content from the initial build and contributed substantial feedback for further development and improvements before the website was ready to go live.

III. Grounding Phase

STAGE 8: ANCHORING NEW APPROACHES IN THE CULTURE

After months of work to launch the new site, it was discouraging to think that the changes and progress made could be undone. To ensure that the changes remained in place, they had to be anchored in a number of ways.

First, as soon as the new site was live, all traffic was redirected from the old sites to the new ones. The old sites were no longer accessible either to the public or to general library staff. The committee also created an online suggestion and problem-reporting portal for library faculty and staff. Feedback and suggestions were encouraged through the portal, and the committee tried to act on the suggestions quickly. The committee also periodically distributed to all library employees a list of suggestions received and the action taken on them. This helped to gain buy-in across the library and also gave more people a sense of ownership in the new site.

Another way the changes were anchored was by creating a permanent website committee that would be responsible for ongoing changes and enhancements to the site. This committee included members of the original website task force and new members from across each of the libraries representing all library departments and ranks. Committee members serve one-year terms, which allows new people to join the committee when others' terms expire. As the website continues to evolve and change, new ways to anchor it will be discovered.

Analysis and Conclusions

In reflecting on the process, several key areas for improvement were identified. For future projects of this magnitude, greater focus should be placed on communication. This is an area of the project that was particularly weak, and better communication would have eased tensions within the library and led to a smoother transition to the new website. Another area in need of improvement was project and time management, specifically allowing more time to undertake complex tasks. Many of the deadlines were self-imposed, and a more careful examination of the project's scope would have better informed the timeline.

The website merger was successful due to a number of strengths, including support from library administration and services from Digital Media. The Dean of UAB Libraries provided the charge for this project and secured a contract with Digital Media to facilitate the creation of the new website. The guidance and expertise provided by Digital

Media during the build proved invaluable. Also, the makeup of the committee and its ability to compromise and work together helped shape the project into a success. There were times when members found themselves at odds regarding the best way to proceed with the project, but these disputes were settled quickly and amicably. The tight timeline could not have been adhered to without the full cooperation of the committee.

The resulting UAB Libraries' website achieved the goal of finalizing the larger libraries merger and providing a single access point for library users. "Combining two very different library websites requires detailed planning and implementation so that the final product fulfills each library's purpose and retains its unique identity while communicating a unified presence."[4] While each library entity within UAB Libraries is now located on pages within the combined website, library.uab.edu, the integrity of the individual entities has been preserved. This aspect of the project was very important to the committee because part of its goal was to create a new website that satisfied everyone while meeting library users' needs. With that goal in mind, the website continues to evolve as the new website committee makes user-focused changes and enhancements.

Following a well-established change model has many benefits, and Kotter's framework for leading change was a helpful tool in reviewing this project. It aided in the identification of successes, and also highlighted key areas of improvement. The lack of consistent communication to library staff was detrimental to the project, and in retrospect, communication across all library channels should be improved. Empowering broad-based action was the other area of the project that went overlooked. If more steps had been taken to empower library employees, the project might not have experienced as much pushback from select staff members. Proactive work in these areas would have encouraged more buy-in from library staff. Kotter's framework for leading change anticipates these issues and offers a plan for preventing them, which makes it a useful tool for planning large-scale change projects. Future UAB Libraries projects will benefit from adherence to an established and clearly outlined change process.

Notes

1. The UAB Libraries website was launched on September 28, 2017, at https://www.library.uab.edu.
2. Darlene Fitcher and Jeff Wisniewski, "Beyond Responsive Design," *Online Searcher* 40, no. 6 (November/December 2016): 67, ProQuest.
3. John P. Kotter, *Leading Change* (Boston: Harvard Business Review Press, 1996), 121, EBSCOhost eBook Collection.
4. Virginia Feher and Kim Mears, "When Libraries Combine: Creating a Georgia Regents University Libraries Website," in *Difficult Decisions: Closing and Merging Academic Libraries*, ed. Sara Holder and Amber Butler Lannon (Chicago: Association of College and Research Libraries, 2015), 202.

Bibliography

Feher, Virginia, and Kim Mears. "When Libraries Combine: Creating a Georgia Regents University Libraries Website." In *Difficult Decisions: Closing and Merging Academic Libraries*. Edited by Sara Holder and Amber Butler Lannon, 201–16. Chicago: Association of College and Research Libraries, 2015.

Fitcher, Darlene, and Jeff Wisniewski. "Beyond Responsive Design." *Online Searcher* 40, no. 6 (November/December 2016): 66–68. ProQuest.

Kotter, John P. *Leading Change*. Boston: Harvard Business Review Press, 1996. EBSCOhost eBook Collection.

Chapter 23

Chaos to Consensus
A Team-Based Approach to Developing Holistic Workflows

Jennifer O'Brien Roper, Jeremy Bartczak, Jean Cooper, Christina Deane, Mike Durbin, Kara McClurken, Elizabeth Wilkinson, and Lauren Work

The University of Virginia (UVA) Library earned a reputation as an innovator in digital libraries in the late nineties as an institution that experimented early and often with faculty and other colleagues to create and share scholarship and research resources online. Located in Charlottesville, in central Virginia, the university is an R1 doctoral institution with a reputation for and pride in the residential experience for undergraduates and excellence in graduate programs. The main library system employs 230 full-time staff members and is administratively distinct from libraries for the professional schools. A particular strength in the humanities led to robust partnerships involving the library with groundbreaking ventures such as the Institute for Advanced Technology in the Humanities (IATH) and the Scholars' Lab. While the library has a well-earned reputation for participation in and leadership of digital humanities projects, an infrastructure for creating and maintaining stable library-managed digital collections was never fully realized. Many different pathways grew to take a collection from idea to dissemination; the solutions were often different for similar types of materials, and no shared understanding of accountabilities developed.

Setting the Change Stage

In early 2017 the library identified the multifaceted digital production workflow as a process in need of significant overhaul. The process of moving digital collections from idea to completion was opaque, both for collections staff wishing to acquire materials or initiate digitization and for processing staff responsible for the underlying work of making these materials available for research and use. After many efforts to increase the quantity and quality of communication between departments, library administration determined that a full review was necessary to create a coherent, replicable, and scalable process for developing and managing digital collections. The result was

the commissioning of a task force with representation from across the library, and the recommendations of that group were made available to all staff before action was approved.

I. Warm-up Phase

STAGE 1: ESTABLISHING A SENSE OF URGENCY

The Electronic Text Center at the University of Virginia was an early player in the creation of digital objects by libraries. However, over time, the functions once unified in that unit were spread out over several departments as the library became responsible for an increasing number of digital resources of varying etiology. Individual units responsible for processing digital collections had a different range of similar but not identical authority and responsibility. The origin and status of the digital accessions differed as well, including in-house digitization of print materials from Special Collections and circulating collections based on intentional collection building as well as patron digitization requests, born-digital materials, legacy digital collections, and newly acquired material with donor expectations for digitization. Many, if not most, of these accessions were not yet publicly disseminated. This lack of access was a distinct point of frustration for all.

In this distributed model, each digital collection was custom-designed. Different evaluation frameworks and processes were in use, based on the various parties involved at the outset. There were no standardized workflows, which resulted in work being omitted in the initial workflow, and later requiring remediation. Additionally, there was no unified prioritization, and units responsible for stages of work on any project had no authority governing their choices. Each unit answered to and received instructions from a different hierarchy. As an example, the Digital Production Group met quarterly with representatives of Special Collections to agree upon prioritization for collection-building digitization for that subset of material. At the same time, the Metadata units received proposals from individual donors who wanted the library not only to accept analog materials, but also to make them accessible electronically. The decisions on accepting these materials rested with Collection Management, an entirely different unit.

STAGE 2: CREATING THE GUIDING COALITION

In recognition of the all-encompassing nature of the stated goal of creating a coherent, replicable, and scalable process for developing and managing UVA's digital collections, the library's Senior Leadership Team authorized the Digital Production Workflow Team to identify issues and propose solutions. The team met for ten weeks between April and June 2017 and reviewed current workflows to acquire, describe, digitize, disseminate, and preserve library-managed digital content.

The group consisted of a mix of managers, who understood relationships between units and larger workflows, and staff who implemented day-to-day operations. This was key to forming an accurate and complete picture of what was happening within and between units and for analyzing roadblocks. Experts in metadata, preservation, repository services, digitization, AV, born-digital, and archival material gathered together to bring their knowledge of the workflows, formats, and best practices for each aspect of the process. A member of the Senior Leadership Team served as a neutral facilitator. A factor in the project's success was the broad composition of the team and the strong desire of the group to have agreed-upon and consistent workflows and strategies for creating, managing, and ingesting digital content.

With this in mind, the team established principles and goals:

- Commit to the establishment, communication, and maintenance of a unified and stable prioritization process.
- Utilize formalized documentation processes and tools.
- Shift from primarily student labor for description and processing to permanent staff.
- Reduce reliance on customized design and increase reuse of standard guidelines.
- Inventory physical materials before material digitization. Full arrangement and description prior to digitization should be preferred.
- Separate patron scanning on demand from collection building at all steps in the process.

The team had credibility across the library because the right people were sitting around the somewhat crowded table. By allowing each unit to determine who should be present, and by being willing to accept additional members, the team was able to gain a complete and accurate understanding about current workflows and sticking points through the entire process. The team was committed to working quickly through each stage of the documentation process, while ensuring that all voices were heard. All were invested in creating positive outcomes for the project and eager to develop consistent workflows and prioritization processes for digital content across the library as a whole.

STAGE 3: DEVELOPING A VISION AND STRATEGY

Because each team member brought a different focus on the current and ideal life cycle for digital collections, time was initially allotted to create a grand unified vision. Near the beginning of the process, the team looked outward at other institutions. Looking outward first helped bring the team to consensus on the important characteristics of a successful program. Several members of the team had prior work experience at peer institutions and were able to describe in depth the practices and process of those organizations. Others researched publicly documented solutions at other libraries to share with the team. Through interrogating the strengths and weaknesses of these approaches with an eye toward applicability to the local culture, staffing, organization, and goals, some main tenets of the strategy emerged. After the environmental scan, the focus shifted to enumerating rough stages of an internal workflow, with individual meetings devoted to each stage.

STAGE 4: COMMUNICATING THE CHANGE VISION

Each member arrived with his or her own critiques of the status quo and a determination to focus on an improved future environment instead of perceived failings with the current state. All projects started prior to the development and adoption of a new workflow were quickly labeled "legacy" projects, and it was understood that the idiosyncrasies of how they were handled should not impede or distract the team from deciding the best path forward. After weeks of regular conversation, the team ultimately arrived at a shared vision. The group communicated internally by email and began using Atlassian's Confluence collaboration software program to collect meeting minutes and resource documents, and to establish agendas. All information was made visible to the full organization. While updates were not pushed out to the organization as a whole, team members could point to the site, and nonmembers interested in the team's work could subscribe to automatic updates when new information was added.

The group met almost every week for three months in order to get through all of the workflow steps and discuss them in some depth, again, documenting each meeting with notes and attached resource documents. By the middle of the summer, the conversations were concluded and the work shifted to the drafting of a report for the administration. A subset of the group, using notes from the discussions, drafted a document outlining findings. The full team reviewed the draft and met again in person to discuss changes, additions, and corrections. A final draft was prepared and sent to the administration for review, followed by a meeting with the administrative team. With only minor changes based on that meeting, the report was sent to all staff detailing thirteen recommendations falling into three major categories:

- **Staffing**—Establish a position dedicated to leadership of digital collections, establish a cross-unit team to oversee prioritization and work planning for digital projects, and staff organization and description appropriately to desired level of output.
- **Documentation**—Create and document policies and procedures for digital collection development, vendor management, preservation actions, and system backup.
- **Systems**—Assess, select, and implement systems for digital project proposal and progress tracking, digital archiving, digitization tracking, metadata creation and storage, digital serials management, and hosting of digital texts.

Following the release of the report was a well-attended all-staff meeting featuring a prepared presentation of report content as well as time for questions and discussion.

II. Introducing New Practices Phase

STAGE 5: EMPOWERING BROAD-BASED ACTION

In the course of the discussion and internal workflow review, the team discovered that the barriers to change fell into three broad categories in need of attention: structure, communication, and ownership. Each of these components arose repeatedly in conversation. Structural barriers included siloed units where projects could be advanced or neglected due to various circumstances of funding, relationships, donors, or areas of interest or focus without broader, library-wide knowledge of those circumstances. The decentralized structure led to a lack of transparent, interconnected systems and an absence of streamlined workflows for processing of digital collections, leading to duplication of effort and customization for all materials, not just those presenting novel or unique content. Fed by the structural obstacles, disjointed communication led to confusion in project handoffs, benchmarks, and expectation for receiving, processing, and dissemination. The compartmentalized nature of collections work did not interface well with the centralized system for processing. There was often conflicting or absent information regarding copyright and licensing concerns, prioritization in relation to financial and personnel resourcing, and no centralized documentation of a project's legal, descriptive, or preservation standing. Finally, it was clear that the lack of ownership and responsibility over the domain of digital collections was crippling to the desired success of stewarding and making these collections accessible. Decisions were not framed in a way that allowed for equitable input and standing from those responsible for the work, nor with a transparent understanding of the circumstances that may move a project forward or cause delay. It was no one person's job to make sure digital collections move from ingest to access. The recommendations addressed these issues to define a successful path to change.

STAGE 6: GENERATING SHORT-TERM WINS

In the team discussions, several decisions led to short-term gains toward the final goals. First, the team agreed to experiment with use of Atlassian's JIRA ticketing system to create a central registry for storing proposals, agreements, and other documentation about projects from idea to completion. The implementation was understood to be iterative as needs surfaced or information was shifted around. The ability to openly track the progress of digital projects through each stage keeps stakeholders well informed in terms of prioritization and action. Next, a team began work on a template framework to establish project-level processing and metadata plans for standardized descriptive workflows. Finally, resources and development time were allotted to investigating a metadata management system to accommodate description for certain formats such as serials and photographs.

STAGE 7: CONSOLIDATING GAINS AND PRODUCING MORE CHANGE

Meanwhile, outside of the group's scheduled meetings, the library hosted the Society of American Archivists workshop "Implementing 'More Product, Less Process,'" which provided a philosophical framework to operate within as we considered the special challenges for efficiently digitizing and describing archival collections at scale. This led to two small experimental prototype digital projects where our approaches for description and dissemination could be tested within a subset of the technical infrastructure. These projects provided examples for future enquiry as the team continued to deliberate technical handoffs, metadata best practices, and optimal user experience.

The recipe to maintain momentum was frequent meetings with focused topics capped off by a consistent and steady project leadership. Including representation from the relevant constituencies within the library and taking the time to begin by outlining the process as it currently existed led to brainstorming questions that needed to be answered in order to move forward. The team recognized that issues resolved in one meeting might be revisited as subsequent questions encroached on an earlier solution. The facilitator kept discussions on track with very focused meeting topics and asking the germane team representative to provide an overview and initiate discussion. By meeting consistently every week, and with the ability to consult detailed notes via Confluence, momentum built as the team constructed a path.

Team members were self-motivated to continue forging ahead in order to create a report outlining the needed changes. The report explained why process change was absolutely necessary for a robust digital workflow. Again, all recognized the need to create a new streamlined workflow that was a more obvious and transparent process for all throughout the library.

As resistance to suggested changes arose, the team either dove into the issues immediately or set up time at the next meeting for deeper discussion. The debates were sometimes lively until arriving at conclusions acceptable to the entire group. In coming together, the relevant stakeholders from each unit tacitly agreed to implement the proposed improved workflow. This report was the blueprint for change that led to the establishment of a permanent Digital Collections Team in late 2017, and in mid-2018, the establishment of a Director of Digital Strategies, a position ultimately filled by the facilitator of the group discussed in this chapter.

III. Grounding Phase

STAGE 8: ANCHORING NEW APPROACHES IN THE CULTURE

The next phase of work began as a new team was established to carry out the recommendations of the working group. The new Digital Collections Team was comprised of some members of the working group, as well as new members. This group began meeting in October 2017, and they continued to communicate through Confluence, on a new site developed for the team and its work. They began work in earnest on the recommendations in the fall of 2017, and that work continues. As milestones in the process are reached by this group, library-wide announcements will be released to alert staff to the new tools and processes this group plans to produce.

Analysis and Conclusions

The Digital Collections Team adopted these strategies intended to address the multifaceted barriers to change. Regardless of the clarity and momentum of the small team, clearly communicating to the larger library staff the existence, goals, and expectations of the new digital collections workflow remained a challenge. This was addressed through the continued open documentation (meeting notes, case studies, decision points, the initial report), as well as presentations about the team and developing workflow during all-staff meetings. Agendas are openly built in Confluence, with notes posted upon meeting completion. Individuals are tagged in the minutes as appropriate, sending a notification to the person, and there are plans to continue to hold one-on-one sessions and small meetings with individuals and teams whose future work would be pragmatically affected by the suggested changes and software that the team is building. An important component of recognizing barriers to change and working effectively to help resolve them is a recognition that these barriers may not be linear, or overcome only once.

The strength of the task force clearly lies in each individual's commitment to a shared solution to separable issues. The willingness to listen to all members, engage in discussion and debate, and compromise was key to the success. Additionally, the commitment involved time: time to prepare for and participate in meetings. In this respect, library administration supported the effort by prioritizing time spent in this pursuit. The work of the task force is considered successful; the recommendations were approved and action begun. The resulting Digital Collections Team is now responsible for maintaining the momentum to bring tangible results in the form of shared process, transparent tracking of progress, and routine dissemination of digital content.

The Kotter framework aligns well with this organic change process. At heart, the framework encourages preparation and intentional discussion prior to firm action. These were key aspects to the UVA change process and foundational to the success achieved. Since the Kotter framework lays out a fairly linear process, the challenge in analyzing the change initiative post-process is the iterative manner in which some parts played out. For instance, while the guiding coalition was established early and remained stable throughout the process, developing and maintaining a shared vision and strategy was continual as new ideas and challenges emerged. Also, culture change is a long process, and anchoring changes takes more than a set of agreed-upon recommendations. Iteration, though, is clear in the tenets of the Kotter framework, and gradual development is what progressed the conversations from review of current state to new positions and creative use of existing tools to bring about change.

Chapter 24

Implementing an Open News and Information System in the Vanderbilt University Libraries

Sara Byrd, Richard Stringer-Hye, and Jodie Gambill

Setting the Change Stage

In the complex environment of a research university library, effective and timely communication between upper-level administration, staff, and the various branch libraries and departments is mission-critical to a successful organization. The change described in this chapter took place in 2017 in the Jean and Alexander Heard Libraries at Vanderbilt University in Nashville, Tennessee. Vanderbilt is a Carnegie R1 research university with 11,782 total full-time students and 4,716 total faculty. The Heard Libraries system consists of nine libraries and a total of approximately 160 staff members.

In many ways, the history of the Jean and Alexander Heard Libraries at Vanderbilt mirrors the history of other academic libraries: a nineteenth-century founding, a devastating fire, acquisition of extensive resources, expansions and renovations of facilities, and the introduction and improvement of computer-based catalogs. Around the year 2008, library staff were basking in the knowledge that reading a daily email digest of "Library Staff News" was cutting-edge communication technology and a sound replacement for the paper and web-based memos that had been issued until that time.

Unfortunately, nine years later, the Heard Libraries' staff members were still getting the same daily email digest. The content was new every day, but the email looked exactly as it had looked when it was first implemented: plain text with long URLs that linked to a publicly available webpage. The emails were simple and old-fashioned, but more important, it was evident that swaths of people were not reading their daily Library Staff

News emails at all. The bottom line: these emails were no longer working. Stagnation and complacency had set in.

Library administration attempted several tactics to improve communication of top-down messages, but results were uneven. Some staff were happy to hear of library news from their divisional supervisors, but trickle-down information-sharing practices resulted in staff in some areas learning key information more quickly than in other areas. It was fairly common to be talking with a colleague from another library and hear of an event or a meeting that hadn't been announced and say, "Why wasn't that in the Staff News?"

A related problem was the library staff intranet, referred to as the Staffweb. Also implemented at the turn of the millennium, the page had evolved over time from an HTML webpage to a Drupal site. In 2012, the library administration decided that the Staffweb should no longer be updated and that all information would be moved to the library's SharePoint website. Due to a combination of problematic implementation and lack of user acceptance, SharePoint has never been particularly effective at managing communication.

A culminating problem was an administrative decision that committee meeting minutes would no longer be shared using the daily email, but would be posted on Share-Point instead. This further weakened the relevance of the Staff News and contributed to its lack of reader penetration.

The change process described in this chapter consisted of a complete re-engineering of the internal communication system and an innovation in the platform and tools that were chosen to implement the new system. The result of the change was a new resource, called Heard Alert, a substantial revitalization of internal communication in the library, and the implementation of a clean, secure, and flexible intranet platform.

The scope of the change involved the entire library system, plus a few important campus stakeholders, eventually gaining the attention of the Vice Provost of Learning and Residential Affairs and the campus communications department.

I. Warm-up Phase

STAGE 1: ESTABLISHING A SENSE OF URGENCY

Library staff frequently complained about the stagnant, closed communications channels and staff intranet. Library administration was never able to make a clear case for improving the Staff News or the Staffweb—it was hard to justify allocating resources to noncritical issues when there were always bigger projects and other problems to solve. What created the sense of urgency, however, was a push from the new University Librarian, who identified communication as a problem and made it a prioritized area of focus. She convened a leadership group retreat in the summer of 2016 to address this problem. An action item that came out of the retreat was to create a short-term task force—specifically not a long-term committee—to make recommendations about how internal communication might be improved.

The Deputy University Librarian convened an Internal Communications Task Force (henceforth ICTF), which began meeting that fall and was given a rather aggressive timeline: recommendations were to be submitted within three months. The team consisted of seven members of the library staff: six librarians and one administrative assistant. All were long-time employees and had been with the libraries for a minimum of ten years. One librarian was a member of the library's IT team, and one librarian was the content manager for the library website.

The ICTF met weekly and worked extensively together over email. To gather data and opinions about usage, they analyzed data from Google Analytics and administered a survey to library staff. To determine effective communications channels across campus, the group reviewed communications tools used in other areas of Vanderbilt University. They looked at a few technology options, such as Slack, to see whether these would be the kinds of solutions that would be willingly adopted by members of the library staff.

The task force found library staff were enthusiastic about the possibility of changes in communication. The survey received a 54 percent response rate, and staff overwhelmingly reported that they were unhappy with current communication in general, and with the Staff News in particular. Library staff strongly preferred to continue getting communications through email but desired a change to a different format and system. A fair amount of criticism was aimed at library administration, with comments that communication from above was often murky, secretive, inconsistent, and unevenly distributed.

The ICTF report made four recommendations to administration:

1. Make regular communication from library leadership a top priority.
2. Enable all library staff to openly post to the Staff News without approval or mediation; restrict access to Vanderbilt ID only, no search engine crawling.
3. Revitalize the Staffweb.
4. Create a central location for calendars.

For the last three recommendations, library administration convened an Implementation Team.

The goals of the Implementation Team were specific to this situation, but if generalized, they are exactly what Kotter recommends in a common goal: *create something sensible to the head and appealing to the heart.*[1]

At this point in the timeline, oversight of the project was moved from the Deputy University Librarian to the Associate University Librarian for Research and Learning.

STAGE 2: CREATING THE GUIDING COALITION

Library administration appointed a chair from the ICTF to lead the Implementation Team. The chair then chose one member from the original task force and one new member from library IT. This was to become the guiding coalition. Kotter emphasizes using careful selection methods to ensure that the key players on a team have a good mix of skills and experience to be effective.[2] The chair selected a team that had worked well together before. One member maintained the library's website, and the other was the Drupal administrator for the Staffweb.

The chair knew that the three team members had a good mix of creativity, pragmatism, and discipline. Each was well-connected and well-respected by library staff across campus, and their work would be taken seriously. They were all savvy enough to avoid landmines in both the technological and political realms. Most important, the three of them all had the main component necessary to create teamwork: trust.[3] Because of the established sense of trust and the group's dynamics, they were able to achieve a high level of productivity while maintaining good spirits.

The Implementation Team was deliberately small. Larger groups tend to have a hard time focusing on a course of action and run the risk of including members that Kotter warns about: big egos, people who create mistrust, and reluctant players.[4]

Although none of the team were in management roles, the group was in a power position—uninvolved peers would not easily be able to block progress. Because the group had the backing of administration, they knew they could expect support from above. The team was given sufficient autonomy to create solutions that would work for the existing library culture and community. Because the ICTF had left the goals sufficiently vague, this allowed the Implementation Team the flexibility to choose which tools to explore.

STAGE 3: DEVELOPING A VISION AND STRATEGY

The team's vision was to increase trust and transparency by creating a culture of open communication in all directions.

The Implementation Team knew that there were two important elements to making sure this part of the project was successful: technology and buy-in from staff.

The team initially hoped to find one tool that would incorporate news, calendar, and intranet resources. Alas, any enterprise solutions available were either prohibitively expensive or incompatible with existing IT structures (figure 24.1).

An unavoidable part of any process is trying out possible solutions that do not ultimately work for that specific situation. The authors feel that it is important to look at these failed attempts, because they often require excessive time. Figuring out when to abandon something is often a delicate balance between idealistic perseverance and stubborn determination.

FIGURE 24.1
Tools the team investigated

An important point in the development of the team's vision was when the ICTF identified and articulated a major problem with the Staff News (figure 24.2). It was simultaneously too open and too closed—available on an open website and crawled by search engines, yet only

TOOLS THE TEAM INVESTIGATED

- **Shared Outlook Calendar:** Already implemented, with extremely low user acceptance due to technological challenges and a clunky interface
- **Microsoft Office 365 Planner / Microsoft Teams:** Campus policies were not conducive to these systems
- **Basecamp:** Good for project management, but too complicated for casual daily interaction
- **Goodbits:** Good for creating a curated newsletter, but had no function to automatically create a daily email from an RSS feed
- **Emma:** Did not support RSS-to-email functionality
- **MailChimp:** Supported RSS-to-email functionality, but did not support an authenticated RSS feed
- **SpringShare Calendar:** Had a robust API, but interface was difficult to navigate; access for all staff would be difficult to maintain
- **Slack:** Excellent for communication, but met with great resistance by some staff who felt that adding another communication channel would be disruptive to their workflow
- **Bedework:** Met all requirements, but funding for a Bedework developer was not approved
- **VU Campus Calendar:** Viewable by the public, which would not work for library-staff-only events, such as birthday celebrations and candidate interview schedules

two people had permission to create posts. This created a situation of low trust and high visibility. The new vision was looking toward a picture of the future where library staff would have a space where any library staff member could share information with other members of the library staff via unmediated post submissions. This would make inroads to create higher levels of trust throughout the library organization.

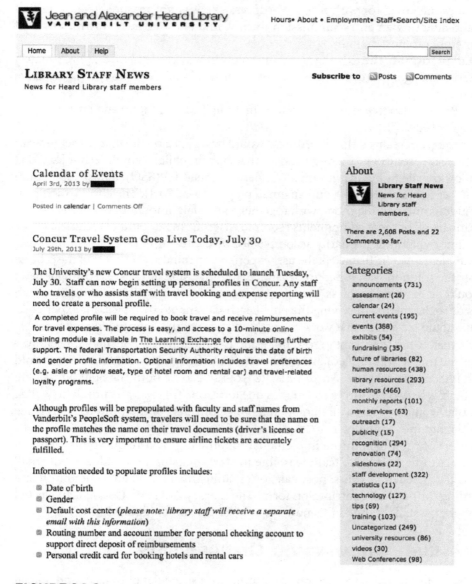

FIGURE 24.2
The old Staff News homepage.

When the team took a hard look at the Staff News, they discovered that the existing technical platform, WordPress, would work well with some changes:

- **Look and feel:** The WordPress theme had not been updated for approximately ten years. A modern theme would make people view the page as more relevant and useful.
- **Who could view:** The existing site was open to the public. Putting the site behind a login would create a sense of privacy.
- **Who could post:** The existing setup allowed only a handful of editors. Making everyone an editor within the WordPress site was not reasonable, but finding and adapting an entry submission form would allow an easy way for any staff member to post an item.
- **Email format:** The existing text-only solution was implemented approximately ten years ago. WordPress had plug-ins that would allow for modern, attractive emails.

WordPress is also free and open-source, making it easy to set up and customize for the library's needs.

Once the team realized that WordPress would be a viable platform, they set to work finding the exact solutions: themes (Suri, with a custom child theme), technology that would allow people to log in with their Vanderbilt-issued ID (SSO), a post submission plug-in (User Submitted Posts), and an email plug-in (MailPoet). The effort to settle on these solutions and making them work together took a fair amount of research and testing. Setting up all of these components required a significant amount of technical expertise and time, which was primarily accomplished by the team's library IT staff member.

The Implementation Team kept the user experience in mind at every step of the process. Whatever the solution was, it had to be simple, intuitive, and attractive. Posting a news item should be easy and painless, even for someone who isn't terribly comfortable with websites or social media. Receiving the email each day should be a pleasant experience: the email should have links that work correctly, include enough information to let people gauge whether or not they want to read more about something, and be mobile-friendly.

After the theme was implemented, the team began migrating content from the old Staffweb intranet so that the WordPress site would become both the Staff News blog and the Staffweb: two resources rolled into one location. This was an entirely new idea, but one that would appeal to all library staff. Once this part of the work fell into place, things began to move rapidly.

A couple of months into the implementation, the big-picture questions were out of the way. At this point, the team was able to start focusing on the dozens of small questions that needed answers: post categories, adjustments to the layout and theme, and wording for the post contribution form. The Library Advisory Council, an elected group of library staff, branded this new system "Heard Alert" (figure 24.3).

STAGE 4: COMMUNICATING THE CHANGE VISION

The Implementation Team worked on communication strategies both large and official and small and political. Official changes included announcing the new service at an all-staff town hall meeting, writing posts for the Staff News, and leading discussions in the Library Advisory Council. Small-scale efforts included political strategizing, such as having private conversations with individuals who expressed hesitant feelings, asking people to post items, and generating buy-in by asking many people to test the system.

Heard Alert
News and Information for Vanderbilt Library Staff

Contribute   Human Resources   Staff Recognition   Technology   Training   Travel   FAQ

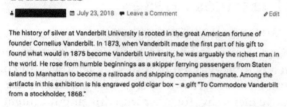

Search

"Vanderbilt Silver" Exhibition Explores University Treasures & Traditions

👤 ▓▓▓▓▓▓   📅 July 23, 2018   💬 Leave a Comment   ✏️ Edit

The history of silver at Vanderbilt University is rooted in the great American fortune of founder Cornelius Vanderbilt. In 1873, when Vanderbilt made the first part of his gift to found what would in 1875 become Vanderbilt University, he was arguably the richest man in the world. He rose from humble beginnings as a skipper ferrying passengers from Staten Island to Manhattan to become a railroads and shipping companies magnate. Among the artifacts in this exhibition is his engraved gold cigar box – a gift "To Commodore Vanderbilt from a stockholder, 1868."

These roots of Commodore Vanderbilt himself paved the way for a tradition of using silver to mark important ceremonies and award recipients at the university. The selection of silver on display draws up memorable moments in the university's history, aims to introduce the vast art of silver making, and in many cases, comes to us directly from the Vanderbilt family

Quick Links

library.vanderbilt.edu

Brightspace

Committees (Sharepoint)

C2HR

Events

ILS Training Portal

ILS Transition Feedback Form

INFORM

FIGURE 24.3
The new Heard Alert homepage.

The Implementation Team demonstrated the new system at an all-staff town hall meeting. This monthly meeting was a place where new plans were often introduced and gave everyone the opportunity to ask questions. The group spoke briefly about the project goals and timeline, and let staff know what to expect. Library staff members were genuinely excited when they saw the prototype of the site.

Saying that anyone can post to a blog is easy; getting people to actually participate is more challenging. The team knew that getting buy-in from staff was extremely important. People were accustomed to having no voice. If they were asked to post something, it was usually an official message, and they had historically sent it to one of the Staff News editors. The new system would be different and exciting because it had the potential to shape an open communication culture. Many people resisted the very idea; "But, what if…" was a common way that people began the phrasing of their question. The Implementation Team decided that they would take a two-pronged attack to people's hesitance:

1. Reminding people, "Your professional reputation is at stake!" A lighthearted tone helped with this, such as the reminder that "If you post about kittens every few days, you are going to be known as That Kitten Guy. Act accordingly."
2. Acting as ambassadors to the new system. They asked people to post things. "That's a great idea! Why don't you post it to Heard Alert?"

Before the page was unveiled to everyone, several people were asked to test the system. The beta testers were the members of the original ICTF. Getting their support was a strategic way to create buy-in for the new system, thus making sure that acceptance of the system would spread. Sadly, there have been instances in the past where an implementation team did not keep the original planners in the loop. This can result in bitterness, subverting the message, and a lack of support, which can ultimately lead to a failure for the initiative. Therefore, the Implementation Team was very careful to respond positively to any changes suggested by the ICTF. One such suggestion was to change the default font color to a darker gray to increase contrast and improve accessibility.

Heard Alert went live in June 2017. In the first year, there were approximately 500 posts from seventy-five staff members. This represents approximately 47 percent of library staff—an excellent participation rate.

II. Introducing New Practices Phase

STAGE 5: EMPOWERING BROAD-BASED ACTION

The initial focus of the project was to create an open communication system whereby any staff member could post on any topic without first seeking approval. In contrast to the previous staff news system, Heard Alert would empower staff to have a voice outside of the normal administrative hierarchy. Together with this empowerment came the responsibility to communicate and be knowledgeable about what had been communicated. Blaming lack of communication on the administrators could no longer be a valid option.

The group made sure to avoid Kotter's "Barriers to Empowerment."[5] In particular, the group was careful to make it as easy as possible for all staff to participate, thus avoiding three of the common barriers to empowerment:

- formal structures making it difficult to act,
- a lack of needed skills undermining action, and
- personnel and information systems making it difficult to act.

One of the group's key goals was that there would be no training required to use the system. The submission form was carefully designed to make posting easy and immediate, as opposed to the old system, which would allow only specific people to make posts. In this brave new world, library staff reported feeling a certain satisfaction when they posted to Heard Alert for the first time: it felt risky, having the newly acquired ability to send a message to everyone. Some people worried that they weren't capable of posting and asked an administrative assistant to post for them, but with a little encouragement, even the least technologically adventurous staff found the posting process to be easy.

During the planning phase, the Implementation Team fought skepticism that staff might post trivial or inappropriate content, but this has not been the case. Not even one post has been censored due to content. Instead, staff feel empowered to share information, and everyone understands the implication of carefully writing and editing the content that they post. The idea that "we are sensible people" has been proven accurate. As Kotter cautions: going forward, it will be important for administration to avoid second-guessing or criticizing posts written by staff.[6] If people are criticized for communication, communication will dry up.

STAGE 6: GENERATING SHORT-TERM WINS

Not long after launching Heard Alert, people began asking for enhancements. Could we enable comments? Could we add a Like button? It was particularly satisfying when these requests were supported by people who were previously skeptical about giving library staff the ability to make unmediated posts. The team was able to enable comments: another short-term win.

Staff asked the team to create posts for them, and with gentle encouragement they were able to see that Heard Alert wasn't hard to use. This gave people a feeling of satisfaction and empowerment. Improved email formatting received lots of positive feedback and was a clear upgrade from the previous email layout. Simply getting a more attractive daily email made people happier and more knowledgeable about their workplace.

The Implementation Team kept up morale and did not get bogged down by the process or the people. It helped to be confident in working on something that was for the good of the staff and that was satisfying.

STAGE 7: CONSOLIDATING GAINS AND PRODUCING MORE CHANGE

Heard Alert was rolled out only one year ago from the time of this writing, so time will tell about its success, but to date it is an unqualified improvement. While it didn't change all systems in the library, it did change the fundamental system by which all staff are glued together in a common enterprise. One interesting observation: when new staff are hired, it's not very long before they post to Heard Alert. This shows that the system is respected and used as the primary communication vehicle by library staff, which is satisfying.

As soon as Heard Alert rolled out, more changes were poised to happen. The team created a technical platform on WordPress to support the spin-off of other intranet sites, giving staff even more options for communication within their units, committees, and groups. The Science and Engineering Library asked for a new intranet tool for its service desk staff, which was implemented successfully. The Access Services group asked for a blog in which they could privately share security information.

Many new menu items have been added to Heard Alert since the rollout. It is now the go-to location for system-wide information for library staff. Monthly birthday announcements had previously been a privacy concern, as staff were not comfortable having their birthdays published on the open web; this system provided a safer alternative. Monthly birthday parties with cake became a morale booster. Things like trainings, funding opportunities, and announcements are posted more often than they were in the old system. This is likely because people don't have to go through the extra step of asking an intermediary to post for them.

In general, the group didn't face much in the way of complacency or resistance. Commitment to each other and to the group was solid, and because of this, the Implementation Team accomplished a great deal.

However, perhaps a few moments of honest reflection are necessary before too much celebration happens. After all, only a year has passed, and Kotter warns us that real change takes many years and must endure staffing changes, reorganizations, and unexpected problems.[7]

III. Grounding Phase

STAGE 8: ANCHORING NEW APPROACHES IN THE CULTURE

Ideally, a well-informed and engaged staff makes for a more effective organization. Heard Alert provides the library with an open system of communication for all staff. Having an open communication system like Heard Alert in place promotes a healthy work culture and improves morale. The next steps for the library may include other open and transparent ways for staff to communicate with each other, and for upper administration to participate as well.

The Heard Alert system is in place and anchored. Its viability is a necessity in that the library urgently needed a staff news platform and intranet. The WordPress platform is easy for library IT to maintain and had the added benefit that it increased knowledge and usage of WordPress in other areas of the library, such as the exhibits program.

The popularity of the service can be seen in continued talk among staff about Heard Alert—"We should post that to Heard Alert," and "Did you see that announcement on Heard Alert?"

The Implementation Team was awarded the 2018 Friends of Vanderbilt University Libraries' Award for excellence in a committee, task force, unit, or other library group. The award honors the work of a team, committee, or task force that developed and followed through on an idea resulting in streamlined workflows, cost savings, enhanced services, or boosted morale in a department, library, or across the libraries. The award recognizes collaborative work and collegiality.

Analysis and Conclusions

Analyzing the process through the Kotter lens helped the team reframe some aspects of the project that may have seemed unimportant or incidental, but that were actually a large part of the project's success, such as the effectiveness of the team. The project team asked the right questions; had the right experience, motivation, and commitment; had buy-in from administration; and found solutions that were both manageable and user-centric. As a small team that had worked together previously, they had a nice mix of skills and experience. They were quite motivated to improve organizational culture and overall morale. The fact that the team knew who to ask for assistance or advice and persisted until the question was answered contributed to the success of this project.

The Kotter framework was not part of the original plan, but it is easy to see how such a method would have been helpful if it were employed from the outset. Although the book emphasized that several phases of the method could be happening at the same time, it would be most useful to create a project plan and checklist while incorporating the advice in *Leading Change*.

Notes

1. John P. Kotter, *Leading Change* (Boston: Harvard Business Review Press, 1996), 59–60.
2. Kotter, *Leading Change*, 57.
3. Kotter, *Leading Change*, 61.
4. Kotter, *Leading Change*, 59–60.
5. Kotter, *Leading Change*, 102.
6. Kotter, *Leading Change*, 112–14.

7. Kotter, *Leading Change*, 143–44.

Bibliography

Kotter, John P. *Leading Change*. Boston: Harvard Business Review Press, 1996.

Chapter 25

Analysis
Technological Change

Colleen Boff and Catherine Cardwell

Libraries
Stephen F. Austin State University (SFA)
University of Alabama at Birmingham (UAB)
University of Virginia (UVA)
Vanderbilt University (Vanderbilt)

Introduction

The libraries at SFA and UVA have reputations for being early and innovative adopters of technologies. While SFA holds this reputation in its community, UVA is recognized nationally for its accomplishments in digital humanities projects. SFA is a small public institution with a Carnegie classification of Basic. Its technological story involved the changes made through its library's Center for Digital Scholarship to reboot its institutional repository, whereas the technological change at UVA, an R1, involved a deep examination of workflows across departments to manage digital humanities projects. The remaining two institutions in this category share the R1 Carnegie classification, but the change story at UAB is one of merging websites at two of its libraries; the change at Vanderbilt is a story of how the libraries re-engineered their internal communication system. Change stories in this category involved multiple libraries or multiple departments and ranged from a technology migration at UAB and Vanderbilt to a redesign of workflows at SFA and UVA. The change at three of the four institutions impacted services designed for external audiences, whereas the change at Vanderbilt was specifically targeted at staff.

I. Warm-up Phase

STAGE 1: ESTABLISHING A SENSE OF URGENCY

SFA was an early but quiet adopter of Digital Commons, an institutional repository (IR) platform. It did so because IRs and open access were emerging trends and, as good stewards, the library staff knew the importance of serving this role for their campus even if the campus did not quite know the value. However, the adoption and implementation of this tool was added to the responsibilities of one librarian and was organizationally not a high priority as it became overshadowed by a website redesign.

After realizing the exorbitant cost per item housed in the IR, the librarians who over-saw the project made a case for more robust support from library administration and librarians and more participation from campus stakeholders in determining the future of the IR. At UAB, a newly hired library dean was given the mandate in 2014 to centralize library operations into one library system. Merging the library websites of two libraries was the last step in this centralization process. The two independently operated websites confused patrons; they were costly for the library to run because it was paying for two instances of the catalog; and they used outdated technologies. The impetus for change at UVA was sparked by staff frustrated with inconsistent practices related to their digital projects. They lacked centralized and cohesive practices across units, which left them with backlogs of analog collections in need of digitization. The backdrop for change at Vanderbilt was spurred by staff frustration and complaints about communication. It took a turnover in the top leadership position for communication among staff to truly become a priority. The new university librarian appointed her deputy university librarian to head up an initial task force of seven members, all of whom had at least ten years of experience. They were given three months to gather data and to make recommendations. They used data from Google Analytics and gathered staff feedback through a survey. Their work resulted in four specific recommendations, which the university librarian assigned to an implementation team.

STAGE 2: CREATING THE GUIDING COALITION

In order to reboot SFA's IR, the associate director was empowered to create the Center for Digital Scholarship by pulling together four staff members from other areas of the library. Together, they actively promoted the capabilities of the IR to individuals and groups of faculty across campus. Once the IR was more popu-lated with a variety of materials, they were able to continue to raise interest and awareness among campus stakeholders. The team at UAB took a slightly different approach to the website merger when the library administration outsourced the work related to the website revision to the UAB campus Digital Media Team. The team conducted a SWOT analysis to gain feedback about the website, and then the library dean formed a website committee with representation from employee groups, departments, and libraries to itemize and categorize all services offered by the libraries. The committee was given a simple charge to merge websites and an ambitious deadline of less than one year to do so. While UAB's goal was to have a small, agile committee in order to facilitate quick decision-making, UVA did the opposite by creating the Digital Production Workflow Team, a group that included many members with knowledge of workflows and appropriate expertise. This was done so that the team had the full picture of all of the disparate processes within the organization. As at SFA, the leadership at Vanderbilt pulled together a small guiding coalition of three to explore and implement a new communication system. The team included two members from the initial task force and a new member from the library's IT unit. These three individuals were hand-picked because they were trusted by the staff at large, worked well together, and had a reputation of creativity and follow-through.

STAGE 3: DEVELOPING A VISION AND STRATEGY

The newly formed unit at SFA unified their efforts as a team by revisiting and revising the mission statement for the IR, which in turn served as their shared vision as a department. They broadened the vision from the IR serving as a depository of print formats to it serving as an archive and showcase of all types of scholarship. The development of a shared vision and strategy at UAB was a bit more complicated and included a review by the committee of the libraries' strategic plan, past usability studies, prior knowledge of the UAB Digital Media team, the results of the SWOT analysis, and an informal review of websites of peer and aspirational institutions. In order to address common complaints from staff and users, the web committee surveyed each unit to determine which of its services it wanted prominently featured on the new website. The committee used this collective feedback to create the structure for the unified site map. As at UAB, the team at UVA looked outward to see what other institutions were doing in order for their vision to coalesce. Through this process, they were able to analyze the strengths and weaknesses of these programs to map out stages in their workflow. They subsequently began to devote meetings to each stage. The initial committee at Vanderbilt identified concrete recommendations to the implementation team, which included a participatory mechanism for sharing news, a revitalized intranet, and a shared calendar. The Vanderbilt team spent significant time at this stage testing a long list of technological tools in the hopes of finding an all-in-one tool, which proved elusive. The strategy they settled on was to go with WordPress, the platform already being used to report news in the organization. However, they devoted a great deal of time customizing it with themes and plug-ins to meet the expectations of the staff.

STAGE 4: COMMUNICATING THE CHANGE VISION

At SFA, the Center for Digital Scholarship team focused on creating a unified presentation of the IR. They stressed that their success hinged on their ability to leverage the relationships each of them had with departmental faculty. This resulted in the IR growing from 279 items in 2012/2013 to more than 6,000 items by 2017/2018. The web team at UAB did not have the benefit of being fully in control of their webpage redesign because they were working with the university's web design team. After the initial visioning process, there was not much communication with library staff or the wider community of users while the campus team was busily working on the landing pages. However, once the pages were ready, feedback forms were placed on the website so users could provide feedback. While the communication at UAB was admittedly spotty, the strategies at UVA were robust, layered, and somewhat unique. To facilitate productive discussion within the group, members were instructed to arrive at meetings ready to talk about ideas to improve the future environment rather than focusing on failures. They decided to label projects that began prior to the processes as "legacy projects" so that members could focus on future work and not get caught up in changing processes related to existing projects. They used Atlassian Confluence, a collaboration software program, to organize their work and make it available to all. They ultimately produced a detailed report with their recommendations and gave it to their library administration and subsequently used this approved report to present to the staff. The implementation at Vanderbilt pursued typical routes of communication, but the strength of the team's communication efforts was attributed to their ability to make strategic and intentional communication decisions. They made sure to circle back to the initial recommending group to not only solicit their help with testing but to gain some buy-in and goodwill among the staff. In addition to making presentations at large staff gatherings, this team worked hard to communicate individually as a way to get staff to contribute to the new system.

II. Introducing New Practices Phase

Stage 5: Empowering Broad-Based Action

A crucial turning point for the Center for Digital Scholarship team at SFA came when they stopped asking faculty to simply deposit their articles and started involving faculty in shaping the scope of the IR. Though this proved to be a fresh start to the reboot of the IR at SFA, the web committee at UAB had the misfortune of their change initiative coming at the end of the centralization of their library system. Though the work got done a bit later than scheduled, they were overly ambitious with their timeline and bundled too many technological changes, including the simultaneous launch of a discovery layer with their web redesign. Other barriers to staff support of the redesign included mixed feelings among staff about outsourcing control of the library website to the campus team. UVA reported communication, especially between departments, as a problem it was trying to solve. Because workflows crossed over departmental lines, projects would get lost in the handoff from one department to another. Funding was sporadic, as was decision-making. As the authors state, "It was not one person's job to make sure digital collections moved from ingest to access." Lastly, the implementation team at Vanderbilt anticipated barriers to staff buy-in and designed the new communication system to be user-friendly and easy to use. They chose to have faith in their colleagues to make reasonable and professional posts, a belief that has proven to be true.

Stage 6: Generating Short-Term Wins

The very metric that served to create a sense of urgency to reboot the IR at SFA also served as the evidence of a short-term win. The cost to host documents in the IR went from $100 a document at the launch of the IR to $5 a document after the hard work of the reboot team. In addition to the growth in the number of items added to the IR each year, other short-term wins included the number of new journals published and the percentage of overall faculty participation. Though it was cause for concern among some UAB staff, the web team saw the decision by the library administration to outsource the creation and maintenance of the website as the first short-term win. The second short-term win was the creation of a new domain address for the website that made the task of centralizing not only the library website but UAB's Springshare products much more seamless. Short-term wins by the UVA team were practical and included the decision to use a project management software program to help them track digital projects. They spent time to establish standardized descriptive workflows, including the investigation of a metadata management system. The Vanderbilt implementation team was encouraged by staff requests for additional improvements to their new communication system, which demonstrated that staff were engaged and actively reading and contributing communications.

STAGE 7: CONSOLIDATING GAINS AND PRODUCING MORE CHANGE

The cycle of change continued at each of these institutions. At SFA, the Center for Digital Scholarship added more and more examples of creative projects hosted in the IR. These were featured during the team's presentations, which sparked even more ideas among faculty about ways to utilize the IR. The website committee at UAB continued their change momentum and worked on various library-related migrations and mergers while the campus Digital Media team was building the website over the summer. These included merging the libraries' two catalogs, creating a unified *A–Z* site for shared databases, and working on a single instance of UAB's Springshare products. The team at UVA tested their framework with two small digital projects that helped them refine their recommendations in their final report. They recommended the establishment of a permanent Digital Collections Team and a director position to lead the group. The new intranet and internal communication blog that the implementation put in place at Vanderbilt is actively being used as more staff are feeling comfortable posting. In fact, the team is getting requests from staff to replicate instances of this enhanced blog to meet additional needs of various working groups in the library.

III. Grounding Phase

STAGE 8: ANCHORING NEW APPROACHES IN THE CULTURE

To truly anchor their IR in the campus culture, the Center for Digital Scholarship team at SFA set their sights on solving a long-standing campus-wide problem by creating a centralized electronic platform to host theses and dissertations. This served only to heighten the value of their IR on their campus. The strategy for solidifying change at UAB and at UVA involved the creation of permanent working groups to continue the work at these two institutions. A permanent website committee was sanctioned at UAB, and the library administration at UVA agreed with the temporary team's recommendation to establish a permanent Digital Collections Team with a dedicated position to lead the group. This signaled to staff that library administration recognized the ongoing work necessary to keep these functions healthy. Finally, staff at Vanderbilt were actively using their new communication platform, which resulted in a more informed staff. In fact, some staff started to see other ways to use the enhanced communication for other work purposes.

Analysis and Conclusions

The technological enhancements made at SFU and UVA are anchored and continue. The work at Vanderbilt has mostly concluded. In spite of all of the hard work by the Center for Digital Scholarship staff, the future of the IR at SFA is tenuous due to four vacated positions out of five that remain unfilled and new library leadership. This suggests that future-facing initiatives such as this that fall outside of core and traditional library roles may become unstable if the shared vision in the organization is disrupted. Not only is this team of one faced with doing less outreach and doing the work of these vacated positions, they now have to strategize about how to make this a library priority once again.

TIPS FOR TECHNOLOGICAL CHANGE

- The amount of work and number of tasks to be completed as a result of the technological change should be considered when the task force, committee, working group, or guiding coalition is formed. The UAB website committee would have benefited from having more members to update and create content for the sub-pages of their newly merged website, especially given the quick turnaround. Although the working group at UVA sounded unusually large, they had a sufficient number of members to spread the workload around.
- The authors' explanation of the characteristics, traits, and qualities Vanderbilt was looking for when constructing its team was very detailed. They reinforced the importance of identifying committee members who are trusted by staff. They stressed the importance of a team that could maintain "good spirits" through the change process while being politically savvy. Vanderbilt's efforts to make thoughtful decisions at this juncture in the change process paid off, given that the implementation team received the Friends of the Vanderbilt University Libraries' award for excellence in a committee, task force, unit, or other working group.
- In a similar vein, the authors stress the importance to UVA of looking to the future and approaching the work with a positive state of mind, which they describe as "a determination to focus on an improved future environment instead of perceived failings with the current state."
- The danger of scope creep on projects involving technology is evident. As demonstrated by UAB, the merger went well beyond just their website and included catalogs, Springshare tools, and a discovery layer. It is difficult to isolate change when it comes to library technology because so many library systems are interconnected and so many of them have a direct impact on users.
- The authors from UAB stressed the importance of communication in the technological change process, especially to stakeholders who are not a part of the change team. The communication challenges were heightened due to outsourcing the library webpage development to the campus Digital Team. Though the library website committee was grateful for the technical expertise this team provided, they simply did not have enough or timely information to share from the Digital Team even though they were willing to do so and had internal mechanisms in place. UVA stressed effective communication among committee members. Taking the extra time to intentionally work through differences of opinion among committee members was likely a contributing factor to their success.
- Project management was a recurring theme among these stories of change related to technology. The use of a project management tool by the UVA team demonstrates the power of using such tools for complex projects. The Vanderbilt authors suggest creating a project plan and checklist based on the Kotter framework. Finally, setting realistic timelines for technological change is critical. Some takeaways from these change stories in particular include the adoption of a project management tool such as Confluence, taking an inventory of the work that needs to be done and by whom, and establishing deadlines for specific phases of the project to be completed.

Conclusion

Analysis across All Groups

Colleen Boff and Catherine Cardwell

This final chapter offers an analysis across all five categories, which include strategic planning, reorganization, culture change, new roles in libraries, and technological changes. Various patterns evolved over the course of many different authors' reflections on these types of change at twenty different institutions in the United States and Canada. Although Kotter's model was originally intended to guide change, it served, in this book, as a valuable tool for analysis and provided a shared language to talk about change concepts.

I. Warm-up Phase

STAGE 1: ESTABLISHING A SENSE OF URGENCY

According to Kotter, "Establishing a sense of urgency is crucial to gaining needed cooperation."[1] He asserts that in order for change to take root, approximately 20 percent of the organization needs to go above and beyond the call of duty to make change happen,[2] but that approximately 75 percent of management need to grasp this sense of urgency.[3] He also asserts that a major reason change fails is due to complacency among the staff. Complacency settles in for a variety of reasons. Chief among them are the following: no visible crisis, ample resources, lack of rigorous performance standards, a rigid organizational structure that focuses on job functions, irrelevant or ambiguous performance outcomes, insufficient performance feedback from external sources, a culture that avoids confrontation, refusal to acknowledge problems, and "too much happy talk from senior management."[4]

The sense of urgency to change was extremely high at a few of the institutions represented among these change stories due to unusual and stressful circumstances related to staff departures. However, for most institutions, the reasons to change were self-imposed and motivated by the need for libraries to stay relevant and become more user-centered on their campuses. Much of the change that took place among these stories was well anchored and successful, though not all of the change had completely unfolded at the time of this writing. Complacency was mentioned most often when there were lags in communication due to waiting for consultants to do their work or when staff needed to be hired or retrained. Though Kotter does not emphasize this among the reasons change

fails, change efforts were tenuous in academic libraries and their outcomes uncertain when top leadership turned over.

The reasons for change in academic libraries among our stories varied and are best analyzed by category. A common thread across many of these stories was the need to centralize operations and reduce redundancies, especially in the larger multilibrary systems. It is clear from analyzing these reasons for change across all categories that libraries still serve their communities in traditional ways, but they are also future-facing and interested in creating environments that are agile, responsive to user needs, and clearly serving in new and exciting roles.

Reasons for Strategic Planning

- To create a more unified, cohesive library organization
- To address holes in organization structure due to vacancies
- To remove barriers between departments
- To improve collaboration within and outside of the library
- To improve communication within and outside of the library
- To refresh an expired, outdated, or nonexistent strategic plan
- To address changes mandated by central administration

Reasons to Reorganize

- To foster collaboration and break down silos
- To address structural problems caused when employee turnover results in permanently vacant positions
- To revise an organizational chart that no longer supports the work of the library or the needs of users
- To retool and respond to changes in the profession and on campus
- To have a seat at the table when important decisions about the library are being made at the university level
- To take advantage of collaborative opportunities
- To relieve the pressure of maintaining traditional services while responding to rapid changes in user expectations
- To eliminate duplicative services
- To address issues related to inconsistent levels of service to patrons
- To meet new expectations established during a strategic planning process

Reasons for Culture Change

- To fix an unhealthy staff culture
- To adjust to a new strategic plan
- To match efforts with a new vision and mission
- To address communication issues among staff
- To provide excellent and consistent services to users
- To be part of a broader planning initiative
- To preserve an appropriate level of services to patrons in spite of chaos behind the scenes

Reasons for New Roles

- To respond to a problem expressed by senior campus leadership
- To lessen internal frustrations of staff with a new workflow, practice, or program
- To address underserved student populations
- To aim for and uphold a reputation of excellence
- To create transformative collaborations
- To change the perception of the library and its ability to serve in new and unlikely roles
- To be a central location for multiple services
- To showcase the many talents of librarians and library employees
- To provide CV-worthy experiences and other experiential learning opportunities for students
- To be open to new possibilities—being in the right place at the right time and stepping up
- To stay informed about developments in the professional literature and acting on them
- To respond to and act on behalf of changing needs of users

Reasons for Technological Change

- To anchor the use of a tool at an institution
- To centralize and merge tech systems
- To remedy broken technological workflows that span multiple units
- To improve staff communication through electronic means

STAGE 2: CREATING THE GUIDING COALITION

Kotter's recommendation to leaders when forming their guiding coalition is straightforward and involves identifying the right people, building trust, and establishing common goals.[5] The guiding coalition must have people with the appropriate positional power, expertise, credibility, and combination of leadership and management abilities.[6] The stories in this book reveal that the guiding coalition needs to include people whom the leadership trusts but also people whom staff trust. Finally, it is critical to build cohesion among the guiding coalition through goal setting and making sure that everyone is unified in the change initiative.[7] The change stories also point to the need for library leadership to carefully consider the size of the guiding coalition.

Library leadership involvement with library-wide change is essential, even if consultants are hired. Middle managers were particularly important when it came to strategic planning, reorganization, and culture change among our stories. They were often the ones involved in the actual implementation of change efforts because of their supervisory responsibilities and their role in overseeing department work, communications, and position responsibilities of individuals. The importance of making sure that middle managers were on the same page with change efforts was stressed on a number of occasions because this group of employees typically serves as the conduit between library leadership and library employees. The change team at the University of Tennessee, Knoxville, lamented the lack of middle management involvement on their team charged with making sure library employees contributed to the goals of the strategic plan. Participation of a middle manager would have helped them establish connections to departmental documents such as annual reports much sooner in the process. Montana State University admitted that it would have benefitted from having its associate dean on the working group due to this person's knowledge of the Balanced Scorecard process. Middle management involvement is especially important when the change involves only a portion of the library, such as a department or unit. It is less likely that library leadership is directly involved with this smaller level of change and typically means that the middle manager is the only person who communicates with library leadership because of reporting structures.

According to Kotter, the guiding coalition should not include people who have big egos, who will undermine the change process, or who are reluctantly on board.[8] Only two of the three head librarians volunteered to navigate the rough waters at the University of Manitoba. A volunteer group under these circumstances was likely the best course of action. In some instances, such as at the University of Florida and Northern Arizona University, the guiding coalitions grew organically and were based on established records of collaboration and good working relationships. In other instances, such as at UCLA and the University of Maryland, the library administration carefully considered committee assignments to ensure appropriate representation of classifications of employees and departments.

Kotter also underlines the need to build trust among the team members and to establish common goals.[9] The interim university librarian at Wesleyan selected three of her trusted colleagues to be a part of her team. At the University of Manitoba, staff trusted the two middle managers who stepped up to form the guiding coalition, which was extremely important given their fear about their situation. The leadership at Vanderbilt was careful to pick a guiding coalition whom staff trusted and who the leadership felt would be politically savvy and good-natured about serving in this capacity.

In most instances, library leadership gave committee charges to the guiding coalitions. In the absence of this, a working group can develop its own guiding principles or goals, as was the case with Montana State University. Some of the consultants were presented with a charge. However, deliverables should be carefully considered and be established with consultants at the outset, especially when it comes to a transition plan once they depart.

The size of a guiding coalition should be carefully considered from the outset. Depending on the nature of change, a larger committee may be warranted when a work-intensive guiding coalition is needed. The guiding coalition at the University of Virginia was large. This served them well because there was a great deal of work to be done. The University of Alabama at Birmingham intentionally set out to have a small group for its website merger with the hope that a smaller group would be agile and able to make decisions quickly. In the end, the group had far more work than they could handle, and admittedly, they would have benefited from a larger guiding coalition from the outset. The other advantage to a larger guiding coalition is that there are more people who are intimately involved with the vision and reason for change, thus broadening the buy-in within the organization. At some institutions, the change was so large that multiple committees were formed simultaneously or one group handed off its findings to another group for implementation. Miami experienced both of these scenarios during its complex library-wide change process.

One last observation about forming the guiding coalition concerns the use of consultants. Several institutions sought help from consultants, typically when the change was extensive and the timeline was short, as was the case at Miami, Montana State University, and the University of Alabama at Birmingham. They frequently helped to gauge staff willingness to change and worked in conjunction with library leadership to set the vision with staff involvement. The stories suggest that when the crisis level was high, particularly at Wesleyan and the University of Manitoba, the need to elevate a leader from within was likely a better choice than adding to staff stress levels by asking them to trust a complete stranger when trust was already unstable.

Stage 3: Developing a Vision and Strategy

At the outset of his book, Kotter explains the difference between leading change and managing change.[10] A firm understanding of the difference between these two roles is essential at Stage 1 and at Stage 3 when it comes to the development of a vision. Kotter defines a vision as "a picture of the future with some implicit or explicit commentary on why people should strive to create that future."[11] While he outlines a visioning process, he asserts that the guiding coalition, including the leader, should be responsible for the creation of the vision and that the vision should convey "a direction for the future that is desirable, feasible, focused, flexible and is conveyable in five minutes or less."[12] There is a wide range of readings, data sources, frameworks, activities, and technology tools used in the visioning stage across our change stories. The editors provide a complete list of these in Appendix C. Some of these same resources were used in Stage 1 to establish a sense of urgency among staff.

Montana State University's experience reinforced the important and critical work that takes place at this stage. Its guiding coalition, including its consultant, reviewed its existing set of value statements and made the intentional decision to deviate from their established timeline in order to revise these. They recognized the importance of slowing down at this stage, even at the expense of additional fees to extend the consultant's time with them.

A particularly prominent theme across the majority of stories included a common vision to improve the user experience. The editors broadly define the users, in most cases, to mean the patrons who use library resources and services. In some instances, they interpret the users to be those internal to the library, such as the staff who benefitted from improvements to the internal communication system at Vanderbilt or improved workflows at the University of Virginia among staff responsible for digitization. Many of the stated goals established to achieve this vision of improved user services were also similar across institutions and frequently included the need to break down silos, to centralize services, to make decisions based on user feedback, to modernize the structural issues in libraries that would enable them to offer innovative services, and to hire or retrain staff to serve in new roles.

STAGE 4: COMMUNICATING THE CHANGE VISION

When it comes to communicating change, Kotter asserts that leaders typically under-communicate at a time when staff have the most questions.[13] He suggests that the best strategies for a guiding coalition to follow are to keep the change message simple and easy to recall by employees, repeat it often, and most important, for everyone on the guiding coalition to be on the same page and to send a consistent message. He also suggests the use of multiple forums and relatable metaphors, as well as the guiding coalition leading by example.[14]

Typical modes of communication across all of these stories included face-to-face meetings with individuals or with groups, presentations to stakeholders, newsletter and email updates, and sharing documents through some type of intranet to keep staff informed. Even among traditional modes of communication, there are decisions to consider. Montana State University branded its emails specific to the strategic planning process in order to make communications about its strategic planning change process distinctive. Some of these change stories clarify when it is important for leadership to meet with staff individually. The deans at the University of Texas at Arlington and at Western Michigan University took the time to do this. This labor-intensive, one-on-one, personal approach may be necessary depending on staff anxiety related to the change efforts and the degree to which the staff is impacted individually.

Traditional means of communicating through face-to-face meetings with the major-ity of staff can be powerful as well. One exemplar that illustrates this is the participatory process of communication used at Montana State University during its strategic plan-ning process. The guiding coalition conducted activities that actively engaged library employees in creating strategy maps and value statements. In other words, Montana State University included the staff in the stage of creating the vision rather than just communicating an already completed draft of the vision out to them. Communication about the change process at Wesleyan was similarly participatory. The interim university librarian at Wesleyan enlisted the help of the staff during a retreat where they worked together to develop project-based goals and concrete action steps. This helped build buy-in, ensured that everyone was on the same page, and made the employees feel as if they were helping to move the organization forward in a time of crisis.

A few unique approaches to communicating the change vision exist in the stories. At the University of Manitoba, where tensions were high due to staff layoffs, the guiding coalition created a communication plan and stressed how important it was for them to communicate frequently with staff to rebuild trust and to contextualize communi-cations that make mention of library and university planning documents. The library leadership at Northern Arizona University intentionally referred to their newly formed UX group as "consultants" to help facilitate communication between this group and the library staff in their endeavors to change from a traditional hierarchical library culture to one where decisions are primarily made through constant feedback from patrons. The University of Virginia employed a notable strategy when the guiding coalition instructed committee members to arrive at meetings ready to talk about ideas to improve the future environment for their digital humanities digitization project, rather than focusing on past failures. Before rolling out their plan to the entire staff, the implementation work-ing group at Vanderbilt circled back to the initial and recommending group to make sure the work of their two groups aligned. Lastly, Miami's timely hiring of a dedicated communications and marketing person to help with consistent messaging about change efforts in its reorganization and strategic planning processes was unusual among these stories.

Conversely, the editors saw evidence of frustration among staff when there were disruptions in communication or infrequent communications, such as with the techno-logical change underway at the University of Alabama at Birmingham. It had outsourced the redesign of its website to the university web design team and, as a consequence, there were stretches of time where communication to the staff was sparse. Miami also expressed frustration at this stage because of a lag time in communication while wait-ing for the consultants to write the strategic plan. In these instances, the library group responsible for change was not fully in control of the change initiative, a potential down-side when working with consultants. Similarly, it is important to maintain communica-tion between multiple working groups during the change process. Change initiatives at several institutions frequently involved multiple committees, where one committee did the planning and another committee was formed for the implementation process. This was the case at Vanderbilt in its reengineering of its internal communication system. The authors attributed part of their success to the implementation group checking in with the recommending group to confirm that their work aligned before rolling it out to the staff.

The categories of change selected for this book suggest that strategic planning, reor-ganization, culture change, and technological change typically cut across multiple library departments and involve intensive communication with the majority of library staff. Certainly, efforts were also made to communicate with external audiences in these change categories but not to the degree that change involving new roles warranted. Communication efforts at Earlham and at West Virginia University, whose stories both address new roles for libraries, were led by a few library champions. Communication about change efforts was primarily with stakeholders external to the library.

Effective Practices

- Brand emails and newsletters specific to the change initiative to differentiate them from other communications.
- Consider one-on-one communications when change impacts individuals and is anxiety-provoking.
- Expedite buy-in through participatory methods, though it may take more time.
- Write a communication plan.
- Communicate a focus on the future rather than a focus on past failures.
- Agree upon communication strategies and expectations with consultants before-hand to ensure an uninterrupted stream of communication with stakeholders.
- Explore ways to bolster communication if multiple teams, committees, or work-ing groups are in place simultaneously or if one team is handing work off to another.
- Consider hiring a dedicated communication and marketing expert if resources permit.

II. Introducing New Practices Phase

STAGE 5: EMPOWERING BROAD-BASED ACTION

This stage of Kotter's change model is about removing barriers that prevent employees from engaging in the shared vision of change. These barriers can come in the form of having ineffective organizational structures, not having the appropriate skills in the organization, not having the right systems in place to get the job done, or having ineffective people in positions of power.[15] The barriers with employees can be addressed through professional development and their involvement in the change process. Kotter also suggests the importance of addressing issues with managers undercutting the change momentum.[16] Investing in the right tools, especially in libraries, can move change initiatives forward as well.

As Kotter suggests, many of the obstacles to change across these stories were structural and related to an organizational alignment.[17] Insufficient staffing at the University of Manitoba and staff turnover at Wesleyan, especially at the top leadership levels, presented extreme cases of staffing barriers, but other institutions also struggled with staff turnover, though to a lesser degree. At institutions such as Western Michigan University and the University of Texas at Arlington, where reorganizations were underway, the leadership had many obstacles to contend with, from working with human resources and unions to changing position descriptions to offering training and professional development to help staff learn new skills. The turnover at the highest levels of library leadership at Wesleyan created a situation where there was interim leadership for long periods. Wesleyan found itself in a holding pattern more often than not while waiting for new leadership to be hired and acclimated before other key positions in the organization could be filled permanently.

Many of the barriers to change across these stories can be attributed to the human response to change. While there were definite themes among these stories, this is an area in the change narratives where in-depth and anonymized interviews could provide more insight into human reaction to change and specific strategies for addressing these emotional responses. Below are the major themes with some advice gleaned from select stories.

Anxiety

- Sudden or unexpected staffing announcements cause anxiety among employees. Such was the case at the University of Manitoba, with the unexpected layoffs of staff, and at Wesleyan, with the sudden and unanticipated departure of the library leader. In both of these instances, library employees who were trusted by staff stepped up to lead during these difficult times. It is doubtful if someone newly hired into these situations would have been able to successfully navigate the emotional toll these circumstances caused for employees. The interim university librarian at Wesleyan was able to push through a particularly troubled and stressful period in her organization because she enlisted a small agile team of trusted colleagues to help her. The University of Manitoba change agents provided direction and regular communications during a tenuous time and helped regain staff trust. They accomplished this through regular and consistent communication that was contextualized and clearly connected to key planning documents.

- Strategic planning invoked anxiety in a few distinct ways. Strategic planning was a daunting task to undertake on top of running a library, especially for those serving on the working committees. Even when consultants were brought in to help, anxiety came into play when the consultants left, as was the case with Miami. In several cases, large complex documents that overwhelmed staff were produced as a result of strategic planning. The guiding coalition at the University of Tennessee, Knoxville, made their document more accessible to busy staff by distilling it into an executive summary.

- Library reorganizations tend to provoke anxiety among staff. While staff are often excited about new leadership, a partial or complete overhaul of the organizational structure usually follows within the first year or two of the leaders' arrival. These change stories provide some strategies for leaders to keep in mind to help staff cope with change related to reorganizations. Miami and UCLA used their detailed strategic planning documents for guidance with their reorganization. The leaders at Western Michigan University and the University of Texas at Arlington provided professional development and training to help staff adjust, while the leadership at Miami provided training for middle managers. Advice garnered from our change stores includes the need to set realistic timelines for staff to adjust to their new responsibilities and the need to time large-scale changes to the organizational structure for when employees are not immersed in intensive work related to the day-to-day operations.

Staff Morale

- The staff morale at the University of Manitoba was particularly low due to staff layoffs. Those who remained felt devalued by library administration and grieved the loss of their colleagues. The leaders of this change initiative tackled this problem by assigning staff more rewarding work, which also helped address perceptions of inequities among employee groups.

- The staff at Wesleyan dealt with a wide range of emotional responses to unrelenting disruption in their organization. In addition to needing to prove their value to university administration, they also had to contend with the unexpected departure of a long-term leader and then the grief of the sudden death of her replacement. The interim university librarian approached this delicate situation by engaging the staff with projects that needed to be tackled and enlisting them to help her move their organization forward.

Buy-in

- Though resistance to change was mentioned several times, most institutions reported only small pockets of resistance rather than large-scale, all-encompassing resistance to change.

- The team at Vanderbilt enhanced the internal communication system by making it simple and easy to use. They also encouraged staff to use the new system and trusted them to do so in a professional manner.
- Getting staff to buy in to change initiatives can be problematic when middle management is not part of the implementation process. Admittedly, this was the case at the University of Tennessee, Knoxville, where the team lacked middle management representation from the outset.
- The institutional repository (IR) team at the Stephen F. Austin State University realized that an effective way to engage faculty with the IR came when they stopped asking faculty to deposit their scholarship and started involving faculty in shaping the IR. They also used the IR to solve a campus problem with their electronic theses and dissertation project.

Burnout

- Change efforts are time-consuming, and it was acknowledged on more than one occasion that employees have their regular work to do on top of committee assignments related to change efforts. The authors at Montana State University recommend providing committee members some type of relief from other duties during the change process.
- The merging of websites at the end of a larger centralization initiative at the University of Alabama at Birmingham also came at a time of great change. To make matters even more challenging, several technological changes were bundled together with an extremely ambitious timeline. To help with this, the decision was made to outsource control of the website to the campus web design department. Though the library was able to provide input on the new design, it did lose control of its website design and maintenance, a solution that was met with resistance from some staff and relief from others.

Frustration

- The two middle managers who stepped up to lead change at the University of Manitoba expressed frustration with the lag time it took for them to get answers from their library administration when they suggested next steps. In this particular situation, it would have been ideal for the middle managers to have more autonomy to act, but this may not have been possible. This does, however, suggest the need for timely decision-making from the highest levels of library administration when staff anxiety levels are so high.
- The director of strategy and planning at West Virginia University expressed frustration over missing an important deadline related to her IMLS grant because an office she had to rely on to complete a promotional video failed to meet a deadline. In the end, this created more work for her since she had to apply for a grant extension. This raises the issue of the frustrations that come with libraries initiating new roles on campus. Change champions at Earlham and at West Virginia University had to secure seed money for their programs while simultaneously

using their short-term wins to promote their programs in the hopes of securing additional and permanent funding sources.

- Interdepartmental communication about digital scholarship workflow was particularly problematic at the University of Virginia. This situation was resolved with the recommendation to hire a person to oversee the newly designed workflow.

Reluctance

- Librarians at the University of Manitoba were reluctant to shift some of their responsibilities to staff even though this was designed to free up some of their time to make room for different work. Such was also the case at Florida State University. The concern among librarians at the University of Manitoba was the fear that they too would be vulnerable to layoffs. For the librarians at Florida State University, the concern was uncertainty about how to fill their vacated time due to ill-defined expectations of what they should do next. In both instances, librarians were able to experiment with new ways of approaching their work and reported better work-life balance after implementing the change.
- Change in decision-making from hierarchical to user-informed at Northern Arizona University was a big culture shift and was met with reluctance among staff. Increased comfort with this new approach came after the UX team was able to make a few changes to the website and prove that the method of involving users in decision-making worked. In fact, the staff grew to appreciate this new approach because changes were made quickly, departmental silos began to dissolve, and the user became central to their work. Librarians at Rice also gained confidence in their customer-service training program after piloting it with the leadership team first.
- To make changes at the University of Maryland, the team used a consensus-building decision-making process and involved everyone in the newly centralized Research and Learning (R&L) department. New initiatives were presented at the R&L heads meetings, vetted by all units within the department, and then presented at open forums.
- The passage of time can work for or against the emotional response of reluctance to change. Resistance to change set in slightly at Miami during periods of waiting to hire staff, whereas staff had time to adjust to the idea of change with lulls in action at Wesleyan.

The authors of these change stories did not provide any evidence of middle management undermining change in libraries, which, according to Kotter, is possible.[18] In fact, middle managers were seen as extremely important to the implementation process.

STAGE 6: GENERATING SHORT-TERM WINS

Kotter explains that short-term wins need to be evident within the first six months of the change initiative in order to hold the attention of employees in the organization.[19] Timing matters, and so does the quality of the "win." These accomplishments need to be unambiguous, highly visible to those who work in the organization, and directly related to the change at hand. These changes don't need to be major, but they need to demonstrate momentum forward.[20]

Examples of Short-term Wins

Strategic Planning

- Merged service points (Miami, Florida State University)
- Adjusted department structures and created a new middle management position (Miami)
- Made small fixes to the organizational structure to improve functions such as collection development (Miami)
- Created new committee structures (Montana State University)
- Increased financial resources (Montana State University)
- Defined projects with action steps (Wesleyan)
- Created an accessible dashboard where staff can self-report their accomplishments (University of Tennessee, Knoxville)

Reorganization

- Switched to a new organizational structure (Miami)
- Hired and onboarded new employees (Western Michigan University)
- Renovated staff spaces and collocated employees in newly formed units (Western Michigan University)
- Conducted team- and community-building activities with staff (UCLA, University of Texas at Arlington)
- Generated new ideas around new vision (University of Texas at Arlington)
- Merged and eliminated some functions (University of Texas at Arlington)

Culture Change

- Changed position descriptions (University of Manitoba)
- Adjusted position descriptions, which resulted in better work-life balance (University of Manitoba, Florida State University)
- Piloted and adjusted the project before presenting it to the staff (Rice)
- Conducted user testing to better understand user needs and habits (Northern Arizona University)

Technological Change

- Increased faculty participation and submissions to the IR (Stephen F. Austin State University)
- Reduced workload thanks to outsourcing web redesign and maintenance (University of Alabama at Birmingham)
- Improved tracking of digital projects through the use of project management software (University of Virginia)

- Responded to staff requests for improvements to its communication system which demonstrated engagement (Vanderbilt)

New Roles

- Generated program growth, which garnered more funding (Earlham, West Virginia University)
- Created new internships (University of Florida)
- Phased in changes to the liaison program in order to incrementally change behaviors (University of Maryland)
- Redefined work of librarians and modernized teaching spaces (University of Maryland)
- Built new relationships with others on campus (Earlham, University of Florida, University of Maryland, West Virginia University)

STAGE 7: CONSOLIDATING GAINS AND PRODUCING MORE CHANGE

At this stage in Kotter's change model, the guiding coalition assesses the smaller wins and continues the momentum of change by identifying larger scale changes that need to be made and by determining who else is needed in the organization to make this happen.[21] Does someone need to be promoted, hired, or urged to move on? The importance of maintaining a sense of urgency for change is stressed at this stage, and project management is emphasized and shared among middle management. Kotter also stresses the importance of examining what he calls interdependencies.[22] A good example of this in the academic library setting might be a call to question why certain data is being tracked if no one is using it or how a processing workflow could be streamlined.

Examples of Ways to Increase Momentum

Strategic Planning

- Created a permanent team to monitor progress toward achieving strategic plan (Montana State University)
- Hired and onboarded new employees (Miami)
- Completed a self-study and a strategic plan (Wesleyan)
- Motivated staff through recognitions, celebrations, and awards (University of Tennessee, Knoxville)

Reorganization

- Rewarded early adopters (Miami)
- Celebrated successes with staff (Western Michigan University)
- Formed a new leadership council and provided leadership development (Western Michigan University)

- Generated flourishing collaboration and communication between departments, eroding silos and changing the culture to one of idea sharing (UCLA)
- Created several new experiential learning initiatives for users, such as a makerspace; developed programs to boost the morale of staff; and hired an associate university librarian (University of Texas at Arlington)
- Created a new library administration position (University of Texas at Arlington)

Culture Change

- Moved away from traditional tasks to concentrate on progress toward new initiatives (University of Manitoba, Florida State University)
- Increased collaborations with others outside the library (Florida State University)
- Gathered more feedback from users (Northern Arizona University)
- Further subdivided and deepened work of guiding coalition (Northern Arizona University)
- Started to see evidence that culture changes were taking root (Rice, Northern Arizona University, University of Manitoba, Florida State University)

Technological Change

- Sparked creative uses of IR with faculty, which diversified and broadened content in the IR (Stephen F. Austin State University)
- Merged catalogs and Springshare products and created a unified database list while webpages were being redesigned (University of Alabama at Birmingham)
- Tested new workflow with two digitization projects (University of Virginia)
- Generated active use of enhanced communication system by employees (Vanderbilt)

New Roles

- Generated continual review of curriculum (Earlham)
- Championed new initiative and enlisted help from librarians to make the program a permanent part of embedded library outreach efforts (West Virginia University)
- Enhanced the application process for internships and added additional CV-worthy experiences for grad students (University of Florida)
- Embedded librarians in departments and the library viewed by students and faculty as the place to go for research assistance (University of Maryland)

III. Grounding Phase

STAGE 8: ANCHORING NEW APPROACHES IN THE CULTURE

Because Kotter's process follows a particular sequence,[23] he reinforces the importance of the final stage.[24] His rationale is that altering a culture involves changes in human behavior, which takes time. Employees within an organization need to see that the changes are superior to the old ways of getting work done, but he also explains that it is important for leaders to frequently remind employees of these changes and to articulate what these changes are in order to actually alter the culture.[25] In most of our stories, the culture described at this stage was different from the one described at the beginning of the change story.

Kotter also underlines the necessity of making staffing changes if there are continued and persistent barriers to change that negatively influence the transformed culture.[26] Though staff were reassigned duties or moved to a different part of the organization among our change stories, mostly due to intentional reorganization, not much evidence exists to suggest that employees were actually removed. This may indeed occur in some academic library settings. However, the presence of tenure, unions, and an overall culture of employee evaluation and continual improvement through professional development make this less likely to happen in academic libraries than in a corporate setting. Many institutions of higher education have human resource departments that will work with managers and leaders to develop performance plans that give employees opportunities to address issues.

Analysis and Conclusions

Readers will find a number of tips in the synthesis chapters written by the editors and placed at the end of each category of change in this book. These suggestions are mostly specific to a certain type of change and are best contextualized within their respective categories.

The editors opened this book with references to two important pieces in the literature: the Dempsey and Malpas article about the future of academic libraries and ACRL's "2018 Top Trends in Academic Libraries."[27] Together, these documents suggest that academic libraries are at a pivotal moment as they make a critical and transformative change from traditional collections-based libraries to service-based models driven by the user experience. When constructing this book, the editors selected the change stories long before writing the introductory chapter. They did not intentionally seek stories that perfectly align with this hopeful picture of the future of academic libraries, yet by chance, that happened. The change described in the twenty stories in this book demonstrates that library leadership is, indeed, actively putting library users at the forefront of their change efforts and aligning user input with library expertise to create vibrant library services, programs, and spaces. It is also worth noting that the editors turned away more than 100 other chapter proposals, many of which put the users in the driver's seat of change.

Collectively, these stories have several implications for libraries. The editors made the intentional decision to include as many stories as possible in the hopes that they would uncover stages in the Kotter model where more research was needed or where library leaders and managers would benefit from professional development. Following are a few of their observations:

- More research and professional development are needed to explore ways to lead the process of creating the vision and strategy for change. The editors wanted more details in some areas of the change stories, but this was particularly true of Stage 3, where authors were asked to talk about creating the vision and strategy for change. There were a few reasons why providing more in-depth details was not feasible. Authors had to tell their story in a concise manner with a word limit as a constraint. In some cases, institutions worked with consultants at this stage and may have been reluctant to go into too much detail over concern about infringing upon the consultants' process. A qualitative study with in-depth interviews of library leaders on this important stage in the change process is recommended.

- Stage 5 is another section where the editors had lingering questions. This is in no way a criticism of contributing authors' change stories. How library leaders navigate barriers to change is a loaded topic and not one that leaders feel particularly comfortable writing about when the names of their institutions and employees are exposed. A research design where responses are anonymized would likely elicit more information about and strategies for addressing the human and emotional response to change, such as resistance to change, anger, fear, and anxiety.

- Finally, as the work of libraries grows more complex, librarians may need additional skill sets in order to do their jobs. Some of the contributing authors expressed the need to know more about project management, UX principles, Design Thinking, setting measurable and realistic program or project goals, conducting usability testing for web design, and mapping complex workflows. This list calls upon expertise in other fields. Some libraries are addressing this by hiring this type of talent and foregoing the traditional credentialing of the MLS. Other libraries look for consultants when they need expertise for a short-term project or support staff participation in the many excellent professional development opportunities offered online. A growing need for different skill sets warrants a careful look at the MLS curriculum and the professional development landscape to equip leaders and librarians with the skills needed to keep up with the quick pace of change.

Use of the Kotter Framework

Kotter's eight-stage model is a more complex change model when compared to some.[28] It is an excellent tool to use for analysis of change in academic library settings for a variety of reasons. The eight stages provided a common language for authors to talk about change; it also provided a consistent way to examine twenty change stories in order to identify patterns of best practices and areas for consideration. A helpful observation about using this framework came from Carroll Wetzel Wilkinson from West Virginia University in chapter 19:

> Using Kotter's eight stages of leading change as an analytical tool has made it possible to see that the change initiative at WVUL [West Virginia University Libraries] to create a sustainable and permanent WVUL_VOP [Veterans Outreach Program] is on its way toward real success.

The twenty change stories in this book, in addition to the growing body of related articles in the professional journal literature, suggest that Kotter's model does indeed help academic librarians grapple with organizational change. This final analysis across all of the change stories provides an opportunity to share the collective experience using the model as a means to examine change.

Organizational change is messy, complex, and unpredictable. The temptation when using a multistep model is to come to believe the illusion that change is tidy and orderly and that the model will have all the answers. Several authors pointed out that the change process at their institutions was not as linear as Kotter's model would suggest and that their change experience did not follow the eight stages in order. In some instances, the stages at their institutions occurred simultaneously or out of order. Though Kotter suggests that the eight stages occur sequentially and typically in the order of his eight stages, he does acknowledge that multiple stages may occur simultaneously. He warns that "skipping even a single step or getting too far ahead without a solid base almost always creates problems."[29] Some authors also pointed out that Kotter does not go into detail at Stage 2 on ways to handle the need for multiple guiding coalitions throughout the change process. However, the most significant shortcoming of using any organizational change model is its inability to help leaders contend with the emotional and human response to change. Diane Klare and Melissa Behney from Wesleyan University summarize it well in chapter 4:

> Library organizations are extremely complex and subject to completely unforeseen forces (e.g., a leader's death). Despite Kotter's framework, bringing about change can be difficult to institute within a precise and logically laid-out model. Humans are complex creatures, and that complexity is evidenced daily as an organization evolves and confronts both planned and unexpected changes.

Kotter's model also does not explicitly include assessment or evaluation of the overall change efforts. He mentions it in Stage 7, but this is in relation to small changes and not to the overall efforts. Libraries typically assess their work, but since the model did not explicitly trigger this analysis and the editors did not add it as an extra prompt, this information was not consistently provided across our change stories. Systems such as the Balanced Scorecard include measurement of success metrics, but the authors were not asked to include these. Readers may consult Appendix B: Information about the ACRL Monograph Project should they want more detailed information about the parameters of the stories.

Together, these disclaimers suggest that the use of and reliance upon a single model, whether for analysis or active use in the change process, is not enough. The Kotter model has been actively used since the early 1990s and remains relevant all these years later. Academic library leaders can safely rely upon it as a reputable and primary framework to facilitate change, but additional expertise and resources will be needed, particularly when it comes to influencing human behavior.

Notes
1. John P. Kotter, *Leading Change* (Boston: Harvard Business Review Press, 1996), 36.
2. Kotter, *Leading Change*, 35.
3. Kotter, *Leading Change*, 48.
4. Kotter, *Leading Change*, 40.
5. Kotter, *Leading Change*, 61.

6. Kotter, *Leading Change*, 57

7. Kotter, *Leading Change*, 66.

8. Kotter, *Leading Change*, 59.

9. Kotter, *Leading Change*, 61.

10. Kotter, *Leading Change*, 26.

11. Kotter, *Leading Change*, 68.

12. Kotter, *Leading Change*, 81.

13. Kotter, *Leading Change*, 85.

14. Kotter, *Leading Change*, 90.

15. Kotter, *Leading Change*, 115.

16. Kotter, *Leading Change*, 112.

17. Kotter, *Leading Change*, 103.

18. Kotter, *Leading Change*, 112.

19. Kotter, *Leading Change*, 21.

20. Kotter, *Leading Change*, 121.

21. Kotter, *Leading Change*, 143.

22. Kotter, *Leading Change*, 142.

23. Kotter, *Leading Change*, 23.

24. Kotter, *Leading Change*, 155.

25. Kotter, *Leading Change*, 156.

26. Kotter, *Leading Change*, 157.

27. Lorcan Dempsey and Constance Malpas, "Academic Library Futures in a Diversified University System," in *Higher Education in the Era of the Fourth Industrial Revolution*, ed. Nancy W. Gleason (Singapore: Palgrave Macmillan, 2018), 78, https://doi.org/10.1007/978-981-13-0194-0_4; ACRL Research Planning and Review Committee, "2018 Top Trends in Academic Libraries: A Review of the Trends and Issues Affecting Academic Libraries in Higher Education," *College and Research Libraries News* 79, no. 6 (June 2018), 286–300, https://doi.org/10.5860/crln.79.6.286.

28. For select examples of additional change models, see Lewin's Change Process of Unfreeze, Change, Refreeze; Doppelt's Wheel of Change; Kanter, Stein and Jick's organizational change model; Bolman and Deal's Reframing Organizations model.

29. Kotter, *Leading Change*, 23.

Bibliography

ACRL Research Planning and Review Committee. "2018 Top Trends in Academic Libraries: A Review of the Trends and Issues Affecting Academic Libraries in Higher Education." *College and Research Libraries News* 79, no. 6 (June 2018): 286–300. https://doi.org/10.5860/crln.79.6.286.

Bolman, Lee G., and Terrence E. Deal. *Reframing Organizations: Artistry, Choice, and Leadership*, 6th ed. San Francisco: Jossey-Bass, 2017.

Dempsey, Lorcan, and Constance Malpas. "Academic Library Futures in a Diversified University System." In *Higher Education in the Era of the Fourth Industrial Revolution*. Edited by Nancy W. Gleason, 65–89. Singapore: Palgrave Macmillan, 2018. https://doi.org/10.1007/978-981-13-0194-0_4.

Doppelt, Bob. *Leading Change toward Sustainability*. London: Routledge, 2010.

Kanter, Rosabeth Moss, Barry Stein, and Todd Jick. *The Challenge of Organizational Change: How Companies Experience It and Leaders Guide It*. New York: Free Press, 1992.

Kotter, John P. *Leading Change*. Boston: Harvard Business Review Press, 1996.

Lewin, Kurt. "Frontiers in Group Dynamics: Concept, Method and Reality in Social Science; Social Equilibria and Social Change." *Human Relations* 1, no. 1 (1947): 5–41.

Appendix A

Call for Proposals
Leading Change in Academic Libraries

Colleen Boff and Catherine Cardwell

We invite chapter proposals for consideration in the publication of a forthcoming ACRL monograph titled *Leading Change in Academic Libraries*. Contributing authors are asked to describe and reflect on a recent change in their academic library in which they worked with others in the organization to reorganize, reengineer, innovate, or initiate a service, program, function or structure in your library. Authors will be asked to use Kotter's (1996) "eight stage process for creating major change" to reflect on their change experience. Criteria for proposals include the following:

- The change experience must have been initiated in the past five years.
- The change experience must have been planned by a working group, team, task force or committee of two or more people.
- The change experience must be in an academic library setting at any type of four-year institution serving undergraduate and/or graduate students in the United States.
- The change experience does not have to be fully implemented or deemed a complete success.

Authors are expected to have expertise and first-hand knowledge of their particular change experience but do not need to have a particular leadership/management title to contribute. While it is not necessary to have used Kotter's model during the change process, we are asking contributors to use this model as a mechanism to explain and analyze their change experience.

Proposals should include the names of all authors and institutional affiliations, identification of primary contact with email address, proposed title of chapter, and an abstract of no more than 500 words.

Authors of accepted proposals will be asked to write a chapter within the range of 12–15 pages, double-spaced, including all text, references, tables, images, and photographs.

Proposal submissions are due to Colleen Boff (cboff@bgsu.edu) by February 28, 2018. If you plan to submit a proposal, please send Colleen a brief email expressing intent to submit. She will send you a link to more information about the project. Questions about this project may also be directed to Colleen.

Editors will respond to proposal contributors by April 15, 2018. Chapters will be due by August 1, 2018. Proposed publication date for monograph is January 2019.

Information about the ACRL Monograph Project

Leading Change in Academic Libraries

Colleen Boff and Catherine Cardwell

We have chosen Kotter's eight-stage change model to structure the change studies in this monograph for a few reasons. First, it provides a uniform framework for readers to rely upon as they move through each change study. Secondly, it provides us with a common language across change studies. Lastly, it provides the editors with a common structure for analysis across change studies. As the editors, our goal is to analyze all of the change studies at each of the eight stages to identify areas of strength in the change process and areas of opportunity for professional development. The complete citation to Kotter's work is Kotter, John P. (1996). *Leading Change.* Boston, MA: Harvard Business Review Press.

It is not necessary to have used this particular framework during the change process. However, we would appreciate it if you could address each of the eight stages in telling your story whether the stage was pertinent to your change process or not.

Important!

Use each of the sections and the headings to organize your chapter. However, the questions are to prompt your thinking. No need to answer the questions directly in your narrative.

Setting the Change Stage

Be sure to include the following in your description of your change experience:
- Name and location of institution

- Size of institution
- Carnegie classification
- What type of change was this? (e.g., strategic planning, assessment, reengineering, reorganization, innovation, starting a new initiative, other)
- What was the scope of the change? (e.g., involved a single unit or department, involved multiple departments within the library, involved the entire library, involved multiple units within the library and on campus, other)

Warm-up Phase

STAGE 1: ESTABLISHING A SENSE OF URGENCY

- What crisis or problem was your team trying to solve?
- What data or information did your team use to formulate this crisis or problem?
- Who was this crisis or problem communicated to?
- Approximately what percentage of the organization/unit was made aware of and believed the crisis or problem?

STAGE 2: CREATING THE GUIDING COALITION

- Describe who was on your team. What were their titles and roles in the organization?
- Were there people who were not on your team that should have been?
- Did the team have a charge and if so by whom?
- Did the team have established goals?
- Did the team have credibility among those outside the team?
- What were the dynamics among the team members?

STAGE 3: DEVELOPING A VISION AND STRATEGY

- Was there a vision to guide the change and if so, who set it and how? "A vision refers to a picture of the future with some implicit or explicit commentary on why people should strive to create that future" (Kotter, 1996, p. 68).
- What specific strategies, plans and/or steps were developed to achieve the vision and what was the timeline?

STAGE 4: COMMUNICATING THE CHANGE VISION

- What did your team communicate about the change?
- With whom did your team communicate about the change?
- How did your team communicate about the change?
- How often did your team communicate about the change?

Introducing New Practices Phase

STAGE 5: EMPOWERING BROAD-BASED ACTION

- What were the barriers to change and how were those dealt with?

STAGE 6: GENERATING SHORT-TERM WINS

- Kotter defines short-term wins as visible, unambiguous, and clearly related to the change effort (p. 121). What short-term wins did your team have and when did these happen in relation to the timeline?

STAGE 7: CONSOLIDATING GAINS AND PRODUCING MORE CHANGE

- Describe the series of changes that took place that cumulatively added up to major change.
- What strategies did your team use to maintain momentum?
- How did the team handle complacency or resistance within the team and/or outside of the team?

Grounding Phase

STAGE 8: ANCHORING NEW APPROACHES IN THE CULTURE

- Is this change experience or any part of it still in place? If so, what strategies were employed by your team to anchor this change? If not, what prevented the change from being anchored?

Analysis and Conclusions

- What areas of the change process did your team do particularly well?
- Where in the change process could you and your team have used some support and what would that support have looked like?
- What did you like/dislike about the Kotter change model?

Summary of Resources Used across Change Stories

The contributing authors identified resources used during the change process at their institutions. Because only major activities are included in this listing, readers may find additional activities referenced in the individual stories. One important caveat to note—resources other than those listed here and in the stories may have been used during the change process at these institutions, but the contributing authors may not have referenced them in their narratives.

Resources are grouped as follows:
- Data Sources and Readings
- Frameworks
- Activities
- Consultants
- Tools and Technology
- Other (used to refer to institutions' specific resources such as strategic plans or websites)

Strategic Planning

MIAMI UNIVERSITY

Data Sources and Readings

- Bell, Stephen P., and John Shank. "The Blended Librarian: A Blueprint for Redefining the Teaching and Learning Role of Academic Librarians." *College and Research Libraries News* 65, no. 7 (July/August 2004): 372–76. https://doi.org/10.5860/crln.65.7.7297.
- Lunenberg, Fred. "Managing Change: The Role of the Change Agent." *International Journal of Management, Business and Administration* 13, no. 1 (2010): 1–6.

- Wharton School of Business. "Is Your Team Too Big? Too Small? What's the Right Number?" June 14, 2006. http://knowledge.wharton.upenn.edu/article/is-your-team-too-big-too-small-whats-the-right-number-2.

Activities

- Steering committee and consultants worked with community to form vision.
- Consultants conducted listening meetings with library departments.
- Formed three additional teams and developed the philosophy, guiding principles, and service categories that became the foundation for the new organizational structure.
- Consultants produced a 260-page integrated master plan.
- Middle managers implemented plan.
- Recruited, hired, and onboarded seventeen new staff members.
- Transitioned employees into new roles.
- Merged reference and circulation desks.
- Re-envisioned collection development duties for librarians.
- Developed team and leadership training plans.

Consultants

- brightspot Strategy
- Perkins & Will

MONTANA STATE UNIVERSITY

Data Sources and Readings

- See change story for a brief literature review about the Balanced Scorecard framework.
- Assessment report of an expired library strategic plan
- LibQUAL survey data
- ClimateQUAL data
- Results from the Northwest Commission on Colleges and Universities
- Data from SOAR survey
- Readings for staff (see note 13 in the change story)

Frameworks

- Balanced Scorecard

Activities

- Offered Balanced Scorecard in-house workshops.
- Working group created their own charge titled "Roles, Responsibilities, and Expectations."

- Consultant worked with the library staff to create value statements, mission, and vision.
- Staff read two articles before filling out SOAR (strengths, opportunities, aspirations, results) survey.
- Consultant held several on-site workshops with staff to develop strategy maps related to strategic objectives (see example in figure 2.2 in change story).
- Formed new UX&A team.
- Created new strategic plan.
- See figure 2.3 in change story for additional initiatives underway.

Consultants

- Martha Kyrillidou, QualityMetrics, LLC

Tools and Technology

- Tableau (data visualization software for strategic plan dashboard)

Other

- *The Montana State University Library Strategic Plan 2018–2024*. https://www.lib.montana.edu/about/strategic-plan/.

UNIVERSITY OF TENNESSEE, KNOXVILLE

Activities

- Created the Strategic Achievement Review (StAR) team to measure progress toward the strategic plan.
- Developed website with dashboard to collect progress toward achieving strategic goals.
- Planned celebrations and awards to recognize staff contributions to the strategic plan.
- StAR team experimented with different methods to get staff to make contributions.

Other

- University of Tennessee, Knoxville. *University of Tennessee Libraries Strategic Plan, 2017–2022*. https://www.lib.utk.edu/about/files/StrategicPlan_Aug2016.pdf.

WESLEYAN UNIVERSITY

Data Sources and Readings

- Data from a library staff survey

- Data from a faculty survey
- Student survey data from institutional research
- Information gathered at two open fora for faculty to share their teaching and research needs
- Benchmark comparison data from external sources
- An analysis from a campus facilities planner about the state of the library facilities
- Bryson, John M. *Strategic Planning for Public and Nonprofit Organizations: A Guide to Strengthening and Sustaining Organizational Achievement*, 4th ed. San Francisco: Jossey-Bass, 2011.

Frameworks

- Association of College and Research Libraries. *Standards for Libraries in Higher Education.* Chicago: Association of College and Research Libraries, 2011.

Activities

- Conducted library self-study using *Standards for Libraries in Higher Education* as framework.
- Conducted library external review.
- Developed library strategic planning with staff.
- Hired a digital projects librarian and created a digital lab.
- Staff began working on pilot projects to move library forward.
- Completed LMS implementation.
- Prioritized vacant positions and began promotions, reconfigurations, and hires related to the reorganization process.
- Responded to turnover in top library leadership position for the second time.

Other

- *Wesleyan University Library Strategic Plan 2016.* https://www.wesleyan.edu/libr/about/2016librarystrategicplan.pdf.

Reorganization
MIAMI UNIVERSITY

Data Sources and Readings

- LibQUAL
- ClimateQUAL

Frameworks

- Design Thinking
- Kristen Hadeed and the "Start with Why" program. https://startwithwhy.com/igniter/kristenhadeed/.

Activities

- Consultants led visioning process with steering committee, and then the library formed two additional working groups.
- Used activities borrowed from improvisational acting class (such as "yes, and…") to build community among working groups.
- Consultant and steering committee developed service philosophy, guiding principles to direct service strategy and vision for new organizational structure.
- Looked at structure at peer institutions.
- Developed new service categories, which became the structure for the departments.
- Hired a new communication and marketing staff member.
- Conducted process mapping activity with one of the working teams to help them visualize complex work processes.
- Completed an integrated master plan that included a space plan, vision, and framework for a next-generation library.
- Created a new hiring plan and began the hiring process.
- Provided professional development training to build teamwork and trust.

Consultants

- brightspot Strategy
- Perkins & Will
- Tom Heuer, a Forsythe Chair in Entrepreneurship and Clinical Faculty from the Miami University Farmer School of Business, and an expert in the Five Practices of Exemplary Leaders Model and its Leadership Practices Inventory.
- Kristen Hadeed, a "Start with Why" facilitator to help build trust. https://startwithwhy.com/igniter/kristenhadeed/.

UCLA

Frameworks

- Görög, Mihály, and Nigel J. Smith. *Project Management for Managers*. Newton Square, PA: Project Management Institute, 1999.

Activities

- Created a user engagement reorganization timeline (see figure 7.1 in change story).
- Analyzed three proposed organizational structures.
- Created and implemented the User Engagement matrix organizational chart (see figure 7.2 in change story.
- Teams and divisions followed the strategic plan guidelines to establish norms, responsibilities, and roles.
- Created opportunities for staff to share ideas such as open mic events and division shout-outs.

- Filled positions.

Other

- *UCLA Library Strategic Plan 2016–19.* http://www.library.ucla.edu/about/administration-organization/strategic-plan-2016-19.

UNIVERSITY OF TEXAS ARLINGTON

Data Sources and Readings

- Data from staff surveys
- Data from ethnographic observations of facility and observed user activity outside the library
- ACRL Research Planning and Review Committee. "2012 Top Ten Trends in Academic Libraries: A Review of the Trends and Issues Affecting Academic Libraries in Higher Education." *College and Research Libraries News* 73, no. 6 (June 2012): 311–20.
- National Survey of Student Engagement (NSSE)
- Student experience survey
- National Association of Colleges and Employers Annual Survey

Frameworks

- Collins, James C. *Good to Great: Why Some Companies Make the Leap—and Others Don't.* New York: Harper Business, 2001.

Activities

- Nine task forces formed and asked to review best practices in several areas at peer and aspirational institutions and to conduct observations of facility usage and user activities outside the library.
- Held a week-long retreat with guiding coalition to review all data and to develop the CXI vision.
- Staff completed two surveys, one to determine staff knowledge, skills, abilities, and preferences, and one to prioritize their top seven job preferences, their bottom five positions, and up to four areas of leadership interest.
- Dean had individual meetings with staff, announced the new organizational chart, and reassigned 94 percent of staff in the organization.
- New leadership team developed a list of forty-nine new initiatives.
- Merged departments and service points; switched to demand-driven acquisitions; eliminated subject-specific collection development practices: and arranged librarian responsibilities by discipline rather than function.
- Created many new programs (see Stages 6 and 7 for complete list).

Consultants

- An outside consultant was retained to help build trust among leadership team.

WESTERN MICHIGAN

Data Sources and Readings

- Staff surveyed at the end of the change process.
- Babrow, Sarah, and Megan Hartline. "Process Mapping as Organizational Assessment in Academic Libraries." *Performance Measurement and Metrics* 16, no. 1 (2015): 34–47. https://doi.org/10.1108/PMM-11-2014-0040.
- Bell, Steven, Lorcan Dempsey, and Barbara Fister. *New Roles for the Road Ahead: Essays Commissioned for ACRL's 75th Anniversary.* Edited by Nancy Allen. Chicago: Association of College and Research Libraries, 2015. http://www.ala.org/acrl/sites/ala.org.acrl/files/content/publications/whitepapers/new_roles_75th.pdf.
- Davis, Jeehyun Yun. "Transforming Technical Services: Evolving Functions in Large Research University Libraries." *Library Resources and Technical Services* 60, no. 1 (2016): 52–65. https://doi.org/10.5860/lrts.60n1.52.
- Ellis, Erin L., Brian Rosenblum, John Stratton, and Kathleen Ames-Stratton, "Positioning Academic Libraries for the Future: A Process and Strategy for Reorganizational Transformation." Proceedings of the IATUL Conferences, 4th plenary session, 2014. Paper 13 (2014), http://docs.lib.purdue.edu/iatul/2014/plenaries/13.
- Garrison, Scott, and Jennifer Nutefall. "Start by Interviewing Every Librarian and Staff Member: The First Step for the New Director." *College and Research Libraries News* 75, no. 5 (2014): 246–53. https://doi.org/10.5860/crln.75.5.9122.

Activities

- New dean interviewed each staff member in the organization using the questions in the Garrison and Nutefall reading.
- Held library-wide strategic planning retreat and identified five major themes.
- Formed two teams, one to create the strategic plan and one to reorganize.
- Conducted process maps.
- Stopped outdated services such as copy center.
- Adopted and implemented new organizational structure.
- Dean met with individuals and gave new departments four months to define work and identify needed talents and skills.
- Adjusted positions descriptions and hired new staff.
- Formed new libraries council.
- Hosted a Library Management Skills Institute for new leaders.
- Surveyed staff to see how the changes were going for them.

Other

- Western Michigan University Libraries. *Strategic Plan 2017–2020.* https://wmich.
  edu/library/about/strategicplan.

Culture Change

FLORIDA STATE UNIVERSITY

Data Sources and Readings

- Conducted a SWOT (strengths, weaknesses, opportunities, and threats) analysis

Frameworks

- Balanced Scorecard
- Open Science Framework

Activities

- Developed six strategies to address research and learning needs of STEM scholars.
- Merged building, circulation, and access management of two of the libraries
  with another.
- Created new service model.
- Changed organizational structure.
- Changed position descriptions.
- Filled vacant positions.

Other

- Besara, Rachel, Renaine Julian, Julia Cater, Ginny Fouts, Kelly Grove, Devin
  Soper, Elizabeth Uchimura, and Trip Wycoff. "STEM II Balanced Scorecard
  Initiative: Final Report," September 18, 2017. STEM II BSCI (FSU), Open Science
  Framework. https://osf.io/5npxh.

NORTHERN ARIZONA UNIVERSITY

Data Sources and Readings

- Used demographic data to develop personas.
- Data through conducting usability studies.
- Data from users through feedback loops such as whiteboard feedback.

Frameworks

- Luchs, Michael G., K. Scott Swan, and Abbie Griffin. *Design Thinking: New Product Development Essentials from the PDMA.* Hoboken, NJ: Wiley, 2015.

- Mootee, Idris. *Design Thinking for Strategic Innovation What They Can't Teach You at Business or Design School.* Hoboken, NJ: Wiley, 2013

Activities

- Created personas to get a better understanding of primary user groups and their needs.
- Conducted usability studies.
- Redesigned website.
- Gathered feedback with whiteboards.
- Did library mapping exercises of library spaces with users.
- Conducted focus groups.
- Subdivided working group into two: UX-Spaces and UX-Web.

Tools and Technology

- Microsoft SharePoint
- A ticketing system for staff to report problems

RICE UNIVERSITY

Data Sources and Readings

- Data from secret shopper activity

Frameworks

- Kotter, John P. *Accelerate: Building Strategic Agility for a Faster-Moving World.* Boston: Harvard Business Review Press, 2014.

Activities

- Organizational and Development Manager visited the library and conducted a "secret shopper" activity.
- Explored existing programs, reviewed literature, created user personas, reviewed customer service videos.
- Used a document titled "Strategy for Service Training Development and Implementation" that borrowed on Seraphim Consulting's "The Road to There" program outlining actions, outcomes, and impacts identified for each actionable item. Seraphim Consulting and Training Solutions. "The Road to "THERE"." Products page. Accessed July 2, 2019. http://www.seraphimconsulting.net/id70.html.
- Used "Dealing with Angry Patrons," an OCLC WebJunction webinar (WebJunction. "Updated Course: Dealing with Angry Patrons." WebJunction. May 18, 2016. https://www.webjunction.org/news/webjunction/updated-course-dealing-with-angry-patrons.html).

- Piloted customer training program with library administration first before conducting it with staff.
- Used ExpressPack cards by Trainers Warehouse as icebreaker to explore good and bad customer service (Trainers Warehouse. "ExpressPack." Accessed May 10, 2019. http://www.trainerswarehouse.com/expresspack.html).

Consultants

- Rice University. Human Resources. Organizational and Development Manager.

UNIVERSITY OF MANITOBA

Data Sources and Readings

- Association of Research Libraries. "Graph 1: Service Trends in ARL Libraries, 1991–2015." From *ARL Statistics 2014–15*. Washington, DC: Association of Research Libraries, 2015. http://www.arl.org/storage/documents/service-trends.pdf.
- Canadian Association of Research Libraries. *CARL Statistics | Statistiques de l'ABRC: 2015–2016, Salaries | Salaires 2016–2017*. Ottawa, ON: Canadian Association of Research Libraries, September 2017, rev. October 24, 2017. http://www.carl-abrc.ca/wp-content/uploads/2017/10/CARL-ABRC_Stats_Pub_2015-16-v2.pdf.
- Creary, Stephanie J., and Lara Rosner. "Mission Accomplished? What Every Leader Should Know about Survivor Syndrome." Conference Board of Canada, executive action report, June 11, 2009 http://www.conferenceboard.ca/e-library/abstract.aspx?did=3084.
- Kotter, John P., and Holger Rathgeber. *Our Iceberg Is Melting: Changing and Succeeding under Any Conditions*. New York: St. Martin's Press, 2006.

Activities

- Reviewed staffing and service models across U15 libraries in Canada and wrote a staffing proposal.
- Implemented a tiered service model that resulted in longer hours of operation but fewer hours of staffed time at service points. Piloted with three libraries and then implemented with remaining eight units.
- Developed a communication plan.
- Developed a "Working Alone Statement" policy.
- Successfully reclassed positions.
- Offered a two-day immersive retreat to refocus librarian model.

New Roles

EARLHAM COLLEGE

Data Sources and Readings

- Association of College and Research Libraries. *The Value of Academic Libraries: A Comprehensive Research Review and Report.* Researched by Megan Oakleaf. Chicago: American Library Association, 2010.
- Earlham College. "Diversity Aspiration Vision Statement." Accessed July 28, 2018. http://www.earlham.edu/policies-and-handbooks/general/diversity-aspiration-vision-statement/.
- Earlham College student retention data, 2006–2012.

Frameworks

- Association of American Colleges and Universities. "Information Literacy VALUE Rubric." Accessed July 28, 2018. https://www.aacu.org/value/rubrics/information-literacy.

Activities

- Worked with campus marketing and communications to promote the LIFT program.
- Collaborated with alumni mentors to work with LIFT students.
- Adjusted curriculum each semester.
- Planned an experience abroad.

Other

- Earlham College. "LIFT: Library Immersion Fellows Teams." Accessed May 24, 2019. http://www.earlham.edu/lift.
- Read more about the LIFT program in Baker, Neal, and Jane Marie Pinzino. "A Reserved Table for First-Generation Students." In *The First-Year Experience Cookbook.* Edited by Raymond Pun and Meggan Houlihan, 59–60. Chicago: Association of College and Research Libraries, 2017.

UNIVERSITY OF FLORIDA

Data Sources and Readings

- Association of Research Libraries (ARL) Position Description Bank.
- George A. Smathers Libraries. *Strategic Directions.* Gainesville: University of Florida, October 2014. http://ufdc.ufl.edu/IR00004144/00004.
- See references to related research published by these authors within their story.

Activities

- Conducted orientations for interns.
- Implemented curriculum vitae and résumé workshops for graduate interns.

Other

- University of Florida, George A. Smathers Libraries. "Smathers Graduate Student Internship Program Guidelines." January 2018. http://cms.uflib.ufl.edu/interns/Index.aspx.

UNIVERSITY OF MARYLAND

Data Sources and Readings

- See a brief review of the literature that informed the change initiative located in Stage 1 of the change story.
- The Library Liaison Task Force examined national trends, emerging literature, and models in place at peer institutions in addition to internal documents and data related to liaison activities.
- The Research Commons Task Force examined national trends, emerging literature, and models in place at peer institutions. They also conducted interviews with stakeholders and other institutions and administered an internal survey to UMD faculty and students.

Activities

- The task forces communicated with standing committees, other task forces, public forums, and email lists. They also held numerous one-on-one conversations, visits to units, and open-door policies.

Other

- Corlett-Rivera, Kelsey, Barbara Dickey Davis, Zaida Diaz, Cynthia Ippoliti, Lara Otis, Karen Patterson, and Nedelina Tchangalova. *Final Report, Task Force on McKeldin Library Research Commons*. College Park: University of Maryland Libraries, July 2013. https://drum.lib.umd.edu/handle/1903/20733.
- Luckert, Yelena, Daniel C. Mack, Svetla Baykoucheva, and Patricia C. Cossard. *Liaison Librarian Task Force 2012–2013, The University of Maryland Libraries, Final Report*. College Park: University of Maryland Libraries, May 31, 2013. http://drum.lib.umd.edu/handle/1903/17456.
- University of Maryland. "Integrated Research Resources on Campus." https://irroc.umd.edu/.
- The UMD Libraries created a "Meet Your Subject Specialist" webpage, with a link to a Google Scholar Profile for each librarian. This webpage also includes anonymous kudos for librarians. Available at https://www.lib.umd.edu/rc/meet-your-librarian.

WEST VIRGINIA UNIVERSITY

Data Sources and Readings

- LeMire, Sarah. "Beyond Service: New Outreach Strategies to Reach Student Veterans." In *Creating Sustainable Community: ACRL 2015, March 25–28, 2015, Portland, Oregon: Conference Proceedings*. Edited by Dawn M. Mueller, 66–71. Chicago: Association of College and Research Libraries, 2015.
- LeMire, Sarah, and Kristen T. Mulvihill. *Serving Those Who Served: Librarians' Guide to Working with Veteran and Military Communities*. Santa Barbara, CA: Libraries Unlimited, 2017.
- Survey data of WVU student veterans' needs and interests and an analysis of its results.

Frameworks

- Ohio State University Libraries. *A Framework for the Engaged Librarian: Building on Our Strengths*. Columbus: Ohio State University Libraries, 2016.
- Association of College and Research Libraries. *Framework for Information Literacy for Higher Education*. Chicago: Association of College and Research Libraries, 2016.

Activities

- Created the Veteran Study Room in the library, which involved remodeling and updates.
- Applied for and was awarded an IMLS SPARKS! grant.
- Identified and enlisted three student veterans (one fellow and two employees) to work on promotion.
- Created a dedicated webpage for program.
- Hired outside firm to produce orientation videos.
- Hosted open houses.
- Hosted a campus visit from Sarah LeMire, a scholar-librarian from Texas A&M University. She delivered one program for the Campus Veterans Advocates group and another program for the WVU Library Leadership Team.

Tools and Technology

- Atlassian's Confluence

Other

- West Virginia University Libraries. Services for Student Veterans website. https://lib.wvu.edu/services/veterans/.
- West Virginia University Libraries. "Resource Guide for Student Veterans." Last updated March 21, 2019. http://libguides.wvu.edu/studentvet.

Technological Change

STEPHEN F. AUSTIN STATE UNIVERSITY

Activities

- Customized presentations to individual departments with consistent messaging.

Tools and Technology

- Bepress Digital Commons (IR platform)

Other

- Stephen F. Austin State University. ScholarWorks website. https://scholarworks.sfasu.edu/.

UNIVERSITY OF ALABAMA AT BIRMINGHAM

Data Sources and Readings

- University of Alabama at Birmingham Libraries strategic plan
- Fitcher, Darlene, and Jeff Wisniewski. "Beyond Responsive Design." *Online Searcher* 40, no. 6 (November/December 2016): 66–68. ProQuest.
- Data from SWOT analysis with staff and other data gathered through environmental scan.

Activities

- Conducted a SWOT Analysis.
- Held town hall–style all-staff meetings.
- Administered Library Services Survey—needs and wants of each library department.
- Reviewed peer and aspirational websites.
- Used data from previous usability studies.

Consultants

- University of Alabama at Birmingham Digital Media, the university's web design unit. Library administration outsourced development and maintenance.

Other

- The UAB Libraries website was launched on 28 September 28, 2017, at https://www.library.uab.edu.

UNIVERSITY OF VIRGINIA

Data Sources and Readings

- Conducted an environmental scan of program characteristics at other institutions.

Frameworks

- Society of American Archivists (SAA). "Implementing 'More Product, Less Process.'"

Activities

- Piloted new workflow with two digitization projects.

Tools and Technology

- Atlassian Confluence (team collaboration software)
- Atlassian.Jira (a ticketing system; issue- and project-tracking system)

VANDERBILT UNIVERSITY

Data Sources and Readings

- Conducted an internal survey with staff.
- Analyzed data from Google Analytics on usage of past communication tool.

Tools and Technology

- WordPress platform and customizations
  - Suri theme for the main site with a custom child theme for sub pages
  - Single Sign-On (SSO)
  - User Submitted Posts (post submission plug-in)
  - Mail Poet (email plug-in)
- Tools the team investigated but did not adopt
  - Shared Outlook calendar
  - Microsoft Office 365 Planner/Microsoft Teams
  - Basecamp
  - Goodbits
  - Emma
  - Mailchimp
  - Springshare Calendar
  - Slack
  - Bedework
  - VU Campus Calendar
  - Microsoft SharePoint

Editor Biographies

Dr. Colleen Boff has worked in academic libraries for twenty-three years and has held a wide range of library management and leadership positions for the past ten years, including program coordinator, department chair, associate dean, and head librarian of a specialized collection. In these capacities, she has contributed to or been at the forefront of leading change in her organization at the department level, library level, and university level. In addition to many conference presentations, she has published several peer-reviewed articles, book chapters, proceedings, and book reviews, which has earned her the rank of professor at her library at Bowling Green State University in Ohio. She recently earned her doctorate in educational leadership and policy studies. The title of her dissertation is "A Quantitative Study of Academic Library Administrators Using Bolman and Deal's Leadership Orientation Framework." Catherine Cardwell, coeditor of this monograph, also served on her dissertation committee.

Catherine Cardwell is the Dean of the Nelson Poynter Memorial Library at the University of South Florida Saint Petersburg (USFSP). She provides leadership for the library, online learning, instructional technology services, and the Center for Innovative Teaching and Learning. A librarian for twenty-four years, Cardwell has served in various leadership positions for twenty-one of those years, from library instruction coordinator to library dean. Because she has worked in several different types of institutions—including Bowling Green State University, a public doctoral university with high research activity; Ohio Wesleyan University, a small private university; and USFSP, a regional comprehensive university—she has a broad understanding of the challenges and opportunities in a variety of academic library settings. Most recently, Cardwell led the library strategic planning effort at USFSP and is currently overseeing its implementation. Her interests include library leadership, integrating information literacy and digital scholarship into the curriculum, creating dynamic and contemporary user-centered teaching and learning spaces, and improving discovery and usability of library resources and services.

Author Biographies

Kenning Arlitsch is dean of the library at Montana State University. In a career spanning a quarter century, he has held positions in library instruction, digital library development, IT services, and administration. His funded research has focused on search engine optimization, as well as measuring impact and use of digital repositories. Arlitsch holds an MLIS from the University of Wisconsin-Milwaukee and a PhD in library and information science from Humboldt University in Berlin, Germany. His dissertation on Semantic Web Identity examined how well research libraries and other academic organizations are understood by search engines.

Neal Baker is Library Director at Earlham College. His professional service currently includes the executive committee of the Private Academic Library Network of Indiana (PALNI), the chair of the *Resources for College Libraries* (RCL) Editorial Board, and work as a Distinguished Bibliographer for the *MLA International Bibliography*. His scholarly publications and presentations span topics that include librarianship, instructional technology, and the science fiction and fantasy genres. His next book chapter is a digital humanities analysis of fifty years of event programming at Gen Con, the longest-running gaming convention in the world.

Jeremy Bartczak is Manager of the Metadata and Discovery Services Unit at the University of Virginia Library. He has an MLIS from Drexel University and an MA in art history from the University of Maryland, College Park. He has worked at the UVA Library since 2012.

Melissa Behney is Director of Library and Learning Commons Services at Middlesex Community College. She was previously the Director of the Science Library at Wesleyan University. Prior to her work at Wesleyan, Melissa held a variety of public service and administrative positions in both libraries and industry. She served as president of the Association of College and Research Libraries New England Chapter (ACRL/NEC) and cofounded its Leadership Development Committee. Her professional interests include changing academic publishing models and their effect on scholarship, learning theory, and leadership. Melissa holds a bachelor of arts in anthropology from Connecticut College and a master of library science from Southern Connecticut State University.

Allison Benedetti is the Director of the Arts, Music, and Powell Libraries at UCLA Library. Before coming to UCLA in 2012 as Librarian for Advanced Research and Engagement, Allison worked for the Society of Architectural Historians, Harvard Graduate School of Design, MIT, and the National Gallery of Art. She is currently the vice-chair of the ACRL Research Planning and Review Committee and a member of the ARLIS/NA Development Committee. Her professional interests include assessment, user-centered library services, and mentorship.

Rachel Besara is the Associate Dean of Libraries at Missouri State University. Until August 2017, Rachel was Director of STEM Libraries at Florida State University, and previous to that was an assessment librarian at Florida State University. Her research interests include library leadership, libraries' role in student success, and Ozark regional history.

Kate Leuschke Blinn is Social Sciences and Data Librarian at Bryn Mawr College. She worked for six years as Academic Outreach Librarian and Social Sciences Liaison at Earlham College. She has worked with first-year first-generation students in the context of the LIFT program since its inception. She has an MLIS from Drexel University iSchool and an MA in the social sciences (cultural anthropology) from the University of Chicago. She teaches course-integrated information literacy and has taught first-year students in seminars focused on reading the *New York Times* as well as on podcasting and autoethnography.

Michelle Brannen is the Media Literacy Librarian, Head of the Studio, and Interim Head of the Scholar's Collaborative at the University of Tennessee, Knoxville, Libraries. Her work focuses on working with students and faculty to incorporate media into their work both for academic assignments and in research. Michelle also serves as a subject liaison librarian for the Journalism and Electronic Media program and the School of Art. Michelle received her master's in information sciences from the University of Tennessee and a BA in music education from Florida State University. Her research interests include how library services can impact and support learning and the creative process, library assessment, and the intersections of civility and diversity in communities.

Maira Bundza is a librarian at Western Michigan University, where her main responsibilities include managing the institutional repository ScholarWorks and developing an open education resources initiative. She has been a reference librarian and involved with assessment and international education on campus. Before coming to WMU, she was the Latvian Studies Center librarian for fifteen years and continues to research Baltic libraries and archives. Maira has a BA in psychology from Cornell University and an MLS from Western Michigan University.

Sara Byrd, now the User Experience Librarian for the National Center for Atmospheric Research Library in Boulder, Colorado, was a librarian at Vanderbilt University for twelve years. She holds a BA degree in fine arts from Cumberland University and an MLS from Indiana University. Her library career has included UX, web management, e-resource management, reference, collection development, circulation, and serving as an IT liaison. She enjoys making complicated things seem simple, using data to tell a story, and sitting down to write a nice SWOT analysis.

Cynthia Childrey has served as the Dean and University Librarian at Northern Arizona University Cline Library since 2002. Prior to arriving at NAU in 1990, she was Management and Economics Bibliographer at Boston University Mugar Memorial Library and received her master's in library science from Simmons College. In 2015 Cynthia received the Polly Rosenbaum award from the Arizona State Library Archives and Public Records in recognition of her leadership, collaboration, creation of innovative learning spaces, development of library services for NAU's online learning programs, and partnerships with libraries and cultural organizations in Arizona.

Judy Consales is Associate University Librarian for User Engagement at UCLA Library. Prior to her work at UCLA, she held management, public service, and training positions in libraries and information companies. Judy is active in various organizations shaping library policies and practices. Her long association with the National Library of Medicine (NLM) includes serving as director of the National Network of Libraries of Medicine—Pacific Southwest Region. She is especially interested in mentoring librarians for future roles.

Jean L. Cooper has worked at the University of Virginia for thirty-five years and currently serves as a cataloger and reference librarian, as well as a genealogical resources specialist. Ms. Cooper earned a BA from Alma College (Alma, MI) and an ML from the University of South Carolina (Columbia, SC). She received the Virginia Genealogical Society's Virginia Records Award in 2009 for her work in indexing the Records of Ante-bellum Southern Plantations microfilm collection.

Christina Deane is the Manager of the Digital Production Group at the University of Virginia Library in Charlottesville, Virginia. She has worked at UVA Library for twenty-six years and received her BA in history from St. Andrews (Laurinburg, NC) and her MA in history from UVA. She also received her MLIS from Florida State University. She has worked in several areas of academic librarianship, including special collections, technology support, and now cultural heritage imaging.

Shirley Dickerson has been the Director of the R. W. Steen Library at Stephen F. Austin State University (SFA) in Nacogdoches, Texas, since August 2007. She has a bachelor of fine arts degree, with an emphasis in performance arts (voice), from SFA; a master of library science degree from Texas Woman's University in Denton, Texas; and a doctorate in educational leadership from Sam Houston State University in Huntsville, Texas. Her library career spans over forty years, during which time she has served in various leadership positions in public, academic, and special libraries. As library director at the R. W. Steen Library, she is responsible for planning, organizing, and directing library service programs in support of the educational and research goals of the university. In her position at SFA, Dr. Dickerson serves on the university Deans Council, Academic Affairs Directors Council, and the Graduate Council. Her research interest is organizational and transformative change in academic libraries. Outside of her professional interests, she relaxes by reading or listening to historical fiction, time travel and espionage stories, and biographies of civil rights activists of the twentieth century. Dr. Dickerson loves to sing and to listen to all genres of music. She enjoys living in the Pineywoods of east Texas with her husband of forty-three years and their three furry, four-legged friends, with frequent visits from their three children and six grandchildren.

Michael Durbin is the technical lead and manager of the Digital Content Management and Dissemination team at the University of Virginia Library. Prior to joining UVA in

2012, he worked in the Digital Library Program at Indiana University. He received a BS in computer science and Japanese from the University of Pittsburgh.

brightspot founder **Elliot Felix** is an accomplished strategist, expert facilitator, and gifted sense-maker, able to understand the most complex of problems through both creative and analytical means. He has directed numerous projects for leading companies as well as higher education and cultural institutions. Elliot has worked with over forty academic and public libraries over his career. He planned three of *Library Journal*'s 2016 "New Landmark Libraries" and is a frequent keynote speaker on the future of libraries and learning. Elliot has led projects for award-winning and innovative libraries such as the Hunt Library at North Carolina State University, Jerry Falwell Library at Liberty University, Miami University, and Georgia Tech's Library System. He oversees an innovative planning process to engage institutions in planning for tomorrow while developing actionable strategies for today.

Jodie Gambill is currently Librarian for Digital Projects at Vanderbilt University Libraries in Nashville, Tennessee. In this role, she does a lot of coding and committee work, with a dash of project management. She is also active in the American Library Association (LITA) and the Tennessee Library Association. She holds a BS in mathematics from Lipscomb University and an MS in information sciences from the University of Tennessee, Knoxville. For fun, she likes to read, run, sing in church choir, and talk to herself on Trello boards.

Julie Garrison is the Dean of Libraries at Western Michigan University. Prior to this role, she served as Associate Dean of Research and Instruction at Grand Valley State University and also held library and information services roles at Central Michigan University and Duke University Medical Center. Julie has published on library leadership and several aspects of library operations over the course of her career. She is an active member in the Michigan Academic Library Association and ACRL and currently serves as an editorial board member of *portal: Libraries and the Academy*. Julie earned a BA from the University of Michigan and her MLIS from UCLA.

Susan Garrison is the Access Services Manager and Education Subject Librarian at Rice University's Fondren Library. She oversees circulation, course reserves, interlibrary loan, security, stacks, and building maintenance, as well as collection assessment and development. Susan is an advocate for change management, process improvement, and service excellence. She holds a BA in communication and an MLS from Rutgers University, and an MBA from the University of Houston—Downtown Campus. She is currently co-chair for LLAMA's Practical and Applied Management Committee and incoming convener for ACRL's Access Services Interest Group.

Jeff Graveline is an associate professor and the Associate Dean for Research and Instruction in the University of Alabama at Birmingham (UAB) Libraries. He is actively involved with the American Library Association and the Alabama Library Association. His research interests include the intersection between copyright law and higher education and leadership in academic libraries. Jeff holds a BA in history from Virginia Tech and a JD and MLIS from the University of Alabama.

Adam Griff is a director at brightspot strategy. He helps universities rethink their space, reinvent their service offerings, and redesign their organization to improve the experiences of their faculty, students, and staff—connecting people and processes to create simple and intuitive answers to complex questions. He has led library projects with a wide range of higher education institutions, including the University of Wisconsin-Madison, Miami University of Ohio, the University of North Carolina at Chapel Hill, Massachusetts Institute of Technology, and the University of Miami.

Jonathan Helmke received bachelor's degrees in political science and business from Wartburg College (1996) and has a master's degree in library science from Indiana University (1997). He is currently the Associate Director for Library Information Services at Stephen F. Austin State University and is leading the implementation of the strategic plan for the library and working with the Scholarly Communications Librarian on various issues concerning the institutional repository. He served as the University Archivist (2011–2016) and Assistant Director for Technical Services and Library Systems at the University of Dubuque (2006–2016) and at Butler University in various capacities, including the libraries' efforts concerning the integration of technology and information literacy into the College of Business curriculum. His research interests include change management and how it intersects with leadership skill development.

Angela Horne is Director of UCLA's Rosenfeld Management Library and Charles E. Young Research Library Humanities and Social Sciences Division. She was previously Associate Director of the Catherwood, Hospitality and Management Libraries at Cornell University, where she led the team responsible for library academic services across the ILR, Hotel, and Johnson schools, including research, instruction, outreach, and collection development activities. She is active in the Special Libraries Association. She is particularly interested in building cultures of connection across organizations as a means to enable innovative, people-based solutions.

Kris Johnson is department head for Learning and Research Services, a large public services unit in the Montana State University (MSU) Bozeman Library. Her department covers everything from circulation and building management to reference, research, and instructional services. In previous professional positions, she was a first-year experience and information literacy librarian, as well as a project manager for a large statewide virtual reference cooperative. While in the latter position, Kris gained formal experience in facilitation and meeting management. Kris's research interests focus on project management, design thinking, and service design and how those concepts and tools play into personnel management and administration.

Renaine Julian is the Director of STEM Libraries at Florida State University. In this role, he oversees a team of science librarians and staff that provide support for STEM scholars across the research and learning life cycles. Prior to that, Renaine served at Florida State University as a Data Research Librarian, STEM Data and Research Librarian, and the Associate Director for STEM Libraries. Renaine has an MLIS, an MS in urban and regional planning, and a BS in political science, all from Florida State University. His research interests include library leadership and administration, scholarly communication, and open science.

Brian Keith is the senior administrator for the areas of human resources, staff development, grants management, facilities and security, and finance and accounting for the Smathers Libraries at the University of Florida. Functions under his direction include recruitment for all library positions; employee relations; compensation plan design and administration; performance management; tenure and promotion administration; and grants administration, including feasibility assessment and pre- and post-award processes. Brian has a distinguished record of service to the profession and has noteworthy accomplishments in research and scholarship.

Emily Kessler is a Senior Strategist at brightspot strategy. She is an experienced leader and management consultant specializing in organizational change and development. Her work is notable for increasing the capabilities, talent, and productivity of mission-driven organizations and leaders. She applies both her design education and her management experience to transform ideas and visions into successful initiatives. Emily is also an accomplished landscape and portrait photographer, which has made her a keen observer of social behaviors and interactions. She has led projects for innovative libraries at institutions such as Tulane University, the University of Wisconsin-Madison, Miami University of Ohio, and Adelphi University.

Diane Klare is the Associate Dean and Library Director of the McDermott Library at the United States Air Force Academy. She was previously the Associate University Librarian for Research and Access Services at Wesleyan University and served twice as the interim university librarian. Her research interests include leadership and management theory and the design of library spaces to enhance the user experience. Diane holds a bachelor of arts in French and a master of business administration from the University of Connecticut, a master of library science from Southern Connecticut State University, and a certificate of advanced study from Wesleyan University. The contents of Chapter 4 in this book represent the author's personal views and not necessarily those of the Department of Defense or the Air Force.

Martha Kyrillidou is principal of QualityMetrics, LLC, a private consulting firm specializing in helping libraries achieve success through strategy development, evaluation, assessment, and R&D activities. Martha developed a series of widely used and known planning and management tools during her twenty-plus years' work at the Association of Research Libraries (ARL), including the StatsQUAL suite of services that encompasses many successful grant-funded sustainable operations such as LibQUAL+, ClimateQUAL, and MINES for Libraries. Martha is an expert on university indirect cost studies. She is a Fulbright scholar, has a PhD from the University of Illinois at Urbana-Champaign, and publishes and presents extensively.

Yelena Luckert is Director of Research and Learning at the University of Maryland Libraries, where she provides leadership in policy creation and implementation, strategic planning, and assessment for liaison librarians program, reference, and instructional services. Luckert's research interests include assessment of academic library services, international librarianship, and Russian and Jewish area studies.

Regina Mays is an associate professor and the Head of Assessment Programs at the University of Tennessee Libraries. Her experience as program manager of the IMLS grant–funded study Lib-Value began a continuing interest in strategic assessment planning, evidence-based decision-making, user experience, and demonstrating library value. A stint as Coordinator of Strategic Planning and Assessment took her love of strategic planning to the next level. In her current position, Mays heads a crackerjack team using leading-edge data science to achieve innovation and excellence in the areas of evidence-based decision-making and demonstration of library value.

Kara McClurken is the Director of Preservation Services at the University of Virginia Library in Charlottesville, Virginia. She received her MLS and her MA in history from the University of Maryland College Park. Prior to working at UVA, she was a Preservation Field Services Librarian at Solinet in Atlanta, Georgia, and a project archivist and preservation specialist in the Sophia Smith Collection at Smith College in Northampton, Massachusetts.

Kevin Messner is the Head of Advise and Instruct at Miami University Libraries. In his twelve years in the Miami Libraries, he has worked as the Head of Branch Libraries, Interim Head of B.E.S.T. Library, Acting Assistant Head of Brill Library, and Biology Librarian. He was previously employed in the University of Minnesota Libraries. Kevin received his BS in zoology from Miami and his MS in LIS and PhD in microbiology from the University of Illinois Urbana-Champaign. His research interests include library space utilization and entrepreneurial service development.

Michael Meth is the Associate Dean, Research and Learning Services, at the Florida State University Libraries. Prior to joining FSU, Michael was the Director of the OISE Library at the University of Toronto. Michael started his career in libraries as the Director of the Li Koon Chun Finance Learning Centre, University of Toronto Mississauga. Michael is a graduate of the University of Toronto's iSchool and the Schulich School of Business at York University. In 2017, Michael coedited a book entitled *Academic Library Management: Case Studies*. Michael is a Senior Fellow at UCLA's Graduate School of Education and Information Studies and has participated in Harvard's Leadership Institute for Academic Librarians.

Lindsay Miller is the Assistant Head of Advise and Instruct at Miami University Libraries, where she has just begun her thirteenth year. She leads a team of student success and instruction librarians and coordinates the library instruction program. She was previously First Year Experience Librarian at Miami Libraries. Lindsay received her bachelor's from Miami University and MLIS from the University of Kentucky. Her research interests include student success and engagement, information literacy instruction, and management of library instruction programs.

Nisha Mody is a Health and Life Sciences Librarian at the Louise M. Darling Biomedical Library at UCLA. She is currently the liaison for the David Geffen School of Medicine and is a member of the Teaching and Learning Functional Team. Nisha previously worked as a speech-language pathologist and IT consultant. Nisha is interested in innovative and critical pedagogy and creating communities. She is an active member in the Medical Library Association and is a proud alumna of the Spectrum Scholarship Program and ARL's Initiative to Recruit a Diverse Workforce.

E. Antoinette Nelson is the Organizational, Wellness and Development Manager and chemistry liaison at The University of Texas at Arlington (UTA) Libraries. Previous positions held since joining UTA in 2000 were Department Head for STEM of the Outreach and Services Department and Manager of the Science and Engineering Library. Prior to working UTA, she was a medical librarian intern at Eskind Biomedical Library at Vanderbilt University and began her professional career as catalog librarian at Cook Library and then as Special Collections Librarian at the William D. McCain Library at the University of Southern Mississippi. She received her MLS from Texas Woman's University in Denton, Texas. Her research interests include organizational excellence and staff development.

Rikke Ogawa is UCLA Library's Director of the Louise M. Darling Biomedical Library and Science and Engineering Library. She started her professional career in 1998 at Lane Medical Library—Stanford University, returning to UCLA in 2006 as Emergent Technologies Librarian. Rikke was a Medical Library Association Board of Directors member (2010–2013) and currently chairs the MLA Communities Strategic Goals Task Force. Her professional interests include scholarly communications, systematic review services, project management, and leadership development in libraries.

Emma Popowich is an associate librarian and Head of the Elizabeth Dafoe Library, Fr. Harold Drake Library, St. John's College Library at the University of Manitoba. Her interests in scholarship include comparative language and literature of Romance languages, as well as library management and administration. Her recent publications include "March's Poetry and National Identity in Nineteenth-Century Catalonia," *CLCWeb: Comparative Literature and Culture* 15, no. 6 (December 2013), https://doi.org/10.7771/1481-4374.2362, and the digital humanities project Reimagining Roussillon, https://emmapopowich.wixsite.com/roussillon.

R. Philip Reynolds is currently in his fifth year as the Scholarly Communication Librarian at Ralph W. Steen Library, Stephen F. Austin State University. Currently he is engaged in publishing several open access journals for the university as well as managing the campus institutional repository, ScholarWorks. He was recently recognized for his twenty years of service at Stephen F. Austin State University. His hobbies include kite flying, refereeing roller derby, and studying the history of China.

Jennifer O'Brien Roper is the Director for Digital Strategies at the University of Virginia Library in Charlottesville, Virginia. She received her MSLS from the University of North Carolina at Chapel Hill and has spent twenty years working in academic libraries to connect scholars to resources.

C. Heather Scalf earned her master of library and information science degree from the University of North Texas while working at the United States Military Academy at West Point. She served in various leadership roles at the University of Texas Arlington Libraries from 2005 until February 2019, leading in the Access Services department and serving as the Director of Assessment. She coordinated qualitative and quantitative assessment projects across the library, in addition to external data reporting. Currently, Heather is the Director of Operations in the Division of Student Success at UT Arlington and is responsible for tactical data reporting for the division and for data analysis to identify student success issues for the schools and colleges. She assists the Associate Vice Provost with strategic planning efforts and assessment to ensure progress toward defined student success targets and with the administrative functions of the division. As an Army veteran, Heather identifies leadership, organizational development, and storytelling with data as key areas of interest.

Andrew See is the Head, User Services and Experience and chairs two cross-functional user experience groups at the Northern Arizona University Cline Library. The UX-Web group currently oversees all virtual services provided through the library, and the UX-Spaces group provides user research regarding the physical use of services and spaces in the library. Andrew received his master's in library and information science at the University of Arizona and is a national presenter on innovation in user data collection and making data-driven decisions.

Jeanette Claire Sewell is the Database and Metadata Management Coordinator at Rice University's Fondren Library. She is actively involved in using metadata to promote library resources in unique and engaging ways, creating everything from digital timelines and coloring books to Twitter bots and LibGuides. Jeanette also serves as the library science subject specialist at Fondren Library.

Manda Sexton is currently the Assessment Librarian for Kennesaw State University in Georgia where she coordinates all information collection, reporting, and implementation of data-driven decision making. Manda also serves as the undergraduate liaison to the College of Education. She previously held the position of Public Services Librarian at the University of Tennessee at Knoxville where she obtained a second master's in educational psychology for adult learners. She previously served on the University of Tennessee Strategic Planning Review team. Her interests include academic library assessment, the future of the librarian profession, and the role of libraries in adult and continuing education.

Aaron Shrimplin is the Associate Dean of Libraries at Miami University, where he is responsible for administrative services, including budgeting, strategic planning, facilities, assessment, communications, and technology. He is a senior member of the libraries' leadership team and enjoys developing and coaching talent throughout the libraries. Aaron joined Miami University Libraries in 1998 and has held various librarian positions. He received his BA in political science from Wittenberg University and his master's in library and information science from the University of Pittsburgh. He is an avid gardener and enjoys investing, doing DIY home improvement projects, and spending time with his family (married with two boys, 11 and 14 years old).

Richard Stringer-Hye is the subject librarian for Earth and Environmental Science and Civil and Environmental Engineering in the Stevenson Science and Engineering Library at Vanderbilt University. He has worked there for twenty-three years. He holds a BA degree in geology from the University of Colorado and an MLIS from the University of Rhode Island. His career in librarianship, mostly in the Vanderbilt University Libraries, has spanned an extremely interesting time period in the history of libraries and information science with the birth and growth of the internet and all things digital.

David W. Swedman is the Montana State University Library's Grants and Assessment Coordinator. He specializes in qualitative, quantitative, and mixed-methods approaches to library assessment, strategic plan creation and implementation, and grant writing and management.

Laurie N. Taylor, PhD, is the University of Florida's Digital Scholarship Librarian. Her work focuses on socio-technical (people, policies, technologies, communities) needs for scholarly cyberinfrastructure. She works heavily with the Digital Library of the Caribbean (dLOC; http://dloc.com/), where she is the Digital Scholarship Director; LibraryPress@UF (http://ufdc.ufl.edu/librarypress), where she is the Editor-in-Chief; Digital Humanities Working Group (http://digitalhumanities.group.ufl.edu/) and the DH Graduate Certificate; and Research Computing (http://rc.ufl.edu/); with these and other activities geared toward enabling a culture of radical collaboration that values and supports diversity, equity, and inclusivity.

Kara Van Abel is a reference librarian and the liaison to the Collat School of Business at the University of Alabama at Birmingham's Mervyn H. Sterne Library. She is an active member of RUSA and BRASS, currently serving as chair of the Business Reference Services Discussion Group. In 2014, she was named an American Library Association Emerging Leader. Kara holds a master's degree in library and information studies from the University of Alabama where she was also a Project ALFA Fellow.

Matthew Vest is the Lead for Outreach and the Music Inquiry and Research Librarian at UCLA. He has also worked in the Music Libraries at the University of Virginia, Davidson College, and Indiana University. He is active in the Music Library Association and the American Musicological Society. His research interests include change leadership in higher education, digital projects and publishing for music and the humanities, and composers working at the margins of the second Viennese School.

Sherri Vokey (https://orcid.org/0000-0002-2396-0413) is the Head of the Neil John Maclean Health Sciences Library and an associate librarian at the University of Manitoba. As a relative newcomer to library management, she has developed a keen interest in the issues relative to adaptive and effective leadership in academic libraries. Her scholarly interests include bibliometrics and research impact, evidence-based practice, and the impact of technology in health outcomes.

Bonita Washington-Lacey is Senior Associate Vice President for Academic Affairs and Registrar at Earlham College. She also is an instructor in religion, specializing in womanist theology. Serving the college in various roles, she has been impactful in designing programs that enhance student success. Serving as the liaison officer for accreditation, she focuses on both assessment of student learning and evidenced outcomes of an Earlham education.

Gary W. White is Associate Dean for Public Services at the University of Maryland Libraries. In his position, he oversees all research, teaching, and access services and is responsible for all public facilities and subject branch libraries. He holds a PhD in higher education from the Pennsylvania State University, an MBA from the University of Akron, and a master of library science from Kent State University. Prior to coming to the University of Maryland, he held a number of increasingly responsible positions in the Libraries at Pennsylvania State University. Gary served as President of the Reference and User Services Section of the American Library Association in 2012 and as editor of *Library Leadership and Management* (2016–2018) and is the author of numerous refereed articles, books and book chapters, and conference presentations and proceedings.

Carroll Wetzel Wilkinson currently serves as the Director of Strategy and Planning at West Virginia University Libraries. She holds a BA degree from Wells College in Aurora, New York, and an MLS from Rutgers, the State University of New Jersey. She has held the academic rank of University Librarian since 1993. Recent previous administrative appointments include Director of Library Strategic Initiatives, September 2014–2017, and Director of Instruction and Information Literacy, August 2006–2014. Her most recent publication is "Building a Library Subculture to Sustain Information Literacy Practice with Second Order Change," *Communications in Information Literacy* 8, no. 1 (Spring 2014): 82–95 (coauthor with Courtney Bruch). The American Library Association's Library Instruction Round Table (LIRT) Top Twenty Committee selected it as a Top Twenty article of 2014.

Elizabeth Wilkinson is Archivist for the Description and Access Unit in the Small Special Collections Library at the University of Virginia. She received both her MA in history and her MLS from Indiana University.

Lauren Work is the Digital Preservation Librarian at the University of Virginia Library, where she is responsible for the implementation of digital preservation strategy at the library. She received her MLIS from the University of Washington.

Doug Worsham is the Lead for the Teaching and Learning Functional Team at UCLA Library and the liaison for psychology and food studies. With a background in instructional design and student-centered pedagogy, Doug is passionately interested in how learners work individually and collaboratively to create knowledge.